BRITISH GOVERNMENT POLICY AND DECOLONISATION 1945–1963

Scrutinising the Official Mind

Frank Heinlein

European University Institute, Florence

With a Foreword by
ROBERT HOLLAND

FRANK CASS

LONDON • PORTLAND, OR

First published in 2002 in Great Britain by
FRANK CASS PUBLISHERS
Crown House, 47 Chase Side
London N14 5BP

and in the United States of America by
FRANK CASS PUBLISHERS
c/o ISBS, 5824 N.E. Hassalo Street
Portland, Oregon, 97213-3644

Website: www.frankcass.com

British Library Cataloguing in Publication Data

Heinlein, Frank
    British government policy and decolonisation, 1945–63: Scrutinising the Official
    Mind. – (Cass series. British foreign and colonial policy)
    1. Decolonization 2. Great Britain – Colonies – Administration 3. Great Britain –
    Foreign relations – 1945– 4. Great Britain – Politics and government – 1945
    I. Title
    325.3′41′09045

ISBN 0-7146-5220-2 (cloth)
ISSN 1467-5013

Library of Congress Cataloging-in-Publication Data

Heinlein, Frank, 1969–
    British government policy and decolonisation, 1945–1963: Scrutinising the Official
    mind / Frank Heinlein.
        p.   cm. – (Cass series–British foreign and colonial policy series, ISSN 1467–5013)
    Revised version of author's PhD thesis at the European University Institute in
    Florence, 1999.
    Includes bibliographical references and index.
    ISBN 0–7146–5220–2
    1. Decolonization–Great Britain–Colonies–History–20th century. 2.
    Imperialism–Government policy–Great Britain–History–20th century 3. Great
    Britain–Colonies–History–20th century. 4. Commonwealth countries–History–20th
    century. I Title. II. Series.
        DA16 .H45 2002
        325′.341′009045–dc21   2001053932

Typeset in 10.5/12.5pt Palatino by *FiSH* Books, London
Printed in Great Britain by MPG Books Ltd, Bodmin, Cornwall

BRITISH GOVERNMENT POLICY
AND DECOLONISATION
1945–1963

CASS SERIES: BRITISH FOREIGN AND COLONIAL POLICY
ISSN: 1467-5013
Series Editor: Peter Catterall

This series provides insights into both the background influences on and the course of policymaking towards Britain's extensive overseas interests during the past 200 years.

Whitehall and the Suez Crisis, Saul Kelly and Anthony Gorst (eds)

Liberals, International Relations and Appeasement: The Liberal Party, 1919–1939, Richard S. Grayson

British Government Policy and Decolonisation, 1945–1963: Scrutinising the Official Mind, Frank Heinlein

Contents

Foreword

DURING THE past 20 years, the end of the British empire after the Second World War has been the subject of a growing and lively literature. First, there were a number of broad synopses; to these were gradually added monographs concerned with events in particular territories and regions; and, during the 1990s, the British Documents on the End of Empire series, courtesy of The Stationery Office, published impressive and bulky volumes of official documentation concerning both individual colonies and the colonial and Commonwealth policies of successive British Governments.

As any fresh historiography unfolds, however, there is a critical need for historians to take stock of the sheer accumulation of knowledge, to check the consistency and persuasiveness of arguments put forward, and to summarise the balance of collective analysis. In the present state of the study of British policy-making in the era of decolonisation, this needs to be done, not by the recitation of already familiar narratives, but by engaging with our increasing awareness of the diversity and changing shape of motivations and methods involved in transfers of power from 1945 through to the 1960s. Frank Heinlein's book is important because it provides just such a comprehensive stock-taking of a complicated and evolving subject.

The achievements of this volume are considerable. Let me identify just a few of them. There are a number of what purport to be broad analyses of decolonisation that on examination are really about a particular region or aspect. In framing his own approach, Heinlein seems equally grounded in East and West Africa, south-east Asia and the Middle East. While some works are based overwhelmingly on secondary reading, and others on some dense patch of archival material, here the secondary and primary sources are blended appropriately together. Often, histories of decolonisation appear, other than by a glancing reference to the Suez episode, or the Cold War, to treat colonial policy (or, come to that, colonial nationalism), as if it had existed in a vacuum. By contrast, Heinlein integrates such themes as sterling crises, pressures emerging from a unifying Europe and superpower rivalries into his account in a serious and sustained way. The Commonwealth association is something of a 'missing ghost' in the literature of decolonisation, often ignored, or made the subject of some modest aside. Here, it is grafted on to the story, and given the importance that it undoubtedly had for contemporary policy-makers.

Heinlein is surely right to argue that there cannot be a single compelling theory as to why the British empire ended, because the factors and forces which operated in the various compartments of imperial and colonial policy – India, the formal colonial empire, the informal empire of the Middle East – were not the same. There was never one indivisible British empire, but many empires within the 'Empire', and each of them had its own networks, and characteristic techniques of management. On the whole, however, the arguments put forward in these pages are not those of an economic determinist. Heinleins emphasis is rather on the degree to which Britain clung to its imperial role so long, not because it was materially profitable, but because it was the role which most suited the self-imagery of its leading political class; and the empire was not dismantled when it ceased to be congruent with commercial interest, but when metropolitan self-imagery gradually flaked apart. Prestige and power, not money, lies at the root of the process. This is surely broadly true, and one is left with a feeling that what we need now is not more accounts of decolonisation in its political guise, but an exploration of the meanings of prestige – or what Lord Palmerston called moral power – in the general context of modern British history, including the ending of empire.

In his conclusions on the future agenda of historiography in this area, Heinlein makes one suggestion which seems particularly apposite. To put decolonisation in its most sophisticated perspective, we now need to engage *historically* with post-independence aftermaths. For example, as yet, we do not have a convincing treatment of the great variety of post-colonial relationships between ex-rulers and ex-ruled. Decolonisation is consequently written about as if the great destination – the culmination of all things – had been independence. Yet it was with what was to come after that everybody – policy-makers in imperial capitals, anti-colonial nationalists, minority groups within plural territories, peasant masses with a still dawning political consciousness – was really thinking about during transfers of power. This great cusp running through the climaxes of decolonisation, and onwards into a world of new states riven with old conflicts, will hopefully be the cutting edge of much new writing during the next few years.

Robert Holland
Institute of Commonwealth Studies,
University of London

Series Editor's Preface

'GREAT BRITAIN has lost an empire, and has not yet found a role'. Thus Dean Acheson, in a speech at West Point on 5 December 1962, attempted to encapsulate the story of the rapid demission of Britain's empire over the previous 20 years. His aphorism provoked an enormous furore at the time. It touched a nerve rubbed raw by anxieties about relative economic decline. But as an account of the end of empire, as Frank Heinlein's masterly overview here shows, it leaves much to be desired.

Narratives of decolonisation have tended to be shaped by a sense of loss and imperial decline, and have sought to explain this by reference to impulses either at the centre or on the periphery. On the one hand, the demission of power was presented as an orderly retreat from empire at the behest of the official mind of the Colonial Office, while on the other it was seen as more of a rout prompted by nationalist pressures, with flags being decorously lowered as riots went on in other parts of the capital city of the newly independent territory. However, both of these approaches focus upon retention or loss of territory as the purpose not only of *imperium*, but as the expression of British interests. This is a profit-and-loss account, which leaves little room for rational readjustment of British interests or the means by which power is projected to achieve them.

Such an approach also runs the risk of imposing artificial divisions on Britain's external interests. The concept of informal empire, for instance, though long integrated into accounts of the high noon of empire, has less commonly been included in interpretations of its demise. One of the strengths of Heinlein's work, by contrast, is to present a consideration of the imperial system – the colonial, the Commonwealth and the informal – as a whole. Furthermore, in this account the operation of this imperial system is integrated into the other concerns of Whitehall, rather than as a by-way for specialist departments and interests. Wider considerations, not least the international politics of the Cold War, are shown as shaping adjustments in Britain's portfolio of imperial interests as much if not more than the familiar push-pull factors of centre or periphery. It could prompt, as Heinlein points out, the carefully managed transfer of power, while long continuing military and financial assistance, as in Malaya. In some cases it could even lead to the decision to stay, as in the excision of the Chagos from Mauritius in 1968 (outside Heinlein's period), with the forced departure of all the inhabitants. In other words, calculations of what best promoted or preserved British interests, rather than the mere retention or loss of territory, were to the fore. Much recent work has focused upon empire as a cultural artifice. Heinlein's great contribution is to remind us that, for British policy-makers, the empire was beyond Britain's shores, was a means to an end rather than an end in itself, and was subservient to their images of Britain and of British interests.

In this account then, empire was not the role, but the means to play a role. And demission of empire, accordingly, was not the end of a role, but an adjustment of the way in which British interests were projected outwards. One facet of this adjustment is apparent from the reactions to Acheson's speech. For the British Prime Minister, Harold Macmillan, then low in the opinion polls and about to journey to Nassau to negotiate the acquisition of Polaris with the Americans, it represented 'One of those rare opportunities...which can be seized with great *internal* political advantage.' The management of comments about empire, just as the management of empire itself, was, as Heinlein shows, accordingly conducted with an eye on Britain's key external relationship with the Americans.

The end of formal empire has too often been seen as the end of the story, a dramatic caesura in Britain's history. Heinlein's more nuanced account points out the difficulties of treating the demission of power as a moment of closure. Rather, it suggests the need to explore the extent to which continuities in the external projection of British interests and relationships persisted using different means in a post-colonial era. Heinlein is right to close by drawing attention to the historiographical neglect, hitherto, of Britain's post-imperial relationships. That is the subject for another book, but one which he has played an important part in paving the way for through the reconfiguring of the end of empire that he offers in these pages.

Peter Catterall
Queen Mary, University of London

Preface

THIS BOOK is a revised version of a PhD thesis defended at the European University Institute in Florence in June 1999. I would like to thank the Institute as well as all the Deutscher Akademischer Austauschdienst (DAAD) for providing the financial and technical assistance to allow me to pursue my research for more than three years.

I am grateful to all those who have read through a rather lengthy manuscript and made detailed and inspiring comments on it. Next to Kirti Chaudhuri, Robert Holland, Bo Stråth and Clemens Wurm, I would like to thank in particular Professor Michael Müller, who provided encouragement when most needed. I have also benefited from the help, advice and criticism of several others, including Stephen Ashton, John Darwin, Richard Griffiths, Frances Lynch, Alan Milward, Richard Rathbone, Peter Robb, Andrew Roberts, Anita Inder Singh, and Mr J.W. and Mrs C. Stacpoole.

I would like to thank the Master and Fellows of Trinity College, Cambridge; the Rhodes House Library; the British Library of Political and Economic Science; and the Trustees of the Liddell Hart Centre for Military Archives, King's College London, for permission to quote from their papers. Every effort has been made to contact the owners of copyright for other documents quoted in this book. Any omissions can be corrected in future editions if copyright owners contact the publisher.

Last, but not least, I would like to thank my wife, Isabelle, as well as my parents for their unwavering support. This book is dedicated to them.

Abbreviations

AFPFL	Anti-Fascist People's Freedom League (Burma)
ANP	Archives Nationales Paris
AVAR	Alexander of Hillborough papers
BARN	Gorell Barnes papers
BoT	Board of Trade
CAF	Central African Federation
CC	Churchill College, Cambridge
CCC	Conservative Commonwealth Council
CCM	Cabinet Committee on Commonwealth Membership
CCOC	Conservative Commonwealth and Overseas Council Papers (Bodleian Library, Oxford)
CDC	Colonial Development Corporation
CD & W	Colonial Development and Welfare
CENTO	Central Treaty Organisation
CM	Cabinet Minutes
CO	Colonial Office
COS	Chiefs of Staff Committee
CPP	Convention People's Party (Gold Coast)
CRD	Conservative Party's Research Department
CRO	Commonwealth Relations Office
DBPO	Documents on British Policy Overseas
ECSC	European Coal and Steel Community
EEC	European Economic Community
EFTA	European Free Trade Area
EOKA	Ethniki Organosis Kyrion Agoniston (National Organisation of Cypriot Fighters)
FNL	Front de Libération Nationale (Algeria)
FO	Foreign Office
GATT	General Agreement on Tariffs and Trade
GNP	Gross National Product
GNWR	Gordon-Walker papers
HMG	Her Majesty's Government
HMGGC	HM Government in the Gold Coast

IBC	India and Burma Committee
ICS	Indian Civil Service
IMF	International Monetary Fund
IOL	India Office Library (London)
JPS	Joint Planning Staff
KADU	Kenya African Democratic Union
KANU	Kenyan African National Union
LHC	Liddell Hart Centre for Military Studies, King's College, London
LSE	London School of Economics
MCA	Malayan Chinese Association
MoD	Ministry of Defence
NATO	North Atlantic Treaty Organisation
NBKR	Noël-Baker papers
NKG	New Kenya Group
NKP	New Kenya Party
OECD	Organisation for Economic Cooperation and Development
OEEC	Organisation for European Economic Cooperation
PRO	Public Record Office (London)
RAB	Butler papers
RHL	Rhodes House Library (Oxford)
SEATO	South-East Asia Treaty Organisation
SWIN	Swinton papers
TANU	Tanganyika African National Union
TCC	Trinity College, Cambridge
TOP	*Constitutional Relations between Britain and India: The Transfer of Power, 1942–47*, 12 vols, ed. N. Mansergh *et al.* (London: HMSO, 1970–83)
UMNO	United Malays National Organisation
UN	United Nations
UNIP	United National Independence Party (Northern Rhodesia)

'To propose that Great Britain should voluntarily give up all authority over her Colonies, and leave them to elect their own magistrates, to enact their own laws, and to make peace and war, as they might think proper, would be to propose such a measure as never was and never will be adopted, by any nation in the world.'

(Adam Smith, *The Wealth of Nations*, Vol. II, London, 1776, p. 224)

'Wise and happy would be the nation which, the first to bend its politics to new circumstances, would consent to see its colonies as allied provinces, and not as subjects to the metropolis.'

(Jacques Turgot, *Mémoire sur les colonies américains, sur leurs relations politique avec leurs métropoles, et sur la manière dont la France et l'Espagne ont du envisager les suites de l'indépendance des Etats-Unis de l'Amérique*, Paris, 1791, p. 31)

— 1 —

Introduction

THIS BOOK provides a study of the views on the Empire-Commonwealth held by British policy-makers from 1945 to 1963, a period that witnessed a profound transformation of the imperial framework created since the early 1800s. It enquires into the economic, geopolitical and strategic importance politicians and civil servants attributed to colonies, overseas commitments and Dominions. The question is not the importance of one territory or the other *per se* – rather it is the importance attributed to the fact that this territory stood in a particular relationship with Britain that was different from that which prevailed in Britain's relations with 'foreign' countries. The book thus investigates to what degree the Empire-Commonwealth *as an institutional framework* was considered necessary and useful to promote British interests. The aim is to evaluate the motives for withdrawing graciously from some possessions while remaining obstinately in others, for maintaining an extensive military presence overseas, and for opening up the Commonwealth. By studying a broad range of debates on general and specific imperial problems, the book highlights the 'official mind' of decolonisation – and late imperialism.[1]

In order to allow a better understanding of the Empire-Commonwealth, the latter has been considered under three headings: formal empire, informal empire and Commonwealth. Unless stated otherwise, the term 'formal empire' is used to describe the ensemble of dependent territories, i.e. colonies, protectorates and trust territories. The term 'informal empire' describes the British position of predominance in the Middle East. This position was not so much based on formal rule or visible coercion, but rather on political influence and military hegemony. In a wider sense, 'informal empire' may include overseas commitments in other regions as well – especially after the transfer of power in Malaya. In this book, depending on the context, both meanings are employed. Finally, 'Commonwealth' means the community of self-governing nations that maintained a loose institutional link with Britain, i.e. Dominion status, after the end of formal rule.

In recent years, there has emerged a considerable body of writing on imperial and colonial policy in the post-war period. However much of it seems to have been written in isolation, with reference only to specific aspects (such as strategic or financial considerations) or selected colonies only. Despite important works such as those by John Darwin, Robert Holland and Ronald Robinson, specialisation still prevails over a more generalist approach.[2] This book does not aspire to provide an all-embracing description of decolonisation or to explain and link developments in the metropole, at the imperial 'periphery' or at the global level.[3] What it does provide is an in-depth study of the importance of the Empire-Commonwealth for Britain's self-image as a great power in the two decades after the Second World War. There are few source-based books covering such a long period, or dealing with the Empire-Commonwealth as a whole. And while there are many books dealing with developments within specific colonies as well as on the international scene, there is little on how Britain perceived the situation, and how it influenced its decisions. The interested reader can make good use of P.S. Gupta's pioneering *Imperialism and the British Labour Government* and Philip Murphy's *Party Politics and Decolonisation*. But the first is not based on archival sources, while the second focuses more on party policy than the government.[4] This book closes the gap by studying imperial policy within a wider chronological and thematic framework from a metropolitan point of view.

There are two further aspects hitherto not sufficiently covered that are studied in this book. First, the role of the Commonwealth for Britain's political, economic and military strategies (particularly in the 1950s and early 1960s); and, second, the various policy-reviews undertaken during Harold Macmillan's first and second premiership. Divergences with prevailing interpretations are essentially fivefold: (1) formal empire, informal empire and Commonwealth are treated as clearly distinct units, each possessing a logic of its own. (2) Decolonisation is not seen as the result of a conscious cost-benefit analysis in the metropole, but rather as a British reaction to the restructuring of the local and international orders. (3) No contradiction is seen between Britain's economic difficulties and its holding on to overseas territories. The explanation for this is seen in the British belief that prestige and a military presence overseas were interdependent as well as inextricably linked to economic and political power. (4) The momentum of constitutional advance in East and Central Africa in the early 1960s is not attributed to a downward reassessment of the political/strategic value of white settlers, but rather to a changed perception of the importance of the African majority and the international situation as well as to emerging local developments. (5) Last, but not least, this book stresses the difficulties of arranging a transfer of power, instead of emphasising any presumed British desire to keep the colonies for their own sake.

Between 1945 and 1963, massive changes were taking place in the relationship between Britain and the imperial 'periphery'. In 1945 Canada, Australia, New Zealand and South Africa still had close economic, political and strategic ties with Britain, while the colonial empire was the largest of its kind.[5] Nobody expected formal rule to end before, at best, a generation. Twenty years later little remained of this imperial splendour. Britain still controlled some smaller territories, but most territories had become independent – some only after bitter struggle, but for the most part surprisingly quickly after more or less peaceful constitutional advance. The Commonwealth was no longer an exclusive club cherished by policy-makers because of the power and prestige it conferred on Britain. By 1965 17 new members, all of them 'non-white' Dominions, had been admitted. Political, strategic and economic cooperation within the club had lost much of its former importance, and the Commonwealth had been transformed from a closely-knit 'white man's club' into a multi-racial 'talking shop'.

While the withdrawal from formal empire was, generally speaking, relatively fast and uncontroversial, the same cannot be said about the informal empire. During the Second World War Britain accumulated huge debts. These so-called sterling balances were, by 1945, equivalent to seven times the value of its gold and dollar reserves.[6] Nevertheless, Britain adopted an imperial policy well beyond its means, maintaining a large-scale military presence in the Middle and Far East. This obliged the British government to make cutbacks at home and prevented it from achieving a balanced budget. The overseas commitments were reduced slowly over the years, but their final demise only took place in the early 1970s. It is often argued that the expenditure incurred for the sake of maintaining this last imperial stand led to the loss of vital resources to the domestic economy. As a result it is claimed that Britain was unable to sustain its position in the competition for an expanding world trade.[7]

The changes and continuities in Britain's relations with the Empire-Commonwealth in the two decades after 1945 thus throw up a wide range of questions. How can one explain the rapid disappearance of a colonial empire Britain had painstakingly built up over centuries? Was it because of a mutation of interest in the metropole, of changes on the periphery, of external influences, or because of a combination of all these factors? Why was the end of colonial rule sometimes an agonising and disorienting experience, but in most cases a *rite de passage* accomplished with 'relative ease and a soothing sense of inevitability'?[8] Why was the transfer of power in most colonies strongly accelerated, often leaving hardly enough time for the preparation of independence? Was decolonisation a real turning point in metropolitan thinking or solely the 'replacing of colonial rule by a relationship which was expected to preserve influence through informal means'?[9] As regards informal empire, one wonders why the struggle to maintain an imperial role, however vestigial, continued for so long? Why did men like Bevin, Eden and Macmillan all persist on 'courses that in important respects proved counterproductive to their own state's interests'?[10] Finally, it is worth investigating why the Commonwealth was diluted by a host of countries that were neither great powers nor had the close racial and cultural links binding the old Dominions to the metropole? What role did policy-makers expect the Commonwealth to play? And what was its importance with regard to Britain's approach to Europe?

Many arguments have been advanced in order to explain the end of empire. In the following pages, we will not attempt to give an exhaustive overview of the vast range of literature,[11] nor will we dwell in detail on such schools of thought as the 'neo-colonialist'[12] or the 'nationalist'.[13] Mass nationalism was an important factor, particularly in India and Indo-China, but it does not explain why most Asian and African countries achieved independence almost simultaneously, even though local circumstances varied strongly. Why did Britain choose to find nationalism irresistible, even where it was far from having developed into a revolutionary force? This phenomenon can only be accounted for when looking at developments in the metropole and the international sphere, as is done by those scholars we will now turn to.

An important group of historians sees the reason for the demise of colonial empire in a recalculation of the benefits formal rule bestowed on the metropole. There are several variations of this approach. While A.J. Hopkins and B.R. Tomlinson argue that, from an economic point of view, the colonial system was no longer *profitable*,[14] D.K. Fieldhouse maintains that formal rule ended because under the changed economic conditions prevailing after 1945 it was no longer *necessary*.[15] Krozewski and Cain and Hopkins see the end of empire as directly linked to Britain's financial interests: 'escape from empire' became increasingly desirable in the 1950s, as Britain's 'tangible material interests' in the colonies waned.[16] The retention of certain territories and the abrupt withdrawal from others is seen as 'largely a matter of a cost-benefit analysis within the framework of the sterling area'.[17]

Robert Holland also sees decolonisation as the result of a cost-benefit analysis, but one simultaneously taking into account economic, strategic and geopolitical aspects.[18] The decisive factor is said to be the supposed drawing-up of an imperial 'balance-sheet'. The first disengagements from formal empire (India, Burma and Palestine) are seen as a 'cutting adrift from dependencies which were net liabilities, and maintaining a grip on those (largely African) possessions which remained bankable assets'.[19] In the late 1950s, the African colonies had also become 'a tiresome disturbance to be sloughed off into independence as soon as possible'.[20]

The latest attempt to explain British decolonisation with the idea of an imperial balance-sheet is a joint article by H.V. Brasted, Carl Bridge and John Kent. The three authors also argue that 'overseas possessions were analysed in terms of the financial or strategic benefits they brought'.[21] But, contrary to Holland, these authors put the stress on the relative increase or decrease in British prestige or status that a particular course of action, from military repression to the abandonment of formal responsibilities, was likely to produce in the international context.[22] Ronald Robinson combines an 'international' approach with the idea of an imperial balance-sheet. He sees the reason for the dismantling of the colonial empire in the changed conditions in the periphery and on the international level.[23] The US insistence on self-determination and awakening nationalism led European policy-makers to reassess the value of their colonies and, finally, to end formal rule. But according to Robinson, changed local and international conditions also allowed the Europeans to achieve their objectives without formal rule. The new, US-dominated world order as well as the establishment of relatively stable African and Asian governments provided security of trade and investment, thus rendering formal empire both unnecessary and burdensome.[24]

Certainly none of these explanations can be said to be completely wrong, and especially in the case of Robinson and Holland, I would agree with many of their arguments. However, this book does not share the widespread assumption that decolonisation was largely the result of a rational reassessment of the benefits the colonies conferred upon Britain. Authors using this kind of argument generally do not differentiate sufficiently between the value of a territory *per se* and its value *as a dependency*. In addition, they discard too easily immaterial factors such as feelings of responsibility, and give pride of place to economic cost-benefit analyses – obviously implying that at one point the colonies *did* provide economic advantages. Decolonisation has to be seen as the result of several interlocking factors making a transfer of power both advisable and possible, rather than the consequence of any realisation that the colonies had 'ceased to matter'. The principal reason of the decision to grant independence was Britain's habit of considering the goodwill of local nationalists as the best guarantee for its interests; the momentum of disengagement in most colonies can be attributed both to local dynamics as well as to changed international conditions.

It is not enough to reconstruct what effectively contributed to British 'power' and what led to its decline. In order to understand British policy, the historian has to go one step further and ask what policy-makers *thought* would contribute to the maintenance or erosion of their country's power. Imperial policy was influenced by a variety of factors, including rising international hostility against colonialism, an increasingly strong desire on the part of the Dominions to become less dependent on Britain, the evolution of a new political consciousness in the colonies and Britain's costly commitment to a welfare state.

Since the post-war period did see massive changes in metropole, periphery and the wider world, due consideration has to be given to these factors. However, in order to understand British policy, the focal point has to shift from the events and changes themselves to metropolitan perceptions of, and reactions to, them. The various factors mentioned above help to understand *why* empire ended. But in order to understand the *when* and *how* as well as the obstinate defence of informal empire, it is necessary to concentrate on the heart of the policy-making process, i.e. upon politicians and civil servants in London. Here the historian has a delicate task to perform, that is, to relate events in the colonies and the wider world to metropolitan perceptions of the importance of empire for Britain's global role. Decisions relating to the Empire-Commonwealth were never made on the basis of prepared economic, strategic or political balance-sheets for individual colonies or with regard to the local situation only. To understand them, it is necessary to look at the whole picture.

This book therefore asks what the Empire-Commonwealth meant to policy-makers in a broader framework of metropolitan decision-making, and how its role changed between 1945 and 1963. It is interested in concepts rather than events or statistics. It focuses on the basic ideas, perceptions and expectations of policy-makers underlying the decisions taken with regard to formal and informal empire as well as to the Commonwealth. Therefore it does not necessarily give a minute, chronological reconstruction of all individual transfers of power (even though various case studies *are* considered), but rather concentrates on the general arguments advanced on the advantages of withdrawing or maintaining the *status quo*. The aim is not to explain individual viewpoints or to link events and developments in a particular colony with the decisions taken in the metropole in response to a specific situation. The object is rather to attempt a comprehensive analysis that pays attention to the mental context within which actions took place.

Although there were sweeping discussions on the future of the informal empire and the Commonwealth throughout the period under consideration, there was never anything comparable with regard to the formal empire. (It has to be borne in mind however that the debates about overseas commitments were never totally separated from those about the colonies.) Policy-makers discussed the specific problems of particular colonies, but never evolved any master plan for future development. Nevertheless a broad outline is discernible by analysing a number of individual cases. Therefore the sections on the informal empire and the Commonwealth follow an outline that differs somewhat from that of the section on the colonies: the latter provides a reconstruction of general discussions as well as several case studies which help to understand the nature of Britain's relationship with the Empire-Commonwealth. In the context of informal empire, policy-makers were concerned, above all, with the amount (or rather the percentage of GNP) to be spent on overseas commitments such as bases and subsidies. Discussions about the Commonwealth, on the other hand, centred above all around the possibilities the club offered to project a certain image of Britain in the world. This accounts for the distinct emphases in debates about each of these aspects.

NOTES

1. 'Official mind' is defined as the sum of the ideas, perceptions and intentions of those policy-makers who had a bearing on imperial policies. The term 'policy-maker' designates politicians and civil servants who were responsible for or had a bearing on the development and execution of imperial policy. These include ministers as well as leading officials from the Colonial, Commonwealth Relations and Foreign Offices; the Treasury; the Board of Trade; the Ministry of Defence and (in some cases), the metropole's representatives in the colonies.

2. John Darwin, *Britain and Decolonisation: The Retreat from the Empire in the Post-War World* (Basingstoke: Macmillan, 1988); Robert Holland, *European Decolonization 1918–1981: An Introductory Survey* (Basingstoke: Macmillan, 1985); and Ronald Robinson, 'The Eccentric Idea of Imperialism, with or without Empire', in W. J. Mommsen and J. Osterhammel (eds), *Imperialism and After: Continuities and Discontinuities* (London: Allen & Unwin, 1986), pp. 267–89.

3. In the following, the term 'metropole' is used to designate the imperial centre, i.e. Britain. 'Periphery' means the dependent territories.

4. Partha Sarathi Gupta, *Imperialism and the British Labour Movement, 1914–1964*

(Basingstoke: Macmillan, 1975); Philip Murphy, *Party Politics and Decolonisation: The Conservative Party and British Colonial Policy in Tropical Africa, 1951–1964* (Oxford: Clarendon Press, 1995).

5.   In the 1940s policy-makers often did not draw any distinction between 'Commonwealth' and 'Empire'. The two terms were considered 'strictly speaking interchangeable'. Sometimes they were used in conjunction, sometimes separately (memorandum on 'Publicity on the British Commonwealth and Empire' by Secretary of State for Dominion Affairs, 9 April 1947. PREM 8/648 (PRO)). 'Empire' and 'Commonwealth' could thus comprise all the colonies as well as the self-governing Dominions. By the 1950s the terms 'Empire' and 'Dominion' were no longer used. In order to avoid the impression of discrimination, London now referred only to the Commonwealth, containing 'fully self-governing members' and 'dependent territories'. In this book a distinction is made between the Commonwealth, understood to mean the association of self-governing nations existing since the inter-war period, and the Empire as the sum total of all dependent territories under British control. Although throughout this book the term 'colony' is used indiscriminately to describe all of Britain's dependent territories (as was done at the time), the constitutional situation was rather complicated. India, Burma, and the Associated States (Grenada, Dominica, St Lucia, St Vincent, Antigua, St Christopher and Nevis) formed part of the Crown Dominions without being 'colonies' in the official sense of the word. The other territories were either classified as 'colonies' (Bahamas, Bermuda, British Guiana, British Honduras, Ceylon, Cyprus, Gibraltar, Jamaica, Malta, Trinidad and Tobago, Southern Rhodesia), 'protectorates' (Bechuanaland, British Somaliland, Northern Rhodesia, Nyasaland, Uganda), 'protected states' (Bahrain, Brunei, Kuwait, Maldives, Qatar, Tonga, Trucial States), 'trust territories' (British Togoland, British Cameroon, Tanganyika), 'mandated territories' (Palestine, Transjordan), and territories under condominium (Sudan and New Hebrides). Some territories were partly colonies and partly protectorates (Gambia, Malaya, Sierra Leone). Some were partly colonies, partly protectorates and partly trust territories (the Gold Coast and Nigeria). (Werner Morvay, 'Decolonization: British Territories', in *Encyclopaedia of Public International Law* (Amsterdam: North Holland, 1987), p. 81 f.)

6.   P.J. Cain and A.G. Hopkins, *British Imperialism: Crisis and Reconstruction, 1914–1990* (London: Longman, 1993), p. 270.

7.   The idea of an 'imperial overstretch' is most vividly formulated in Paul Kennedy, *The Rise and Fall of the Great Powers* (New York: Random House, 1987). After the Second World War, the percentage of GNP Britain devoted to defence expenditure was proportionately always higher than in any other Western power except the United States – although Britain was almost constantly on the brink of a financial crisis. Admittedly, informal empire accounted only for part of military expenditure, but even as late as 1965, with hugely reduced commitments, 15 per cent of all defence expenditure went east of Suez. The book will not discuss whether in economic terms, any 'imperial overstretch' was really responsible for Britain's decline. For an interesting introduction to this debate see Karen A. Rasler and William R. Thompson, *The Great Powers and Global Struggle, 1490–1990* (Lexington, KY: University Press of Kentucky, 1994).

8.   Robert Holland, 'The British Experience of Decolonization', *Itinerario*, 20 (1996), p. 51.

9.   John Kent, *British Imperial Strategy and the Origins of the Cold War 1944–49* (Leicester: Leicester University Press, 1993), p. x. The term 'decolonisation'

can be understood to mean much more than a constitutional development; here it is defined as the transfer of all government functions from the administrating power to local authorities. In most cases this is preceded by constitutional advance in several stages. Outward signs of this advance are changes in the composition of the legislative council. Elected members gradually gain control and replace the elements nominated by the governor. When there is also an elected majority in the executive council, and the legislature has achieved control over the executive by appointing its own members (usually called ministers), 'responsible government' (or internal self-government) has arrived. Full self-government is reached when ministers take over the running of all government departments.

10. Dane Kennedy, 'The Expansion of Europe', *Journal of Modern History*, 59 (1987), p. 338.

11. A good introduction can be found in John Darwin, *Britain and Decolonisation: The Retreat from Empire in the Post-War World* (Basingstoke: Macmillan, 1988).

12. Some scholars believe that independence was but a device to exploit the African and Asian peoples more effectively. This 'neo-colonialist' theory was above all discussed in the 1960s and 1970s; in recent years, it has somewhat sunk into oblivion, at least in its cruder form.

13. Some historians working on specific colonial societies regard the influence of nationalism and resistance to colonial rule as most important. According to A. Low, M. Twaddle and B. Porter, Britain was 'hustled and harried out of most of her old colonies'. (Bernard Porter, *The Lion's Share: A Short History of British Imperialism, 1850–1995* (London: Longman, 1996), p. 342.) J. Hargreaves even argues that it would be possible to write a history of decolonisation based solely on the biographies of Nehru, Ho Chi Minh or Nkrumah. (John D. Hargreaves, 'Les techniciens de la décolonisation: l'évolution de la politique de la Grande-Bretagne en Afrique, 1936–1948', in *Les chemins de la décolonisation de l'empire colonial français: Colloque organisé par l'IHTP les 4 et 5 octobre 1984* (Paris: Centre Nationale du Recherche Scientifique, 1986), p. 84.)

14. Anthony G. Hopkins, *An Economic History of West Africa* (Harlow: Longman, 1973); Brian R. Tomlinson, *The Political Economy of the Raj 1914–1947: The Economics of Decolonization in India* (Basingstoke: Macmillan 1979).

15. D.K. Fieldhouse, *Black Africa 1945–80: Economic Decolonization and Arrested Development* (London: Allen & Unwin, 1986).

16. Gerold Krozewski, 'Finance and Empire: The Dilemma Facing Great Britain in the 1950s', *International History Review*, 18 (1996), p. 68. P.J. Cain and A.G. Hopkins, *British Imperialism: Crisis and Deconstruction, 1914–1990* (London: Longman, 1993).

17. Gerold Krozewski, 'Sterling, the "Minor" Territories, and the End of Formal Empire, 1939–1958', *Economic History Review*, XLVI (1993), p. 241.

18. Robert F. Holland, *European Decolonization 1918–1981: An Introductory Survey* (Basingstoke: Macmillan, 1985), p. 301.

19. Robert Holland, 'The Imperial Factor in British Strategies from Attlee to Macmillan, 1945–63', *Journal of Imperial and Commonwealth History*, XII (1984), p. 169.

20. Robert Holland, 'Did Suez Hasten the End of Empire?', *Contemporary Record*, 1 (1987/88), p. 39.

21. H.V. Brasted, Carl Bridge and John Kent, 'Cold War, Informal Empire and the Transfer of Power: Some "Paradoxes" of British Decolonisation Resolved?', in M. Dockrill (ed.), *Europe within the Global System 1938–1960: Great Britain, France, Italy and Germany: From Great Powers to Regional Powers* (Bochum: Brockmeyer, 1995), p. 11.

22. Brasted, Bridge and Kent, 'Cold War', p. 23.
23. Ronald Robinson, 'Imperial Theory and the Question of Imperialism after Empire', *Journal of Imperial and Commonwealth History,* XII (1984–85), p. 43.
24. Wm Roger Louis and Ronald Robinson, 'The Imperialism of Decolonization', *Journal of Imperial and Commonwealth History,* XXII (1994), p. 495. John Darwin also explains decolonisation by changes at the metropolitan, the peripheral, and the international level. Contrary to Robinson, however, Darwin stresses the influence of Britain's political and strategic interests rather than international developments. He sees an attempt to transform formal into informal empire: the post-war breakdown of the conditions which had favoured the existence of colonial empires led the British to opt for 'indirect forms of influence and control'. (John Darwin, *The End of the British Empire: The Historical Debate* (Oxford: Blackwell, 1991), p. 121.)

— 2 —

The Empire-Commonwealth under the Attlee Governments

THE INFORMAL EMPIRE – THE MIDDLE EAST AND OTHER OVERSEAS COMMITMENTS

BECAUSE OF BRITAIN'S enormous financial and economic difficulties in 1945, the Treasury called for a radical reassessment of Britain's military commitments. The Prime Minister, Clement Attlee, supported this, arguing that, for a combination of strategic, economic and political reasons, Britain should give up the Middle East and the eastern Mediterranean. Foreign Secretary Ernest Bevin and his officials, as well as the military, strongly resisted. For them, any sign of weakness would only invite Soviet inroads and provoke other countries to prey on British assets. In the end the latter group prevailed, not least because Attlee realised that the hoped-for new world order had failed to materialise. In order to prevent further Soviet expansion and to maintain the special relationship as well as a strong pound, the government therefore vowed to maintain its commitments. Over the following years, 'what we have we hold' thus remained the motto governing British actions, at least with regard to informal empire.

'CUTTING A DASH IN THE WORLD' – ATTLEE VS BEVIN AND THE CHIEFS OF STAFF (1945–47)

Labour's victory in the elections of 1945 was linked to many high hopes and expectations of new policies. Indeed the government set out to make far-reaching changes, at least on the national level. However, as far as foreign and imperial affairs were concerned, there was strong continuity – even though circumstances might have justified some radical changes. The war had left Britain the world's largest debtor nation: £15 billion was owed to the United States, and more than £3 billion to countries within the sterling zone. The foreign deficit amounted to one-tenth of the total national product. But despite the heavy material and financial losses inflicted upon Britain during the war, policy-makers continued to see their country as a world power. The assumption that Britain had not ceased to be a Great Power was 'part of the habit and furniture of our minds: a principle so much [at] one with our outlook and character that it determines the way we act without emerging itself into clear consciousness'[1] – a feeling that was never seriously challenged over the next two decades.

While there was general agreement as to Britain's continuing importance on the international scene, there were considerable disagreements about the extent to which 'empire', and in particular the costly overseas commitments, were necessary to maintain this status. In general, the colonies were not considered a major burden on the Exchequer. Abandoning them was considered incompatible with Britain's moral duty, but also contrary to British interests: it would lose Britain vital sources of raw materials and open new opportunities for Soviet expansionism. More important in terms of money and manpower spent on them, but also with regard to Britain's claim to the role of a world power, were the so-called overseas commitments, i.e. bases and troops stationed overseas. Whereas the Foreign Secretary and the military stubbornly opposed any withdrawal, a relatively small group around the Prime Minister and the Chancellor of the Exchequer argued for a partial reduction of these commitments.[2] During the war, the Treasury had begun to press for a reassessment of the nation's commitments: these were considered beyond Britain's means and often not in its interest. This pressure intensified once hostilities (and US aid through the lend-lease programme) had ended. The new Chancellor of the Exchequer, Hugh Dalton, argued that military expenditure had to be reduced drastically and rapidly or else US and Canadian credits would be exhausted by early 1949; the government would then have no alternative but to cut rations and reduce employment through restrictions on the import of machinery and raw materials – a course which was hardly defensible in public.[3] However, not only did general military expenditure need to be reduced, overseas commitments also had to be cut. Unless the countries of the Middle East and south Asia could be persuaded to lend Britain money for its troops to be stationed there, it would have to move them out.

According to Dalton, the country could not afford to devote such a large proportion of its finance and manpower to defence.[4] It was more important to have enough workers for the export production that was to help reduce the country's enormous deficits. The losses of earnings from overseas investments, adverse terms of trade, and a decline in invisible earnings (especially shipping) meant that a 75 per cent rise in exports over pre-war levels was needed to balance the nation's trade. The Cabinet should stop debating the country's economic prospects in 'an atmosphere of emotional impatience and intellectual levity', and concentrate on the essentials, i.e. the need to ensure economic survival:

> Some of my colleagues seem not to realise at all the serious outlook for the next few years, nor the sort of measures which must be taken if this country … is, at the least, to scramble through these years, without a first-class economic and political disaster.[5]

Britain was vainly trying to do more than it could. Unless it relaxed, the result would be rupture. In these 'hard and heavy years of transition', the government should think of national defence not only against the more distant possibility of armed aggression against British interests or possessions in some far-off part of the world, but also against the immediate risk of economic and financial overstrain and collapse.

For Dalton it was quite clear that Britain could not and should not go on holding responsibility for people claiming their freedom, however incompetent they were to govern themselves. It would be 'a waste both of British men and money to try to hold down any of this crowd against their will'. They had to be allowed to find their own way, 'even through blood and corruption and incompetence of all kinds, to what they regard as "freedom"'.[6] Often Western rule was necessary to prevent chaos or a communist take-over. But the 'brave little United Kingdom' had long borne more than its fair share, both in peace and war. Therefore it was much more tightly stretched than others were, and it was only fair if its allies took over part of the burden. Only by transferring part of the burden to the United States was it possible to get relief in a significant way: 'We must at all costs avoid deluding either the Americans or ourselves into thinking that we can do things which in fact we cannot do. We are already severely overstrained.'[7]

Attlee also called for a reassessment, but his motives differed somewhat from those of Dalton. Largely on strategic grounds he advocated abandoning the Middle East and the Mediterranean, which he considered 'only an outpost position'.[8] Given Britain's huge overseas deficit and the changed international environment, imperial strategy should be adapted to the modern conditions of three-dimensional warfare. In the age of nuclear weapons and long-range bombers, the Empire-Commonwealth – a creation of sea-power – was not a unit that could be defended by itself. Britain had special interests in the Middle East, but was not in a position to defend the area against a determined land attack. The time saved by the use of the Mediterranean route for the purpose 'presumably of reinforcing India' was not worth the cost. In any case it was doubtful whether Britain would be able to keep this route open in case of war. Communications with south-east Asia and Australia could be maintained by use of the Cape route or the Panama Canal. The government had to consider very carefully how to make the most of its limited resources. It should not, 'for sentimental reasons based on the past', become a hostage to fortune. A withdrawal from the Mediterranean and the Middle East would allow the shedding of some particularly heavy and unwelcome burdens. British Somaliland, for example, had always been 'a deadloss and a nuisance'. It was only acquired as part of the scramble for Africa. Of course there would be 'the sentimental objection to giving up a piece of the Empire, but otherwise it would be to our advantage to get rid of this incubus'. Rather than as a power looking eastwards to the Mediterranean, Britain should be considered an easterly extension of a strategic arc stretching from Europe across North America to Australasia.[9]

Attlee was not only willing to shed existing commitments, but also reluctant to take up new ones. When the Cabinet discussed whether Britain should take over the Italian colonies, he argued against such a move. He could see 'no possible advantage to us in assuming responsibility for these areas'. They would involve Britain in immediate loss, and 'the more we do for them the quicker shall we be faced with premature claims for self-government. We have quite enough of these awkward problems already.' Taking over Cyrenaica or Eritrea would saddle Britain with an expense it could ill afford. The former Italian colonies should be handed over to a friendly power or be put under collective trusteeship in order to make sure they did not come under Russian control. Britain, however, had no positive interest in taking them over:

> Why should we have to bear it? Why should it be assumed that only a few great powers can be entrusted with backward peoples? Why should not one or other of the Scandinavian countries have a try? They are quite as fitted to bear rule as ourselves. Why not the United States?[10]

Attlee's ideas were based on a desire to fit Britain into the new world order he expected to crystallise around the United Nations.

International cooperation through the UN and a common defence policy with the United States were to replace the old empire-centred thinking, at least with regard to the Middle East:

> The British Empire can only be defended by its membership of the United Nations Organisation … If the new organisation is a reality, it does not matter who holds Cyrenaica or Somalia or controls the Suez Canal.[11]

In addition, the Prime Minister wanted to develop a new kind of relationship with countries which had hitherto been treated as dependencies. Goodwill and influence were to take the role of force and coercion. One example of this kind of thinking was the transfer of power in India. Another example was the treaty re-negotiation with Egypt concerning the Suez base. The Prime Minister insisted that Britain could not retain its base by force. British interests would only be impaired if it insisted on remaining against the will of the Egyptians. Britain should not alienate 'genuine nationalist feeling', be it in India, Persia or Egypt, by clinging to 'the old technique of obtaining concessions and insisting upon exact compliance with their terms'.

However, Attlee was not an anti-imperialist. He was ready to defend Britain's imperial heritage – provided he thought it worth the effort. While he wanted to get rid of Somalia, south-east Asia was to be defended at all costs. Failure to meet the threat to the security of Hong Kong or Malaya, he feared, would seriously damage Britain's prestige in Asia. And while he wanted to reduce external commitments, he backed Albert Alexander, Minister of Defence, and Bevin against Dalton's demand for an accelerated run-down of the armed forces. He also feared repercussions on Britain's standing in Washington if the country should default too openly on its international commitments.[12] What Attlee had in mind was a concentration of the British defence effort upon those areas and communications considered vital, i.e. the United Kingdom, the United States, the white Dominions, south-east Asia and sub-Saharan Africa. Commitments in other parts of the world, most notably the Middle East, should be cut. The aim was to create a neutral zone, putting a 'wide glacis of desert and Arabs between ourselves and the Russians'.[13]

The Foreign Office (FO), supported by the Colonial Office (CO), the Commonwealth Relations Office (CRO) and the Chiefs of Staff, systematically opposed Attlee's ideas. All of these took for granted the necessity of a global presence. Lack of resources was not seen as a hindrance. Until 1947 the conviction prevailed that Britain's economic and financial problems were only provisional and could be overcome with 'skill and good fortune'.[14] Thus it was neither necessary nor desirable to relinquish existing commitments. According to the FO, Britain's privileged relationship with the United States was due mainly to its global presence.[15] Withdrawal might lead other countries to assume Britain was only a secondary power that could be treated as such. It would be particularly disastrous if the United States drew such a conclusion. Britain's international standing and the stability of sterling depended to a large extent on the special relationship.[16]

The result of showing weakness would be a disastrous loss of confidence in sterling and the destruction of any hope of preserving Britain's position as head of the Commonwealth. Moreover, other countries might confiscate British assets or occupy British territory. Giving up external obligations was therefore not feasible. Britain had to demonstrate that it could overcome its difficulties; it must not be seen to give in. This applied in particular to Egypt, 'an immense African country with a hysterical people' where a little firmness would get Britain at once over its present difficulties.[17] Contrary to the arguments put forward by Attlee, FO officials maintained (somewhat unconvincingly) that growing hostility to Britain was 'largely due to the long series of concessions which we have made to Egypt over the last twelve months without exacting any immediate return'.[18] In Egypt, this was interpreted as a sign of Britain's growing weakness. It was essential to counter this impression by a strong showing.

Bevin shared his officials' attitude. He saw Britain's international commitments as directly linked to its standing. Attlee's proposals as well as Dalton's demands for decisive cutbacks in defence spending met with his 'mulish resistance' and he systematically opposed anything which smacked of relinquishing power.[19] For Bevin, the presence of British troops overseas was necessary to command Soviet respect and to maintain the country's reputation. Any reduction would have an immediate impact upon his bargaining power at the diplomatic table. Relinquishing positions in the Middle East and the Mediterranean would not only lead the United States 'to write us off', but also threaten the 'life-line' of the empire. Any withdrawal would enable the Soviets to establish themselves at the vital sources of petrol and across Britain's lines of communications to the east.[20] Attempting to reach an agreement with the Soviet Union in order to prevent this would be 'to repeat on a larger scale the errors made at Munich' – paper guarantees or the creation of neutral zones did not suffice to contain Moscow.

According to Bevin, the aim of Soviet policy was to establish communism throughout the world. The Soviets were trying to achieve this by the continued aggressive promotion of their ideas by all means short of war. A 'firm and realistic' policy was necessary to prevent Soviet miscalculations as to Britain's real strength.[21] There was already a major communist drive in progress in south-east Asia; sooner or later the Soviets would also make a drive against Britain's position in Africa and the Middle East. Britain had to remain in control of its empire. Giving up any part of it would lead to the rest being controlled by communism.[22] If Britain withdrew, it would be difficult to persuade lesser powers to play a part in the regional defence against communism or to interest the United States in taking over some of its commitments. Economic difficulties must not be allowed 'to stampede us into withdrawals of our outposts throughout the world'.[23]

The Middle East was of particular importance to the Foreign Secretary. Britain had to maintain its presence to prevent the area from falling under Soviet control. Withdrawing at the present moment was 'sheer madness'.[24] The region was not only of strategic, but also of enormous economic importance: if it was properly developed, it might take the place of India.[25] An estimated £150 million worth of goods were exported to the region, and by 1951 it would provide more than 80 per cent of Britain's oil supplies. From the trade point of view, the Middle East was 'probably worth between one and one and a half million men employed to this country'.[26] But the question of withdrawal was also linked to the maintenance of Britain's standing 'as a World Power and therefore as a Great Power'. The attention the United States paid to Britain's strategic and other opinions (as well as to its requirements), was 'directly due to our hold on the Middle East and all that this involves'. Therefore a withdrawal would have incalculable strategic and economic consequences. If Britain were seen to withdraw for lack of military strength, it would join the ranks of the other lesser European powers and be treated as such by the United States.[27] The Dominions would turn towards the United States, while other states would no longer respect Britain. Unless Britain demonstrated that it was determined to maintain its position, the United States would feel compelled to interest itself in the Middle East. It would also refuse the vital financial and political support on which Britain counted.[28] For all these reasons Britain had to retain a firm hold on the Middle East. This could only be achieved by 'tangible evidence of our ability to move forces into the area in an emergency'.[29]

All this did not mean that Bevin was necessarily opposed to the principle of independence. The Foreign Secretary stood firm on Sudanese self-government and was willing to consider Libyan independence because in these cases, Britain's strategic interests seemed better served by autonomous regimes than by formal rule. But Bevin believed that in many other areas withdrawal would endanger British interests, either directly through Soviet penetration or indirectly because of the consequences for Britain's standing in the world. Britain should maintain its presence, but not attempt to dominate the locals. The aim had to be to find a *modus vivendi* by making them realise that their interests were not necessarily contradictory to those of Britain. The governing aim, in the Middle East as elsewhere, should be

> not to dominate its people or dictate how they shall live, but to preserve them against any other domination, to help them to help themselves towards political stability and social advance, to make them feel that their interests coincide with ours, and thus to secure the fullest possible measures of cooperation from them in matters of policy and in arrangements for defence.[30]

In many cases, however, this was not feasible without the maintenance of some military presence. While the long-term objective should be the establishment of a system of friendly partnership between East and West, the short-term objective had to be the containment of communist expansion.

The Chiefs of Staff fully supported the Foreign Secretary. They regarded the retention of Britain's position in the Middle East as one of the three 'cardinal requirements for the future defence of the British Commonwealth'.[31] Bases and other facilities in the area were essential for the rapid deployment of troops in case of global war. If these bases were lost, Britain would have to fight from an 'outer ring', i.e. North America, South Africa, Australia and New Zealand. With the exception of Britain, there would be no air bases from which to launch the strategic air offensive on which British strategy relied until the late 1940s to achieve deterrence in peace and defence in war.[32] The Middle East was essential to provide imperial defence with the necessary depth in case of a Soviet aggression.[33] If Britain cut its commitments and thereby lost the capacity to intervene, the Middle East as well as the Mediterranean would sooner or later be dominated by the Soviet Union. A withdrawal would thus undermine the strategic foundations of imperial defence, i.e. command over the sea and air, the exercise of which required a chain of firmly held bases.

In January 1947, faced with a threat of resignation by the Chiefs of Staff, Attlee gave up his plans for an extended withdrawal from the Middle East.[34] Bevin won the upper hand, although some cutbacks had to be made: on 14 February 1947 the Foreign Secretary announced that the Palestine mandate would be transferred to the United Nations. At the same time, Britain withdrew from Greece. Finally, Bevin and Alexander also had to give ground to the demands for a substantial reduction of the armed forces. Despite these withdrawals, the Middle East continued to assume an important position in British strategy. In the evolving Cold War context even the Prime Minister began to consider it as important. By 1948 he accepted that it was 'now more than ever' necessary, from the strategic aspect, to keep Britain's foothold in the eastern Mediterranean and the Middle East.[35] Attlee realised that the new world order he had hoped for was not likely to materialise in the near future. The United Nations could not guarantee peace and stability, the United States was still reluctant to carry a larger part of the British burden, and the Soviet Union seemed poised for further expansion. To defend British interests it seemed necessary to maintain a worldwide military presence and formal rule, wherever there was no likelihood of a sufficiently strong indigenous government replacing British administration.

'What We Have We Hold': The Last Years of the Labour Government (1948–51)

The conviction that Britain had to maintain its commitments in order to ensure its strategic, political and economic survival continued to dominate British thinking for the rest of the Attlee government – despite increasing financial difficulties. The assumption that Britain could overcome its problems within a relatively short period was dealt a particularly heavy blow by the convertibility crisis of 1947, which followed on the heels of an economic crisis the preceding winter.[36] Just two years later, there was another crisis which made it necessary to devalue sterling from £1:00 = US$4.03 to £1:00 = US$2.80. Although this move temporarily helped British exports, it led to considerable dissatisfaction in the rest of the sterling area.[37] The outbreak of the Korean War in June 1950 dealt another heavy blow to British recovery. The government feared that the conflict would spread to other areas and launched the largest rearmament programme ever planned in peacetime. Rearmament estimates more than doubled from the 1949/50 level to £1,555 million in January 1951. This programme proved a crushing burden on the Exchequer and substantially reduced the amount of British goods available for export. But the government feared that, without it, the United States would refuse Britain protection. It also firmly believed that the special relationship with the United States, the strength of sterling and

Britain's international commitments were all interlinked; any unjustified reduction of the latter would trigger off an unstoppable crumbling process that would destroy the whole fabric.

In the early 1950s policy-makers dropped all plans of transforming Britain, in conjunction with the Commonwealth and western Europe, into a third power and gave clear priority to the development of Britain's relations with the United States. The United States' leadership of the Western world was recognised and welcomed, but it was hoped that Britain would be able to exert a decisive influence on US policy-making. This did not mean that policy-makers were now more willing to consider a withdrawal from overseas commitments – quite the contrary. The informal empire continued to hold an important position in the official mind, both because of its presumed importance for Britain's economic interests and because of its symbolic value. Indeed the realisation of their nation's weakness strengthened the determination of British officials to hold on to areas still under their control.

A good example of the kind of thinking predominating in Whitehall towards the end of the Attlee administration is an FO paper reviewing Britain's 'world responsibilities inherited from four hundred years as an Imperial Power'.[38] It began by analysing the factors underlying British policy: the United Kingdom was not a self-sufficient economic unit, but depended on trade with the Empire-Commonwealth and other countries. There was no global security system, and Britain was faced with a serious external threat. The main objective of foreign policy therefore, had to be to maintain the country's position as a world power while maintaining the highest possible standard of living. Communist expansion had to be resisted, *inter alia*, by making sure the nations of the Middle East and Asia were 'stable, prosperous and friendly' allies. These objectives involved several obligations and responsibilities. The colonies had to be maintained, developed and defended. Britain had to make a major contribution to the maintenance of sea and air communications across the world while independent states which might fall victim to Soviet expansionism had to be backed up militarily and economically.

The paper identified the Middle East as the most important region for British interests, followed by south-east Asia. The strategic value of the Middle East resulted from its importance as a base for strategic air offensives, its oil reserves and its position as a barrier for the defence of Africa, while Asia mattered as a dollar earner and as a sterling source of raw materials. Withdrawal was not feasible. There was no other power apart from Britain capable of linking these areas to the West and of creating some kind of regional association capable of effective resistance against communist expansion.[39] The Middle East as well as south-east Asia were of direct value to Britain, and had therefore to be kept within the British sphere of influence through an active and visible presence. But other, less important areas (such as the West Indies), should not be given up light-heartedly either. Even a partial shedding of obligations would mean a severe contraction of influence without any appreciable reduction in defence costs.

Britain could not support its population and balance of payments by commercial means alone, 'unsupported by political prestige or influence'. Its economic, military and political position had to be regarded as a whole in terms of world confidence and credit. Any withdrawal would have an adverse effect on Britain's economic position: most notably, rendering impossible the continued existence of the sterling area. Countries which now earned foreign exchange for Britain would become either its customers or (more likely) its competitors. The effect of such a development would be cumulative. The break-up of the sterling area would gravely undermine Britain's credit and would further reduce its overseas earnings, particularly those from invisible exports. As a result there would be a heavy fall in the standard of living. Communism would move into the areas evacuated by Britain. The special relationship with the United States would be broken. According to the paper's pessimistic conclusions, the picture of 'splendid isolation on a peaceful and prosperous island' was illusory. Withdrawal from overseas commitments would lead to 'a progressive descent into weakness' that would be impossible to arrest even by the most ingenious means. Britain's various obligations were widely interdependent. The abandonment of any one of them would start 'a crumbling process', which would destroy the whole fabric.

The paper underlined that not to withdraw was less dangerous than evacuation. But it was only possible if the standard of living in the United Kingdom was lowered. Though this decline would still be less than that resulting from a wholesale withdrawal, it would also be hard to sell to the public. The problem, officials mused, was to determine how far external obligations could be modified or transferred to other shoulders without impairing Britain's world position and without sacrificing the 'vital advantages' which flowed from it. It was clearly impossible to withdraw safely from any major obligation if this meant leaving behind a vacuum. Some savings might be effected by sharing certain responsibilities with other Commonwealth countries. But any reduction should be as gradual as possible. Britain could not relinquish its responsibilities unilaterally. The only way in which it could safely reduce the stress on its resources was to transfer some of the burden to its allies, or find suitable local collaborators. The consequences of too sudden 'a relaxation of grip' on overseas commitments were said to be incalculable. The presence of troops in particular had to be maintained as far as possible. They instilled 'just that element of fear and respect for power so ultimately necessary for the maintenance of our position'. By their simple presence they lent power and prestige to Britain.[40]

The views presented in the FO paper continued to dominate British political thinking throughout the 1950s. In particular, the informal empire in the Middle East remained of paramount importance: for policy-makers in London, it was the key argument in favour of Britain's claim to world-power status and to a special relationship with the United States. The interdependence of overseas commitments, a strong pound, the special relationship with the United States and Britain's international position was taken for granted. Being seen to abandon any commitment prematurely, i.e. before it was taken over by a friendly power or secured in another way, was expected to lead to disastrous consequences for Britain's economic, military and political standing.

Conclusion

The Second World War left Britain facing massive economic and financial problems. Dalton and Attlee called for a reduction of overseas commitments in order to reduce the strain on national resources. While the Chancellor of the Exchequer considered empire a waste of money, the Prime Minister wanted to concentrate resources in sub-Saharan Africa, south-east Asia and the white Dominions. According to Attlee, the traditional imperial system no longer offered adequate protection for British interests. The United Nations, as well as cooperation with indigenous nationalists, would ensure that British interests were protected properly. Attlee's proposals were vehemently opposed by Bevin and the Chiefs of Staff. They argued that Britain's power and economic well-being depended on the maintenance of a worldwide presence. To withdraw from the Middle East would not only jeopardise Britain's lines of communications, but also its access to the region's vital oil resources. Many independent nations would lose heart and succumb to communist subversion. Others might be encouraged to prey on British assets. The Dominions would turn towards the United States, which would probably stop its financial and political support for Britain, thus putting at risk the stability of sterling. As a result, Britain would play only a subordinate part in international affairs and suffer unpredictable economic damage.

In 1947 Attlee abandoned his plans for a widespread withdrawal from the Middle East and moved towards Bevin's position. Commitments in Greece and Palestine were cut, but the overall position remained unchanged. Britain's financial difficulties grew stronger, but policy-makers were determined to maintain the status quo. Since the United Nations failed to provide an effective global security system, ministers came to regard the special relationship as the ultimate reference point. To ensure that the United States continued to treat Britain as its closest ally, they thought it necessary to maintain all overseas commitments. Otherwise Britain's economic, strategic and political position would be damaged beyond repair. Sterling, the special relationship and world-power status were thought to be interdependent, hinging on the informal empire. Even minor withdrawals would start a crumbling process destroying the whole edifice; therefore all commitments were to be maintained.

THE FORMAL EMPIRE

After 1945 there was no departure from the broad lines of foreign and imperial policy established before and during the war. The same applied to the colonial sector. Despite some brash talk about a socialist colonial policy, Labour's approach was far from revolutionary. The new government had neither a timetable nor a precise agenda for retreat from colonial empire – apart from the (rather hazy) idea of granting independence to India. Circumstances on the spot led policy-makers to end the formal empire in south Asia much earlier than planned. But in the smaller territories and the settler colonies of East and Central Africa there was hardly any change. The development plans fostered in 1947/48, as well as the continuing support of white immigration in East Africa, demonstrate that Labour knew fairly little about the situation in the colonies themselves, and did not always care as much about the natives as party propaganda would have liked international opinion to believe. Nonetheless, the roots of the decolonisation wave of the 1950s and 1960s can be traced to the late 1940s.

Colonial Policy

Labour's 'New Approach'
During its first year in office, the new government did little to distinguish its colonial policy from that of its predecessors. The CO's approach was to proceed slowly and to rely on local institutions to

train Africans and Asians in managing their own affairs. This changed in late 1946: policy-makers felt that the internal situation in many colonies as well as the state of international opinion (not to mention the public relations of the Labour Party) demanded a new approach, particularly for Africa. Once the difficulties of the immediate post-war period had been overcome, they began to look for alternatives to traditional policy. One driving force behind this search was Andrew Cohen, head of the CO's Africa division. Cohen (as well as many other officials) expected a rapid growth of political consciousness among colonial populations – even if for the time being there were only rudimentary traces of it. In Nigeria and the Gold Coast, the educated classes were already asking for more rapid progress towards self-government, and (as the precedent of India seemed to show) this demand would become more insistent as time went on. The 'rains of nationalism' had not yet burst into full flood, but policy-makers were confident that the moment was not far off – and once it had come, the aim had to be 'not to dam the flood but to divert it into useful channels'.[41]

According to British perceptions, nationalism could be a positive force, stabilising weak states against communism, but it could also go out of control: 'Exploited or dissatisfied nationalism produces a state of mind in which any sense of grievance, injustice or inferiority is magnified out of all proportion.'[42] This could lead to a state of unbalance 'amounting in the worst cases to hysteria'. Since nationalism was a dynamic on the upsurge that could not be stopped, it had to be directed into 'healthy and legitimate' channels of cooperation. The aim accordingly was the creation of the sort of 'healthy' nationalism with which the British could hope to deal. This was to happen by making 'reasonable concessions ... without conceding any points which are genuinely essential'.[43] Policy-makers realised that a demand for independence could rarely be countered by rational arguments. Instead of opposing it, they tried to make sure that the gradual advance to self-government did not lead to open conflict. Nationalism was to be met with diplomacy and cooperation, not intervention and force.

Creech Jones, Colonial Secretary since October 1946, shared this official view. He set up a committee that was to consider the possibility of a more rapid political, economic and social development in the African territories. The resulting Caine–Cohen Report (authored by Sydney Caine and Andrew Cohen), submitted in May 1947, announced the CO's intention to introduce an efficient and democratic system of local government in the colonies. Educated Africans should, whenever possible, be brought to participate in native administration. This was to be their 'school for national government', providing the basis for an extension of African representation in the legislative councils.[44] Local government was to be accompanied by the Africanisation of the civil services. Education and development were to enable the colonials 'to stand on their own feet without support, to manage their own affairs without supervision, and to determine their own future for themselves'.[45] By constructing a political pyramid with a firm base in local government, it was hoped, there was a good chance that London had dug out 'an adequate system of political irrigation channels' before the rains of nationalism burst into full flood. This would allow the CO to remain in control of the timetable and to secure the goodwill of local nationalists. The aim was to win enough time for proper development of the colonies so that British rule could be ended without any deterioration in the social or economic situation.

Despite the concerns of some governors, there is no sign that the government envisaged conceding independence (as opposed to internal self-government) in the near future. Creech Jones and Cohen might have called for a new approach to colonial questions, but at least in one respect their policy did not differ significantly from that of their predecessors – the timetable. The Labour governments never laid down when formal rule was to end. Circumstantial evidence points to a rather long period: probably a few decades less than envisaged before the war, but still in the distant future. The colonies were to be prepared for soundly based self-government, representative and beneficial to all. Since this social, economic and political development had to have a long-term character, the common assumption until the end of the 1940s was that colonial rule might continue for decades, if not for generations to come.[46] However, British rule was generally considered to be for the good of the natives first of all, and it was never intended to last forever:

> We must not dream of perpetual possession, but must apply ourselves to bring the natives into a state that will admit of their governing themselves in a manner that may be beneficial to our interests as well as their own, and that of the rest of the world.[47]

In Africa the period before self-government could be granted was expected to be even longer than in most other parts of the empire. Britain had no intention of 'jeopardising the security, well-being, and liberty' of its colonial subjects by a premature withdrawal.[48] It was committed to Indian self-government and would grant it in the near future. The rest of Asia was to follow after some decades. The

Africans, however, were nothing like as civilised or advanced as the Asians. They still had 'a long way to go' before they could reach independence.[49] In West Africa self-government had to wait until territorial unity had become a reality, and the political leaders representative of, and responsible to, the people. In East Africa self-government would not be granted before the African majority could take its full part along with the European and Asian immigrant communities. Predictions as to the length of the period necessary for such a development were said to be idle. Officials estimated that in the Gold Coast, the territory where Africans were most advanced politically, internal self-government was unlikely to be achieved in much less than a generation. In other territories the process was likely to be considerably slower.[50]

Labour's colonial policy was clearly evolutionary, not revolutionary. After the non-interventionist (and low-cost) policies of the interwar period, the stress was now on development and preparation of the colonies for self-government. Independence was not expected to come about in the near future since the territories simply were not ready for it. Withdrawing British rule (and protection) too early, it was assumed, would only lead to chaos and invite Soviet interference as well as international criticism. However, there was no doubt that most colonies would sooner or later achieve independence. The only question was whether they would 'break away entirely' from the Commonwealth or whether they would 'part from our tutelage on such good terms that they choose to continue some form of association'.[51]

To understand Labour's policy it is necessary to make one proviso: not all colonies were expected to reach independence. Instead dependent territories were classed into three groups: firstly, those potentially capable of achieving independence; secondly, those which could combine with others to form units capable of independence and thirdly, those which fell in neither of these categories. The Labour governments (as well as their Conservative successors) aimed at creating states that were, in British eyes, big enough to survive economically and militarily, and to play a certain role on the international scene. Policy-makers were convinced that smaller territories could not exist on their own. They had either to be governed and protected by a greater power, or, wherever possible, be grouped together in order to achieve independence as a federation. Not only would this ensure the territories' survival, but it would also help restrict the number of Commonwealth members. The club would thus remain an association of relatively important states, thus bolstering British prestige. The Gold Coast, Nigeria and a Malayan

Federation were the only colonies that were expected to attain independence in the foreseeable future. Others might follow, provided they joined a federation. Among them were the East and Central African territories as well as the Caribbean islands. Last, but not least, there were the smaller territories which would have to remain under British sovereignty for an indeterminate period, either because of their strategic importance (Gibraltar, Malta, Cyprus, Aden) or because they were too remote to link up with any other territory (Gambia, St Helena, the Falkland Islands, the Pacific territories).

Marching to the 'Third British Empire': the Development of Colonial Resources

The Labour government launched an extensive (if somewhat incoherent and ill-founded) programme of political and social development which was to be for the good of the colonies. But policy-makers hoped that it would also be possible to use colonial resources to foster metropolitan recovery. In particular, African raw materials were to help close the dollar gap. Large-scale projects were launched in order to boost the production of groundnuts or eggs in spite of opposition from the CO. After the initial enthusiasm had passed (and millions of pounds been lost on unsuccessful projects), policy-makers realised that it was not possible to bring about the rapid development they had hoped for. This as well as the stabilising world economy led them to abandon their attempts to recreate an imperial economy. Once more the colonies were considered merely a responsibility, not an asset.

The 1945 Colonial Development and Welfare Act (CD & W) provided £120 million for the colonies, to be spent over ten years. Policy-makers were eager to claim that British imperialism was dead, 'in so far as it ever existed, except as a slogan used by our critics'. The money provided under the CD & W Act was to prove this.[52] However, policy-makers still thought empire could be used to further metropolitan interests. In the immediate post-war period, they tried to ease Britain's economic and financial problems by drawing on colonial resources. Because of the United Kingdom's huge dollar deficit, trade with non-sterling countries was extremely difficult.[53] The colonies came to be seen as a means of re-establishing Britain's economic independence from the United States. The rapid maximisation of colonial commodity production became an *idée fixe* among most ministers and, to a lesser degree, officials. Plans for a *mise en valeur* of the colonial empire were not new. What was new was the scale on which development was to be undertaken. The sterling crisis of 1947 led to a sharp increase in the attention being paid to colonial resources. In August 1947 the Colonial Development Corporation (CDC) was set up. Its task was to 're-establish and indeed improve upon the pre-war position in which exports of primary produce from the colonies to America were among our principal earners of dollars'.[54] Large-scale development projects were to provide even more food and raw materials for the dollar-starved metropole than had hitherto been made available through bulk purchase agreements. His Majesty's Government (HMG) would invest considerable sums but it was expected that these investments would yield rapid and high returns. The idea of colonial development was hijacked effectively for the good of the British economy.[55]

Ministers were aware that this policy was somewhat contradictory to Labour's professed intentions regarding the colonies. An incautious or incidental disclosure without proper justification, they thought, would come as 'something of a shock' to government supporters and expose HMG to 'very damaging misrepresentation'.[56] Labour ministers (like their Conservative successors) therefore were very careful to present their policy in such a way as to avoid anything that might appear as an indiscriminate exploitation of colonial resources. All development schemes were to demonstrate that their general purpose was the raising of the living standards of the local populations *as well as* obtaining foodstuffs, minerals and raw materials required by Britain. Without this Britain would have to fight against 'quite baseless charges' at the United Nations.[57] Despite these concerns, the principle of developing colonial resources for the good of the metropole was not in doubt – not least because the United States itself encouraged Britain to pursue its efforts in that field in order to prevent another global depression.[58]

The CO alone opposed the planned large-scale development on *moral* grounds. Other officials, especially the Board of Trade, also objected, but mostly on technical grounds. Creech Jones and his officials acknowledged that it was important to keep overseas payments to a minimum, but pointed out that this did not justify action which was contrary to 'the policy of opposition to Colonial exploitation' consistently advocated by the Labour Party. Development was essential to put Britain in a strong position *vis-à-vis* its critics, both on the international scene and at home, who might otherwise accuse it of neglecting its *protégés*.[59] But if the government even *appeared* to be abusing political sovereignty to secure financial advantages at the expense of the colonies, it would unquestionably lead the empire's peoples 'to think that they can get fair treatment only by complete political independence'.[60] Britain's policy should be free from any taint of exploitation. The colonies were not British estates which could be exploited at will – primary production had, above all, to be for the good of the colonies themselves.

The CO felt sincerely committed to develop the colonies for their own sake. When the Treasury proposed to cancel some of the colonial sterling balances, officials rejected the idea immediately. It would mean exacting a forced contribution from territories that ought to have been assisted as generously as Britain's resources permitted.[61] The government could not promise £120,000,000 for colonial development and simultaneously contemplate a cash surrender of precisely the same amount. It would be as impolitic as it would be immoral to take from the colonies with one hand what was given to them with the other: 'nineteenth century conceptions of empire' such as those which seemed to linger on in the Treasury or the FO were totally inappropriate.[62] Unfortunately it was on the economic side that the CO had least control over policy. Officials were always at the mercy of other departments which framed policy in this respect. For example, Creech Jones's memorandum calling for higher prices for colonial producers never went to Cabinet owing to persistent opposition from the Ministry of Food and the Treasury to anything implying higher charges for the government or domestic consumers.

Notwithstanding the CO's opposition, throughout 1947–48 ministers had ambitious ideas about how the colonies could help Britain restore its balance of payments and remain a great power. They had high hopes of getting food and raw materials out of 'many hitherto far too neglected parts of the colonial territories'.[63] Bevin was one of the most enthusiastic supporters of such ideas. Closer trade relations with the Commonwealth as well as an intensified effort for colonial development were to provide raw materials and manu-factured goods from sterling sources.[64] These could be used to buy dollar goods for Britain, while the producers could be paid in sterling. It was believed that Britain would thus make the United States 'dependent on us, and eating out of our hand, in four or five years'.[65]

Africa lay at the heart of the plans proposed by Bevin (and other policy-makers) for an imperial *mise en valeur*. The continent came to be seen as the core of Britain's possessions, offering a wealth of resources waiting to be tapped. Its rapid development was encouraged not only to help the British economy but also to turn the colonies into 'an asset and not a liability as they largely now are'.[66] Typical of the way many policy-makers thought at the time is a memorandum Viscount Bernard (Field Marshal) Montgomery wrote after a tour through various colonies. Montgomery called for a 'master plan' for the development of Africa, which, he claimed, contained everything the British needed: raw materials, labour, food and power.[67] These resources should be developed with the Commonwealth and the rest of the empire serving as market. The African would not suffer in the process. In any case, he was 'a complete savage' incapable of developing the continent himself. Attlee was 'much interested' and Bevin called for a 'serious and urgent study' of Montgomery's ideas.[68]

Only the Colonial Secretary condemned Montgomery's 'astonishing superficiality' and 'amazing ignorance'. Montgomery's proposals, he claimed, ignored political realities as well as the development towards self-government which had been initiated. Imposition of the 'grand design' would conflict with Britain's declared policy of devolution and certainly fail to secure local cooperation.[69] There was 'a very great danger' in talking too much about the possibilities and prospects of colonial development. What was really going to happen would be much smaller than the 'flood of weekend speeches on the boundless possibilities of developing the Empire' suggested. There was little likelihood in the next few years of substantial results either in raising the standard of living of colonial peoples or in increased supplies to the metropole.[70] To secure development on the scale envisaged by Montgomery, the government would have to provide capital and consumer goods on a much larger scale than at present. In order to be able to use the continent's natural wealth, much preparatory work had to be done: for example, infrastructure was often inappropriate or completely missing, qualified manpower was scarce, and basic knowledge of what could be achieved, how and at what cost, was at best rudimentary – problems that were also ignored by other 'adepts' of imperial development. Most important for Creech Jones, however, was probably the fact that Montgomery clearly did not care very much about the fate of the locals.

In 1948 an increasing number of policy-makers began to realise that colonial development was a complex process that could not be hastened overnight. After the costly failure of the Tanganyika groundnuts project and the Gambia egg scheme, policy-makers grew increasingly disillusioned with the prospects of imperial development, particularly since the two above-mentioned failures were no exception: many other sites as well gave cause for anxiety.[71] Henceforth, discussions in Whitehall on what was achievable became noticeably more sober – plans like those of Montgomery were now passed over in silence. Slowly but surely it was realised that turning the colonies into profitable estates was much costlier and more difficult than expected. Any hopes ministers may have harboured for a rapid development of imperial resources were finally shattered when, in March 1951, the economic policy committee authoritatively informed them that there was no prospect of a large-scale increase in colonial production.[72] There was a long way to go before 'anything remotely resembling an investor's paradise' would appear.[73] Without the basic services the colonial field was bound to remain unattractive for external investment of any kind. The whole conception of imperial development as the solution to all difficulties was mistaken.[74]

Paradoxically, the constant warnings by officials did not quite have the beneficial effect for the colonies they had hoped for. Once ministers had accepted that development was a difficult business unlikely to yield any high returns, CO demands for the allocation of more resources met with rather frosty replies – a metropole in dire straits could not afford to dissipate scarce resources on its poor dependants. The Treasury, in particular, offered stiff resistance. However, even the Treasury was aware of the importance of granting at least some aid. Cut-backs would lead to accusations that HMG was seeking some fundamental changes in its relations with the colonies, to the disadvantage of the latter.[75] Officials acknowledged that the United Kingdom had 'a political and moral responsibility' for promoting the colonies' development. If there was no improvement in the standards of living, some territories would be subject to strong political pressure from local communist parties. A rapid falling off in the current rate of investment might cause unemployment and should therefore be avoided. An adequate rate of development, however, would help to ensure the colonies' political stability and prosperity, which in its turn would enable the colonies to meet their liabilities arising from Britain's past investment.[76] Apparently, development aid was never wholly disinterested.

By the early 1950s, the idea of developing the empire in order to restore Britain's balance of payments had disappeared from the minds of most policy-makers. US help through the Marshall Plan, the stabilisation and liberalisation of world trade as well as the realisation that colonial development was likely to be very costly and slow, all contributed to the virtual disappearance of the original enthusiasm. The idea was shortly revived when the Conservatives took office. One of Oliver Lyttelton's earliest requests was for a Cabinet paper indicating the possibilities of increasing colonial production of food-stuffs and raw materials, and of re-routing colonial exports 'so that more of their existing production comes to this country instead of going to other less laudable destinations'.[77] But his officials advised that, except for a few commodities such as copper, cotton and sugar, the chances of increasing colonial supply to Britain were very limited. Much depended on public and private investment, none of which was likely to be made to a sufficient extent. The greatest problem of colonial development was an improvement of agriculture and food production for the locals themselves. Cash crops and mining could not be pressed to the neglect of this basic need.[78] It was not simply a matter of extracting 'one or two useful materials for which there may be short term increases in demand'. Nor could development be achieved through a few large-scale projects directed from London.

Lyttelton accepted these arguments. In the following years his major preoccupation was not with the supposed riches of the colonial empire, but the need to attract US capital to finance its development.[79] Henceforth, very little was heard of imperial development. Not only had the colonies proved to be unsuitable for large-scale projects, but the United States also continuously prodded Britain towards free trade under the General Agreement on Tariffs and Trade (GATT). Furthermore, because of international pressure and local discontent, it was not possible to maintain artificially low prices for colonial produce: by 1951 the United Kingdom was generally paying open market prices for such produce.[80]

Plans for the development of an imperial army met the same fate as those for economic development. For some time after the war it was hoped that troops from the colonies could relieve part of the burden resting on the British army. After some initial enthusiasm, officials quickly realised that none of the remaining colonies could provide an imperial army. Any increase in the size of colonial forces was primarily dependent on the provision of finance, equipment and training staff from Britain – neither of which London was able or willing to provide to the extent needed.[81] The size of colonial forces was also limited by the fact that in many territories, there was no surplus manpower. The findings of the CO were corroborated by the Chiefs of Staff: an increase in indigenous troops would affect neither the size of British forces overseas nor the scale of Britain's strategic reserve. Stationing coloured troops in territories such as Gibraltar or Cyprus would be subject to considerable objections by the local population, while using African troops in Korea or Malaya would not be profitable.[82] In addition, it might also lead to conflict with British soldiers: widespread rank-and-file prejudices had already led to an 'unfortunate series of racial incidents'.[83] Even though the proposal continued to be aired annually by a small group of Conservative and Labour back-benchers, official interest in a colonial army had disappeared by the early 1950s.

In the years that followed, the colonies came to be regarded largely as a responsibility (if not a burden) rather than an asset. They had to be defended and developed, and Britain was criticised for its position as a colonial power. What now came (again) to matter most was to ensure that no hostile power (in particular the Soviet Union) gained control of these territories, and that Britain could come out 'with honour'. This trend is well illustrated by developments in south Asia.

The Legacy of War: South Asia

As shown above, Labour had few concrete ideas of what to do with the colonies. Only with regard to south Asia were there somewhat precise ideas. India was to attain independence after about five to six years. Burma and Ceylon were to follow with some delay. They were more advanced than the African territories, but not ready for self-government. Burma, in particular, was first to recover from the ravages of Japanese occupation. However, things developed in a totally different way.

'Coming Out with Honour': India

At the beginning of the nineteenth century, the Viceroy George Curzon proudly proclaimed that as long as Britain ruled India, it was 'the greatest power in the world'.[84] Less than half a century later, this belief in the importance of governing India had all but evaporated. After the war, the British were rather desperate to find a solution that would allow them an honourable withdrawal from the subcontinent. In August 1947 the Raj was ended – contrary to the ideas held by Labour in 1945 – without any treaty regulating Anglo-Indian relations after the transfer of power. Nonetheless, policy-makers by no means considered that their 'pre-war objectives' had been defeated or that India had been 'lost to the empire', as some authors seem to imply.[85]

Before the war, Labour had pledged to grant independence, but there were no plans of how to deal with the problems of the princely states and the Muslim League.[86] Once in office, Attlee and his colleagues set out to fulfil their pledge: fresh elections were to be held, and an all-Indian assembly was to work out a new constitution. Once it was ready, British India was to become independent. At the same time, a union with the States was to be created. Partition was not envisaged. The new government was apparently determined to end British rule in India. This was felt to be a moral obligation. But it was also thought to be in Britain's interest to gain a partner rather than a colony which had to be ruled at the price of local resistance and international criticism. Ministers were willing to move ahead, but had not taken into account the many obstacles still remaining. There was neither a clear timetable nor any contingency planning. The government believed that there was plenty of time to make the necessary arrangements for independence – such as Indianising army and administration, both of which still depended heavily on British personnel. Until mid-1946 the Cabinet expected the transfer of power to be several years away. Recruitment for the Indian Civil Service (ICS), for example, continued as late as August 1946. Labour's initial insouciance was partly due to its ignorance of the local situation and partly to the expectation that close cooperation would continue after the end of formal rule, as in the other Dominions. Supposedly, this made it superfluous to develop detailed plans.

The government's main objective was to avert administrative chaos and to secure an orderly transfer of power to a stable, unified India, coupled with 'satisfactory defensive arrangements'.[87] British thinking was dominated by the risk of a global war against the Soviet Union. It was assumed that such a conflict was likely to break out sooner or latter, and that it was essential to deny the Russians access to south Asia. Therefore power was to be transferred only if the subcontinent's defence could be ensured. Britain's strategic interest was 'not so much that we ourselves as an empire should possess this, that or the other country, but that we should deny to our potential enemies territory from which they could threaten our sea communications'.[88] The British feared that without their protection, India would easily be overrun. This would lead to Soviet control of the Middle East and the Indian Ocean. That is why the independent state demanded by the Muslim League was not thought to be feasible: its creation would not only reduce the two successor states to 'ramshackle' creatures, but would also make it impossible to organise an effective defence against Russia.[89]

The elections of 1946 confirmed Congress and the Muslim League as the two leading parties. However, neither showed any sign of being willing to cooperate with each other, since their demands for a strong centralised state and Pakistan, respectively, were mutually exclusive. Meanwhile communal tensions increased. The viceroy Lord Wavell warned that the Muslims would not cooperate under the present proposals and that the probable result of setting up a constitution-making machinery against their will would be civil war. There was no time to hope for the gradual evolution of a political agreement. The run-down administrative machine, the scarcity of manpower and resources and mounting intracommunal tensions called for a speedy solution:

> Things out here seem to get worse and worse, and I do not think I am an alarmist in thinking that we in India will be extremely lucky to get through till June next [1946] without serious trouble. Everything points to the absolute necessity of some solution being found.[90]

The civil services were losing heart, Warell warned, and there were even signs of demoralisation in the Indian army.[91] If the Indian forces ceased to be reliable, however, the British alone would not be able to control the situation or to protect essential communications. To regain control, 'nothing short of an organised campaign for the reconquest of India' would be necessary – an option the Viceroy as well as the government immediately discarded as unrealistic.[92] Even if Britain were able to suppress a violent attempt to oust it from the sub-continent, it would be very difficult to maintain authority afterwards. All positions of responsibility in the administration would have to be occupied by British officials. This would make it necessary to start recruitment 'on a scale never before attempted'.[93]

Having realised that the Indian parties could not be persuaded to accept the existing proposals, in March 1946 HMG sent a team led by Sir Stafford Cripps, A.V. Alexander and Lord Pethick-Lawrence to negotiate an agreement. After interviewing the leaders of the two major parties, the delegation presented five alternatives: Britain could withdraw as soon as possible; it could announce its withdrawal for 1 January 1947, thus allowing the Indians at least some time to prepare for independence; it could appeal to the United Nations; it could try to maintain British rule by force; and last but not least, it could choose to transfer power in the Hindu provinces in southern and central India, while maintaining control in the north-western and north-eastern provinces with a Muslim majority.[94]

The Cabinet excluded as unrealistic any attempt to maintain British control in the face of open revolt. Major reinforcements could be provided only at the cost of reducing security in other areas that were considered more important to British interests, for example, Palestine or Greece.[95] In addition, domestic and international opinion would be hostile to any attempt to extend British rule by force. The same applied to unconditional withdrawal, an option that would plunge the subcontinent into chaos and civil war. This would be an inglorious end to Britain's long association with India. Opinion abroad and at home would regard it as a policy of scuttle unworthy of a great power.[96] Withdrawal would thus weaken Britain's international position because it would be interpreted as 'evidence of a decline in British power and resolution'.[97] It would also adversely affect Britain's prestige and influence in the Middle and Far East, inducing the locals to put up less resistance to Russian pressure. Therefore it was essential to avoid at all costs 'a policy of scuttle and humiliation'.[98] Any appearance of weakness might well precipitate the troubles ministers wished to avoid: it would 'arouse very strong reaction[s] in this country and the Dominions and have a most serious effect on our international position'.[99] Britain had to avoid at all costs a situation it was apparently not able to control anymore: 'It must be clear that we were going freely and not under compulsion'.[100]

Ministers resolved that Britain would maintain its responsibilities until the Indians could find a basis for accepting its offer of independence, i.e. transfer of power to a united India with a federal constitution. The Cabinet Mission (i.e. the team led by Cripps, Alexander and Pethick-Lawrence) was once more to try to hammer out a compromise. Surprisingly enough, the three ministers did reach an agreement, reflected in an optimistic statement, and left India on 29 June 1946. While the Cabinet was confident that the road ahead was now clear, the Viceroy continued to point to the risk of civil war, arguing that the basic problems were unchanged. His warnings seemed to come true when, at the end of July, the Muslim League withdrew its acceptance of the Cabinet Mission's proposals. Unperturbed by this turn of events, London went ahead, filling for the time being the League's posts in the Indian government with Congress members.

The Viceroy once more advised that Britain could not afford to stay on much longer. The administrative machine was 'extremely weak' and the few Europeans remaining in the services were tired and dispirited.[101] The loyalty of the Indian civil servants was bound to be tempered by thoughts for the future. The ICS, formerly the 'steel frame' of the Raj, was now dangerously thin on the ground.[102] Because of these difficulties, Wavell argued that the Cabinet should accept his breakdown plan. Contingency planning was vital: 'We cannot safely continue to drift without a clear idea of how and when we are to leave.'[103] It was suggested that Britain should, at the latest by 31 March 1947, announce its intention to withdraw gradually to the north-western and north-eastern provinces, transferring power only in provinces with a clear Hindu (and Congress) majority. Then it could try to reach a compromise in the remaining provinces or transfer them to the League. By March 1948 the withdrawal from the whole of India would be complete. According to Wavell, this middle course between repression and scuttle would allow Britain to get out safely and without major losses in case the Indians did not reach a compromise. But it was hoped that the announcement of the plan alone would suffice to coax them into agreement.

Ministers acknowledged that the withdrawal from India had to take place in the near future, but they did not appreciate the Viceroy's plan for a military-style evacuation.[104] They thought that a statement on the lines proposed by Wavell would destroy any prospect of an ordered and peaceful transfer of power. The army would disintegrate, and there was a high risk of total administrative breakdown. As soon as the withdrawal was announced, everybody would start 'scrambling for position'. It would become impossible to control the subcontinent. Moreover, a withdrawal on the lines proposed by Wavell would create the impression that Britain had been forced out of India, thus inflicting irreparable damage upon its (as well as the government's) prestige. It was essential therefore to avoid civil war and partition.[105] India's unity and its security were closely linked, and Britain had a stake in both. The Soviet Union would certainly take advantage of an unprecedented opportunity to establish itself in a position from which it could threaten the whole fabric of the empire.[106] Leaving India without a stable successor state would jeopardise communications with Australia and New Zealand as well as oil transports from the Persian Gulf.[107] A withdrawal into provinces with a Muslim majority would fail to satisfy Britain's strategic needs and result in civil war. From a military and political perspective Wavell's plan was therefore 'completely unacceptable'.

In the autumn of 1946 the situation worsened considerably, with communal tensions growing ever stronger. In October there were major massacres in eastern Bengal, and in November the governor of Bihar reported riots, which left 5,000 people dead. Britain now had the responsibility for India without the power to enforce law and order – an embarrassing position with potentially fatal results for Britain's international standing. At last this was also recognised in London. In December 1946 ministers prepared a statement declaring that it was Britain's intention to hand over power by 31 March 1948.[108] Should the constituent assembly by this date not be representative of the whole of India, power would be transferred to governments that were deemed representative of different parts of the country. Although this was against British interests, ministers consoled themselves with the view that it was the only way of ensuring a dignified withdrawal. They were all 'very tired', and at numerous meetings the same arguments had been 'raised and chased round and round'.[109] Since withdrawal was inevitable, ministers thought it essential to make the best of it. The announcement would present the withdrawal from India as 'the final stage in a deliberate policy of encouraging India's development towards self-government, to which successive Governments in this country had subscribed for the last thirty years', i.e. not as an abdication, but as the fulfilment of Britain's mission in India. The government should not excuse its action, but rather claim credit for it.[110]

Bevin vehemently opposed this decision. The Viceroy should be replaced with 'somebody with courage who, even if he were the last man left there would come out with dignity and uphold the British Empire and Commonwealth'. Not only was India going, the Foreign Secretary warned, but Malaya, Ceylon and the Middle East were going with it, with tremendous repercussions on the African territories. What Britain needed was a new General Gordon, not another Dunkirk. Attlee should not give way to this 'awful pessimism'. The government was knuckling under at the first blow, thus losing all international respect: 'We appear to be trying nothing except to scuttle out of it, without dignity or plan.'[111]

The Prime Minister replied firmly that it was not possible to stem the tide. The Raj depended on tens of thousands of lesser functionaries whose loyalty was waning by the week. The government was in no way scuttling out. For economic, military and political reasons alike, London could not afford to commit British troops to a long series of operations in India. Therefore, it was essential to leave as long as an ordered withdrawal was still possible.[112] Attlee called on Bevin to propose a 'practical alternative'. Characteristically, the Foreign Secretary did not reply. His reaction was emotional, based on a certain image of how Britain should behave, not a rational assessment of the possibility of maintaining British rule – a fact he finally had to acknowledge.

The statement's publication was postponed when Congress suddenly gave in to demands made by the League. In the meantime, Wavell came to be blamed for the political stalemate in India: his soldierly mind allegedly was not 'supple' enough to deal with the subcontinent's intricate problems. Attlee prepared to replace him with Lord Louis Mountbatten, who urged the Prime Minister to accept a speedy transfer of power. The statement announcing the British withdrawal by June 1948 should be made even if there was an agreement between Congress and the League. It was of paramount importance to set a time limit. Otherwise the Indian public would suspect an escape clause, and the government would be accused of '"scuttling" without having the guts to admit it'.[113] Ministers still hoped for a compromise and were not yet willing to issue the statement. They realised that once a date had been set, there would no longer be a safeguard against partition. It was only when the League announced its boycott of the constituent assembly that ministers decided to cross the Rubicon. On 20 February 1947 the statement was read in the House of Commons. One month later Mountbatten arrived in Delhi.

Having been in India for three weeks, Mountbatten realised that even those who had predicted a reprieve of only 18 months had been too optimistic: there was practically no hope of a compromise, and the time remaining until a total collapse of British rule was much shorter than assumed. Mountbatten now argued that the transfer of power should take place within a few months, with partition being accepted as a last resort.[114] Anything else would lead to a civil war which would be impossible to control. The Viceroy underlined that fortunately, Congress had indicated its desire for India to become a Dominion, at least until a new constitution had been worked out. This was 'the greatest opportunity ever offered to the Empire'. Not only did it permit a speedy transfer of power, but it also increased Britain's prestige and ensured future defence collaboration.[115] On 22 May 1947 ministers endorsed Mountbatten's recommendation. In order to prevent 'widespread and uncontrollable communal disturbances', the Viceroy was to try one last time to reach an agreement.[116] If this attempt failed, he was to announce that power would be transferred to two separate governments within three months.

On 3 June Mountbatten announced that the transfer of power to a Congress-dominated 'Hindustan' and a League-controlled 'Pakistan' would take place on 15 August 1947. The following weeks were spent in hasty preparation for independence, most of the time being taken up by the demarcation of the new boundaries and the partition of army, administration and other assets. Mountbatten managed to coax most of the princely States into a union with one of the two Dominions – with the noticeable exceptions of Hyderabad and Kashmir. The latter lapse, in particular, poisoned Indo-Pakistani relations for many years, thus destroying any hope for peaceful cooperation between the two states. In the weeks immediately following the transfer of power, riots and massacres erupted all over northern India. Hundreds of thousands of Indians were killed, and millions lost their homes. Indian units were seldom able (and often unwilling) to interfere, while British troops had strict orders to act only in self-defence. Nonetheless, policy-makers were content with the results of Mountbatten's manoeuvring: Britain could withdraw in an honourable fashion, and the subcontinent did not drift into 'a foreign and hostile orbit'.[117] India was partitioned, but the successor states maintained the Commonwealth link. Thus there was no immediate need to work out a new constitution and pass it in parliament, while administrative and military assistance could continue. At first it was also hoped that India and Pakistan would both accept Mountbatten as their common governor-general. Supposedly, this would create 'conditions favourable to an ultimate union of all the Indias'. The British (in particular the Viceroy himself) hoped until the last that the unity of the subcontinent could ultimately be re-established.[118] The underlying assumption presumably was that once a Muslim state was conceded, the League would be reluctant to destroy the unity of the subcontinent. Jinnah's decision to become governor-general of Pakistan, and then the conflict over Kashmir, destroyed this fanciful scheme.

In London, the highly complex administrative difficulties, refugee movements and bloodshed resulting from partition were considered regrettable, but inevitable. Attlee and his ministers knew as well as the Viceroy that the situation was chaotic, and that the difficulties arising from partition had been aggravated by the short time in which it took place. But Britain had avoided a scuttle, and the transfer of power seemed to enhance its prestige and standing. Ministers consoled themselves that 'at least we have come out with honour instead of, as at one time seemed likely, being pushed out ignominiously'.[119] The transfer of power in 1947 differed strongly from the plans the government had envisaged in 1945. Nevertheless, it was not considered a defeat. Policy-makers were convinced that independence would not mean the end of Anglo-Indian collaboration, but rather a new chapter of it. As long as there was a stable successor government maintaining friendly relations with Britain, the transfer of power did not have to damage vital British interests. Because of its presumed future dependence on Britain for defence (as well as administrative and technical know-how), India was expected to follow its lead on all major issues of foreign policy.[120] A paper written in July 1946, following an order by Wavell to draw up a cost-benefit analysis of independence, demonstrates this attitude.

The paper concluded that the main advantage derived by Britain from its control of the subcontinent was strategic. The greatest asset was India's manpower, followed closely by its contribution in war material.[121] But Britain could no longer afford to *pay* for these assets as it had done during the Second World War. In addition, India had made it clear that it no longer wanted its troops to be used to support Britain's 'imperialist' policy in the Middle or Far East. Even where Indian troops were still available (as in Burma), their value was highly doubtful as they could probably not be employed against anything resembling a popular uprising for freedom. Participation of an independent India in Commonwealth defence would be of greater value than British control of the subcontinent. On the economic side, the paper continued, India was of some importance, but this did not necessarily depend on British rule. The United Kingdom was 'a natural market' from which Indian importers would continue to seek their requirements, and British technical and management skills were highly valued.[122] In the sphere of international prestige Britain would gain by transferring power, provided it was done in an orderly and friendly manner. If the subcontinent lapsed into chaos, however,

Britain would lose trade, strategic advantages and prestige. Since none of this seemed likely in August 1947, British officials thought they had every reason to congratulate themselves.

Ministers at first thought it necessary to make the transfer of power conditional on a treaty. Later on this was quietly dropped, since Indian goodwill and Commonwealth membership came to be seen as a better guarantee for British interests than any written agreement. At first Attlee was still determined to secure Britain's strategic interests by treaty. But the Cabinet delegation and the Viceroy advised against making the transfer of power conditional on any concessions of this kind. They believed that India would itself ask for a defence agreement and probably even Commonwealth membership, provided it was not forced into it.[123] There was a much better prospect of 'India remaining in the Empire' if independence were not bound to any conditions. British aims could only be secured through goodwill, not pressure. Cripps, in particular, insisted that it was not realistic to imagine that there could be any arrangements permanently to guarantee British interests.[124] After some hesitation the Prime Minister accepted these arguments and overruled Bevin, Lord Listowel and the military, all of whom still wanted a treaty. Attlee also opposed the proposal to leave British troops in India after independence. The military argued that this would stabilise the country and help Britain to maintain its influence with neighbouring states. Mountbatten, however, pointed to Egypt where there were widespread demonstrations against the presence of British troops, and advised against any such plan. Attlee followed his advice and ordered all British troops to be withdrawn after 15 August 1947.[125]

The Chiefs of Staff also eventually acknowledged that it was not realistic to insist on a defence agreement. There were two reasons: first, given Britain's weakness it could not afford to let negotiations break down; therefore none of its needs could be classified as essential.[126] Second, past experience showed that even where military treaties were secured, their public nature rendered them ideal targets for nationalist attacks. Therefore it was probably better not to insist. To compensate for the lack of an agreement, the military at first wanted to retain the Nicobar and the Andaman Islands under British sovereignty.[127] But the Cabinet followed Mountbatten's argument that any attempt to retain the islands under British control would lead to an 'absolute flare-up throughout the length and breadth of India'.[128] Indian friendship was more important than any strategic short-term gain. However, the issue did not lead to major discussions. There was general agreement that control over the Maldives (which were not a part of British India) would be retained for the foreseeable future, providing necessary air and naval facilities in the Indian Ocean.[129] The Raj had thus, at least in British eyes, been ended rather successfully, without jeopardising vital interests and seemingly opening the way for close collaboration between Britain and India. There were no comparable feelings about the transfer of power in India's eastern neighbour, Burma.

'Scuttling without Having the Guts to Admit It': Burma

Unlike its position on India, Labour had not pledged itself to grant independence to Burma. Labour's policy was that developed by the War Cabinet, i.e. to help the local population 'to secure full self-government within the Empire at the earliest practicable date'.[130] Elections to a constituent assembly were to be held after three years of direct rule. Self-government would be attained, at the earliest, after five or six years, the minorities in the frontier areas staying subject to a special regime. After several years of Japanese occupation, the country's infrastructure and administration had to be re-established; in addition there were large groups of armed underground fighters (many of whom had sided with the Japanese until a few months before the end of the war). Nonetheless, it was assumed that a return to 'normal' political life would be possible without any major deployment of manpower or resources.

Contrary to policy-makers in London, Mountbatten, then head of the South-east Asia Command (1943–46), advocated a new approach. He suggested the promise of immediate independence to Burma upon the restoration of civil government.[131] The Japanese decision to grant a measure of independence had left its trace. Therefore Britain could not just go back as before, but had to 'strike out on some new line' if she was to find a place in Asia again. The war had let loose a number of nationalist movements which were likely to react upon each other. All the European powers in Asia had to be ready to make deals with them. These were the 'signs of the times'.[132] The establishment of friendly relations with the younger generation of Burmese nationalists therefore was an urgent task (and, as later in India, Mountbatten assumed he was particularly predisposed to achieve this). In Burma this new generation was represented by Aung San's Anti-Fascist People's Freedom League (AFPFL).

Governor Reginald Dorman-Smith was convinced that the policy outlined by Mountbatten was 'wrong from every point of view'.[133] Instead of working with former Japanese collaborators, Britain should favour those Burmese who had not betrayed their masters. The AFPFL paid only lip service to democratic ideals and conducted a repressive policy against other parties.[134] Ministers tried to find a middle way between these two positions. While they were eager not to drive Aung San and his (armed) followers underground, they were also not willing to contemplate Burmese self-government in the near future, particularly not outside the Commonwealth. British officials would make no progress with 'the very astute politicians' with whom they had to negotiate by playing their hand from a position of weakness, i.e. by making too many concessions right at the beginning:

> We shall find it difficult enough to play even from strength! But the moment they think that we are out to bring them in at any cost and that we are prepared to go one inch beyond the limits set by HMG ... they will have us on the run. That is a state of things that the Cabinet would be most reluctant to see come about.[135]

The AFPFL was to participate in political life, but not to the exclusion of other forces. Constitutional advance would be gradual, just as in other colonies. This policy was implemented after the restoration of civil government in October 1945. Dorman-Smith set up an advisory council to which he also invited the AFPFL.

Ministers had hoped that the situation would stabilise over time, but in the spring of 1946 the political climate was still tense: security was weak, strikes and demonstrations continued to flare up all over the country, and the AFPFL insisted on a rapid transfer of power. London grew increasingly uneasy about the 'extremely confused' situation and replaced Dorman-Smith with Hubert Rance.[136] Shortly after his arrival in Rangoon the new Governor had to face a strike by local police. His reaction was to start consultations with the AFPFL. He was reluctant to concede all its demands, knowing that this would have meant handing over the country to 'a number of (largely) untried politicians with a strong Communist trend'. But he considered concessions necessary to avoid open rebellion. Britain had neither enough troops to deal with such a situation nor the support of world opinion; therefore it was vital to act swiftly.[137] Rance's move seemed to have been the right decision: Aung San negotiated a settlement, and the situation calmed down. Within four weeks, however, tension began to rise again, with the AFPFL demanding even wider powers.

The Cabinet advised the governor to do his best 'to put the brake on': he should not make too many concessions so as to avoid repercussions on the delicate negotiations going on in India. But while ministers were anxious to slow down advance, Rance pressed for further acceleration. According to his view, the AFPFL was the only party that could keep a government going without being paralysed by strikes.[138] The remaining Indian troops would be largely withdrawn by February 1947. But even before that date it would be virtually impossible to employ them: any uprising would probably be presented by its organisers as one for freedom from British 'oppression', thus attracting international and, in particular, Indian support. British reinforcements were not available. Therefore the maintenance of order by military force had to be ruled out.

According to Rance, the AFPFL could not afford to wait: its influence would keep declining so long as it could be represented as 'poor clients of His Majesty's Government waiting for crumbs to fall from their master's table'. To hold it off was to expose it to the fate of the Mensheviks: it would be 'devoured' by less cooperative extremists. But once the government negotiated with the AFPFL as the national representatives its influence would grow again. There was a new spirit of nationalism abroad – 'tempered and restrained, but quite unyielding'. Britain had either to come to terms with it quickly, or prepare to hold Burma by force. Developments in Indonesia were closely watched in Burma: the situation had much in common, except that the Indonesian leader, General Sukarno, had attained his position by force.[139] Britain still had the possibility of securing an orderly transfer of power in Burma, but the longer a settlement was delayed, the greater the danger of extreme elements gaining the upper hand.

The advice given by Rance was contradictory. He pointed to the strength of AFPFL and warned of a second 'Indonesia'. On the other hand he depicted concessions as the only means of protecting 'moderate' nationalists such as Aung San. Ministers recognised the lack of coherence and hesitated. In the meantime Aung San made new demands: Britain was to announce before 31 January 1947 that Burma would be independent within a year. At the same time, the AFPFL-dominated executive council was to be recognised as the national government. Despite his dislike of 'a caucus with no electoral mandate', Pethick-Lawrence advised the Cabinet to invite a Burmese delegation. The situation in Burma was deteriorating rapidly; any delay would lead to anarchy and rebellion.[140] Ministers agreed and sent an official invitation. Having received the latter, the AFPFL stepped up its demands. The delegation would only come to London if the British government announced publicly that the purpose of the visit was to prepare for an interim government with full powers, and that the forthcoming general elections would elect a constituent assembly for the whole of Burma, i.e. *de facto* power was to be transferred without prior elections and without any stipulations for the protection of minorities.

Pethick-Lawrence advised his colleagues to accept these demands.

British troops available were totally inadequate to control Burma for much longer, let alone to deal with a widespread rebellion. It was essential to reach a speedy solution.[141] To give in now, even to an apparently exaggerated demand, would probably retain Burmese friendship and render possible the continuity of British trade and influence. Open strife, however, would ruin prospects for a long time. Since the government had just decided to announce the withdrawal from India, it was neither desirable nor realistic to try to maintain British rule for much longer. It would be wise to give Burma the same option as India and take the risk of 'her exercising it in an unwise way'.[142] The British were dealing with 'a body politically immature, singularly lacking in experience of the outside world', and with no appreciation of the difficulties their country would have to face without British support; but the British would reach nothing by trying to reason with the Burmese. The AFPFL was not the ideal partner for a transfer of power. Under normal circumstances, HMG would avoid committing itself at this stage. Unfortunately though, Britain's position was far from strong and it had to take certain risks.

Pethick-Lawrence's advice did not go unopposed. The Colonial Secretary pointed to possible repercussions on Ceylon and Malaya. In Ceylon, in particular, an orderly transfer of power would be rendered difficult, if not impossible, since Ceylonese politicians would at once demand independence.[143] According to Alexander, the government risked being manoeuvred into a 'humiliating position'. The devastation caused by the war had made Burma less ready for self-government than other territories. Britain should assume its responsibilities rather than run away from them.[144] Alexander and Creech Jones were opposed by other ministers who argued that, if the principle of independence was sound for India, it was also sound for Burma. The British had persuaded the Dutch, 'much against their original inclination', to accept a settlement involving almost complete independence for Indonesia. It would seem odd if Britain tried to take a different line in Burma and it would achieve little by doing so. All the evidence was that the AFPFL was the only political force with which the government could come to terms. Whatever his failings, Aung San had shown 'a considerable degree of moderation and statesmanship' in the last year, preferring to attain his ends by constitutional means.[145] Refusing to transfer power would make it necessary to hold the country by force for some years. The result would almost certainly be to ensure that Burma left the empire as soon as it could.

The last part of the argument is most revealing: if Britain granted independence immediately, it was hoped, Burma would still remain in the Commonwealth (and thus Britain's sphere of influence). If Britain tried to hold the country by force, however, the Burmese would sever all ties with Britain once they had achieved independence, as inevitably they would, sooner or later. A majority of ministers was convinced that concessions were vital to maintain local goodwill which, in its turn, was of crucial importance for Anglo-Burmese relations after independence. There was not much to be gained by trying to maintain formal rule by force, and there was little the government could do against the AFPFL that would not hurt British interests even more than a transfer of power.[146] In addition, there was no longer any reason to fear repercussions on the nego-tiations in India as ministers had already decided to announce the transfer of power by mid-1948. After some hesitation ministers therefore accepted Aung San's demands.[147] There was some heart-searching on the question of whether the transfer of power should be made conditional on written safeguards. A majority of policy-makers thought that Burmese goodwill was the most effective safeguard for European enterprises and investments. Written safeguards would be of little use. The same applied to Britain's defence requirements: these could not be obtained by compulsion or legal clauses, but only by goodwill.[148]

The London Conference held in January 1947 resulted in a partial transfer of power: Aung San was in charge of the interim government, the governor only being present at meetings involving his special powers. The question of Commonwealth membership was left un-settled (even though the Burmese made it quite clear that they were *not* ready to accept Dominion status). Not much time was spent on the fate of the frontier areas. Since Britain would not be able to fulfil her pledges once Burma had become independent, these 'small, poor and land-locked states' were to come under the direct control of Rangoon.[149] This was clearly contrary to earlier assurances, but did not much disturb policy-makers in London. The creation of a strong centralised state able to resist communist subversion was considered more important.

In the general elections held in April 1947 the AFPFL won a majority in 88 constituencies (out of 91). Britain was thus able to claim that power had been transferred to a democratically elected government – even though vital concessions had been made *before* the elections, thereby putting Aung San and his party in an incomparably strong position *vis-à-vis* potential rivals. Britain promised to provide a military mission free of charge for three years. In return, Burma agreed to allow Britain the use of various airbases, ports and air transit rights.[150] This agreement met the limited needs of the Chiefs of

Staff, namely a Commonwealth monopoly of defence relations and transit facilities. On 4 January 1948 the transfer of power was completed. Ministers were more or less content with the outcome, despite the near-complete surrender to the AFPFL, which left the country's various minority populations (most importantly the Karens) at the mercy of Rangoon. The terms of independence had been largely dictated by Aung San, but at least Britain had avoided a military confrontation, which would have made it impossible to disengage for a long time.

An Exemplary Transfer of Power: Ceylon

Ceylon achieved independence at about the same time as India and Burma, but the transfer of power in the island was markedly different. It was not the result of strong indigenous pressure coupled with Britain's unwillingness (and inability) to deploy scarce resources, but an attempt to ensure harmonious cooperation with the island's comparatively moderate nationalists. The case of Ceylon is of particular interest, since the British came to consider the island a model of successful decolonisation: the end of formal rule not only did not harm Britain's military or economic interests, but enhanced its international prestige and standing. In addition, it was Britain, not local nationalists, who determined the timetable as well as the modalities of the transfer of power. Policy-makers hoped that the feat might be repeated in other colonies and did their best to secure 'more Ceylons and fewer Burmas'.[151]

In 1942 the Ceylonese had been promised responsible government after the end of hostilities, leading (at an unspecified date) to full Dominion status. Before long, the Ceylonese expressed discontent with this vague promise: in 1945 Ceylon's leading political figure, Dudley Senanayake, demanded the immediate granting of Dominion status. Lord Soulbury, author of the 1942 report, supported him. A unique opportunity had arisen to make permanent 'the good feelings' existing towards Britain and the Commonwealth. It would be a tragedy to repeat in Ceylon any of the colossal mistakes made in Ireland: 'To hit the golden mean between caution and magnanimity is perhaps impossible but I believe that in the long run giving too much and too soon will prove to be wiser than giving too little and too late.'[152] The Governor of Ceylon put forward similar arguments. The government should promise full Dominion status within five years. If no clear statement was made, there would be further agitation. Concessions would have to be made sooner or later, and there was a risk that they would appear to have been obtained by threats and intimidation. HMG had 'a golden opportunity by the exercise of a little courage now, of making a generous and spontaneous gesture to Ceylon which, in the long run, would pay a handsome dividend'.[153] The Cabinet, however, considered it premature to grant Dominion status to Ceylon before India and Burma. Six years after the introduction of the new constitution there would be a further review of the constitutional issue.[154] Self-government (with reserved powers in respect of defence and foreign policy) would thus be reached by the mid-1950s at the earliest.

For the time being, Senanayake accepted the rebuff. But when, in February 1947, India was promised independence within 18 months, he demanded the same for Ceylon. Creech Jones informed his colleagues that he had 'no doubt whatever' that the Ceylonese desire for independence was strong and genuine. In case of another rebuff, Senanayake might lose control of the nationalist movement and be replaced by more radical left-wing elements. Therefore he recommended that Senanayake's demand be met. He argued that Senanayake was a realist who recognised that Ceylon was too small to stand on its own feet without outside assistance; he would keep his country in close alignment with Britain and the Commonwealth.[155] The granting of Dominion status was an excellent opportunity to demonstrate that Britain's colonial policy was not 'an empty boast' and that Commonwealth membership was not reserved for people of European descent. If the matter was correctly handled, Britain's interests would be secured through the end of colonial rule, not its maintenance – an achievement which would 'confound our critics' who accused the government of 'squandering the Empire'.

Bevin vigorously opposed the proposal. While he was endeavouring to hold on to the Middle East, Creech Jones was undermining Britain's position in Asia by letting go of the whole of the Indian Ocean.[156] The repeated use of the word 'independence' was dangerous since 'Eastern people' attached a different meaning to it. The countries of the Middle and Far East were watching every move made by Britain, and if she went any further her 'moral authority' in the whole area would be lost. The 'constant desire to make further pronouncements' should be resisted. The pressure for constitutional advance would lessen if the government took a firm line. First, the existing constitution should be operated; then certain guarantees concerning defence, external affairs and the protection of minorities should be laid down in a binding agreement. Only then should there be further advance. There was strong support in Cabinet for Bevin's view that it would be 'unwise to reach a hurried decision'. The government should not expose itself to the criticism of acting precipitately in response to an overture from a party leader on the eve of an election, and of ignoring the position of the minorities whose interests had hitherto been carefully safeguarded – two blunders which had already been committed in the case of Burma. Immediate and far-reaching concessions might be interpreted as a further indication of weakness. Senanayake might not keep his promise, and the government would encourage demands for similar concessions elsewhere.

What weighed most in the minds of ministers, however, was the fear of prejudicing Mountbatten's delicate negotiations in Delhi. Early in June 1947 the situation changed decisively when the Congress and League, led by Jawaharlal Nehru and Mohammad Ali Jinnah, respectively, finally accepted Mountbatten's proposals involving partition and independence by mid-August. All of a sudden, holding on to Ceylon was no longer considered necessary. On the contrary, it was now assumed that a speed-up would help the moderate Senanayake maintain his position – and secure favourable terms for military and other agreements. After India's independence, the island might come under strong pressure from its northern neighbour affecting its willingness to enter such agreements. Therefore it was essential to act quickly. Independence would foster local goodwill and boost Britain's prestige as a benevolent colonial power, while leaving unharmed its vital interests, i.e. those in the military sphere. Some ministers wanted to make the transfer of power conditional on adequate protection of the island's ethnic minorities, but most Cabinet members feared that this would only lead to a deterioration of Anglo-Ceylonese relations. To insist on safeguards would involve considerable delays without necessarily doing any good for the people concerned – Britain had to put its interests first. On 3 June 1947 the Cabinet decided to hold independence talks with Senanayake.[157]

The Chiefs of Staff were anxious to secure British defence requirements by some form of agreement. According to the military, the retention of facilities was vital for adequate defence security in any future war.[158] Loss of facilities would seriously weaken Britain's control of the Indian Ocean. In order to make sure the base was at Britain's disposal, the Chiefs of Staff wanted to maintain, at least in reserve, the right to intervene in matters of internal security.[159] The CO acknowledged the necessity of a treaty, but advised that it was better not to mention the possibility of a British intervention in an independent Ceylon. However, they assured the Chiefs of Staff, the wording of the relevant article in the defence agreement had been left 'sufficiently vague' to cover the possibility.

The CO was confident that Ceylonese politicians would see sense in matters of defence: Senanayake and his followers acted on the 'tacit assumption' that, for all practical purposes, the United Kingdom would have the last word, particularly in an emergency. But they did not 'altogether like harping in writing on the fact'.[160] The precise terms of the agreement were less important than the spirit underlying it. British defence relations with Ceylon would depend upon mutual confidence: this could not be written into a document and certainly could not be forced out of Ceylon as the result of a treaty. Only if independence was conceded soon, and without too many strings attached, were the Ceylonese likely to remain cooperative. In the end the Chiefs of Staff dropped their claim, probably being satisfied that the continued presence of British troops would suffice to stabilise the situation.[161]

A general election in the summer of 1947 confirmed Senanayake's position. In November 1947 the Ceylon Independence Bill passed the House of Commons, and early in 1948 Ceylon became fully self-governing. The British assumed that the transfer of power would help to maintain close relations rather than destroy them. At first, these hopes seemed to be justified. A few months after independence Patrick Gordon-Walker, Parliamentary Under-Secretary of State for Commonwealth Relations, reported that Ceylon was settling down as 'a genuine Dominion'. Ceylonese politicians were extremely friendly and wanted to maintain and deepen the British connection. The administration was firmly in control and had even been strengthened by the transfer of power. Britain could help it by preserving the right approach: 'If we treat them strictly as a Dominion, they will behave very like a loyal colony: whereas if we treat them as a Colony we may end in driving them out of the Commonwealth.'[162] By the end of the 1940s, Britain considered the transfer of power in Ceylon to have been exemplary. The timetable had been shortened considerably, but policy-makers were confident that constitutional advance in other colonies should follow the same path. Ceylonese goodwill had been safeguarded, and Britain's interests were secured while it gained international respect for its liberal policy. It was assumed that this could be repeated in other 'normal' colonies,[163] provided Britain managed to maintain a working relationship with suitable local collaborators. Two cases where this tendency was particularly evident were in Malaya and the Gold Coast.

'Normal' Colonies

Malaya

Malaya had also been occupied by the Japanese. Contrary to Burma, however, there was no vociferous independence movement. The Malay community was above all anxious to avoid political and economic domination by the Chinese minority.[164] The Chinese minority aimed first of all to gain citizenship rights, not independence. Because national unity was not yet well developed, the British expected the advance to self-government to be sluggish: in the late 1940s, it was generally assumed that it would take at least 25 years. A long preparation was to ensure that British economic and defence interests were properly secured through a stable successor state: Malaya had great importance for the sterling area as a major dollar earner (through its rubber and tin exports), while Singapore (which was to be federated with the colony) was a crucial military base.

There were some voices calling for a more rapid advance. Most important among them was that of Malcolm MacDonald, Governor-General for south-east Asia. He argued that by making early concessions the Malayan government would retain 'full trust in British leadership'.[165] Otherwise Britain would once more lag behind local opinion. Nationalist movements were growing all over Asia. Britain's influence depended largely on how successful it was in retaining their confidence. At the moment Britain was not regarded as a reactionary imperialist power. On the contrary, Britain's reputation, as a result of developments in India, Ceylon and Burma, was very high.[166] If this was to continue, Britain had to come to terms with Asian nationalism wherever it was encountered. If Britain waited too long, 'our hand may be forced (as it is being forced elsewhere in the Empire)'.[167]

For MacDonald, it was better to run the risk of Britain's own choosing than to wait until 'the mere pressure of events' hurried the government into action. In the past, political evolution in the dependent territories had almost always been accompanied by considerable hostility to the United Kingdom. Malaya, 'if wisely guided', might constitute an exception to this rule. The Malays must not be left entirely on their own until they could keep their end up against the Chinese and other immigrant communities. But the proper way of enabling them to stand on their own feet was to encourage them in political development. Thus self-government might lead to a strengthening rather than a weakening of ties between the two countries.[168]

Lord Killearn, the FO's special commissioner to south-east Asia, did not share MacDonald's optimism. According to him, far too much emphasis was laid on constitutional change (a stance which was rather representative of the FO generally at the end of the 1940s).[169] The polyglot population of the country was not yet very politically minded. But under the 'continual high pressure of salesmanship' the local 'irresponsibles' would begin to look on political advances as 'the panacea for all ills'. Britain ought to pay more attention to the real problems confronting Malaya. Fostering constitutional advance without heeding the country's social and economic development would lead to 'political agitation in all sorts of extreme and un-balanced forms'. There would be an outcry for self-government as the cure-all, and when that happened the CO would have to bear a share of the responsibility because it had so persistently overstressed the importance of 'political "independence"'.

There was also strong resistance to rapid change within the Malayan administration. The Governor, Edward Gent, claimed that the Malays did not want British rule to end because they were afraid of communism and Chinese domination. The disturbances in India had opened the eyes of 'thinking people' to the dangers inherent in a British withdrawal.[170] It was no doubt desirable to emphasise 'for external consumption' that the aim of British policy was self-government. But the first object in Malaya had to be the restoration of confidence.[171] Although this resistance at times proved cumbersome, it did not keep the CO from pressing ahead with its plans for constitutional advance in order to retain Malay goodwill. Its determination to do so was only strengthened by the upsurge of terrorist activities all over the country which led the Governor to declare an emergency in June 1948.

Policy-makers were immediately convinced that the trouble was communist-instigated.[172] The 'campaign of terror' in Malaya was not perceived as a national movement, but as 'part and parcel of the general offensive at present being waged throughout Asia by militant Communism'. The government sent more than 40,000 troops to restore order – an effort considerably stretching metropolitan resources. Bevin pointed out that it would be 'most inconvenient, to say the least', if incidents occurred in other territories which required movements of troops to restore order.[173] Sending further reinforcements would turn the country into 'a bottomless pit devouring all our resources and thus playing straight into Russia's hands'.[174]

The British were determined to defeat the guerrilla movement. But they realised quickly that the solution did not lie in the military sphere alone: it was essential to find a political solution as well.[175] Constitutional concessions were to undermine the support for the insurgents and incite the Malays to bear a greater share of the defence burden. It would also make it easier to fend off international criticism, since Britain would visibly be fighting for the freedom of the locals. Accordingly, ministers developed a double-edged strategy which combined the guerrilla campaign with an increasingly accelerating approach to independence. This strategy unfolded over the years, and the timetable of Malaya's constitutional advance was constantly shortened.

In 1949 self-government was still expected to be 15–20 years away.[176] One year later MacDonald, the new Colonial Secretary, James Griffiths, and High Commissioner Henry Gurney agreed to shorten the timetable to 10–15 years.[177] The process would inevitably be accelerated by factors over which Britain had little or no control. First, a new generation of Malayan leaders who were in favour of quickening the pace would soon come to the fore. Second, because of the communist take-over in China, the agitation against British rule was likely to gain in strength. Once Indo-China had achieved complete self-government, Malaya would be the only remaining dependent territory in south-east Asia. The pressure of Asian and 'world opinion as expressed through UNO [United Nations Organisation]', would be irresistible to local politicians.[178] The danger therefore lay in progress being too slow rather than too rapid. If the government wanted to avoid 'another Indonesia', it was 'vitally important' to keep in step with political leaders.[179] The government should not commit itself to a definite period of time, but maintain a flexible approach. The secret of success apparently lay in

> pursuing a policy that always carries the agreement of the local Asian leaders, exercising our influence to slacken the pace, so that they may have time to fit themselves for their responsibilities, but accommodating ourselves to the requirements of the situation.[180]

Thus, in the early 1950s Britain was ready for Malaya's rapid advance to self-government although as yet there was no strong indigenous demand for such a development. The British intended to anticipate any pressure for independence. They wanted to ride the tide before it had even had time to build up. The lessons of India and Ceylon had been learned. The transfer of power in Malaya was to be the result of harmonious collaboration, not bitter strife.

The Gold Coast

The desire to 'ride the tide' was also present in the Gold Coast. Of Britain's four West African colonies, the Gold Coast seemed the most suitable candidate for constitutional advance: the population was relatively developed, the territory was rather well off thanks to its cocoa production, and there were no major racial divisions. The territory's progress towards self-government was seen as exemplary for other African territories.[181] Therefore, particular attention was paid to events in this colony.

At first there was no discernible nationalist movement, and it seemed as if political, social and economic development would follow the plans laid by the CO. This changed when, in February 1948, the colony was rocked by the outbreak of the so-called Accra riots.[182] The riots were largely a protest against inflated prices for consumer goods, but most British officials perceived them as the birth pangs of a new political consciousness. The Governor, Gerald Creasey, thought it best not to impose tranquillity by 'restrictions and controls backed by the sanction of the armed forces'. Rather, he tried to eliminate the causes of the disturbance by political means.[183] An African committee was set up to make recommendations about constitutional change. The committee produced a formula calling for a much larger elected assembly, universal suffrage and devolution of much of the Gold Coast's internal affairs to local politicians. The government accepted this recommendation, calculating that it would help to calm the situation while leaving untouched the foundations of colonial rule – control of external affairs and defence. While local self-government was to be conceded relatively quickly, independence was to follow much later.

British plans were disturbed when Kwame Nkrumah founded his Convention People's Party (CPP), which, by insisting on self-government in the near future, managed to attract considerable popular support. British officials regarded Nkrumah's activities with deep mistrust, since they undermined the position of traditional political forces inclined to cooperate with the colonial state.[184] No direct links to communist organisations could be detected, but British officials still feared that the CPP would serve the long-term interests of communism by destabilising the country. Nkrumah's party was condemned as a 'relatively small body of zealots, partly composed of fanatical "anti-imperialists" and nationalists, and partly of gangsters'. Despite their dislike, British officials did not intervene in Nkrumah's political activities. Officials hoped that Nkrumah would act as a bog-eyman, frightening moderate Africans into cooperation with the government.[185] Alas, in June 1949 Nkrumah began to spread the slogan of 'self-government in 1949'. British officials concluded that nothing but a showdown would contain Nkrumah: in early 1950 he was jailed for advocating strikes, boycotts and demonstrations.

In order to counter Nkrumah's influence, the government set up a committee that was to consider further constitutional reform. The resulting report called for stronger African participation in government affairs while retaining ultimate responsibility in the Governor. The CO received this recommendation with delight. It seemed to demonstrate that African and British interests need not necessarily conflict. Enhanced participation in administrative and political tasks would lead to a 'steady (and healthy) growth of "national" spirit'.[186] A great deal of the 'emotional nonsense' talked about self-government would disappear, since politicians would be busy with their new responsibilities.[187] The country could thus be prepared for independence, while Britain remained in control of the speed of constitutional advance. The Colonial Secretary strongly advised his colleagues to accept the report's recommendations: they represented a victory for moderate opinion and offered the chance to secure peaceful collaboration. Implementation of the report would positively influence the course of events in the Gold Coast, but also in many other territories, for a long time to come.[188] Not to implement it, however, would alienate the moderates and strengthen the extremists. It was better to make concessions voluntarily than be seen to give in only grudgingly and as a result of African pressure – an advice fully endorsed by ministers.

The new constitution was introduced in 1950. In the ensuing elections (the first elections in an African colony under universal suffrage), the CPP won a land-slide victory – much to the dismay of British officials. However, it was considered advantageous to go along with the prevailing political feeling, 'however crude it may be'.[189] In February 1951 the Governor Charles Arden-Clarke released Nkrumah and appointed him 'Leader of Government Business'. Nkrumah still demanded Dominion status in the near future, but signalled his readiness to cooperate. Thereafter British opinion about him changed slowly for the better. But no matter whether British officials liked him or not, there seemed to be no alternative to Nkrumah: the Governor advised officials that if the CPP government were to fall, it could only be replaced by a government of even more extreme nationalist tendencies. At the time there was no organised opposition, and a power struggle took place between extremist elements of the CPP and its more moderate leaders. Britain had only one dog in its kennel, and the whole question was whether the tail would wag the dog or the dog the tail: 'It has a very big tail and not much guts. All we can do is to build it up and feed it vitamins and cod liver oil; and, as soon as the opportunity offers, some of the tail must be docked.'[190] It was vital to help Nkrumah become the nucleus of a more moderate party attracting to it 'the more sober responsible elements'.[191]

Governor Arden-Clarke tried to make policy-makers in London understand the difficulties faced by African politicians. What is remarkable is how precisely his arguments matched those put forward by the Burmese administration several years earlier: the general problem of the CPP government, he wrote, was to avoid going to such lengths as to oblige HMG to administer a rebuff, and to avoid the criticism that, as a government committed to their election promises, they did not go far enough. It was almost certain that extremists would try to out-flank the CPP government by putting forward extravagant demands. The government therefore might be forced to move 'more rapidly than ideally we should wish'.[192] Nkrumah was 'a highly volatile character', but his rivals were an even greater danger. Only by making concessions would it be possible to retain a degree of control. If the people of the Gold Coast felt they had self-government in matters of local interest, they would be less likely to agitate for it in 'the wider fields in which … they have not the experience or resources to exercise independence'. Moreover, the key to future relations between Britain and the Gold Coast was the maintenance of goodwill, and this depended primarily on the extent to which officials could convince the Africans of Britain's good intentions.[193] The way things were going in the Gold Coast was 'theoretically, over-hasty political advance' – but it was the only way of preventing more extreme demands and a head-on clash.[194] Officials and ministers eagerly embraced the Governor's view. As a result, events in the Gold Coast took a turn few would have expected a year earlier, and constitutional development was considerably accelerated.

The Last White Dominion: Settler Colonies in East and Central Africa

While the Gold Coast moved towards internal self-government, there was no such development in Kenya, Tanganyika or Northern Rhodesia. This was due not only to the lack of vociferous nationalist movements but also to the assumption among British officials that policy in West Africa would differ widely from the one in East and Central Africa where there were substantial minorities of European residents. The Labour government had no clearly defined policy for ending colonial rule in these territories: they were to be united in two federations and thus become self-governing members of the Commonwealth. But no timetable was laid down, nor was it stated what the status of the white minorities would be. The years under Labour thus brought little change in East and Central Africa. In public, to explain the slow advance, policy-makers incessantly pointed to the locals' backwardness: the 'average' African allegedly was of 'the mental calibre of a British child of ten'.[195]

Such considerations might have played a role. But a more important explanation for Britain's sluggish approach to constitutional advance in East and Central Africa was the presence of European minorities. After all, underdevelopment alone did not keep the government from setting other colonies on the road to self-government. The problem was that Britain did not want either Kenya or Southern Rhodesia to achieve unqualified independence under the white settlers. This might have meant the establishment of a South African-style regime – a development Britain felt morally obliged to prevent, but which was also expected to be detrimental in the era of the Cold War. At the same time, it was feared that a transfer of power to the African majority would have disastrous consequences for the whites, leading them to rebel against British rule. In order to prevent either of these developments, the government promoted 'multi-racial' societies and the establishment of a federation, between the Rhodesias and Nyasaland in Central Africa, and Kenya, Tanganyika, Zanzibar and Uganda in East Africa. Uniting territories with relatively strong white minorities, i.e. Kenya and Southern Rhodesia with others that lacked significant settler communities was designed to make it possible to check attempts by the Europeans to establish a South African-style regime – while offering them an economic unit big enough to achieve satisfactory development.

However, while officials wanted to prevent white settlers from gaining unrestricted control of local affairs at the expense of the Africans, independence was generally expected to arrive under a white-dominated government. Moreover, nothing was done to stop European immigration – it was even encouraged. The idea of creating a new white-dominated Dominion obviously died hard. In May 1946 a 'Plan for the Peopling of our Empire' was transmitted to Bevin. The paper, written by A.C. Wilkinson, who was a former soldier apparently distinguished by his cricket performances against New Zealand, claimed that throughout the empire, there were 'millions of empty acres, capable of supporting millions of human beings'.[196] The state should therefore encourage and support immigration on a large scale. Immigrants were to be settled in model villages, each of them having 'a really good Club, which will also serve as the village pub; where the men can get their beer, and the women their gin!'

Obviously stimulated by this and similar proposals, Bevin argued for the systematic settlement of East Africa: Britain had lost the United States by trying to stop expansion in that country – attempting to stop it in Africa would mean to lose this continent as well.[197] It was doubtful whether in the face of the 'ever growing economic and demographic needs' of Europe, Britain would be able indefinitely to protect the natives against white immigration. Attlee signalled his consent and called for further exploration of the matter: 'While I am aware that there are large regions at present uninhabitable, ... I cannot believe that it is right that these great areas of the earth's surface should continue to contain so few inhabitants.' Bevin, he suggested, should launch a special investigation into the possibilities of increasing white settlement.[198] Most other policy-makers agreed: it was generally assumed that Britain's traditional demographic dynamism would continue, that the surplus population would have to emigrate, and that the colonies were the right place to receive them.[199] Britain could thereby become nearly self-sufficient in food, and at the same time secure the continued loyalty of the Empire-Commonwealth.

Creech Jones was one of the few to warn of the consequences of continuing European settlement, especially in East Africa where it would cause serious political trouble.[200] Despite his protests, immigration continued on a rather large scale. For other ministers, the natives were a secondary factor. They thought it more important to develop the colonies and to strengthen the British element against rival groups of immigrants (in the case of Central Africa, against the massive influx of Afrikaners). Between 1945 and 1951, more than 700,000 citizens migrated from the United Kingdom to other parts of the Empire-Commonwealth, a large number of them under government-sponsored schemes.[201] Many of them went to the old Dominions, but Africa, too, received its share. In Southern Rhodesia, the white population thus rose from 55,400 in 1935–36 to 221,500 some 20 years later; in Northern Rhodesia, the number of Europeans increased from 9,900 to 74,500.[202] In Kenya, their number increased from 17,900 to 55,700; in Tanganyika, from 8,400 to 20,500; and in Uganda, from 1,900 to 10,800. Some of the new arrivals were administrators and technicians who would be expected to remain only a few years. But in all these territories land was still being taken up for settlement. Government-aided farm-settlement schemes, which enabled European settlers to develop the fertile areas of Kenya reserved for them, remained in operation until the end of the 1950s, and, until 1958, advertisements continued to appear in British newspapers urging readers to settle in East Africa.[203]

Labour favoured migration despite less than favourable circumstances in Britain – labour shortages and fears of a declining birth rate – and in the colonies – there were seldom the millions of empty acres ministers talked about, especially in Kenya where the scarcity of land was one of the major African grievances. That migration was fostered despite these unfavourable circumstances demonstrates how little thinking with regard to East and Central Africa had developed since the 1920s. Colonies in this area were still considered assets that could be developed and colonised at will, with little or no attention paid to the indigenous population. However, the enthusiasm for the large-scale settlement of Europeans faded in the late 1940s. Policy-makers realised that most countries were not apt to receive more immigrants. In addition, population growth in Britain slowed down, thus eliminating the alleged need to find a safety valve for demographic pressure. However, the principle that white emigration to Africa was legitimate and should be encouraged was not seriously questioned before the late 1950s.

Imperial Residue: Smaller Territories

While most of Britain's larger colonies were ultimately to achieve self-government, there was to be no lowering of the Union Jack in many of the smaller territories. British officials and politicians alike believed that some territories could never be fully self-governing. Independence, it was argued, could only be granted if a territory was economically viable and capable of defending its own interests. It was dangerous for smaller territories to nurse 'illusions of independent grandeur', since the 'ornament' of self-government would not last for long.[204] In a number of territories it would also jeopardise Britain's vital strategic interests. Policy-makers therefore strove to find a status that would allow British rule and protection to continue while satisfying local and international demands for more political rights.

The concept of the so-called 'smaller territories' was very vague: it was generally understood as referring to island and fortress territories, as well as to colonies whose population, size or economic strength were considered insufficient to sustain independence. This is only a rough indication though, since the rather fluent term of viability was never clearly defined.[205] Among the territories considered not viable were British Guiana, British Honduras, Gambia, the High Commissioner's Territories in South Africa, Sierra Leone, Uganda, as well as most of the island territories. The so-called 'fortress territories' were Gibraltar, Malta, Cyprus, Aden and Singapore. In certain other territories of no direct strategic importance, Britain had to retain some control because their occupation by an unfriendly power was expected to be detrimental to Britain or its allies. Among these were the Pacific islands covering Australasia, the Falkland Islands and Somaliland. Last but not least, there were territories whose retention was thought important for the maintenance of Britain's prestige and influence. A prime example of this category was Hong Kong: throughout the whole post-war period, the retention of the city-state was said to be necessary 'chiefly for reasons affecting our prestige'.[206]

Some territories united various qualities that made them, in British eyes, unsuitable for independence. The most prominent example was probably Cyprus. The Greek Cypriots demanded *enosis*, i.e. union with Greece, a claim strongly supported by the Greek Orthodox

Church, the most powerful social force in the island. The Turkish-speaking minority, however, which made up 20 per cent of the population, was strongly opposed to it. The Cypriot question thus not only touched upon Britain's strategic interests and standing in the Middle East, but also upon its relations with Greece and Turkey. When the Cabinet discussed the issue in February 1947, the Minister of Defence was in favour of a 'firm decision' to maintain British sovereignty.[207] There was no guarantee that India would remain within the imperial defence system or that Britain could maintain its foothold in the Middle East. Therefore, it was very important to retain Cyprus as a base for Commonwealth defence. Moreover, to cede the only British territory in the eastern Mediterranean, even if accompanied by the retention of all necessary strategic facilities, would be regarded as a manifestation of weakness. This, it was argued, may persuade Turks and Arabs that their future lay with the Soviet Union. The Colonial Secretary was worried about the danger of 'drifting into another Palestine', but he accepted that unless there was somebody who could 'bounce' the Cypriots into cooperation in Mountbatten style, Britain had to maintain its position.[208]

Bevin was 'somewhat torn in two': he disliked the idea of giving up Cyprus, but believed that the demand for *enosis* was serious.[209] It would be difficult to ignore it in view of the fact that India and Burma had just been promised independence. Opposing the Cypriot demand would not only damage Britain's international standing, but also weaken the anti-communist government in Athens. Above all, Cyprus might take Britain to the United Nations, where it would be in a vulnerable position. Attlee, however, thought it was 'now more than ever' necessary to 'keep our foothold in the Eastern Mediterranean'.[210] The government should say rather firmly that Britain intended to remain in control, and try to wean the Cypriots from 'the delusion of Greek nationalism'. The demand for *enosis* was but froth and would die away as soon as the Cypriots realised that Britain would not give in – a rather surprising stance, given Attlee's insistence on rapid Indian independence and his call for a withdrawal from the Middle East. Apparently neither the Prime Minister nor his Foreign Secretary can be said to have been, as a matter of principle, for or against formal rule overseas.

One CO official was 'a little puzzled' by the ministerial reaction: the government wanted Britain to hold on to the island because of its strategic value – but in the context of the Cold War, Cyprus was 'a vulnerable salient'.[211] Most officials, however, were in favour of maintaining formal rule, even those in the FO. Nobody believed that Cyprus, once given the opportunity, would not unite with Greece, and the sympathy of the Greek government was considered less important than Turkey's participation in a Middle Eastern defence scheme. The withdrawals from India and Palestine as well as the difficulties in Egypt reduced the number of available bases and generated a fear of losing control over the whole Middle East. At the end of the 1940s, policy-makers were therefore determined to stay in Cyprus until the strategic reasons for doing so were no longer valid – and no one could say when that would be.[212]

Despite the confidence displayed in public, policy-makers realised that they were not likely to get the smaller territories' permanent dependence 'across with the Colonies as a purely negative concept'. The need to act was not very strong yet: for a large part the indigenous people were thought to be content to remain under British administration.[213] Nonetheless, a solution had to be found: international criticism would one day also focus on the smaller territories. Therefore, British officials tried to devise a status which would, on the one hand, allow the United Kingdom to preserve control over defence and foreign affairs, while on the other hand providing it with the means of an escape from the 'stigma of colonialism'.[214] In December 1948 a committee was appointed to develop the idea of a status short of independence. Officials discussed the 'Tongan model' of a fully autonomous country in treaty relationship with Britain, which would provide external security. It was concluded, however, that for most smaller territories Britain would have to continue to hold some responsibility for internal affairs: in territories where the bulk of the population was 'economically weak and politically immature', internal self-government might involve 'the abandonment of the people to the dictation of a dominant group which would be free to indulge in tyranny and corruption without let or hindrance'.[215] The committee therefore developed a new status of 'Island or City State': Britain would retain responsibility for external and internal affairs, little would change for the territories except their designation as 'colonies'.

The idea was deemed 'attractive intellectually but academic and un-English' by the governors of the territories concerned. If the new status became the climax of constitutional evolution, it would lead to unrest. In October 1951 the governors' comments were put before the incoming Colonial Secretary, Oliver Lyttelton, who rejected the proposal. Another idea, that of a new 'satellite status', proposed by Charles Jeffries, shared the same fate.[216] The Bahamas, Bermuda, the Gold Coast, Kenya, Malaya, Mauritius, Nigeria, Northern Rhodesia, Sierra Leone, Singapore, Tanganyika and the West Indies were to be accorded 'satellite status', allowing them some degree of internal self-government. The other territories were to remain Crown colonies, with the option of one day acceding to 'satellite status'. Jeffries' proposal received no positive echo, but it is another indication of the ideas about limited self-government prevailing in Whitehall until the early 1950s. Like many of his colleagues, Jeffries assumed that the Gold Coast, Nigeria or Malaya would never (or at least not for a long time to come) be able to control their own defence and foreign policies.

Conclusion

Labour set out to implement a new approach to the colonies: they were to be properly developed and the natives were to learn to govern themselves. Independence would be granted once the colonies were ready for it, i.e. after 30 to 40 years at the earliest. During this period colonial resources were to be developed for the good of the metropole *and* the periphery. However, the difficulties encountered by large-scale development on the spot rapidly destroyed the high hopes of turning the colonies into an asset. By the end of the Attlee governments, most colonies were seen as a burden on the Exchequer. The major reason for holding on to them was a sense of responsibility as well as the feeling that to abandon them would damage Britain's prestige: there seemed to be no alternative to formal rule but chaos. In general, once the international political and economic environment had stabilised, policy-makers mused, there were no cogent reasons to hold on to empire – but no cogent reasons to abandon it prematurely either.

In India, the deadlock between the two major parties, which took place against a background of rising communal tension, an increasingly weakened administrative machine, a lack of troops and international opinion clearly opposed to British rule, finally led the government to opt for partition and rapid withdrawal. Although the aims set in 1945 were not reached, policy-makers did not think in terms of failure: they had not only avoided involvement in a civil war, but had also 'come out with honour' – the dreaded 'scuttle' had been avoided. While the transfer of power in India could thus still be presented as a success, the same could not be said of Burma. There, the terms of the transfer of power were dictated by Aung San and the AFPFL. Burma's independence clearly was a scuttle rather than the result of any planned policy. Ceylon, however, demonstrated that it was possible to control decolonisation and to use it for Britain's own ends. Power was transferred very rapidly, since it was assumed that British interests were better secured by independent (but loyal) nationalists than by formal rule. To wait until the country was perfectly prepared for self-government would only create ill will and jeopardise British interests. Early independence, it was assumed, would secure Ceylonese goodwill – and thus British influence.

A policy similar to the one implemented in Ceylon was also pursued in the Gold Coast and Malaya. In the first case, it was the sudden upsurge of nationalist demands which led Britain to accelerate constitutional development beyond anything imagined feasible immediately after the war. In the case of Malaya, there was as yet no strong demand for independence. But policy-makers were confident that it would arise sooner or later. Therefore they did their best to pre-empt any negative developments. Indo-China and Indonesia were considered as warnings of what might happen if Britain tried to stem the tide. The outbreak of the emergency only strengthened British determination to reach a political solution in agreement with moderate political forces.

While major colonies without white majorities thus advanced towards self-government under a democratically elected native government, policy-makers had not yet made up their mind about East and Central Africa: they wondered whether they should give preference to the creation of a new white Dominion or African emancipation. White immigration was still tolerated and even encouraged. But the government (and, in particular, the CO) did not want the Africans to come under the unrestricted control of the settlers. Such a development was not considered in accordance with Britain's trust. The result was a policy full of contradictions. In theory, the aim was the creation of multi-racial societies allowing blacks and whites to live in harmony. In practice, very little was done to achieve that aim.

As regards the smaller territories, policy-makers still believed that it would be possible (and necessary) to maintain formal rule for a considerable time to come. While most territories concerned did not (yet) object to their status, policy-makers were aware that it would sooner or later lead to problems. Officials therefore tried in vain to develop a status that would allow British protection and control to continue, but would remove the 'stigma' of colonialism.

THE COMMONWEALTH

Empire by Proxy? The Commonwealth under Labour

Most of Britain's colonies did not simply attain independence, but became 'self-governing within the Commonwealth'. Policy-makers attached great importance to this, especially in the early years after the Second World War. The club was considered an important factor contributing to Britain's prestige and standing in the world. Pethick-Lawrence, for example, thought it essential to avoid any suggestion that Burma could achieve self-government outside the Commonwealth: 'Whatever may happen hereafter, self-government within repeat within Commonwealth ... is as far as His Majesty's Government can undertake to take matter [*sic*].'[217] At the same time, there were fierce debates about who should be admitted as a new member. Many feared that the admission of Asian and African nations would destroy the homogeneity of the association, which until the end of the war had effectively been a 'white man's club' and overwhelmingly 'British'.

The terms 'Commonwealth' and 'Dominion' never had their precise meaning laid down. The Balfour report of 1926 had defined the 'Dominions' as freely associating states, autonomous within the empire, equal with each other and Britain, and owing allegiance to the Crown. The 'Commonwealth' was defined as the community of Dominions and the United Kingdom.[218] But the meaning of these terms varied depending on the circumstances and the actors using them. In fact they were 'balls played by different players for different purposes at successive phases'.[219] In the immediate post-war years, 'empire' and 'Commonwealth' were closely linked, often even synonymous. When a country attained self-government within the Commonwealth, it nevertheless remained 'within the Empire'. In later years, the term 'empire' (like the terms 'Dominion' and 'Dominion status') gradually fell into disuse, the word 'Commonwealth' being used instead to designate the totality of colonial and self-governing territories that were a part of it.[220]

Despite this change of nomenclature, it was always presumed in the metropole that Britain would still have a special position: as *primus inter pares*, its voice would weigh more than others and it would naturally give guidance in political, military and economic affairs. There was another reason for blurring, at least in terminology, the difference between empire and Commonwealth (or colony and Dominion): this ambiguity proved a convenient means of cloaking, *vis-à-vis* the domestic and the international public, the true changes in power relations taking place between Britain and its colonies. But the term 'empire' (like 'colony') also disappeared because it was no longer an appropriate term. The United States was traditionally opposed to it, and the international climate after 1945 created even stronger incentives to look for new terms stressing partnership and free cooperation rather than domination and exploitation.[221]

The Commonwealth lacked any institutional framework, and even in Britain there was a huge variety of views on what the

Commonwealth was or what it *should* be. Accordingly, descriptions of it tended to be vague and evasive.[222] The links uniting the Commonwealth were said to be intangible and indefinable. Its members adhered to certain absolute values and shared a certain way of life that had many local differences, yet gave a general sense of community. Constitutional forms were not decisive – what counted were the spiritual links, which had grown out of a common historical and cultural background, as well as common interests.[223] In fact the Commonwealth was more an abstract concept than a reality. It may be compared to a screen upon which different viewers could project their ideas and expectations simultaneously, without disturbing others. What is clear is that the British considered the Commonwealth a convenient framework for projecting a certain image of Britain, especially in the United Nations, and for ensuring collaboration with the Dominions. The absence of any rules was not considered a disadvantage since it allowed great flexibility. Moreover, it was feared that any attempt to institutionalise the Commonwealth would not only lead some members to leave; it would also reveal the club's lack of coherence and strength.

For the Attlee administration, the Commonwealth was an 'essential ingredient' in ensuring Britain's status in the context of an uncertain world emerging from six years of global conflict.[224] Diplomatic support by the Dominions as well as the claim to represent them in international affairs were seen as important factors which enhanced Britain's standing in the world. The military assistance of the Commonwealth was to contribute to Britain's survival in case of global war, while trade based on imperial preferences was to ensure Britain's economic survival if the world economy suffered a recession, as it had after the First World War. The Commonwealth was seen as the solution to most problems facing Britain in the post-war period. For some time the FO even nursed a vision of the Commonwealth as a 'Third World Power', equivalent to the Soviet Union and the United States. Bevin hoped that the Commonwealth could act as a duplicate of the United Nations on a smaller scale, i.e. as the core of a new world order with a privileged position for Britain.[225]

These ideas had to be dropped by the end of the 1940s, when the Dominions demonstrated that they were not willing to follow the ideas developed by British officials in London. Nevertheless, the Commonwealth continued to be seen as an essential pillar of Britain's great power status. Despite its lack of institutional coherence it was still assumed that the club could play an important role in world affairs – not least as the incarnation of a specifically 'British' world order. This is the idea behind Attlee's statement that some form of association with others for security and greater prosperity is the desire of many peoples. The League of Nations and the United Nations organization express this desire, but the one great practical example of how complete freedom and independence can be combined with inclusion in a greater whole is the British Commonwealth of Nations.[226]

The Commonwealth connection continued to be seen as an important means of safeguarding Britain's strategic interests. Members presumably recognised the necessity for close collaboration; they would, it was hoped, automatically support each other because they believed that any threat to the security of one nation affected the security of the rest of the community. Policy-makers hoped that this would act as 'an effective deterrent to any potential aggressive action'.[227] For military planners, too, the Commonwealth continued to assume an important strategic role – even though the North Atlantic Treaty Organisation (NATO) increasingly gained weight as the body which would have to bear the brunt of European (and British) defence against a possible Soviet onslaught.[228]

While its political and military aspects remained important for policy-makers throughout the 1940s, the Commonwealth increasingly lost its economic role: world trade stabilised and the Dominions demonstrated their reluctance to extend imperial preferences; moreover, GATT prohibited new preferences. Nonetheless the individual members of the Commonwealth remained important trading partners; and imperial preferences were still more advantageous than most-favoured-nation status. In addition, the Commonwealth was expected to act as a political framework for the sterling area. The Commonwealth also remained an important destination for migrating Britons. Between 1945 and 1951 more than 700,000 citizens migrated from the United Kingdom to the Empire-Commonwealth. The government supported this migration despite less than favourable circumstances at home, that is, an acute labour shortage and fears about the declining British birth rate, which led to the appointment of a Royal Commission on population.[229] Ministers defended this policy by arguing that migration reduced the number of civilians to be protected in case of war, and at the same time strengthened the empire's manpower resources.[230] Migration was also said to invigorate the links between Britain and the Dominions. If the government allowed the percentage of 'British stock' in the Dominions to diminish, Britain's future strength, influence and safety (which depended to a large extent on the Commonwealth) would be affected in unpredictable ways.

Most of the hopes placed in the Commonwealth in 1945 did not materialise. Under the Attlee governments, the Commonwealth's character and composition changed considerably: the 'hard-rock' foundation of Britain, Canada, South Africa, Australia and New Zealand was joined by three new members (India, Pakistan and Ceylon), whereas Ireland dropped out. In order to allow a republican India to remain in the club, the Crown link was abandoned. These changes initiated a profound transformation of the Commonwealth from a 'white man's club' to a 'minor UN'. The following section will analyse British motives for accepting it.

The Admission of South-Asian Members

India

India, Burma and Ceylon were the first non-European colonies to attain independence from Britain after the Second World War. The question whether they should be offered membership in the Commonwealth was vehemently disputed in London. Not only did they not share the 'sentimental bonds' linking Britain to the so-called 'old' Dominions but the situation was also complicated by India's declared intention of becoming a republic. This would sever its constitutional link with the British Crown and thus render continued membership impossible. If it wanted to retain India in the Commonwealth, Britain would have to forego its insistence on the Dominions' allegiance to the Crown. Since the link to the Crown was thought to have a high symbolic value, the question of whether Asian countries should be admitted to full membership led to heated debates in London – debates that indicate how much importance was attached to the Commonwealth in the post-war period.

Attlee was particularly involved in these debates. He considered Commonwealth membership essential for future cooperation between Britain and India, and called for a review of the club's constituent entities.[231] In his view, a political decision was required. The critical position in south Asia left no time for a 'lengthy examination by constitutional lawyers'. The old empire had gone, but the new Commonwealth had not yet found its shape. Britain had to find a formula that would enable the greatest number of independent units to adhere to the association 'without excessive uniformity in their internal constitutions or in their relationship to Great Britain, the Commonwealth and one another'. A phrase such as 'Associated States of the Commonwealth' might provide an umbrella under which a number of independent states could be brought together – Britain, Eire, the old Dominions, Southern Rhodesia, India, Burma and

Ceylon. Attlee was supported by Mountbatten, who considered the Indian desire to stay in the Commonwealth as 'the greatest opportunity ever offered to the Empire'.[232] The empire, he believed had to change with the times and become a 'somewhat looser form of association'. If India did not want the Crown link, then Britain should do its best to allow it to stay in without the link. This would result in a 'terrific world-wide enhancement of British prestige', an intensification of Indo-British relations and the 'completion of the framework of world strategy from the point of view of Empire defence'.[233] Viscount Addison and Gordon-Walker were equally strong advocates of concessions: 'There is perhaps no country in the world potentially more important to us, except the US, than India with its vast population, immense trading possibilities and key position in Asia.' It would be a tragedy if the government failed to retain India in the club.[234]

The Chiefs of Staff also thought it important to retain India, mainly because of the bases that India would make available.[235] Moreover, through Indian participation in staff meetings and liaison arrangements the country would be integrated into the Commonwealth defence system. The resulting military support might be the only effective deterrent against a Soviet advance into the subcontinent.[236] British defence requirements might also be met if India entered into a treaty with the United Kingdom. But the best way to secure lasting cooperation was to retain India as a member.[237] Most British officials were equally in favour of retaining India. The Dominions Office especially championed the cause of enlargement. It acknowledged that Indian politicians were not as cooperative as older members of the Commonwealth, but pleaded that relations were exceptional. Britain needed time and a great deal of patience while the 'heady wine of "freedom"' was still having its effect.[238] Membership would enable Britain and the Dominions to exercise 'a useful steadying influence' on the young Indian state, keeping it out of the Soviet camp.[239] India's departure would be regarded as a weakening of the Commonwealth, and its example might be followed by Pakistan, Ceylon and Malaya. Retaining India would, however, enhance the club's standing, particularly in the eyes of potential aggressors.[240] Besides, the whole question was linked to Britain's concurrent attempt to achieve the leadership of a Western Union that would be sufficiently powerful to be independent, both politically and economically, of both the Soviet and the US blocs. Therefore the Commonwealth had to be 'as large and as powerful as we can make it'.[241] Commonwealth membership would help retain India in the sterling area and preserve the imperial preferences covering 30 per cent of British exports to India.[242] India's demotion from Commonwealth status to most-favoured nation, however, would make British businesses liable to much higher taxation than at present.

Not all policy-makers thought it worthwhile to weaken traditional Commonwealth links in order to retain India. Resistance was to be found above all in the FO. It argued that the essence of the Commonwealth relationship lay in a common outlook on world problems, based on the inheritance of a common cultural tradition and an origin from a common stock. The emblem of this unity was recognition of the Crown. If a nation was not prepared to recognise this emblem, it did not apparently share the common heritage which made the Commonwealth an effective reality. Watering down the Crown's importance would weaken the emotional bonds which had hitherto been 'a powerful influence' in holding the club together.[243] Australians and New Zealanders, as well as some of the Canadians and South Africans, had reached 'the point of explosion at any further whittling away of the bonds of the Commonwealth'. No concessions should be made to those who wanted to go the way of Eire. Otherwise the links with the old Dominions would be destroyed.

India would not accept any of the unwritten obligations of membership but would conduct its affairs on the basis of the 'most ruthless self-interest'.[244] Its admission to the Commonweath would undermine the Commonwealth's unity, and Britain would lose the old Dominions without retaining the new. This would destroy any prospect of transforming the Commonwealth into a 'third force'. India would be more of an embarrassment than an asset.[245] Instead of acquiring Dominion status, it should be made to enter into a special treaty relationship with Britain.[246] The strength of the Commonwealth in world affairs lay in 'the natural harmony' of its components, and India would certainly not conform to this. Even from an economic point of view, Britain would hardly lose anything if India left. Except for certain preferences, Britain had no specific trade advantages in countries 'merely because they are within the Empire'.[247]

The arguments of both sides were contradictory and seldom based on verifiable facts – mainly because nobody had hitherto made a study of the real advantages provided by Commonwealth membership. In fact, officials found that there was 'very little authoritative literature' on the subject.[248] In order to provide ministers with a conclusive answer, a working group of FO, CRO, CO, Treasury, BoT, Home Office and MoD officials prepared a paper on the implications of India's membership. The working group concluded that on political grounds, some objections were valid, but that all the military and economic considerations tended in favour of India's membership.

Any attempt to create an inferior form of relationship would not only alienate India, but would also be resented by the older members of the Commonwealth.[249] Some of the old Dominions might prefer the status of an associated state, thus throwing the inner and outer groups of the Commonwealth out of balance. The existing informal ties would have to be replaced by formal agreements. In the ensuing negotiations serious difficulties were likely to arise. India, Pakistan and Ceylon would certainly resent any implication that it was not open to them to attain equality with the white Dominions. If they were to be retained in the British sphere of influence, they had to be treated like all other members.[250] It was more advantageous to admit them to full membership than to lose their goodwill and see them cutting every link with Britain.

When ministers discussed the issue, Bevin was 'extremely defeatist' and repeated the arguments brought forward by his officials: it was not worth keeping India in because it would not be sincerely committed to Britain – 'but we to it'.[251] But Attlee as well as most of his colleagues were in favour of keeping India in, even if this meant the end of the Crown link. On political, strategic and economic grounds they thought it important to retain India. Every effort should be made to achieve this.[252] India's departure would not only be a disastrous blow to the prestige and influence of the Commonwealth, but would also gravely affect the economic position of the United Kingdom and the sterling area.[253] A secession would end all hopes of creating 'an example of the free, democratic association of different races', in contrast with the communist world in which the different races were held together by 'force and fear'.[254] Moreover, India's departure might have a 'corroding and disintegrating effect' upon the old Commonwealth. If India was retained it was likely that the relationship between Britain and its former colony would grow closer in the years to come. Accepting a republican Dominion might even lead to the return of the Irish Republic and Burma – an argument revealing a considerable extent of wishful thinking.[255] After lengthy debate ministers therefore decided to admit a republican India. On 27 April 1949 the Commonwealth prime ministers' conference in London accepted India's request to allow it to remain in the Commonwealth as a republic. Henceforth, India would owe no allegiance to the British Crown, but simply recognise the British monarch as head of the Commonwealth. Even though it was hoped at the time that India would settle down as a normal Dominion, its anti-colonial stance and fierce criticism of British policy soon proved this wrong. India's admission thus led slowly but surely to a transformation of the Commonwealth.

Burma and Ceylon

While ministers were willing to abandon the Crown link in order to retain India, there was no such flexibility with regard to Burma. This intransigence demonstrates that, at the time, the Commonwealth was not considered merely a façade that concealed political realities. In the late 1940s, Attlee and his colleagues still hoped that membership in the club would lead to close cooperation and allow Britain to exert a guiding influence over the Dominions. Since Aung San and his followers (contrary to Nehru) did not hide their intention of cutting loose from the metropole, policy-makers thought it advisable not to 'spoil the ship for a ha'pence of heretics': it was better to let Burma secede in order not to destroy the intimacy of the club.[256] While Mac-Donald predicted that the country's departure would be the beginning of 'an immense decline' of British prestige in the region, to Pethick-Lawrence the advantages of retaining Burma appeared 'relatively slight'.[257] Whereas in early 1946 he had still considered it essential for Burma to attain self-government only within the Commonwealth, he was less than eager to retain it one year later – probably because there was no longer any danger of creating a precedent for India. Even if Burma remained in the club, he underlined, this would not in itself have ensured that her policy would be 'in the same instinctive harmony with our own as have invariably been those of the white Dominions (other than Eire)'. Burma was a small country and its inclusion in the Commonwealth was not likely to offer sufficient advantages to outweigh the disadvantages. They would undertake obligations towards Burma flowing 'automatically' from membership while prejudicing 'essential features' of the Commonwealth as hitherto understood.[258] The same view prevailed in the Dominions Office: in principle, officials thought it undesirable to see any part of the empire secede. On the other hand, it was argued, there were 'serious embarrassments' in having members who enjoyed the advantages without carrying any of the obligations. Burma was nothing like as important as India and did not warrant the creation of a special category of membership.[259] It was preferable to secure Britain's (not very important) strategic and economic interests through a treaty. Even if the Burmese went 'outside the Empire', they would probably still wish to remain on close and friendly terms with Britain.[260] These views prevailed in the Cabinet, and Burma left the Commonwealth on becoming independent on 4 January 1948.

Contrary to the case of India and Burma, there was never any major discussion whether Ceylon should be allowed to remain in the Commonwealth – even though officials briefly toyed with the idea of offering it an inferior status. It was taken for granted that the island would always be a 'loyal and willing member', and that its accession would prove advantageous to the whole club.[261] Ceylon was no great power, but offered important air and sea bases for the protection of the imperial 'life-line' through the Indian Ocean. Its politicians were eager to maintain the Commonwealth connection and would follow the lead given by Britain. Retaining the island in the club, it was assumed, would help maintain and even strengthen its links with Britain. Only some FO officials wanted to keep Ceylon out, arguing that the island was not 'British'. But their resistance waned quickly once it emerged that India would stay in. There was no point in excluding Ceylon if its much bigger northern neighbour was allowed in. The CRO was in favour of Ceylon's admission, but insisted that in the future membership should not be granted unless the country concerned was able to defend itself. No colony should be allowed to seek the advantages of Dominion status while still retaining a colonial status in defence matters, for example, by reliance on the Royal Navy: 'The full insurance rate should be paid: there are no reductions'.[262] Otherwise the Commonwealth would end up being an association of countries depending on the United Kingdom for their defence, thus weakening the club's standing in the world. Ceylon should remain an exception justified by the particular circumstances in south Asia.

Conclusion

In 1945 the Commonwealth was a loose association between Britain and the Dominions of Australia, Canada, Ireland, New Zealand and South Africa. It lacked institutional strength, but policy-makers considered it an important political instrument: the club was thought to enhance Britain's international standing, particularly in the United States, and to act as a deterrent against potential aggressors. The vagueness of the links between members was considered an advantage rather than a drawback. It allowed recalcitrant members like South Africa to be retained while putting a veil over the association's real strength. Policy-makers feared that any attempt to formalise the club would lead to serious difficulties.

In 1947–48 the Commonwealth was enlarged through the admission of India, Pakistan and Ceylon. Policy-makers in the FO were against this decision since they wanted to keep the club 'white' and 'British'. At the time, they still assumed that the Commonwealth could be transformed into a 'third force'. The old Anglo-Saxon intimacy apparently needed to achieve this would be spoilt by the admission of 'brown' Dominions which did not share the other members' sentimental links with Britain. However, most officials and ministers thought it advantageous to retain India. They assumed that this would enhance Britain's as well as the Commonwealth's standing, keep India in the British sphere of influence, ease future cooperation, and ensure the subcontinent's defence against the Soviet Union. Moreover, it would enable the Commonwealth to provide a political framework for the sterling area as well as a model for the organisation of international relations. India's departure, however, would deal a heavy blow to Britain's economic, strategic and political interests throughout Asia. Therefore, it was decided to abandon the Crown link rather than to witness the departure of India.

The debate about India's admission demonstrates how many expectations policy-makers projected onto the Commonwealth in the post-war period – on the side both of Bevin and the FO as well as of Attlee and Cripps. The latter group eventually gained the upper hand. A majority of policy-makers believed that the new multi-racial Commonwealth would enhance Britain's international standing and help promote its interests. It was to be more than a mere façade hiding the realities of the transfer of power. It was to offer a model for a new world order, securing Britain's prestige and influence while making it unnecessary to rely on coercion and force. The discussions about India's admission to the Commonwealth thus demonstrate Britain's willingness to put relations with its former colonies on a new footing. Most policy-makers had an astonishingly liberal concept of a new world order based on mutual respect and cooperation. For them, there was never any serious thought of using the Commonwealth as a new guise for the old empire.

NOTES

1. Oliver Franks in the *Listener* 52/1314, 11 November 1948, p. 788, quoted in Philip Darby, *British Defence Policy East of Suez, 1947–1968* (London: Oxford University Press, 1973), p. 22.
2. Memorandum 'The first aim of British foreign policy', Bevin to Cabinet, 4 January 1948. CAB 129/23 (Hyam, *Labour Government*, II, 142).
3. Memorandum Dalton to Cabinet (CP (46) 53), 8 February 1946. PREM 8/195 (PRO).
4. In 1946, the armed forces still had 1,900,000 trained men and 100,000 under training, and 16.1 per cent of GNP was spent on defence expenditure. (Until the mid-1970s, it was customary to calculate the British military burden by dividing the military budget by the GNP at *factor cost*. Since then, the GNP at *market prices* has been used as the denominator. References in the text are, in accordance with contemporary practice, to defence expenditure at factor cost.)
5. 'Note on a Difference of Opinion', Dalton to Attlee, 20 January 1947. MS Attlee dep. 49, fol. 86–91 (Bodleian Library).
6. Dalton Papers, Dalton diary, entry for 20 December 1946. I/34 (LSE); Winster to Creech Jones, 14 February 1947. Mss.Brit.Emp. s 332, 54/2 (RHL).

7. Brief 'British Overseas Obligations', E. Plowden to Cripps, 25 April 1950. T 232/167 (*DBPO* ser. II, vol. II, no. 36).
8. Attlee to Bevin, 1 December 1946. FO 800/475 (Hyam, *Labour Government*, III, 279); memorandum 'Future of the Italian Colonies' (CP (45) 144), Attlee to Cabinet, 1 September 1945. CAB 129/1 (PRO).
9. Memorandum 'Future of the Italian Colonies' (DO (46) 27), Attlee to Cabinet defence committee, 2 March 1946. CAB 131/2 (Hyam, *Labour Government*, III, 276).
10. Memorandum 'Future of the Italian Colonies' (CP (45) 144), Attlee to Cabinet, 1 September 1945. CAB 129/1 (PRO).
11. Ibid.
12. Dalton Papers, Dalton diary, entry for 8 August 1947. I/35 (LSE).
13. Report 'Strategic Position of the British Commonwealth' (DO (46) 47), Chiefs of Staff to Cabinet defence committee, 2 April 1946. CAB 131/2 (Hyam, *Labour Government*, III), 321 Dalton papers, Dalton diary, entry for 22 March 1946. I/34 (LSE).
14. John Saville, *The Politics of Continuity: British Foreign Policy and the Labour Government, 1945–46* (London: Verso, 1993), p. 153.
15. Memorandum, 'Effect of Britain's External Financial Position on Foreign Policy', 9 February 1945. FO 371/45694, quoted in Jim Tomlinson, 'The Attlee Government and the Balance of Payments, 1945-1951', *Twentieth Century British History*, 2 (1991), p. 55.
16. Memorandum by Sargent, 1945. FO 371/50912, quoted in Stuart Croft, *The End of Superpower: British Foreign Office Conceptions of a Changing World, 1945–51* (Aldershot: Dartmouth Press, 1994), p. 4.
17. Minute by Smart, 10 October 1946. FO 371/53257, quoted in W. Travis Hanes, *Imperial Diplomacy in the Era of Decolonization. The Sudan and Anglo-Egyptian Relations, 1945–56* (Westport, CT: Greenwood Press, 1995), p. 71.
18. Sargent to Bevin, 28 March 1947. FO 371/62943, quoted in Hanes, *Imperial Diplomacy*, p. 111.
19. Dalton papers, Dalton diary, entry for 8 August 1947. I/35 (LSE).
20. DO 10 (46) 2, 5 April 1946. CAB 131/1 (Hyam, *Labour Government*, III, 322).
21. Bevin to Attlee, 9 January 1947. FO 800/476, quoted in John Kent, 'The British Empire and the Origins of the Cold War, 1944–49', in Anne Deighton (ed.), *Britain and the First Cold War* (Basingstoke: Macmillan, 1990), p. 177.
22. Bevin to Creech Jones, 22 September 1948. CAB 21/2244 (PRO).
23. Memorandum by Minister of Defence (CP (49) 245 annex), 18 October 1949. CAB 129/37 (3) (PRO).
24. Minute by Mallet, 14 July 1949. FO 371/73892, quoted in Wm Roger Louis, 'Libyan Independence, 1951: The Creation of a Client State', in Prosser Gifford and Wm Roger Louis (eds), *Decolonization and African Independence. The Transfers of Power, 1960–80* (New Haven, CT: Yale University Press, 1988), p. 168.
25. Bevin to Attlee, 9 January 1947. FO 800/476, quoted in William Roger Louis, *The British Empire in the Middle East, 1945–51: Arab Nationalism, the United States and Post-war Imperialism* (Oxford: Clarendon Press, 1984), p. 740f.
26. Minute by Bevin, 10 January 1948. FO 371/69192, quoted in Saville, *The Politics of Continuity*, p. 133.
27. Memorandum, 'Strategic Implications of an Independent and United Libya' (COS (49) 381), 10 November 1949. DEFE 5/18 (PRO).
28. COS 144 (47) 1, 21 November 1947. DEFE 4/8 (Kent, *Egypt*, I 108)
29. 'World Strategic Review' (JP (48) 70), draft report by COS for Cabinet defence committee, 11 September 1948. DEFE 4/16 (Hyam, *Labour Government*, III, 326).

30. Memorandum, 'Imperial Security in the Middle East' by Minister Resident, Middle East, 2 July 1945. FO 371/45270, quoted in Bernd Ebersold, ' "Delusions of Grandeur": Großbritannien, der Kalte Krieg und der Nahe Osten, 1945-1956', in Hans-Heinrich Jansen and Ursula Lehmkuhl (eds), *Großbritannien, das Empire und die Welt: Britische Außenpolitik zwischen 'Größe' und 'Selbstbehauptung', 1850–1990* (Bochum: Brockmeyer, 1995), p. 147.

31. CM 6 (47) 3, 15 January 1947. CAB 128/11 (PRO).

32. 'World Strategic Summary for Use in Informal Discussions with Commonwealth Representatives', 30 October 1947. JP (47) 139 (final), quoted in Richard Aldrich and Michael Coleman, 'Britain and the Strategic Air Offensive Against the Soviet Union: The Question of South Asian Air Bases, 1945–9', *History*, 74 (1989), p. 401.

33. 'Future Defence Policy' (COS (47) 5), 23 January 1947. DEFE 5/3, quoted in Bernd Ebersold, *Machtverfall und Machtbewußtsein: Britische Friedens- und Konfliktlösungsstrategien, 1918–1956* (Munich: Oldenbourg, 1992), p. 153.

34. Raymond Smith and John Zametica, 'The Cold Warrior: Clement Attlee Reconsidered, 1945–7', *International Affairs*, 61 (1985), p. 251.

35. Memorandum, 'Constitutional Reform in Cyprus' (CA (47) 21), Attlee to Cabinet Commonwealth affairs committee, 22 December 1947. CAB 134/54 (Hyam, *Labour Government*, III, 236)

36. Anthony Adamthwaite, 'Britain and the World, 1945–1949: The View from the Foreign Office', in J. Becker and F. Knipping (eds), *Power in Europe? Great Britain, France, Italy and Germany in a Post-war World, 1945–1950* (Berlin: de Gruyter, 1986), p. 20. In December 1945, the United States had provided Britain with a loan of $3.75 billion – on condition that the pound sterling was made convertible after two years. When free convertibility was implemented, it was followed by a strong increase of the dollar drain as all countries with sterling reserves hurried to exchange them into US currency (Scott Newton, 'Britain, the Sterling Area and European Integration, 1945–50', *Journal of Imperial and Commonwealth History*, XIII (1984/85), p. 166). It is estimated that the drain rose from $60 m in the first six months of 1947 to $300m between 1 July and 20 August 1947. By mid-August only $850m remained of the US loan. In order to avoid a collapse, convertibility had to be suspended on 20 August 1947 – an embarrassing revelation of the international lack of confidence in sterling. (Allister E. Hinds, 'Sterling and Imperial Policy, 1945–1951', *Journal of Imperial and Commonwealth History*, XV (1986/87), p. 155.)

37. The sterling area comprised all colonies and Dominions (bar Canada) as well as some non-Commonwealth countries. Britain acted as banker to the system. At the outbreak of the Second World War, the convertibility of sterling had been suspended and free movement of goods and payments was confined to the sterling area. Dollar transactions were managed through a pooling system under British supervision, and members accumulated sterling balances whenever their exports were not matched by imports. This system lasted well into the 1950s. In the late 1940s and early 1950s, the sterling area ran up increasing deficits with the dollar area because of the spending of Britain and the Dominions. The colonies, on the other hand, maintained a substantial surplus, partly because of high commodity prices and partly because of import restrictions.

38. Memorandum, 'British Overseas Obligations' (PUSC (50) 79 final 2nd revise) by Permanent Under-Secretary's committee, 27 April 1950 (*DBPO* ser. II, vol. II, no. 43).

39. Memorandum, 'The United Kingdom in South-East Asia and the Far East',

Permanent Under-Secretary of State's committee, n.d. (October 1949). CO 967/84 (Stockwell, *Malaya*, II, 196).

40. Memorandum, 'British influence in Egypt today' by J. Hamilton, 18 September 1950. FO 141/1398 (Kent, *Egypt*, II, 178).
41. H. Cooper to Blackburne, 13 October 1947. CO 537/5133, quoted in Frank Furedi, 'Creating a Breathing Space: The Political Management of Colonial Emergencies', *Journal of Imperial and Commonwealth History*, XXI (1993), p. 99; memorandum by R. Robinson, n.d. (March 1947). CO 847/38/3, quoted in Hyam, 'Africa and the Labour Government', p. 149.
42. T. Lloyd to W. Strang, 9 September 1952. CO 936/217 (Goldsworthy, *Conservative Government*, I, 6).
43. Jasper to Thomson, 4 August 1948. DO 142/10 (PRO).
44. 'Constitutional Development in Africa': African Governors' Conference, draft minute 5 (2nd session), n.d. (November 1947). CO 847/73/7 (Hyam, *Labour Government*, I, 67).
45. Burns to Colonial Service Staff, 14 March 1947. CO 554/152/1 (Rathbone, *Ghana*, I, 17).
46. Larry J. Butler, 'The Ambiguities of British Colonial Development Policy, 1938–48', in Anthony Gorst, Lewis Johnman and W. Scott Lucas (eds), *Contemporary British History 1931–61: Politics and the Limits of Policy* (London: Pinter, 1991), p. 131.

    This long-term perspective on the timing of self-government is underlined by the expansion of the number of civil servants employed, and the ambitious plans for a new purpose-built office near Westminster Abbey. Before the war, the CO had been staffed by 465 civil servants: by 1950, the number had increased to 1,289. In addition, more than 6,300 men were recruited into the administrative service during the first Labour government (J.M. Lee, *Colonial Development and Good Government: A Study of the Ideas Expressed by the British Official Classes in Planning Decolonization, 1939–1964* (Oxford: Clarendon Press, 1967), p. 37). The speed at which locals were trained for responsible posts in colonial administrations also leads to the conclusion that independence was not expected to come about in the near future: a 1948 commission thought that the 98 senior government posts held by Africans out of a total of over 1,300 in the Gold Coast represented 'a fair increase', even though proportionately it represented little advance on the 1925 figure of 27 out of 500 (J.D. Hargreaves, *Decolonization in Africa* (London: Longman, 1988), p. 108f.).
47. Attlee in the parliamentary debate on Indian independence, quoted in Tomlinson, *Political Economy*, p. 152. Actually these were not the Prime Minister's own words: he was quoting Mont Stuart Elphinstone, a British official in India who had done much to promote popular education and local administration.
48. Statement by Attlee in the House of Commons, 13 April 1949, quoted in Alpha Mohamed Lavalie, 'The Transfer of Power in Sierra Leone: British Colonial Policy, Nationalism and Independence, 1945–61', unpublished PhD thesis, University of London, 1989, p. 16 f.
49. Note by Attlee, n.d. (1942). CAB 118/73, quoted in Hyam, *Labour Government*, I, p. XXIII.
50. Memorandum, by A. Cohen, n.d. (March 1947). CO 847/36/47238/1 (47), quoted in J.W. Cell, 'On the Eve of Decolonization: the Colonial Office's Plans for the Transfer of Power in Africa, 1947', *Journal of Imperial and Commonwealth History*, VIII (1979/80), p. 246.
51. Rita Hinden, *Empire and After: A Study of British Imperial Attitudes* (London: Essential Books, 1949), p. 187.

52. 'Projection of Britain Overseas' (OI (46) 10), proposed statement as revised by Mr Morrison for committee on overseas information services, 17 August 1946. CAB 124/1007 (Hyam, *Labour Government*, I, 68).

53. Diane B. Kunz, *British Post-War Sterling Crises* (Austin, TX: University of Texas Press, 1992), p. 7.

54. Memorandum by Parliamentary Under-Secretary of State for the Colonies (CP (47) 242), 23 August 1947. CAB 129/20 (PRO).

55. Britain's lack of dollars was not the only reason for the heightened interest in colonial produce: in the immediate post-war period, economic experts expected the world shortages of food and raw materials to last for much longer than they actually did. Using the ample natural resources of the colonies was designed to help Britain avoid being drawn into another global depression (George C. Peden, 'Economic Aspects of British Perceptions of Power on the Eve of the Cold War', in Becker and Knipping (eds), *Power in Europe?*, p. 257).

56. Brook to Attlee, 14 January 1948. PREM 8/923 (Hyam, *Labour Government*, II, 121); memorandum by Rees-Williams, March 1948. FO 1110/20 (PRO).

57. Minute, 'Definition of Functions of Colonial Development Corporation and Overseas Food Corporation', Bevin to Attlee, 4 October 1947. FO 800/444 (Hyam, *Labour Government*, II, 84).

58. Telegram, Bonnet (Washington) to Paris, 5 July 1948. 457 AP 120 (ANP).

59. Minute by Creech Jones, 18 January 1947. CO 537/1651 (Hyam, *Labour Government*, II, 164 introduction).

60. Draft memorandum, 'Prices of Colonial Export Products' by Creech Jones, March 1947. CO 852/989/3 (Porter and Stockwell, *British Imperial Policy*, I, 42).

61. CO note, n.d. (1946). Mss.Brit.Emp. s 332, 44/1 (RHL).

62. Memorandum, 'A Federal Solution for East Africa', by A. Dawe, July 1942. CO 822/111, quoted in Ronald Robinson, 'Andrew Cohen and the Transfer of Power in Tropical Africa, 1940–1951', in W.H. Morris-Jones and Georges Fischer (eds), *Decolonisation and After: The British and French Experience* (London: Frank Cass, 1980), p. 54.

63. Lord Addison to Mackenzie King, 9 April 1948. Addison papers, quoted in Partha Sarathi Gupta, 'Imperialism and the Labour government of 1945–51', in Jay Winter (ed.), *The Working Class in Modern British History: Essays in Honour of Henry Pelling* (Cambridge: Cambridge University Press, 1983), p. 108.

64. Bevin to Attlee, 16 September 1947. FO 800/444 (Hyam, *Labour Government*, II, 140); memorandum 'The First Aim of British Foreign Policy', Bevin to Cabinet, 4 January 1948. CAB 129/23 (Hyam, *Labour Government*, II, 142).

65. Dalton papers, Dalton diary, entry for 15 October 1948. I/36 (LSE).

66. Memorandum by J. Strachey (CP (47) 10), 4 January 1947. CAB 129/16 (Hyam, *Labour Government*, II, 116).

67. Memorandum 'Tour in Africa, Nov.–Dec. 1947' by Montgomery, 19 December 1947. DO 35/2380 (Hyam, *Labour Government*, II, 104).

68. Attlee to Montgomery, 21 December 1947, and Bevin to Attlee, 22 December 1947. PREM 8/923 (Hyam, *Labour Government*, II, 104).

69. Note by Creech Jones, n.d. (January 1948). Mss.Brit.Emp. s 332, 4/4 (RHL); memorandum by Creech Jones, 6 January 1948. DO 35/2380 (Hyam, *Labour Government*, II, 106).

70. Minute by S. Caine, 9 November 1947. CO 877/31/5 (Hyam, *Labour Government*, I, 69); M. Flett (Treasury) to E. Melville (CO), 30 June 1952. CO 537/7858 (Goldsworthy, *Conservative Government*, III, 404).

71. CO memorandum, 'Colonial Development Corporation', n.d. (October 1951). CO 537/7847 (Goldsworthy, *Conservative Government*, III, 452).

72. Minutes of Cabinet economic policy committee, 9 March 1951. CAB 134/228 (Hyam, *Labour Government*, II, 103).
73. E. Melville (CO) to M. Flett (Treasury), 27 June 1952. CO 537/7858 (Porter and Stockwell, *British Imperial Policy*, II, 12).
74. Creech Jones to Cripps, 19 November 1949. CAB 124/122 (Hyam, *Labour Government*, II, 99).
75. Minute by J. Crombie, 8 December 1952. T 220/262 (Goldsworthy, *Conservative Government*, III, 471).
76. Note by L. Bristow, n.d. (21 August 1954). T 229/865 (Goldsworthy, *Conservative Government*, III, 420).
77. H. Poynton to C.G. Eastwood, 1 November 1951. CO 537/7757 (Goldsworthy, *Conservative Government*, III, 359); memorandum 'Possibilities of Increasing the Supply of Colonial Foodstuffs and Raw Materials to the United Kingdom', Lyttelton to Cabinet, 12 November 1951. CAB 129/48 (Goldsworthy, *Conservative Government*, III, 360).
78. CO brief for Churchill, n.d. (December 1951). CO 537/7597 (Goldsworthy, *Conservative Government*, III, 398).
79. Minute by Lyttelton, 22 May 1952. CO 537/7844 (PRO).
80. Charles F. Feinstein, 'The End of Empire and the Golden Age', in Peter Clarke and Clive Trebilcock (eds), *Understanding Decline: Perceptions and Realities of British Economic Performance* (Cambridge: Cambridge University Press 1997), p. 224.
81. Memorandum, 'The Share of the Colonies in Defence' by Trafford Smith, 24 October 1951. DEFE 7/415 (Goldsworthy, *Conservative Government*, I, 1).
82. Minutes by J. Martin and A. Cohen, 2 August 1950. CO 537/5324 (Hyam, *Labour Government*, III, 336).
83. CO paper on racial prejudice, May 1946. CO 537/1224, quoted in Gupta, 'Imperialism', p. 116.
84. Quoted in Bishwa Nath. Pandey, *The Break-Up of British India* (Basingstoke: Macmillan, 1969), p. 1.
85. Nicholas Owen, 'The End of Empire 1945–51', *Contemporary Record*, 3 (1990), p. 16; David K. Fieldhouse, 'The Labour Governments and the Empire-Commonwealth, 1945–51', in Ritchie Ovendale (ed.), *The Foreign Policy of the British Labour Governments, 1945–1951* (Leicester: Leicester University Press, 1984), p. 91.
86. In 1945, India consisted of 593 separate administrative units – 582 autonomous Indian states and 11 British provinces. Britain could only end formal rule over the 11 provinces; the States were (at least in theory) free to choose whether they wanted to join any Indian successor state or become independent. The Muslim League demanded an independent state – Pakistan – for the Muslims of the subcontinent.
87. CM (46) 55 (confidential annex), 5 June 1946. L/PO/12/2 (*TOP*, VII, 455).
88. A. Nye (Madras) to Mountbatten, 2 May 1947. R/3/1/152 (*TOP*, X, 282).
89. Note, 'The Viability of Pakistan' by Pethick-Lawrence, 13 February 1946. L/P&J/10/21 (*TOP*, VI, 427).
90. A. Rowlands to D. Monteath, 20 November 1945. Mss.Eur.D.714/71 (*TOP*, VI, 221).
91. Wavell to Pethick-Lawrence, 13 November 1945. L/PO/10/22 (*TOP*, VI, 208). A letter from Killearn to Ismay is a good example of the way officials on the spot saw their situation. Recalling his service in Bengal, Killearn stated that he had 'no vain regrets over Dacca': it was a 'foul place and a filthy climate, no amenities of any sort, endemic disease of all kinds, ... no health station, not an Englishman or woman to talk to. And for what?' Killearn complained that he and his men were paid inadequate transfer

expenses, had only four months home leave in five years, and 'a loss of at least £120 a year of pensions for life' (Killearn to Ismay, 16 August 1947. ISMAY 3/7/8 (LHC)).

92. Record of meeting of Cabinet delegation and Wavell on 16 May 1946. L/P&J/5/337 (*TOP* VII 296); paper 'Internal Situation in India' (COS (45) 667 (0)), Chiefs of Staff to Cabinet, 1 December 1945. L/WS/1/1008 (*TOP*, VI, 256).

93. Memorandum, 'What Will Happen if the Cabinet Mission Does Not Achieve a Settlement?' by J. Thorne, 5 April 1946. R/3/1/109 (*TOP*, VII, 60).

94. Cabinet delegation to Cabinet Office, 3 June 1946. L/P&J/5/337 (*TOP*, VII, 442).

95. CM (46) 55 (confidential annex), 5 June 1946. L/PO/12/2 (*TOP*, VII, 455).

96. CM (46) 108 (confidential annex), 31 December 1946. R/30/1/9 (*TOP*, IX, 235); record of a meeting of Cabinet delegation and Wavell, 16 May 1946. L/P&J/5/337 (*TOP*, VII, 296).

97. Memorandum, 'Situation in India and its Possible Effect upon Foreign Relations' by Foreign Secretary (CP (46) 222), 14 June 1946. L/PO/6/112 (*TOP*, VII, 528).

98. A.V. Alexander to Bevin, 1 June 1946. AVAR 5/11 (CC).

99. Attlee to Cabinet delegation and Wavell, 6 June 1946. L/P&J/10/22 (*TOP*, VII, 465).

100. CM (46) 104, 3 (confidential annex), 10 December 1946. L/PO/6/112 (*TOP*, IX, 181).

101. Memorandum by Wavell, 30 May 1946. L/P&J/5/337 (*TOP*, VII, 407).

102. Minutes of Governors' conference, 8 August 1946. Wavell papers (*TOP*, VIII, 132). There were only some 500 British officials in the ICS (out of a total of more than a thousand) and 500 more in the police. The Governor of the Central Provinces and Berar reported that he had 17 European ICS officers, including three Judicial officers, and 19 European members of the Indian Police. These figures excluded people serving in the government, but included people on leave. This handful of Europeans had to deal with over 18 million people living in an area of 100,000 square miles (H. Twynam to Wavell, 26 November 1945. L/P&J/5/194 (*TOP*, VI, 239)).

103. Wavell to Attlee, 30 October 1946. R/30/1/8a (*TOP*, VIII, 531).

104. Record of a meeting held at 10 Downing Street on 23 September 1946. L/P&J/10/45 (*TOP*, VIII, 354). In August, 4,000 Hindus were killed in Calcutta. These massacres were followed by reprisals in Bihar in which 7,000 Muslims died.

105. Report, 'India – Military Implications of Proposed Courses of Action' (DO (46) 68) by Chiefs of Staff, 12 June 1946. R/30/1/7 (*TOP*, VII, 509).

106. Hollis to Monteath, 13 March 1946. L/WS/1/1044 (*TOP*, VI, 521).

107. Wavell to Pethick-Lawrence, 13 July 1946 (*TOP*, VIII, 26 annex II).

108. Pethick-Lawrence to Attlee, 21 December 1946. L/P&J/10/46 (*TOP*, IX, 216).

109. Dalton papers, Dalton diary, entry for 20 December 1946. I/34 (LSE).

110. Attlee in the House of Commons, 10 July 1947, quoted in N. Mansergh (ed.), *Documents and Speeches on Commonwealth Affairs, 1931–52*, Vol. 2 (London: Oxford University Press, 1953), p. 689; note by Mountbatten, 11 February 1947. Mountbatten papers (*TOP*, IX, 378).

111. Bevin to Attlee, 1 January 1947. R/30/1/8a (*TOP*, IX, 236).

112. Notes by Attlee, n.d. (November 1946). R/30/1/9 (*TOP*, IX, 35); Attlee to Bevin, 2 January 1947. PREM 8/564 (*TOP*, IX, 237).

113. Mountbatten to Attlee, 17 February 1947. Mountbatten papers (*TOP*, IX, 415).

114. Minutes of Governors' conference, 15 April 1947. L/PO/6/123 (*TOP*, X, 147).

115. Mountbatten to Ismay, 8 May 1947. R/3/1/153 (*TOP*, X, 360).

116   Memorandum 'Indian Policy' by Prime Minister (CP (47) 158), 22 May 1947. L/PO/6/121 (*TOP*, X, 516).

117.   COS (47) 134 (0), 26 June 1947. L/WS/1/1091 (*TOP*, XI, 362).

118.   COS (47) 62nd, 12 May 1947. L/WS/1/1030 (*TOP*, X, 416).

119.   K. Harris, *Attlee* (London: Weidenfeld & Nicolson, 1982), p. 385.

120.   F. Wylie (United Provinces) to Wavell, 19 February 1946. L/S&G/7/904 (*TOP*, VI, 447).

121.   'Note on the Results to the British Commonwealth of the Transfer of Political Power in India', July 1946. Wavell papers (*TOP*, VIII, 26).

122.   Anita Inder Singh, 'Economic Consequences of India's Position in the Commonwealth: The Official British Thinking in 1949', *Indo-British Review*, 11 (1984), p. 107.

123.   Cabinet delegation to Prime Minister, 15 May 1946. L/P&J/10/42 (*TOP*, VII, 291).

124.   Pethick-Lawrence to Lascalles, 7 March 1946. L/P&J/10/21 (*TOP*, VI, 505); report 'India – Military Implications of Proposed Courses of Action' (DO (46) 68) by Chiefs of Staff, 12 June 1946. R/30/1/7 (*TOP*, VII, 509).

125.   Mountbatten to Listowel, 4 July 1947. R/3/1/82 (*TOP*, XI, 511).

126.   Hollis to Monteath, 13 March 1946. L/WS/1/1044 (*TOP*, VI, 521).

127.   IB (47) 28th meeting, 28 May 1947. L/P&J/10/79 (*TOP*, X, 553); COS (47) 76, 16 June 1947. L/WS/1/1032 (*TOP*, XI, 221).

128.   Viceroy's personal report, 12 June 1947. L/PO/6/123 (*TOP*, XI, 162).

129.   Report, 'Maldive Islands' by joint planning staff, Chiefs of Staff committee (JP (47) 117 (final)), 12 September 1947. CO 537/3769 (PRO).

130.   Memorandum, Secretary of State for Burma to Cabinet, 29 August 1946 (IB (46) 29). L/PO/9/11 (Tinker, *Burma*, I, 678).

131.   Draft letter, Mountbatten to Churchill, 26 October 1944. WO 203/5261 (Tinker, *Burma* I, 51, appendix A).

132.   Cabinet Office to Mountbatten, 13 February 1946. CAB 121/1954 (Stockwell, *Malaya*, I, 71); Meiklereid to FO, 27 December 1946. FO 371/53970, quoted in Martin Shipway, 'British Perceptions of French Policy in Indochina from the March 1946 Accords to the Inception of the Bao Dai Regime 1946–1949: A Meeting of "Official Minds"?', in Charles-Robert Ageron and Marc Michel (eds), *L'ère des décolonisations: Sélection de textes du colloque 'Décolonisations: comparées', Aix-en-Provence, 30 septembre–3 octobre 1993* (Paris: Karthala, 1995), p. 87.

133.   Dorman-Smith to Pethick-Lawrence, 27 August 1945. M/4/1239 (Tinker, *Burma*, I, 252).

134.   Dorman-Smith to Pethick-Lawrence, 10 September 1945. Mss.Eur.E 215/8 (Tinker, *Burma*, I, 269).

135.   Pethick-Lawrence to Dorman-Smith, 26 October 1945. Mss.Eur.E 215/7, quoted in Nicholas Tarling, 'Lord Mountbatten and the Return of Civil Government to Burma', *Journal of Imperial and Commonwealth History*, XVI, 2 (1982/83), p. 222.

136.   Attlee to Pethick-Lawrence, 3 May 1946. L/PO/9/16 (Tinker, *Burma*, I, 483).

137.   'Appreciation of the Situation as at 2359 Hours, Sunday 15 September 1946 by Sir Hubert Rance'. L/PO/9/15 (Tinker, *Burma*, II, 18); Rance to Pethick-Lawrence, 16 September 1946. PREM 8/143 (Tinker, *Burma*, II, 20).

138.   Rance to Pethick-Lawrence, 8 November 1946. M/4/2621 (Tinker, *Burma*, II, 97).

139.   Rance to Pethick-Lawrence, 16 November 1946. M/4/2615 (Tinker, *Burma*, II, 108); official note 'Indonesia and Burma', 4 October 1948. PREM 8/734 (III) (PRO).

140.   Note by G. Laithwaite, 16 November 1946. M/4/2621 (Tinker, *Burma*, II,

109); memorandum, 'Policy in Burma' (IB (46) 40), Pethick-Lawrence to India and Burma committee, 22 November 1946. L/PO/9/11 (Tinker, *Burma*, II, 112).

141. South East Asia Land Forces to War Office, 13 January 1947. L/WS/1/1053 (Tinker, *Burma*, II, 179). The text of the telegram is strangely reminiscent of advice given earlier by Mountbatten. It is not inconceivable that the former commander of the South-East Asia Command played a role in its formulation.

142. Memorandum, 'Burma: Constitutional Position' (CP (46) 448), Secretary of State for Burma to Cabinet, 9 December 1946. M/4/2621 (Tinker, *Burma*, II, 129).

143. CM (46) 104, 10 December 1946. M/4/2621 (Tinker, *Burma*, II, 130).

144. IB (46) 10, 19 December 1946. M/4/2621 (Tinker, *Burma*, II, 144).

145. Minute by Murray, 7 November 1947. FO 371/63457, quoted in Shipway, 'British perceptions', p. 94.

146. Brief, 'British Interests in Burma' by Bevin, n.d. (June 1948). PREM 8/715 (PRO).

147. CM (46) 107, 19 December 1946. M/4/2621 (Tinker, *Burma*, II, 145).

148. Draft note of a meeting with the Burma sub-committee of the imperial policy group of the Conservative Party held at the Burma Office, 23 May 1944, quoted in Nicholas Tarling, '"An Empire Gem": The British Wartime Planning for Post-War Burma, 1943–44', *Journal of South-East Asian Studies*, 13 (1982), p. 326.

149. Pethick-Lawrence to Rance, 19 October 1946. M/4/3025 (Tinker, *Burma*, II 67); Rance to Pethick-Lawrence, 2 January 1947. M/4/2804 (Tinker, *Burma*, II 157).

150. Richard J. Aldrich, 'British Strategy and the End of Empire: South Asia, 1945-51', in Richard J. Aldrich (ed.), *British Intelligence, Strategy and the Cold War, 1945–51* (London: Routledge, 1992), p. 288.

151. African Governors' conference paper, AGC 17, n.d. (November 1947). CO 847/6/4 (Hyam, *Labour Government*, I, 64).

152. Lord Soulbury to Hall, 5 October 1945. CO 54/986/6 (Hyam, *Labour Government*, I, 3).

153. H. Moore to Hall, 25 September 1945. CO 54/986/6/3 (De Silva, *Sri Lanka*, II, 295).

154. CM 30 (45) 3, 11 September 1945. CAB 128/1 (PRO).

155. Memorandum by Colonial Secretary, 29 April 1947. PREM 8/726 (PRO).

156. Bevin to Creech Jones, 20 May 1947. CAB 118/29 (Hyam, *Labour Government*, I, 26).

157. CM 51 (47) 4, 3 June 1947. CAB 128/10 (PRO).

158. Report by Chiefs of Staff, 5 May 1947. PREM 8/726 (PRO).

159. 'Ceylon Defence Requirements', draft report by Joint Planning Staff (JP (47) 63 (0) (revised draft)), 30 May 1947. CO 537/2217 (PRO).

160. M.A.W. to C. Jeffries, 19 May 1947. CO 537/2217 (PRO).

161. IB 43 (47), 28 July 1947. PREM 8/726 (PRO).

162. Memorandum by Parliamentary Under-Secretary of State for Commonwealth Relations (CP (48) 91), 17 March 1948. CAB 129/26 (PRO).

163. The term 'normal' colonies is used to designate those territories that had no substantial white minorities or strategic importance, and that were esteemed big enough to achieve independence on their own.

164. According to a 1947 census, the Malays made up 49.5% of the population, the Chinese 38.4%, and Indians another 10.8%. These figures excluded Singapore where three-quarters of the population were Chinese. (Clyde Sanger, *Malcolm MacDonald: Bringing an End to Empire* (Liverpool: Liverpool University Press, 1995), p. 277.)

165. MacDonald to Hall, 25 May 1946. CO 537/1529 (Stockwell, *Malaya*, I, 92).
166. MacDonald to Creech Jones, 27 June 1947. PREM 8/950, (I) (PRO).
167. Minute by H. Bourdillon, 23 January 1948. CO 537/2177 (Stockwell, *Malaya*, I, 37).
168. CO note 'Future Political and Economic Developments in Malaya', n.d. (September 1948). CO 537/3746 (Stockwell, *Malaya*, II, 167); H. Bourdillon to Bennett, Seel, Poynton, 25 June 1947. CO 537/2568 (PRO).
169. Killearn to Sargent, 20 February 1947. FO 800/274 (PRO). Killearn had been appointed special commissioner for south-east Asia a short time after Malcolm MacDonald had been nominated Governor-General. MacDonald, linked with the CO, was to ensure coordination of policy and administration throughout the territories under his authority, i.e. Malaya, Singapore, Sarawak, North Borneo and Brunei; Killearn was to advise the FO on problems affecting the conduct of foreign affairs in south-east Asia. This overlap in responsibilities was only ended when MacDonald took over Killearn's functions and became Commissioner-General for south-east Asia in 1948.
170. Note by W. Linehan, 2 March 1948. CO 537/3746 (Stockwell, *Malaya*, II, 139).
171. Gurney to Lloyd, 24 February 1949. CO 537/4741 (Stockwell, *Malaya*, II, 177).
172. Memorandum, 'The Situation in Malaya' (CP (48) 171), Creech Jones to Cabinet, 1 July 1948. CAB 129/28 (Stockwell, *Malaya*, II, 153).
173. Memorandum Bevin to Cabinet, 18 October 1949. CAB 129/37 (1) (Hyam, *Labour Government*, II, 152).
174. DO (50) 32, 29 April 1950. CAB 131/9, quoted in Karl Hack, 'Screwing Down the People: The Malayan Emergency, Decolonisation and Ethnicity', in Hans Antlöv and Stein Tønnesson (eds), *Imperial Policy and Southeast Asian Nationalism 1930–1957* (Richmond: Curzon Press, 1995), p. 88.
175. Memorandum 'Political and Economic Background to the Situation in Malaya' (DO (50) 94), Griffiths to Cabinet defence committee, 15 November 1950. PREM 8/1406/2 (Stockwell, *Malaya*, II, 227).
176. McNeil to Mayhew, 2 April 1949. FO 371/76049, quoted in A.J. Stockwell, 'Insurgency and Decolonisation during the Malayan Emergency', *Journal of Commonwealth and Comparative Politics*, 25 (1987), p. 71f.
177. Minutes of 15th Commissioner-General's conference, 7 June 1950. CO 537/5961 (Stockwell, *Malaya*, II, 218).
178. 'Political Developments in Malaya', CO brief for Rees-Williams (October 1949). CO 967/84 (Stockwell, *Malaya*, II, 195).
179. Minute by Rees-Williams, 7 January 1949. CO 537/3746 (Stockwell, *Malaya*, II, 174).
180. Memorandum 'The Military Situation in Malaya', Strachey to Cabinet Malaya committee (MAL C (50) 21), 17 June 1950. CAB 21/1681 (Stockwell, *Malaya*, II, 220).
181. Minute by A. Cohen, 5 September 1949. CO 96/800/1 (Rathbone, *Ghana*, I, 57).
182. Creasy to Creech Jones, 28 February 1948. CO 96/795/6 (Rathbone, *Ghana*, I, 21). On 28 February, a demonstration by unemployed ex-servicemen began marching on government house. When the police opened fire to stop the parade, two men were killed and five wounded. This led to violent clashes between demonstrators and the police. At the same time, large crowds plundered shops in Accra.
183. Memorandum by R. Scott, 5 March 1948. CO 96/795/6 (Rathbone, *Ghana*, I, 25).
184. Despatch R. Scott to Creech Jones, 10 March 1949. CO 537/4638 (Rathbone, *Ghana*, I, 42).
185. Minute by L. Gorsuch, 23 March 1949. CO 537/4638 (Rathbone, *Ghana*, I, 42); minute by E. Hanrott, 18 March 1949. CO 537/4638 (Rathbone, *Ghana*, I, 42).

186. L. Gorsuch to R. Saloway, 11 November 1949. CO 96/812/4 (Rathbone, *Ghana*, I, 70).
187. Minute by E. Hanrott, 21 June 1949. CO 537/4638 (Rathbone, *Ghana*, I, 47).
188. Minute by A. Cohen, 5 September 1949. CO 96/800/1 (Rathbone, *Ghana*, I, 57).
189. Minute by E. Hanrott, 14 February 1950. CO 537/5816 (Rathbone, *Ghana*, I, 80).
190. Arden-Clarke to Cohen, 12 May 1951. CO 537/7181 (Rathbone, *Ghana*, I, 99).
191. CO note of a meeting with Arden-Clarke, 9 January 1952. CO 554/298 (Rathbone, *Ghana*, I, 112).
192. Arden-Clarke to Gorell Barnes, 24 September 1952. CO 554/371 (Rathbone, *Ghana*, II, 119); Cohen to Mackintosh, 11 June 1951. CO 537/7181 (Rathbone, *Ghana*, I, 100).
193. Memorandum 'Anglo-French Relations in West Africa' by A. Cohen, 20 November 1951. CO 537/7148 (Goldsworthy, *Conservative Government*, I 114); minute by C. Jeffries, 10 October 1949. CO 96/800/1, quoted in Hyam, *Labour Government*, I, p. xxxvi.
194. T. Lloyd to J. Macpherson, 5 March 1953. CO 554/254 (Rathbone, *Ghana*, II, 123).
195. Ismay to Kennedy, 9 February 1952. DO 121/146, quoted in Ronald Hyam, 'The Geopolitical Origins of the Central African Federation: Britain, Rhodesia and South Africa, 1948–1953', *Historical Journal*, 30 (1987), p. 164.
196. 'A Plan for the Peopling of our Empire, and its Consequent Development' by A.C. Wilkinson, May 1946. FO 800/443 (PRO).
197. Minutes by Sargent and Bevin, 3 August 1948/n.d. FO 371/69153 (Hyam, *Labour Government*, II, 127 introduction).
198. Attlee to Bevin, 29 October 1946. PREM 8/458 (PRO).
199. Minute by H. Tizard, n.d. (November 1947). FO 800/444 (PRO). Tizard was the government's chief scientific adviser. In minutes to the Prime Minister, Alexander and Noel-Baker signalled consent with his ideas.
200. Creech Jones to Attlee, 5 February 1948. CO 537/3631 (Hyam, *Labour Government*, II, 122).
201. Kathleen Paul, '"British Subjects" and "British Stock": Labour's Post-war Imperialism', *Journal of British Studies*, 34 (1995), p. 251.
202. J. Forbes Munro, *Britain in Tropical Africa, 1880–1960. Economic Relationships and Impact* (Basingstoke: Macmillan, 1984), p. 51. Many of the new settlers came from South Africa, but there was a considerable number originating directly from Britain: from 1946 to 1950, nearly 37,000 British immigrants arrived in the Rhodesias, while about 40,000 came from South Africa (CP (51) 122, appendix to annex I, 3 May 1951. CAB 129/45 (PRO)).
203. Alison Smith, 'The Immigrant Communities (I): The Europeans', in D.A Low and Alison Smith (eds), *History of East Africa*, Vol. 3 (Oxford: Clarendon Press, 1976), p. 459.
204. A.W.S. to H. Lintott, 19 December 1958. DO 35/7873 (PRO); STCC (59) 2nd meeting, 24 March 1959. CAB 134/2505 (PRO).
205. In 1950, for example, Nigeria and the Gold Coast were named among the smaller territories (note by C. Jeffries (STC (50) 20), 27 April 1950. DO 35/2218, quoted in W. David McIntyre, 'The Admission of Small States to the Commonwealth', *Journal of Imperial and Commonwealth History*, XXIV (1996), p. 252).
206. Memorandum, 'The Future of the UK in World Affairs', Treasury, FO and MoD officials to Cabinet policy review committee (PR (56) 3), 1 June 1956. CAB 134/1315 (PRO).
207. CM 20 (47) 6, 11 February 1947. CAB 128/9 (Hyam, *Labour Government*, III, 231).

208. Note on a meeting with A. Wright, 20 July 1951. CO 537/7453 (PRO); minute by M. Fisher, 31 January 1951. CO 531/7453 (PRO).

209. Winster to Creech Jones, 17 September 1947. CO 537/2484 (PRO).

210. Memorandum, 'Constitutional Reform in Cyprus', Attlee to Cabinet Commonwealth affairs committee (CA (47) 21), 22 December 1947. CAB 134/54 (Hyam, *Labour Government*, III, 236).

211. Minute by J. Bennett, 21 January 1948. CO 537/4035 (ibid., 238); minute by J. Bennett, 13 June 1950. CO 537/6228 (Hyam, *Labour Government*, III, 244).

212. Minute by G. Bateman, 7 January 1950. FO 371/8776/RG1081/41, quoted in Robert Holland, 'Never, Never Land: British Colonial Policy and the Roots of Violence in Cyprus, 1950–54', *Journal of Imperial and Commonwealth History*, XXI (1993), p. 153.

213. Brook to Prime Minister, 5 October 1955. PREM 11/1726F (PRO).

214. Memorandum, 'Future of the Smaller Territories', CO to working party on smaller colonial territories, 20 March 1959. CAB 134/2505 (PRO).

215. Lloyd to Liesching, 4. December 1951. DO 35/2218, quoted in McIntyre, 'Admission of Small States', p. 253.

216. Note by Jeffries (STC (50) 20), 27 April 1950. DO 35/2218, quoted in McIntyre, 'Admission of Small States', p. 252.

217. Secretary of State for Burma to Governor of Burma, 23 February 1946. M/4/2593 (Tinker, *Burma*, I, 404). The Commonwealth is an informal association that emerged in the 1920s. At first it comprised the self-governing Dominions of Canada, South Africa, Australia, New Zealand, Ireland, and, unofficially, Southern Rhodesia.

218. Roger J. Moore, *Making of the New Commonwealth* (Oxford: Clarendon Press, 1987), p. 3.

219. W.H. Morris-Jones, 'The Transfer of Power, 1947. A View from the Sidelines', *Modern Asian Studies*, 16 (1982), p. 18; for more information on the changing meaning of the word 'Commonwealth' see David McIntyre, *The Significance of the Commonwealth, 1965–90* (Basingstoke: Macmillan, 1991), pp. 13–16.

220. Sometimes the term 'independent Commonwealth' was used to designate the association of self-governing states, as opposed to the 'dependent Commonwealth', i.e. the colonies. In this book, the term 'Commonwealth' always denotes the group of self-governing nations (as opposed to the dependent territories).

221. It was only in 1958 that 'Empire Day' was changed into 'Commonwealth Day'.

222. See the report, 'Publicity on the British Commonwealth and Empire' by Empire publicity sub-committee, n.d. (February 1947). PREM 8/648 (PRO).

223. CRO memorandum, 'The Probable Development of the Commonwealth over the Next Ten or Fifteen Years', June 1956. CO 1032/51 (PRO).

224. D.W. Dean, 'Final Exit? Britain, Eire, the Commonwealth and the Repeal of the External Relations Act, 1945–1949', *Journal of Imperial and Commonwealth History*, XX (1992), p. 397.

225. Memorandum (CP (49) 208), Bevin to Cabinet, 18 October 1949. CAB 129/37 (1) (Hyam, *Labour Government*, II, 152).

226. Attlee in the House of Commons, 10 July 1947, quoted in Mansergh, *Documents and Speeches 2*, p. 689.

227. 'India – Defence Requirements. Brief for Negotiations' by Chiefs of Staff, July 1947. L/WS/1/1046 (*TOP*, XII, 219).

228. COS paper 'Strategic Summary', 16 October 1947. DEFE 4/8, quoted in Anita Inder Singh, 'Post-Imperial British Attitudes to India. The Military Aspect, 1947–51', *Round Table*, 296 (1985), p. 361.

229. Peden, 'Economic Aspects', p. 247.

230. Memorandum, 'Problems of Emigration from the United Kingdom with Particular Reference to Movement to the Commonwealth', June 1950. LAB 13/281, quoted in Paul, 'British Subjects', p. 269.
231. Prime Minister to Lord President, Foreign Secretary, President of the Board of Trade, Minister of Defence, Lord Chancellor, Dominions Secretary, Colonial Secretary, 14 May 1947. CAB 21/2278 (*TOP*, X, 436).
232. Mountbatten to Ismay, 8 May 1947. R/3/1/153 (*TOP*, X, 360).
233. Minutes of staff meeting, 9 May 1947. Mountbatten papers (*TOP*, X, 366).
234. Memorandum by Lord Privy Seal, 3 November 1947. CAB 134/54, quoted in Singh, 'Post-Imperial British Attitudes', p. 360.
235. Memorandum, 'The Defence of the Commonwealth' (DO (47) 23) by COS, 7 March 1947. CAB 131/4 (PRO).
236. CRO memorandum, 'Military Advantages to India and Pakistan of Remaining in the Commonwealth', August 1948. DO 142/341 (PRO).
237. Report 'Military Implications of India's Possible Future Status' (JP (49) 19) by JPS, 17 February 1949. DEFE 4/20 (Hyam, *Labour Government*, IV, 400).
238. Thomson to Turnbull and Baxter, 7 August 1948. DO 142/10 (PRO).
239. Report, 'India's Future Relations with the Commonwealth' (GEN 276/6) by official committee on Commonwealth relations, 22 February 1949. CAB 130/45, quoted in Anita Inder Singh, 'Keeping India in the Commonwealth: British Political and Military Aims, 1947–49', *Journal of Contemporary History*, 20 (1985), p. 475f.
240. Minute by A. Joyce, 27 August 1948. DO 142/356 (PRO).
241. India Office memorandum, 'Future Relations of India and the British Commonwealth', 3 February 1947. L/P&J/10/122 (*TOP*, IX, 338).
242. F. Turnbull to G. Laithwaite, 16 December 1948. DO 142/137 (PRO).
243. CR (48) 1, 3 April 1948. CAB 134/118 (PRO); Brook to Attlee, 22 October 1948. PREM 8/950 (II) (PRO).
244. H. Duncan Hall to Noel-Baker, 11 October 1948. NBKR 4/111 (CC); minute by F. Turnbull, 24 August 1948. DO 142/356 (PRO).
245. CRO minute, 31 August 1948. DO 142/356 (PRO); draft letter by F. Turnbull, 4 October 1946. L/P&J/10/122 (*TOP*, VIII, 409).
246. G. Gater to D. Monteath, 6 December 1946. L/P&J/10/122 (*TOP*, IX, 171).
247. A. Nye (Madras) to Mountbatten, 2 May 1947. R/3/1/152 (*TOP*, X, 282).
248. A.N. to Laithwaite and Commonwealth Secretary, 31 January 1956. DO 35/5012 (PRO).
249. Report, 'Commonwealth Relations' by official committee on Commonwealth relations, n.d. (September 1947). CAB 134/117 (PRO).
250. 'Note on Stent's Memorandum' by Gordon-Walker, 15 March 1948. GNWR 1/7 (CC).
251. Gordon-Walker diary, entry for 10 February 1949. GNWR 1/7 (CC).
252. CR 1 (49), 7 January 1949. CAB 134/119 (PRO).
253. Cabinet committee on Commonwealth relations (CR 2 (49) 2), 8 February 1949. CAB 134/119 (Hyam, *Labour Government*, IV, 398).
254. Report by Chiefs of Staff committee on 'Implications of War between India and Pakistan', 6 April 1950. PREM 8/1450 (PRO).
255. Minute, 'The Link with India', Gordon-Walker to Attlee, 31 December 1948. PREM 8/1008 (PRO).
256. Macmillan to Foreign Secretary, 6 March 1960. PREM 11/2925 (PRO).
257. MacDonald to Colonial Secretary, 27 June 1947. PREM 8/950 (I) (PRO); memorandum (BUK (47) 13) by Secretary of State for Burma, 9 January 1947. CAB 133/3, (Tinker, *Burma*, II, 173).
258. Secretary of State for Burma to governor, 24 May 1947. CAB 134/117, quoted in Moore, *Making of the New Commonwealth*, p. 99.

259. Minute by A. Morley, 20 May 1947. M/4/2677, quoted in Nicholas Tarling, *The Fall of Imperial Britain in South-East Asia* (Singapore: Oxford University Press, 1994), p. 190.
260. G. Laithwaite to D. Monteath, A. Henderson and Secretary of State for Burma, 29 April 1947. M/4/2677 (Tinker, *Burma*, II, 340).
261. Governor of Ceylon to Colonial Secretary, 7 March 1947. CO 882/30 (De Silva, *Sri Lanka*, II, 382).
262. 'Note by the Commonwealth Relations Office on the Defence Aspects of Further Grants of Independent or Semi-Independent Status within the Commonwealth', 14 March 1951. CO 537/7098 (PRO).

— 3 —

The Empire-Commonwealth under Churchill and Eden

THE INFORMAL EMPIRE

MOST HISTORIANS agree that Conservative Party policy in the early 1950s was 'not properly conceived and followed through'. Probably the only realistic option at the time was a gradual reduction of overseas commitments. But it is not entirely correct to state that this strategy 'never received a fair trial' by Conservative policy-makers.[1] The withdrawal from the Suez base and the move towards greater mobility initiated in 1954 were important steps towards lightening the imperial burden. However, since they considered Britain's overseas stance as a whole, it never occurred to policy-makers to consider complete withdrawal from any specific area. It was assumed that it was not possible to evacuate, for example, the eastern Mediterranean without starting a crumbling process that would inexorably destroy Britain's hold over the Persian Gulf and the Indian Ocean as well. The Churchill and Eden governments were eager to reduce overseas commitments. But they thought that this was a difficult process needing delicate handling. For them, Britain's economic strength depended directly on its political and military performance on the international scene. Therefore, they considered it vital to maintain all overseas commitments.

Ministers thought that the stability of sterling, the special relationship and Britain's international standing were interlinked, and that all depended on the informal empire. Giving an impression of weakness would lead to an unstoppable decline, with catastrophic consequences for Britain's well-being. If the governments under Winston Churchill and Anthony Eden are to be criticised, then it is for their belief in sterling's dependence on a strong showing (a belief they shared with their predecessors as well as their successors) rather than for anything that resulted as a logical consequence from it. For the same reason it is also necessary to nuance Holland's statement that the

Suez operation was 'only' preoccupied with prestige and therefore 'desperately at odds' with economic concerns.[2] Policy-makers saw no contradiction between prestige and economic interests. For them, the two were rather intimately linked.

'A Luxury We Can No Longer Afford?' Imperialism in the Early 1950s

When the Conservatives arrived in office in October 1951, they were faced by a multitude of economic and financial problems. One of the most urgent of these was another balance-of-payments crisis brought about by Labour's rearmament programme in the wake of the Korean war. According to the new Chancellor of the Exchequer, R.A. Butler, the financial crisis facing the government was 'worse than 1949, and in many ways worse even than 1947'.[3] In the very first memorandum to be placed before ministers, he pointed out that the external deficit was growing at a rate of £700 million a year. Despite these enormous difficulties, many policy-makers still believed that Britain could hold the tide. The spectre of declining economic, military and political power strengthened rather than weakened their resolve to maintain the country's worldwide commitments. The new government had no intention of caving in to the various pressures facing it. For ministers, the real problem was not whether great-power status should be maintained, but how this could be done at an affordable price. It was acknowledged that, at least in material terms, Britain had ceased to be a first-class power. But the continuing difficulties led to a hardening of the government's determination to maintain Britain's worldwide presence rather than to retreat to 'shorter and more defensible lines'. Any kind of unnecessary withdrawal, it was feared, would lead to a loss of prestige which, in its turn, would lead to a loss of power and a dangerous weakening of sterling. Hence, it was essential to avoid anything which might be regarded as an indication that Britain's strength and influence were failing.[4]

While this stance was shared by an overwhelming majority of policy-makers, it did not go totally unopposed. As under the Attlee governments, it was again the Chancellor of the Exchequer who called for a reassessment – using arguments that were nearly identical to those used by his predecessor. Butler argued that it was above all the external deficit which threatened the position of sterling. The only chance of preventing irreparable harm was to restore confidence in Britain's ability to deal with its financial weakness. He called for import cuts, monetary measures, as well as drastic reductions in government expenditure especially in the defence budget projected by Labour, which he believed was too big for the nation's means.[5]

Overseas commitments as well as the size of the armed forces had to be reduced in order to allow economic recovery. FO and MoD papers did not even 'glance' at the balance-of-payments aspects, although it was essential to reflect what Britain could really afford: 'With shrunken assets we have accepted commitments which are not only far greater than before the war, but many of which are non-productive'.[6] The figure of 850,000 men in the armed forces was much too high given the fact that Britain was already losing civilian contracts to Germany and Japan. The percentage of the GNP devoted to defence expenditure, that is, 10 per cent, was also too high. The government had to undertake badly needed productive investment at home and to build up reserves. For this it was essential to get a considerable trade surplus, which could only be achieved by lightening the burden on the economy of defence and overseas expenditure.[7]

Macmillan opposed Butler's proposals vehemently, arguing that Britain's economic survival largely depended upon world confidence in sterling – and this hinged upon 'our ability to maintain ourselves as a great Power'.[8] A reduction of overseas commitments would therefore prove to be a false economy. Instead of accepting responsibilities without claiming privileges – 'a luxury we can no longer afford' – Britain should use its empire for economic recovery by developing alternative supplies of food and raw materials, which in the sterling area until now had been obtained from non-sterling areas. According to Macmillan, the present level of spending had to be maintained. In some areas it might even be necessary to spend more. This applied in particular to the Middle East: if the fuel needs of the United Kingdom during the next 20 years were to be met, imports of oil had to be trebled. Therefore Britain had to make sure that oil continued to be produced by British firms, flowed to Britain at an acceptable price – and could be paid for in sterling. What was needed was not a parsimonious debate about saving some pounds here or there, but 'the fearless proclamation' of a policy that would reinspire the masses and restore their pride and confidence: 'This is the choice – the slide into a shoddy and slushy Socialism, or the march to the third British Empire.'[9]

Eden also argued against any withdrawal from Britain's 'world responsibilities inherited from several hundred years as a great Power', repeating the basic lines laid down in the FO paper of 1950.[10] There was no global security system, and Britain faced a strong threat from the communist world. The main objective of British foreign policy, therefore, had to be to maintain the country's position as a world power while maintaining the highest possible standard of living in the metropole. The United Kingdom was not a self-sufficient economic unit, but depended on trade. Therefore Britain had to make a major contribution to the maintenance of sea and air communications across the world. The colonies had to be maintained, developed and defended. The independent states in the Middle East and Asia had to be backed up militarily and economically, otherwise the Russians would move in, and the United Kingdom's international status would be affected:

> It is evident that in so far as we reduce our commitments ..., our claim to the leadership of the Commonwealth, to a position of influence in Europe, and to a special relationship with the United States will be, *pro tanto*, diminished.[11]

Even small withdrawals would lead to a loss of standing. Britain had to avoid this at all costs, for power was not to be measured in terms alone of money and troops (both of which the United Kingdom was already short of): 'a third ingredient is prestige, or in other words what the rest of the world thinks of us'.[12] According to this logic, any kind of retreat equalled a loss of prestige and thus power. And loss of of power meant not only political, but also economic decline.

According to the perception of policy-makers like Eden and Macmillan, the government was faced with a dilemma: on the one hand, the United Kingdom was not strong enough to carry out the policies needed if it was to retain its position in the world. On the other hand, any show of weakness would have repercussions on this position. Military and political weakness reacted on each other. Making one false move might lead to the crumbling of the whole edifice. In order to avoid being drawn into such a vicious circle, the government had to make every conceivable effort to avoid a policy of 'surrender'. If Britain accepted a lesser role, it would necessarily be 'so modest as to be intolerable'. In order to cope with the difficult situation she should share its burden with others. Britain was already working towards the construction of international defence organisations for the Middle East and south-east Asia. It should now persuade the United States to assume 'the real burdens in such organisations, while retaining for ourselves as much political control – and hence prestige and influence – as we can'.[13] Shedding the burden was to be a very gradual and inconspicuous process in order not to damage Britain's position and influence in the world. At the same time, expenditure in the domestic social sector was to be reduced as well. It was important to avoid the impression that Britain was seeking to transfer part of its military burden to its allies only to preserve intact its welfare state.

These arguments put forward by Macmillan and Eden are revealing of the way in which they conceived of Britain's position in the world: economic power resulted from Britain's status as a great power, not vice versa. International confidence in sterling was crucial. To maintain it, Britain had to act as a great imperial power – even if this threatened to break its (financial) back. Without a strong pound, the sterling area would break up, the Commonwealth would disintegrate, and Britain would cease to be a centre of international financial and commercial exchanges. This would not only have disastrous economic consequences for a country which depended on imports of fuel and food and was unable to pay for them in dollars – it would also damage its political standing.[14] And since Commonwealth central bankers had made it clear that any further devaluation (like the one in 1949) would spell the end of the sterling area, it was considered crucial to maintain a strong pound – not by implementing the cuts proposed by Butler, but by trying to make a 'strong showing' in the world.

Eden and Macmillan were supported by military officials who argued that Britain's economic position had to be restored if it was to hold its 'full status and influence as a major partner of the United States in world affairs'.[15] But it was impossible to restore (and preserve) this position unless Britain could maintain its standing as a strong military power. Britain's overseas commitments, its international status and its economic strength were all inextricably linked: 'Our standing of living stems in large measure from our status as a great power, and this depends to no small extent on the visible indication of our greatness, which our forces, particularly overseas, provide.' Yielding even a small part would lead to a chain-reaction. All over the world, Britain was under the greatest pressure to hand over its responsibilities. Any evidence of readiness to quit would start a landslide which would be impossible to control.[16]

Persuading the United States (and the Dominions) to bear a greater share of the burden would only be successful if Britain was able to demonstrate that it was making the maximum effort possible. If it defaulted too flagrantly on its obligations (as it would have to under the cuts Butler had called for), its allies would be dissuaded from helping: 'The reactions not only on our military but also on our economic position might well be catastrophic.' Therefore reductions of overseas commitments should only be made if this did not create the impression that Britain was unable or unwilling to perform its global role.[17] Other aspects were the need to prevent the further spread of communism as well as the protection of British assets, both of which depended on the presence of British troops. Britain had many enemies, and if it relaxed its grip 'scarcely a British interest outside the United Kingdom' would survive.

In the end, massive resistance forced Butler considerably to water down his proposals. Nonetheless, the need to adapt commitments to scarce resources persisted. Accordingly the military began to look for ways of reducing the huge expenditure on overseas troop deployments. One solution was to mothball bases in peacetime to which troops could be flown out in an emergency, an idea implemented in the Suez base in 1954. This was to be complemented by the creation of rapid intervention forces, which would be rendered highly mobile by air transport, and would be located at strategic centres, that is, in the United Kingdom, the Middle East and Malaya. Such a redeployment would not only reduce the expenditure of foreign exchange, but also pre-empt trouble provoked by the presence of British troops in countries with a hostile population.[18] In addition, everything possible was to be done in order to reduce the demands on the British army. Since Britain could no longer carry the whole burden alone, it had to find a satisfactory means of sharing it with others. In dependent territories this meant building up local forces, in independent countries the creation of regional defence alliances.[19]

The Churchill and Eden governments were determined to maintain Britain's overseas commitments. At the same time, it was acknowledged that it was not feasible to defend all of them by force. Already in the 1940s, many officials and politicians had hoped that coercion and intervention would be replaced with influence and cooperation. Eden also believed that intervention would ultimately undermine rather than sustain British influence. He attempted to act in agreement with Asian and African rulers, not against them. Concessions were acceptable – provided they did not appear as a humiliation of Britain. This was most marked in the case of Egypt: in the early 1950s, the Foreign Secretary had aimed at an agreement which would allow Britain an honourable way out of the Suez base, but in 1956 he was most anxious to 'teach [Gamal Abd'al] Nasser a lesson' because he felt that Britain had been insulted.

When the Cabinet discussed the future of the Suez base in 1953, Eden advocated a flexible approach. According to the Foreign Secretary, Britain could no longer hope to maintain its position by the methods of the nineteenth century, 'however little we like it'.[20] In most Middle Eastern countries, the tide of nationalism was rising fast. If Britain was to maintain its influence, it had to harness these movements rather than struggle against them. Since the Egyptians regarded the Suez base as a military occupation by foreign troops, it no longer served Britain's strategic purposes. Britain could undoubtedly deal with any attempt to eject it by force, but the base would be of little use if there was no local labour to man it. Moreover, a military campaign against Egypt would be costly in terms of money, manpower and publicity. Rather the government should retreat in an honourable way as long as it still could do so: 'if we seek to hang on we may end by being expelled, and that would be humiliating'.[21] In view of Britain's limited resources, it was essential to utilise its strength in the most economical way. The aim had to be to secure Britain's strategic interests while avoiding open conflict with the Egyptians.[22]

In clear opposition to Eden, Churchill advocated a firm stand. What happened in Egypt would set the pace for the rest of Africa and the Middle East. Leaving control of the Suez Canal to the Egyptians was 'another stage in the policy of scuttle which began in India and ended at Abadan'.[23] For Churchill, it was better to break off negotiations than to make concessions:

> We should not be afraid on a matter of importance or principle to let the negotiations fail. That would be much better than weakly yielding to either Egyptians – or Americans. It is comforting in this affair to remember that there are few countries in the world weaker than Egypt. We are for the first time negotiating from a position of strength.[24]

Britain's position was weakened because the Attlee government had 'flinched' from doing this in India or Persia – Churchill was confident, though, that the whole trend would be reversed by firing 'the decisive volley'.[25] The other ministers, however, thought that on military grounds, it made sense to go ahead with the negotiations. In October 1954 the terms and timetable of the British withdrawal from the Suez base were agreed upon. The United Kingdom would evacuate all its troops from Egyptian territory by the spring of 1956, while Nasser indicated a tentative willingness to cooperate on matters of regional strategy. British technicians would maintain the Suez base, and Britain would have the right of re-entry in case of war. Eden's approach was probably the most realistic one, given Britain's weak position in terms of both international law and its capacity to maintain a large contingent in Egypt against local resistance. Nonetheless, the Foreign Minister was sharply criticised by a small but vociferous group of Conservative MPs who accused him of scuttle and appeasement – a reproach Eden would be eager to avoid in the future.[26]

'We Must Cut Our Coat According to Our Cloth': First Attempts at a Policy Review

The withdrawal from Suez and the move towards greater mobility were important steps towards reducing the strain on the British budget, but they did not suffice. In 1955 there was yet another sterling crisis, which could only be met by an emergency budget. When Harold Macmillan took over as Chancellor of the Exchequer in September 1955, he soon discovered that the situation was '*much worse*' than he had expected.[27] In a joint memorandum Macmillan and the Minister of Defence therefore expressed their disquiet. Britain appeared to be spending a great deal of money to provide defences that were 'little more than a facade'.[28] The burden this placed on the national economy was a cause of weakness rather than of strength. In order to prevent any further degradation, government expenditure should be reduced by some £100 million, while sterling balances should be significantly increased. Since the end of the Second World War, Britain's position had grown stronger, but it was still precarious: 'We are like a man with an increasing income who is always living beyond it.' Despite the massive amount of aid received from the United States over the past ten years, Britain's gold and dollar reserves were lower than immediately after the war. In the future, there would be less help, and the United Kingdom would have to face the prospect of repaying its loans from the United States and Canada at the rate of £80 million per annum until the year 2000. Ministers and officials should therefore carefully study Britain's vital interests in peacetime and establish by what means they could best be safeguarded. Eden (who had replaced Churchill as Prime Minister in April 1955), liked the paper and advised a working group of officials to elaborate the points put forward by Macmillan and Walter Monckton.

Early in June 1956, Treasury, FO and MoD officials presented a joint memorandum on 'The Future of the UK in World Affairs'.[29] Despite a modernist rhetoric, the paper basically repeated the points made in earlier FO papers. Ever since the war Britain had tried to do too much, often acting on the brink of economic collapse. Unless there were substantial reductions in claims on the national economy, Britain's capacity to play an effective role in world affairs would be destroyed. Officials listed three steps which had to be taken to secure Britain's survival as a great power: first, it had to be established where the country's vital interests lay and what had to be done to secure them; second, the government should ensure that more resources were put into home investment and the build-up of reserves and less into consumption; and finally, dispensable overseas commitments should be shed, but in an orderly way, preferably by transferring them to the United States or the Dominions. In doing the latter, the presentation of Britain's case would be of the greatest importance.

The worst possible impression would be given if the government failed to convince others that the changes it was making were designed 'not merely to safeguard our own living standards but to help us play an effective role in world affairs and in particular to meet the Russian threat'. The presentation of Britain's case mattered not only because of possible political repercussions. Even more important were the financial ones. Maintaining the international value of sterling was 'a matter of life and death'. Failure to do so would be fatal to British interests. One of the main foundations of world trade and finance would be removed, leading to 'a period of great confusion and depression' favourable to communist expansion. Standards of living in Britain would plummet and the effect on the political cohesion of the Commonwealth (and thus, indirectly, on Britain's international standing) would be disastrous.

Apart from the stability of sterling, Britain had an essential economic interest in the Middle East and south-east Asia. The former mattered because of its oil resources, the latter because of its dollar earnings, which helped bolster up the sterling area. Africa mattered mostly for strategic reasons and because of Britain's responsibilities towards the continent's population. Whereas formal rule ensured that British interests in Africa were for the time being relatively safe, the response in the Middle and Far East had to be adapted to local circumstances. British policy should aim to promote stability and help the locals acquire 'a vested interest in their own freedom and the desire and ability to resist Communism'. The same applied to the Middle East. The uninterrupted supply of oil depended more upon the 'friendly co-operation' of the producing and transit countries than their defence against an external threat. Therefore the government should increase the resources dedicated to economic and technical assistance in order to counter hostile influences.

In many areas it would be possible to substitute cheaper non-military measures for some of Britain's expensive military commitments. These non-military measures included education, information services, British Council activities, economic aid and the training of officers in intelligence and police work.[30] They were to be complemented by 'a worthwhile contribution' to the build-up of the nuclear deterrent. Since conventional forces mattered less after the advent of the hydrogen bomb, Britain should concentrate on the area which would best allow it to maintain its prestige. The United States would then be more likely to help defend British interests generally while also paying more attention to British views. In addition, greater reliance should be placed on sending troops out in cases of emergency and less on having forces available in the theatre all the time. The move towards greater mobility initiated in the early 1950s, was to be continued without, however, making any precipitate withdrawals.[31]

Eden intended the memorandum to serve as the starting point for a ministerial review of national policy.[32] Once it was completed, he established a policy review committee consisting of himself, Foreign Secretary Selwyn Lloyd, Macmillan, Monckton and Lord Salisbury. The review was to take into account the adjustments to be made in British policy in the light of the changes in the 'methods, if not the objectives, of the Soviet Union' – and of Britain's dire financial situation. The period of foreign aid from the United States was ending, and Britain now had to cut its coat according to its shrinking cloth. The government had to find the means of increasing by £400 million a year the credit side of the United Kingdom's balance of payments.[33] Despite these ambitious objectives, the ministerial committee did little more than confirm the official findings. It concluded that the main threat to the United Kingdom now was political and economic rather than military. Britain could no longer rely solely on the threat of military force to attain political stability: it had to devote much more of its non-military resources to this end.[34]

Despite this high-sounding rhetoric, no radical reassessment was made. The assumptions for future planning outlined by the committee were far from revolutionary, and actually confirm traditional lines of policy. They gave priority to maintaining North American involvement in Europe, developing closer cooperation with the United States and Canada and fostering the cohesion of the Commonwealth. No review of colonial policy took place: it was considered impossible to say in advance which colonies might attain independence 'in so long a period as fifteen years'.[35] Power was to be transferred as soon as the territories concerned were ready for it. Any precipitate withdrawal, either from the colonies or other overseas commitments, was considered detrimental to Britain's wider interests.

The policy review hardly presented any new features; but even the few changes it might have produced were shelved with the onset of the Suez crisis: for the next four months events in Egypt absorbed most of the time and energy of senior policy-makers.

'Piracy' on the Nile: Britain and the Suez Crisis

The ill-fated intervention in Egypt was closely linked to the sense of impending financial crisis described above. In this context, the feeling of losing influence in the Middle East (and on the international scene) played a crucial role: the Anglo-French operation was to demonstrate that Britain was still a country the world had to reckon with. By mid-

1956 British policy-makers feared that they were losing their political hold in the Middle East, with immeasurable consequences for Britain's prestige, the stability of the pound as well as the security of British investments and Middle Eastern oil supplies. These anxieties had built up during the year preceding Nasser's nationalisation of the Suez Canal Company. For British officials, pan-Arab nationalism under Egyptian leadership threatened to roll up British influence all over the Middle East.[36] When Nasser nationalised the Suez Canal Company in July 1956, this was considered one in a long series of humiliating experiences suffered by Britain for which Egypt was responsible. Egypt seemed to have no intention of honouring the spirit (or what Britain presumed was the spirit) of the 1954 agreement. Ministers considered it essential to send a clear signal.[37]

Eden especially considered it vital to react: in his eyes, a policy of appeasement would lead to nothing but further aggression: 'our best chance is to show that it pays to be our friends' – and dangerous to be Britain's foe.[38] Tolerating Nasser's act of 'piracy' would imperil the United Kingdom's economic survival. Not only did the canal carry two-thirds of Britain's oil supplies – other countries might be encouraged to prey on British assets. Attlee's failure to take 'a strong line' in the Abadan crisis had already severely weakened the country's ability to influence events in the Middle East – another failure might be lethal.[39] Only military action could produce 'a salutary effect throughout the Middle East and elsewhere, as evidence that United Kingdom interests could not be recklessly molested with impunity'.[40]

The ignominious history of the joint Anglo-French intervention is too well known to be recounted here. What shall be attempted instead is a brief analysis of the impact the Suez crisis had on Britain's imperial and colonial policy. Even though the Suez crisis was certainly not the decisive watershed that Brian Lapping claims it to be, the defeat of the joint Anglo-French operation helped to drive home three facts: first, the dependence of Britain's delicate financial situation on volatile international markets; second, the weakness of Commonwealth solidarity; and, finally, the determination of the United States not to provide propaganda ammunition for the Soviet Union.

The Suez crisis revealed in a very drastic manner to what degree Britain's foreign and imperial policies were restricted by the disparity between the government's ambitious ends and its financial means. While British troops occupied the canal area, dollars and gold drained from the Bank of England at an alarming rate. On 20 November 1956 Macmillan informed ministers that the loss of these reserves by the end of the month could run as high as $300 million (out of some $2,000 million) and that as a consequence, sterling might cease to be an international currency.[41] Ironically, one of the main reasons for the intervention in Egypt had been the government's belief that a failure to confront Nasser would jeopardise the sterling exchange rate. The military operation nearly led to the disaster it had been designed to prevent. The Suez crisis thus laid bare, both at home and abroad, Britain's fundamental financial weakness and strengthened those policy-makers who argued that it was essential to restore international confidence through strict savings. In a letter to the Chancellor of the Exchequer, the Governor of the Bank of England underlined how important it was to reduce the strains on the national economy: 'We have over the last five years been able to maintain our position on a see-saw, retaining just adequate confidence in the currency by a slender margin. After the events of the past few months I do not believe this is good enough.'[42]

But the Suez crisis demonstrated more than just Britain's financial weakness. Some Dominions remained silent, while others (especially India) launched a vociferous attack against the military operation. This lack of solidarity demonstrated to what degree the Commonwealth had ceased to be an instrument which could be used to foster Britain's foreign policy aims. Moreover, the Soviet Union rattled its nuclear sabre of Britain and France, threatening Soviet intervention if the Europeans did not withdraw – a move not countered by any US promise of support. The United States also refused to stand by Britain in the United Nations. On 24 November, the General Assembly resolved by 63 votes to five, to demand the immediate withdrawal of Britain and France from Egypt – the United States was among the 63. The United States also let it be understood that it would not act in support of sterling until Britain had shown that it was conforming to the UN resolution. Since US support was vital for Britain, it was clear that Britain could not afford to maintain a situation to which US and world opinion were opposed. The Suez crisis thus demonstrated that no military operation could be successful 'unless national, Commonwealth and Western world opinion is sufficiently on our side'. Britain could never again resort to independent military action, outside British territories, but possibly even within them, without being sure *at least* of US acquiescence.[43]

Conclusion

The incoming Conservative government under Churchill faced an impressive range of economic and financial difficulties. Butler called for massive cuts in government expenditure, most notably in the military sector, in order to cope with these difficulties. Economic recovery would be impossible as long as Britain attempted to maintain the full range of her overseas commitments. Macmillan and Eden opposed these demands. For them, any reduction of overseas commitments would prove futile. Britain's economic survival was said to depend on world confidence in sterling, and this in turn hinged on Britain's ability to maintain herself visibly as a Great Power. For Eden, Macmillan and most other policy-makers, the country's economic, diplomatic and strategic strength depended to a large extent on what others thought of it. Any rash withdrawal would start an erosion which would be impossible to stop. The informal empire was vital to preserve sterling, the special relationship, Britain's leadership in the Commonwealth and her influential position in Europe, while also serving as a barrier to Soviet expansionism and as a protection for British assets and possessions.

The partisans of informal empire acknowledged that some reductions had to be made, preferably by shifting part of the burden to the United States. But they insisted that cutbacks had to be made very cautiously in order not to create the impression that Britain was a paper tiger in retreat. This is the background to the policy-review Eden ordered in 1955: it was to study ways of reducing government expenditure without damaging Britain's image abroad. The results were rather uncontroversial: expensive military commitments should increasingly be replaced by cheaper means of maintaining Britain's influence and protecting its assets. These means included economic and military assistance, information measures, and last but not least, the courting of moderate nationalists in order to achieve their 'friendly co-operation'. Following the report's advice, Eden at first strove to find political solutions to conflicts such as that over the Suez base as 'precipitate military actions' were of no use to reach a lasting settlement.

Ironically, it was under Eden's premiership that Britain launched such a precipitate military action. Eden's decision to intervene in Egypt was due to the feeling that Britain was increasingly losing ground in the Middle East. Therefore it was considered important to take a strong line in order to prevent further erosion. But rather than stabilise the situation, the use of force pushed Britain back to the brink of financial collapse. The failure of the Anglo-French intervention thus served to drive home three factors: first, London could no longer afford to launch a major military action without being assured of the United States' acquiescence; second, the Commonwealth could no longer be counted on to support Britain; and third, the country's finances had to be put on a sound basis if Britain wanted to maintain confidence in sterling despite informal empire. While the first two points were accepted by all policy-makers, it was particularly the last point which took time to set in.

THE FORMAL EMPIRE

Whereas the Conservatives considered it vital to maintain a firm stand on the informal empire, their approach to colonial affairs soon turned out to be astonishingly flexible and relatively liberal. This interpretation is not generally accepted: many historians continue to believe that Tory rhetoric can be automatically equated with Tory politics. Goldsworthy, for example, sees the period 1951–57 as one of continuity in which the Churchill and Eden governments tried as much as possible to keep 'change within bounds'. According to Goldsworthy, this approach was counter-productive, since it produced circumstances which led Macmillan to end the colonial empire too hastily.[44]

I do not share this view. The Conservative governments were at first less enthusiastic than their socialist predecessors about the colonies' advance towards self-government, but they did nothing to slow down the pace of constitutional advance. In Malaya, the Gold Coast and other territories, the timetable drawn up by Labour was even considerably shortened. Lyttelton and Alan Lennox-Boyd did not attempt to hold back the tide – rather they tried to ride it wherever they thought it appropriate and possible. Like their Labour predecessors, the Conservatives were reluctant to put aside their old loyalty to the settlers. But this loyalty was never exclusive – the responsibility for the fate of the Africans was taken seriously, even though actual policy was often hesitant and contradictory.

The explanation for the sudden ending of colonial rule under the second Macmillan government is not to be found in any delaying tactics of the Churchill or Eden governments. Rather it has to be sought in developments on the local and international scene at the end of the 1950s. Until then, however, policy-makers thought it possible and necessary to maintain formal rule over the settler colonies in Africa as well as the smaller territories.

'Riding the Tide': Colonial Policy under the Tories

From Restoration to Acceleration

While in opposition, Labour's colonial policy seemed too liberal to many Conservatives. Criticism was voiced more or less loudly, in particular by such eminent figures as Churchill and Lord Salisbury. They agreed with the goal of leading the colonies towards self-government, but thought that Labour was going too fast, particularly in Africa, by adopting 'a half-baked policy towards the natives in order to appease ignorant Left Wing opinion'. All that would result from the transfer of power to ill-prepared indigenous politicians was a breakdown of law and order or communist infiltration.[45] The only way of preventing this was to maintain, wherever possible, Western control through 'firm and just government'. Britain had to train the backward areas under its tutelage until they were able to shoulder the full responsibilities of government – a process which was likely to last decades, if not centuries.[46]

In the early 1950s, many Conservatives were disturbed by the situation prevailing in the empire: it seemed to have 'drifted downhill since the war'.[47] The Attlee government was suspected of wanting 'to abdicate at all cost', its policy allegedly being a 'breach of our trust'. Lord Swinton reported being told by a former member of the Egyptian Civil Service that 'all the African officers [were] saying that the line they had been given was Self-Government in double-quick time: some of them were even talking about a Mountbatten timetable'.[48] This claim has no historical foundation, but it reflects the anxieties prevailing in the Conservative Party before it was confronted with the practical difficulties facing any government, whatever its political orientation, in the colonial sector.

Despite their criticism most Conservatives acknowledged after some time in office that the principles underlying Labour's colonial policy were sound. At first they regretted that 'the policy of assisting dependent peoples to attain self-government had been carried forward so fast and so far'.[49] The advance towards self-government should not be stopped, but slowed down. This, however, was easier said than done. Lyttelton, the new Colonial Secretary, pointed out that 'the ever-improving communications of our century, ... the rapidity with which news and propaganda can now be spread, and above all the increasing education and literacy of all people' made it impossible to hold political development at the speed envisaged before the war. The situation in Britain, the colonies, and the world at large left no alternative but to make concessions:

> Fifty million islanders shorn of so much of their economic power can no longer themselves expect to hold dominion over palm and pine on the nineteenth century model of power and paternalism which made us the greatest nation in the world.[50]

The British could regain their 'pinnacle of fame and power' only by transforming the empire into a community of freely associating nations, the Commonwealth. They could not hope to maintain formal rule against the open resistance of the local population. Even the appearance that Britain was departing from its liberal colonial policy would have unfortunate repercussions throughout the empire. Therefore there should be no change from the colonial policy initiated by Labour – a demand accepted by most new ministers, including Churchill.[51]

At first sight this is rather astonishing, since the new Prime Minister had 'an instinctive hatred of self-government in any shape or form', disliking 'any country or people who want such a thing or for whom such a thing is contemplated'.[52] For Churchill, the end of the Raj was an 'abject scuttle', and he urged the French to resist being 'Dutched-out' of Indo-China by 'the same sloppy United Nations methods as lost Indonesia'.[53] But while he demonstrated his dislike in public of anything which might reduce the extent of the formal empire, in reality Churchill took relatively little interest in colonial affairs. Thus, while being averse to the process of devolution, he did nothing to resist it. At times, Churchill even opposed the empire lobby, for example, as in the case of Malcolm MacDonald. MacDonald's term as Commissioner-General had expired in May 1952, but Churchill extended it three times until 1955 despite a campaign among Conservative MPs, military men (especially Montgomery) and journalists to ensure that the appointment was not renewed. In November 1942 Churchill made the emphatic statement that he had not become 'the King's first Minister in order to preside over the liquidation of the British Empire' – ten years later, it was under his very premiership that constitutional changes in the colonies continued and gained momentum.[54]

Even Commonwealth Secretary Lord Swinton, whose ideas were close to those of Lord Salisbury, accepted willy-nilly that 'these lesser countries', i.e. the Gold Coast, Malaya and Nigeria, would 'continue in their progress towards "independence" (though I would hope at a less rapid rate than under the Socialist Government), however little they are really fitted for [it]'. Statements and declarations by ministers established that the government was committed to grant self-government within the Commonwealth when it was satisfied the colonies concerned were fit for it. The Colonial Office should seek, by 'judicious and carefully timed concessions of progressive self-government in domestic affairs', to forestall premature demands for independence, while at the same time avoiding the appearance of 'weakly yielding to extremist pressure'. In the end, however, the speed would depend on the strength of local demands, not timetables set by British officials.[55]

But despite their acceptance of constitutional advance, Swinton as well as Lyttelton hoped that colonial politicians would not be over-anxious to assume 'the responsibilities as well as the privileges of external independence' if their 'reasonable aspirations towards internal self-government' were satisfied. They would probably be satisfied with having opportunities of representation when matters affecting their interests were discussed in the Commonwealth. Thus it might be feasible to come to an agreement whereby the grant of independence would be accompanied on the side of the Africans by voluntary surrender to Britain of control over their foreign relations and defence. This would satisfy 'their *amour-propre* so far as status was concerned', while making sure the territories remained under British control and protection. This was considered important for two reasons: first, to prevent their falling victim to hostile influences and second, to protect the Commonwealth from being swamped by 'lesser territories' with no significance on the international scene.[56]

Swinton and Lyttelton were not the only ones hoping that, with some modifications, British control could be maintained for quite some time to come. In the early 1950s, many policy-makers still expected that despite constitutional concessions, the nature of power relations between metropole and colonies would remain unchanged. The locals were to attain self-government in 'matters that really touch them', while Britain would continue to control essential functions like defence and foreign affairs.[57] The problem was to ensure that the locals were satisfied that they had won the essentials of self-government – 'while we are satisfied that *we* have got the essentials of ultimate control'.[58] Autonomy could thus be conceded as long as Britain retained ultimate control. Promising as such schemes seemed in theory, most policy-makers acknowledged after a while that the locals were not likely to accept them. Nkrumah and other West African politicians showed 'an unwelcome interest' in foreign affairs and defence which would be impossible to satisfy with half-hearted measures.[59] Owing to the advice given by their officials, Lyttelton and Swinton realised that it was not feasible to deny the *arcana imperii*. This did not imply the recognition of a general principle, though. In the case of smaller territories, the idea of granting only internal self-government had some attraction. Policy-makers expected that in most of these territories, the population would be content to remain under British administration.[60] Even in the case of Nigeria and the Gold Coast it was assumed until the late 1950s that the new rulers would continue to collaborate closely with London. However, from mid-1953 onwards it was acknowledged that, at least in the case of larger territories, full independence would have to be granted sooner rather than later.

Thus, despite the concern voiced by Eden and others on taking over, most colonies advanced towards self-government at the same rate, if not faster, as under Labour. After a short period of orientation, Conservative ministers came to the same conclusions as their predecessors: even though it was not always palatable, there was no way, or any point in keeping territories without (white) minority problems or major strategic importance from attaining independence. The logic of events led them to end formal rule in Malaya and the Gold Coast much earlier than originally planned. Soon after taking over, the Conservatives began to have second thoughts about the wisdom of an evolutionary approach and accelerated the transfer of power in those territories where there seemed to be a strong enough demand for it. In order to avoid a conflict with nationalist leaders, policy-makers often acquiesced to concessions which 'we all recognise to be, theoretically, over-hasty political advance'.[61] They could have spun out the process, but the risk to good relations after independence, ministers calculated, would not be worth taking.[62] Most policy-makers acknowledged that, 'of course', the Gold Coast or other territories were no more ready for independence than one's teenage daughter was ready for the proverbial latch-key. Nor would they be any more ready, if at all, in five or ten years. Traditional policy was to dole out 'small doses of additional responsibility, keeping if possible one step ahead of demand'.[63] But at best such a policy could maintain a state of uneasy equilibrium. In the international environment of the 1950s, it was impossible to adhere to an ideal timetable. The answer was to skip the intervening stages and give the people 'the chance to learn the responsibility in the only possible way, i.e. by having to exercise it'. In order to maintain the goodwill of 'the more responsible political leaders', Britain had to move 'more rapidly than ideally we should wish'.[64]

Theoretically, it was best for the colonies to advance smoothly and gradually towards self-government, with particular attention being paid to the maintenance of administrative and political efficiency. But policy-makers realised that if they wanted the colonies to maintain close links with Britain after independence, it might be necessary to accelerate the transfer of power. The pace would be determined far more by public pressure than by British opinions of when self-government should be granted. The Africans wanted to be their own masters, even if this meant a temporary fall in government standards.[65] Material difficulties were not in themselves sufficient to arrest countries which had been bitten by the 'nationalistic bug'.[66] Under Labour as under the Conservatives, accelerated constitutional advance was thus considered the best means of retaining goodwill and of preventing violent confrontations. Policy-makers were not

ready to resist demands for self-government as long as the nationalists in question were non-communist and cooperative. Only in
territories where there seemed to be a risk of communist subversion
or where wider strategic interests were at stake did Britain intervene
militarily.[67]

Explaining the Strange Death of Conservative Colonialism

There are several interlocking (and interacting) factors that explain the
willingness of Conservative ministers to accelerate the constitutional
development of 'normal' colonies beyond anything even progressive
Labour politicians had thought advisable as recently as a decade
earlier. First, there was the emergence of nationalist movements
throughout the empire. Tories and socialists alike agreed that it was
essential to retain the goodwill of Africans and Asians in order to
safeguard British interests after independence. Because they were
afraid of driving colonial nationalists into more radical positions, they
often made more concessions than was originally thought appropriate.
At first it had been hoped that gradual concessions would appease
leaders such as Nkrumah. Soon officials realised, however, that those
nationalists cooperating with the British could not hope to maintain
their position for very long if they did not step up their demands.
Politicians who appeared not to try to keep pace with the constitutional
advance of 'pace-maker' territories, such as India, risked being
outflanked by more extreme elements. Even moderate nationalists had
to demand an early end of formal rule since they risked being
denounced as British stooges – even if they knew that their country
was not yet ready for independence. This logic was acknowledged by
British ministers. But it was always hoped that the early transfer of
power could be compensated for by continued cooperation and assistance after independence. British officials were convinced that, at least
in the case of 'normal' colonies, it was better to move too fast than too
slow: the latter, they feared, might drive local leaders into communist
collaboration or favour radical elements.[68] This applied to all
territories, but in some it was of particular relevance: both Malaya and
the Gold Coast were major dollar earners and held large sterling balances. The transfer of power in these two colonies can thus *inter alia* be
seen as an attempt to dissuade them from leaving the sterling area or
withdrawing their balances over-hastily – even though this was not
considered very likely because of the drawbacks it would supposedly
have for these countries.[69] However, since a certain risk existed, it was
considered wiser to take pre-emptive measures.

Officials and politicians inevitably justified the acceleration of
constitutional advance with the rapidly growing strength of

nationalist demands. But British policy cannot be understood without reference to other factors. In Malaya, for example, the British chose to find local nationalism irresistible, even though it was as yet quasi non-existent. Apart from the desire to remain on good terms with the right kind of nationalists, there were several other reasons explaining the eagerness to remain ahead of events. The first (closely linked to the point made above) was the impression that after the death of Stalin, and the end of the 'hot phase' of the Cold War, a new phase had begun – one in which the struggle was not for direct political control, but for the hearts and minds of Asians and Africans. In the 1950s, the colonial empire thus became 'a vital "cold war" battleground'.[70] To frustrate demands for self-government, it was feared, would drive nationalists into the arms of Moscow. The FO was especially concerned about mounting evidence that the Soviet Union was giving higher priority to African affairs. Officials discerned 'a concerted plan' to follow up the Soviet thrust into the Middle East in order to open up another front in the Cold War.[71] The Colonial Office also worried that the Soviet Union would use every means at its disposal to increase its influence, notably by courting 'disappointed nationalism'.[72] The best strategy seemed to avoid friction from the outset. If containment was to be effective, it had to enjoy the widest possible measure of support – it was no use trying to break communist leaders if there was nobody to step into their place. For British officials, the best way of providing a 'constructive answer' to communism was a liberal colonial policy.[73] Decolonisation thus became an inherent part of cold war politics.

Another factor which influenced British colonial policy in the 1950s was anti-colonialism. Already in the 1940s, officials had remarked on the heightened international attention paid to colonial affairs. Self-determination had been one of the rallying cries of the Anglo-American alliance, which was also increasingly adopted by the Soviet Union and the non-aligned states.[74] In the late 1940s, there was as a consequence enormous international interest in colonial questions, with 'the alleged "colonialism" of HMG' subject to fierce attacks by the Soviet Union, Cuba, Egypt and India.[75] British officials acknowledged that international opinion disapproved of the state of dependence and demanded the rapid grant of 'self-government in whatever form'.[76] But it was still assumed that, at least in the crucial case of the United States, public opinion might be 'educated' on the advantages of colonialism.[77] By the 1950s, however, anti-colonialism had gained in strength and proved a constant source of irritation, not least because of India's efforts at denouncing Western 'imperialism' wherever possible.

The rising strength of international anti-colonialism was a reflection of several developments, most importantly the deepening of the Cold

War and the emergence of non-aligned states. As a result, the British empire found itself in a world in which colonialism was 'increasingly unpopular and the use of force to maintain it no longer practical politics' – at least if Britain wanted to retain the support of its allies.[78] Policy-makers continued to argue that the demand for an early end to colonial rule took no account of fitness for self-government. However, they were no longer able to ignore it. The FO, in particular, warned that the international antipathy towards colonialism was such that it had become 'a concrete and important factor' affecting the government's ability to maintain 'satisfactory foreign relations'. The mere names 'Colonial Office' and 'colony' became 'a serious handicap'.[79] Therefore British policy-makers were eager to remove what was increasingly considered 'the stigma of "colonialism"'.[80] At first it was hoped that this could be achieved by a simple change in terminology: in-convenient words such as 'colony' were to be replaced with 'a more positive concept carrying with it an alternative terminology'.[81] But soon it was acknowledged that a mere change of name would not put an end to the attacks on Britain. It was necessary to make visible changes in the constitutional relations between Britain and its colonies.

Anti-colonialism was not only a problem for Britain's international relations: policy-makers realised that negotiations on colonial affairs in the United Nations could gravely impair Britain's ability to control constitutional advance. The international political atmosphere encouraged nationalists and led to increased demands for self-government.[82] Such interference was of particular importance in the case of the trust territories, i.e. Togoland, Cameroon and Tanganyika. Apparently, the time had passed when Britain could afford to dismiss international criticism.[83] Hostile debate in the United Nations could foster and encourage local opposition, and render the implementation of a certain policy impossible. To ignore international opinion would stimulate even more criticism and influence the attitudes of indigenous politicians, thus reacting on Britain's ability to carry the policies through. Therefore it was important to give evidence of steady constitutional advance in order to 'keep the Trusteeship Council reasonably sweet'.[84] It was acknowledged that the United Nations had to be taken into consideration, but officials were determined at least to *appear* to be in control: 'The last thing we would like to happen is that the United Nations should appear to gain credit for forcing any changes which we may make.'[85] Britain had to take the initiative and make concessions rather than wait until the pressure built up.

The three factors described above played an important role. But British colonial policy cannot be understood without reference to the permanent scarcity of resources facing all governments of the time. Lack of military manpower was one factor: Malaya, Kenya, and (from 1955 onwards) Cyprus, required binding substantial numbers of troops to be permanently deployed. Any further strain would have made it necessary to reduce vital commitments elsewhere. Britain had difficulties maintaining its NATO obligations. It was feared that to default any further on these obligations would lead the United States to withdraw from Europe, with drastic consequences for British strategy and the special relationship. This as well as constant financial difficulties made it necessary to avoid any costly counter-insurgency measures. The need to bolster colonial budgets in Kenya or Malaya showed that it was not only crucial to have local collaborators who could bear part of the burden, but even better, to avoid armed conflict from the outset: 'It is much more expensive to deal with disasters like Mau Mau than to prevent them happening.'[86]

The broad outline of colonial policy was determined by a combination of various motives and events, which have been described above. A further factor that gained relevance in the mid-1950s was the dynamics of decolonisation in the periphery: advance towards self-government in one colony almost automatically led to demands for comparable concessions in other territories. Another problem in this context was the administrative factor. The difficulty of maintaining the morale of a 'dying service' was not restricted to India. In Africa and the rest of Asia as well, the problem was 'how to kindle and maintain the zeal of officers ... when the logical conclusion of the political policy is that the Service which they are joining is a dying Service'.[87] Once it became clear that many territories would attain independence in the near future, few young men were willing to join the CO's services. Those already in the service began to look elsewhere for more promising careers. Indeed, it became increasingly difficult for colonial governments to find qualified personnel: in West Africa, for example, the percentage of unfilled administrative posts rose from 34 in 1951 to 83 four years later.[88] To prevent a collapse while Britain was still responsible for its colonies, it was considered preferable to transfer power – even if local administrations were not yet sufficiently prepared.

'Normal' Colonies

Malaya

The example of Malaya demonstrates clearly how the various factors outlined above led to a speeding-up of the transfer of power. In the immediate post-war period, Malaya had been expected to reach self-government within three decades. The emergency as well as regional and international developments led to a revision of this timetable. Policy-makers soon realised that constitutional concessions were a means to win 'the minds of the people'.[89] From 1952 onwards, the military situation clearly developed in favour of Britain. Officials in Britain and Malaya believed that there would soon be growing pressure for 'swifter progress towards self-government', and feared that it would be difficult to keep the momentum under control. Once more Britain was anxious not to miss the tide. In December 1952 General Gerald Templer proposed a 'tentative time-table', scheduling self-government for 1960 – although, as he pointed out, there was as yet 'no real desire' for independence amongst any community.[90] The country lacked political leaders and there were no political parties of the type required to operate a parliamentary system. Nonetheless, Templer favoured moving ahead: unless there was an early an-nouncement of the intention to prepare for federal elections, HMG would appear to have lost the initiative. Popular demand might still be weak, but it was sure to grow. It was better to take the initiative rather than wait until there was widespread public demand (which might well be exploited by the communists).

The CO agreed: in 1953 it expected Malaya to assume 'a substantial measure of local autonomy' after eight to ten years while acknowledging that constitutional development might be further accelerated by factors beyond its control.[91] This willingness to accelerate constitutional development was not only linked to the situation in the colony: Britain was equally concerned with events in neighbouring Indo-China where France was fighting a losing battle. It was feared that a deterioration in Indo-China would have serious repercussions on the rest of Asia: Thailand and Burma would probably fall to the communists, and it would be extremely difficult to hold the rest. The fear of a knock-on or domino effect was reduced when the United States began heavily to subsidise the French mili-tary effort.[92] On the other hand, Britain doubted whether a communist take-over could be averted only by the kind of 'pre-cipitate military actions envisaged by the Americans'.[93] For British officials the problem was as much political and economic as military. If containment was to be effective, it had to enjoy the active support of the local population. The surest way to achieve this was gradual self-government. It might lead to a deterioration in the ad-ministration, but it kept moderate politicians 'on our side'. If progress towards self-government were delayed, however, Britain would quickly lose their confidence.[94]

In 1953 the local population cautiously began to voice demands for independence. The leaders of the two main political parties, the United Malays National Organisation (UMNO) and the Malayan Chinese Association (MCA), agreed to fight federal elections as a joint Alliance. This agreement put them in a rather strong negotiating position *vis-à-vis* Britain, which was, in any case, willing to accelerate constitutional development. Following demands made by the UMNO–MCA alliance, the British High Commissioner agreed that after the elections, scheduled for July 1955, nominated members of the legislative council (32 out of a total of 99 members) would be selected in consultation with the leaders of the elected majority. This was an important step towards self-government, especially since all the parties contesting the elections committed themselves to secure rapid independence. CO officials therefore expected that after the elections, pressure would mount rapidly. This in itself was not considered a bad thing; but British officials feared that unless they managed to retain control of this process, there would be 'extravagant and competitive claims' for early self-government, which would take no account of the fact that Malaya would for some time to come be 'quite unable' without outside help to defend itself, maintain internal security or even to balance its budget.[95] Officials were determined therefore to persuade local politicians of the urgency of making 'satisfactory arrangements to ensure their survival against hostile forces before they proceed to the more congenial task of discussing the next stage of developments towards internal self-government'. To leave the matter until there was strong nationalist pressure might prejudice the satisfactory outcome of negotiations with regard to bases and the responsibility for internal and external defence. Provided these issues were satisfactorily resolved, however, the advance to self-government could be accelerated.

The elections of 1955 gave the Alliance parties (now joined by the Malayan Indian Congress) all but one of the elected seats – and thus, thanks to the 1954 agreement, also control over the nominated ones. The Colonial Secretary promptly agreed to negotiations on independence and invited a Malayan delegation to London. In Cabinet, he argued in favour of far-reaching concessions: the Alliance politicians would come with one object in mind, namely to obtain a promise of independence, almost certainly with a date attached to it. They would go 'with the eyes of the whole country fixed on them', knowing that, unless they came back with what they were asking for, there would be widespread disappointment and dissatisfaction.[96] They would return to Malaya without the necessary determination to fight communism, and anti-British elements would gain the upper hand. But if the moderate Alliance remained the 'voice of the masses', the process of change would continue to be peaceful and constitutional, causing the least possible upset to the country's economy and security – and Anglo-Malayan relations.[97] Ministers should therefore go 'a very long way' with the delegation in order to establish an atmosphere of goodwill and understanding.[98] Britain's ability to retain Malaya in the Commonwealth depended largely upon its capacity to convince locals that it was entirely sincere in its promises of independence. That is why the transfer of power could not be postponed for much longer.[99]

The Colonial Secretary assured his colleagues that it would be possible to secure satisfactory agreements on defence and 'the other issues of particular concern to us' if an early transfer of power was conceded. Even more important, however, were the resulting goodwill and cooperation which were the best guarantee to secure British interests after independence.[100] In any case, Britain would have to grant self-government sooner or later: it could not hope to govern the country without 'at least the acquiescence of the majority of the population'. And this it would not enjoy for long unless the colony was allowed to make rapid moves towards self-government. There was therefore 'every advantage in granting quickly what is asked of us and using the goodwill which may be expected to flow from that to secure conditions which we want'.[101] Internal self-government should be conceded as soon as possible, with control of internal security retained for the time being. All remaining powers were to be transferred two years later.[102] According to Lennox-Boyd, it would be dangerous to wait any longer:

> Faced with a hostile public, at least unco-operative and perhaps quickly turning to active opposition, we should find ourselves benefitting [sic] only the Communists; and sooner rather than later we should have to concede in the most unhappy circumstances what we could earlier have granted with an air of generosity, the support of world opinion and the promise of loyal co-operation. The tide is still flowing in our direction, and we can still ride it; but the ebb is close at hand and if we do not make this our moment of decision we shall have lost the power to decide.[103]

The French example in Indo-China had shown what could happen if the tide was missed. The choice therefore lay between the 'bloody and disastrous consequences' of hesitating and meeting the demand for constitutional advance fast enough to retain a guiding influence.[104] Britain's long-term objective in Malaya was to secure a cooperative and reliable ally. The best chance of attaining it lay in granting independence.

Salisbury accused Lennox-Boyd of 'giving way all along the line': the Cabinet should not be induced by fear of adverse world opinion to move more rapidly than was in the interests of the peoples concerned.[105] Most ministers, however, agreed with the Colonial Secretary. For them, world opinion as well as the goodwill of Malaya's politicians did indeed matter more than the possible repercussions of British policy on the locals. Power should be transferred in the near future. There was some debate as to whether or not an attempt should be made to obtain written safeguards for Britain's economic and strategic interests.[106] The Colonial Secretary, the Chancellor of the Exchequer and the President of the Board of Trade argued that the Malayan leaders could not be expected to enter into an agreement which would limit their freedom of action in such matters as taxation. Moreover, such safeguards would be of little value if a government which wished to pursue a discriminatory policy towards British interests were eventually to come to power. The example of India showed that a formal agreement was of limited value. The difficulties which British nationals in south Asia had encountered after independence were not of the sort that could have been avoided by an agreement. What really mattered was the recognition of mutual interests. Goodwill was the only guarantee that was likely to survive the first few years after independence.[107] The Cabinet agreed to give further consideration to the possibility of securing some assurances in the course of the forthcoming negotiations, but did not make the transfer of power conditional upon them. Ministers assumed that there would be a far greater chance of getting Malayan cooperation if Britain refrained from over-stating its demands in the first instance.[108]

As expected, the Alliance leaders who attended the conference in London in January 1956 demanded a transfer of power by 31 August 1957 – 'while at the same time privately acknowledging that in practice this target is not feasible'.[109] Following the advice given by the CO, the transfer of power was not made conditional on any agreement, nor was any attempt made to retain bases or any part of Malayan territory under British sovereignty – London did everything to maintain local goodwill. This strategy was rewarded: despite their insistence on independence, the Malayan parties were willing to continue close cooperation. They indicated their intention to remain in the Commonwealth and the sterling area, and – very much to the delight of officials and ministers – concluded an agreement containing satisfactory assurances on external defence, internal security, finance and the position of expatriate officials. In exchange, Britain promised considerable assistance in connection with the emergency and the building up of the Federation's armed forces. It was clear that independence would not change the substance of Anglo-Malayan relations.[110]

The British readiness to grant independence was not due to a decline of the colony's importance. On the contrary, Malaya remained important for four reasons: it was a source of essential raw materials and a 'very substantial' dollar earner; it received large amounts of private investment; it provided important bases and it was the symbol of British influence in the area.[111] Britain still had considerable long-term interests in the economic and defence fields, but policy-makers opined that these were best secured by establishing a stable non-communist government, 'with the trappings and most of the substance of independence', which would be friendly towards the United Kingdom, and remain a member of the Commonwealth and sterling area. To achieve this, the timetable of constitutional progress was subordinated to the need of preserving local goodwill. Political evolution in the dependent territories had almost always been accompanied by considerable hostility to Britain, even if this was only a passing phase. Britain thought that there was a good chance that Malaya, 'if wisely guided', would constitute an exception to this rule.[112] Early independence, it was assumed, would strengthen rather than weaken the country's ties with the metropole. The ability of the Alliance leaders had not yet been fully proved, but British policy-makers were convinced that the additional experience indigenous politicians would gain in a longer period of transition would far outweigh the loss of goodwill that was expected to flow from any insistence upon such a delay.[113] The same logic applied to the problem of Malayan nation-building: British officials knew that the different races were far from showing the degree of unity which was deemed to be necessary for the achievement of independence. However, they also realised that the time needed to reach it was simply not available. Therefore they opted for an early transfer of power, hoping Malaya would prove stable enough to allow the gradual emergence of racial unity.

Indeed, it seemed as if the end of formal rule in Malaya facilitated cooperation between the two countries: political, military and economic links remained very strong. After a visit in 1959 Lord Home reported enthusiastically that politicians in Kuala Lumpur recognised clearly where their 'true friends and interests' lay. Cooperation with Britain was 'exceptionally close' and Britain's influence 'very extensive'. If Britain approached the relationship with its former colony 'in a sympathetic way', the Federation should continue to be 'a much more than usually reliable friend in this crucial part of Asia'.[114] Malaya seemed to prove that rapid decolonisation, if handled correctly, could be a useful tool.

The Gold Coast

The arguments brought forward to justify Malaya's rapid advance to independence were also used in the case of Nigeria and, in particular, the Gold Coast. Until 1950 the British expected the Gold Coast to advance at a relatively leisurely speed. This changed when Nkrumah and his party won an overwhelming electoral victory. Governor Arden-Clarke now began to advocate a speed-up of constitutional development, fearing that otherwise there might be violent clashes with the CPP. In this he was supported by Cohen, who urged the new Colonial Secretary, Lyttelton, to make concessions in order to preserve local goodwill. Confronted with this advice, Lyttelton did not hesitate long to implement it. In February 1952 the Colonial Secretary proposed changing the title of the 'Leader of Government Business' (a reference to Nkrumah) to 'Prime Minister'.[115] The Prime Minister would preside over the Gold Coast cabinet in the absence of the British Governor, and the latter would consult with Nkrumah before nominating African ministers.

These changes were said to be of name rather than of substance, since they would not go materially beyond recognising what was already the *de facto* position. If they were not conceded, however, it would be difficult to hold back demands for immediate self-government. The Labour government had apparently failed 'properly to assess the strength of nationalist aspirations, and to retain the confidence of the people and the initiative for ordered constitutional advance'. If the government failed again to recognise the strength of local nationalists, there might be new riots. But if the concessions were made, there was a good chance of 'a policy of ordered progress by successive stages' being successfully pursued. At the moment there was a deep fund of goodwill towards the United Kingdom, and the British connection was highly valued. But the Colonial Secretary warned that any attempt to block constitutional advance would produce disastrous results. It would ensure that, when power was eventually transferred, it would be handed over to a local leadership predisposed towards an anti-British policy.[116] If the titular concession were made, however, there was at least a chance of delaying more important constitutional changes in order to allow time for African ministers to gain 'a further sense of responsibility and knowledge of government'. No guarantee could be given that the proposed steps would 'lead us where we want'. All that the Colonial Secretary could guarantee was that not to take them would 'certainly lead us to where we do not want'.

The Cabinet approved Lyttelton's recommendation on the understanding that the changes conferred no more than 'an appearance' of greater authority on Nkrumah. For some time it seemed as if things would go ahead at the speed envisaged by British officials. But after a while the Governor advised that more concessions were required if the Gold Coast was to continue to be governed by consent. There was growing pressure for an all-African cabinet. The responsibility for finance and perhaps justice should be transferred to African ministers, while, the governor would take over direct responsibility for defence, foreign affairs and certain police matters. The Colonial Secretary forwarded these recommendations to the Cabinet, and advised his colleagues to accept them.[117] Nkrumah's demands were far-reaching; but in order to avoid a 'head-on clash' it would be better to accelerate constitutional development. Failure to do so would only hasten the demand for immediate independence and bring to an end settled government by consent.[118] It was wiser to err on the side of conceding too much too early than too little too late: self-government ('however amateurish or corrupt') was better than good colonial government.[119] The Africans had their eyes fixed on the future, not the present. Therefore political advance could not wait until the people were ready for it. The Cabinet discussed Lyttelton's proposals in May 1953. Negotiations were authorised, but the view was strongly expressed that Britain should not go beyond turning over the portfolios of justice and finance. This, it was hoped, would encourage more moderate politicians to line up on the British side.[120]

The acceleration of constitutional development in the Gold Coast was not welcomed by everybody. The colonial administration of Nigeria, in particular, pointed to the dangers inherent in such a move. Southern politicians regarded it as a national disgrace that Nigeria should be constitutionally more backward than the Gold Coast, and therefore outbid each other with demands for constitutional advance. It was better to refuse rapid constitutional advance, both in Nigeria and the Gold Coast. There would certainly be a sharp reaction amongst the local press and 'subversive elements'. But a firm stand would be welcomed by a considerable majority of the Nigerian population, and the security situation would remain manageable. The government should think twice about making concessions: once a country was set on the road towards responsible government it was very difficult to hold the position at a transitional stage – and once the threshold had been crossed in one colony, others would have to follow suit.[121]

The CO acknowledged the Governor's concerns, but thought it more important to remain ahead of events in the Gold Coast than to take into account possible ramifications in other territories. It was feared that collision with Nkrumah would have even graver repercussions on Britain's position in Nigeria than 'acquiescence ... in what we all recognise to be, theoretically, over-hasty political advance'.[122] The international repercussions of such a clash would weigh at least as heavily as the risk it posed to the maintenance of good relations between Britain and the Gold Coast. Refusing early self-government would create worse conditions than its acceptance. The tide could not be stopped. Nigeria's advance towards self-government would undoubtedly be accelerated by events in Accra, but this was the price to be paid. CO officials assured the Governor of their sympathy, but refused to heed his advice.

In the summer of 1953 policy-makers finally realised that it was impossible to devise any constitution which would satisfy nationalist aspirations while retaining ultimate power in British hands – even though it was still hoped that Africans would remain susceptible to British influence. Once this had been accepted, independence was only a matter of time, not of principle.[123] The biggest worry for policy-makers now was not so much Nkrumah's democratic credentials or his country's fitness for self-government but whether Nkrumah and his crew would prove to be the staunch anti-communists they were expected to be. Lyttelton advised that Gold Coast ministers should be persuaded to take 'certain specific actions', which could be regarded as indicative of 'a real and enduring desire' to prevent the expansion of communist influence.[124] In fact, Arden-Clarke reported a few days later that the Gold Coast cabinet had taken a series of measures to contain communism.[125] These measures may, to a large extent, have been aimed at Nkrumah's rivals, communist or not, but they sufficed to reassure British officials.

Early in 1954 a new constitution was introduced, providing an all-elected legislative assembly, and a totally Africanised cabinet appointed on the advice of Nkrumah. In elections held in June 1954 the CPP won 72 out of 104 seats. Arden-Clarke argued once more for a further acceleration. The 'rapid and reasonably successful' transition to near-complete internal autonomy had convinced the Africans that they could manage their own affairs. This and the pace of events in the Sudan had combined to create a state of mind which made the Africans look to the attainment of independence in about the middle of 1956, i.e. two years earlier than assumed in 1953.[126]

Arden-Clarke argued that while it might be possible to spin out the process and delay independence until the middle of 1957, it would not be without recourse to expedients which would seriously diminish African goodwill. The benefits of such a delay would in no way compensate for the damage it would do to relations after independence. In the short run, the Gold Coast would certainly make many blunders: there was likely to be 'considerably less wisdom and restraint' in domestic affairs and a certain amount of irresponsibility in foreign policy, not least because of the high dependence on expatriate officers, whose exodus would gain momentum. But that was the only way in which a fledgling nation could learn 'to use its wings'.[127] Possible administrative and political weaknesses could not be the determining factor in the timing of independence.[128] Local politicians were aware of the problems awaiting them and would privately be glad of a delay. But they had to fulfil their pledges to the electorate if they did not want to be overtaken by extremists. Ministers were convinced by Arden-Clarke's arguments and decided that power would be transferred in early 1957.

Repeated reports about corruption and mismanagement by the CPP as well as the emergence of a vociferous Ashanti-based opposition movement demanding a federal constitution led Lennox-Boyd for a short while to reconsider the timing of the transfer of power. In November 1955 he informed Cabinet that it was now 'most unlikely' that independence could be conceded as foreseen.[129] Senior European staff had not yet been replaced with trained African elements, and ministers had not yet dealt firmly enough with corruption. Until it had been demonstrated that a majority of the people were in favour of immediate independence, there could be no question of the 'final and irrevocable step' being taken. In July 1956 a new general election was held in order to establish whether Nkrumah really had the backing of the population. The result was a clear majority for the CPP and a 'disappointing failure to produce an Opposition strong enough to frighten the Government'.[130]

Thus the last impediment on the way to independence was now an intervention by the Chancellor of the Exchequer, Harold Macmillan: he tried to convince his colleagues to defer the date of self-government in case this involved the risk of the colony's sterling balances, amounting to nearly £100 million, being withdrawn for investment elsewhere.[131] The Colonial Secretary pointed out that the Gold Coast authorities were already free to withdraw their balances from Britain. Moreover, one of the prime objectives of British policy was to hand over power 'in a spirit of amity and goodwill' so as to ensure that Ghana maintained a friendly attitude towards the United Kingdom and the Commonwealth in general. Therefore it was not sensible to try to delay independence on financial grounds.[132] To do so would only make a withdrawal of the sterling balances more likely. Furthermore, Nkrumah's repeated pleas for British aid after independence demonstrated that he was not likely to do anything which would, in the long run, jeopardise his own interests.[133]

Despite the decision taken in Cabinet, the Gold Coast's advance towards independence was viewed with mixed feelings. Commonwealth Secretary Lord Home in particular was 'full of forebodings' about the whole 'experiment'. The CO mounted a defence of its policy, but in private Lennox-Boyd admitted that there were 'disturbing features' about political life in the Gold Coast.[134] The Africanisation of the administration was not sufficiently advanced and the country contained

> no substantial uncorrupt middle-class and no other reservoir of talent and experience to protect the common people from exploitation by the very inexperienced and not necessarily high-minded politicians they have voted into power.[135]

However, for the Colonial Secretary, there was no viable alternative to the policy then being pursued. Britain should rather concentrate on keeping the country stable after independence. The only way of countering Soviet attempts to undermine internal stability and penetrate the Gold Coast by economic means, was aid.[136] The territory was the first African country to achieve independence within the Commonwealth. Its future would profoundly influence political development throughout the empire.

Once the novelty of self-government had worn off, the British would find that the goodwill they had earned by conceding independence would wear 'pretty thin' unless it was backed up by aid.[137] Admittedly the grant of aid to a Dominion would set a pattern for the future. But this had to be weighed against the risk that Ghana, upon independence, would find itself 'falling between two stools', being neither eligible for further funds from the CDC, nor in a position to raise a market loan in London. It would be 'unfortunate politically, and wrong in principle', to leave the Gold Coast simply to sink or swim.[138] The Soviet Union would certainly use this opportunity to win a foothold in Africa. Prophylactics were cheaper than therapeutics: granting some aid in order to keep the country out of the communist orbit was much cheaper than counteracting the effects of a communist take-over.[139] At the time, no favourable decision was taken. Even though the Gold Coast received some aid, no general principle was acknowledged. Chancellor of the Exchequer Macmillan was not willing to make available the unspent balances of the Gold Coast's existing Development and Welfare allocations, amounting to about £1 million.[140] The future Prime Minister apparently considered that Britain had already done enough for its African wards.

On 6 March 1957 the Gold Coast achieved independence,

seemingly in perfect harmony with its former colonial masters. On balance the grant of independence seemed a good deal for Britain: the Gold Coast had no strategic importance, was likely to remain in the sterling area and seemed solidly anti-communist. The transfer of power took place without any major friction and enhanced Britain's international standing as a liberal colonial power. This, it was assumed, would reduce anti-colonialist pressure and strengthen Britain's position in the United Nations. It was hoped that Ghana's independence would be seen as a proof of the virtues of British policy and as a reason for other countries to moderate their criticism – at the time, nobody expected that Ghana's arrival on the international scene would have such a galvanising effect on the anti-colonial lobby, with grave repercussions on British policy over the following years.[141]

East and Central Africa

Whereas the Churchill and Eden governments accelerated the transfer of power to democratically elected governments in Malaya, the Gold Coast and other territories, they were less convinced that this was the right solution for colonies with white minorities. Like their socialist predecessors, the Conservatives believed that there could be no uniform policy for the whole of the empire, let alone Africa. In the context of West Africa, the objective of self-government was straightforward enough. There were difficult questions of timing due to 'somewhat conflicting subsidiary objectives' – on the one hand, the desire to ensure that self-government was not attained at the expense of social and economic progress or at the price of bad or oppressive government; and on the other, the anxiety that locals should feel that self-government was attained 'with our help, not in the face of our obstruction'. But these questions belonged to the tactics, not the strategy of politics. There was not much doubt that 'in a world in which "colonialism" is increasingly unpopular and the use of force to maintain it no longer practical politics', the wisest thing was to end formal rule. In West Africa, therefore, only the question of the timing of further political advance remained.[142] In East and Central Africa, however, the objective of self-government (and black majority rule), 'whilst retained as an ideal', had to give way before the objective of partnership between the various races.

The problem was the presence of sizeable European minorities which, throughout the 1950s, continued to grow, mainly through immigration. In the Rhodesias and Nyasaland alone, the number of Europeans rose from 169,000 in 1950 to more than 287,000 ten years later.[143] By the end of the 1950s, Kenya had around 68,000 settlers (one in 93 of Kenya's total population); Northern Rhodesia, 72,000 (one in 31); Southern Rhodesia, 207,000 (one in 13); whereas Nyasaland had only 8,300 (one in 328) and Tanganyika 22,330 (one in 408).[144] The rights of minorities were of minor importance in the case of Burma, India or the Gold Coast. There Britain was not ready to delay the transfer of power for the sake of minorities because it feared losing the goodwill of the majority. In East and Central Africa, however, the presence of white minorities was the cause of considerable difficulties. While Britain wanted to prevent the whites from coming under the sway of South Africa, it was also keen to ensure that they were not forced to live under an African-majority regime. The best way to achieve this was believed to lie in the promotion of 'multi-racialism' and the creation of a federation.

The ground for the Central African Federation had been prepared under the Labour governments. In 1953 the Rhodesias and Nyasaland were finally brought together. In public the stress was on the economic advantages of a closer union between the raw materials and the work-force of the three territories. But the government's main incentive was the desire to keep Southern Rhodesia away from South Africa. Both Labour and Conservatives agreed that one of Britain's prime aims on the African continent was the containment of the Union of South Africa.[145] Its influence and territorial sovereignty had to be prevented from spreading further north – without prejudicing relations with Britain, which were to remain as cordial as possible. The emancipation and political advancement of the African had to remain a major objective, but 'we must not subordinate all else to it'.

There was the danger that, to avoid domination by Africans, the whites in East and Central Africa would throw in their lot with the Union. This grave danger had to be avoided, even at the cost of protests from African and Asian communities against the appeasement of the white minority. To offend the whites might make it impossible effectively to protect the non-Europeans against a South African-style native policy. Salisbury's policy might have been far from ideal, but it was much better than anything South Africa would impose. The expansion of South Africa, both economically and through Afrikaner emigration, constituted 'a serious and imminent threat' to the independent existence of the Rhodesias.[146] It undermined their British way of life and gravely prejudiced race relations. Should the government, intentionally or by default, throw the whites into the arms of Pretoria, 'our whole work in Africa' would be undone.[147] The Central African territories were 'potential American colonies – very loyal, but very determined to have their own way'. Southern Rhodesia was the test case: it would inevitably be drawn either northwards or southwards. Britain had to ensure the pull came from the north. Otherwise Britain would 'immensely increase the attractive power' of the Union's policy for white communities in neighbouring colonies. Southern Rhodesia's defection might trigger off a chain reaction in Northern Rhodesia, Kenya and the neighbouring Belgian and Portuguese colonies.

Britain had to defend its reputation as 'a champion of liberal Western civilisation'.[148] Any move which could be construed as an endorsement of Pretoria's racial policy could bring Britain into serious conflict with international and domestic opinion. On the other hand, for economic and strategic reasons, links with South Africa had to be preserved. A Central African Federation was considered the best way to keep British colonies out of the Union's orbit without offending the latter. It would solve the region's economic problems while keeping its white populations out of South Africa's sphere of influence. The federation would be dominated by Southern Rhodesia, but constitutional advance and African land rights in Nyasaland and Northern Rhodesia would be controlled by Britain – after all, federation was not to be a mere extension of Salisbury's brand of apartheid into the other two territories. This was to secure the support of African opinion, which, at least in Nyasaland and Northern Rhodesia, tended to see the federation as a scheme for entrenching white preponderance.

The Central African Federation (CAF) was established in August 1953. While the CO was in charge of Northern Rhodesia and Nyasaland, contacts with Southern Rhodesia and the federal government ran through the CRO. The CAF was expected to achieve independence in 1960, under a white federal government, but not against the wishes of the African population. It was hoped that time would lead the whites to moderate their stance *vis-à-vis* the Africans. The CO, in particular, was determined not to grant independence before the whites had won the Africans' confidence. Proposals to transfer power in the CAF at the same time as in the Gold Coast were rejected. But surely no one was talking of African majority rule at this time. The aim was still a 'multi-racial society' – with an enduring core of European leadership, however small numerically.

In East Africa, there were strong African objections against federation. These objections could not be overruled as easily as in Central Africa – not least because the United Nations was expected to be critical of anything that would impede Tanganyika's progress towards self-government.[149] No federation was established. It was hoped, though, that at some later point it might become possible not only to keep Kenyan Europeans out of Pretoria's sphere of influence, but also to entrench the effective protection of white individual and property rights. Since the white minority in East Africa was much smaller than that of the Rhodesias, it was clear that it would not be possible to prevent African majority rule in Uganda or Tanganyika, and perhaps even in Kenya. However, in a federation, each territory would have a vested interest in preserving stability in the other territories. Thus any attempt by one government to expropriate European settlers might be resisted and restrained by the other territories because of the economic consequences to the federation as a whole.

Tanganyika and Uganda had only very small numbers of European settlers. Theoretically they could have been granted independence at about the same speed as the West African territories. But policy-makers believed that this would create an unwelcome precedent, making it difficult to resist similar claims in Kenya. Kenya was a particular case where constitutional development should be as slow as possible.[150] The settlers were not strong or numerous enough to launch a 'Mombassa Tea Party', and the size of the African and Asian population made self-government on Southern Rhodesian lines, i.e. with a purely white government, impossible. But the settlers were not willing to accept equal rights for the Africans – and presumably strong enough to resist any attempt to impose it. Therefore it was vital to find a framework that would allow different races to exist alongside each other. African opposition could not be brushed aside as easily as in the CAF, but it was not possible to ignore white opinion either. Fortunately, until the mid-1950s, British officials believed that in East Africa nationalism was still 'a slow growing plant'. Kenya's Mau Mau uprising, for example, was not perceived as a nationalist movement. It was seen as an atavistic tribal rising – 'more hooliganism than a deep political convulsion'.[151] It was hoped that some token concessions would suffice to satisfy African demands for participation in political life and act as 'a curb on extreme African nationalism'.[152] This would leave enough time for multi-racialism to develop.

Britain's belief that it would be possible to slow down constitutional advance in East Africa was shaken in late 1956 when the Governor of Tanganyika proposed a decisive change of policy. He advised that for strategic reasons, communists and anti-colonialists were planning to make 'a dead set' on the Belgian Congo and Tanganyika.[153] Therefore it was vital to act immediately: as the white minority had not shown itself capable of political leadership, it was necessary to devise a programme of constitutional change that would reflect a move from the concept of a multi-racial society to that of a preponderantly African state. The CO at first hesitated. Experience seemed to show that once a policy agreeable to the Africans had been announced, they would begin to agitate for its achievement almost immediately. Moreover, the announcement of African-majority rule in the near future would certainly cause 'something like a panic' in Kenya and nip in the bud the first signs of the adoption of 'a more sensible racial policy' by the whites in Central Africa.[154] On the other hand, officials thought, it might be worth making some concessions in order to 'capture' the Tanyanyikan leader, Julius Nyerere. He seemed 'a moderate and sensible chap, liable to tailor his opinions to his audience, but nevertheless worth sweeping into the fold'. It would be fatal if he was allowed to become 'a dissident and disruptive voice'.[155] The repercussions of such a development would certainly be worse than possible pressure to move faster in Kenya.

By early 1957, the CO was determined to accelerate Tanganyika's advance to self-government under African-majority rule. For the time being, however, nothing should be said about the future of Tanganyika as 'an "African State", a "primarily African State" or even a "fully democratic state"' in order not to provoke similar demands in Kenya. Despite the new approach, Tanganyika was not scheduled to become fully self-governing before the mid-1970s (followed after a considerable delay by Kenya and possibly Uganda). Apparently, the clocks in East Africa were still ticking slower than elsewhere.

Smaller Territories

In the early 1950s policy-makers continued to believe that the smaller territories would never be able to achieve independence. This was due to the impression that they simply could not survive without British rule. Independence would only lead to chaos and misery, provoke international criticism of Britain and invite Soviet interference. In the case of fortress territories, policy-makers believed, formal rule had to be maintained in order to guarantee access to the strategic facilities after independence. Because of rising domestic and international pressure, especially with regard to Cyprus, several attempts were made at finding a status which could be presented as the ultimate stage of development for such colonies while preserving British control of defence and external affairs. One such attempt was the suggestion that a new constitutional goal of 'statehood' might be established. The designation 'state' was to be conferred as an honourable distinction upon certain territories which could show 'reasonable economic stability, an established form of representative government and proof of self-government in domestic affairs'.[156] The departments concerned concluded that the idea was not viable. There was hardly anything to distinguish 'statehood' from the penultimate stage of constitutional development, which was usually reached by a territory on the road to self-government. It would not be accepted by the population concerned or international opinion. The working group had no alternative proposal, though, and the problem continued to attract official attention.

H. Bourdillon of the CO proposed the smaller territories' incorporation into the United Kingdom. These territories, he argued, were not isolated from 'the fierce pressures of nationalism and anti-colonialism'.[157] Once the larger territories had become independent, the smaller ones would come into the full glare of world publicity as 'the last bulwarks of Imperialism'. Even if they reached a high degree of internal self-government, their status would still carry 'the marks of enforced and permanent inferiority'. The result would be the loss of loyalty and goodwill which were 'the final safeguard' of British interests. This would be particularly dangerous in fortress territories. In the last resort Britain would have to hold these territories by force. Like Cyprus, they would become 'strategic liabilities instead of strategic assets'. In order to prevent this, they were to be offered union with the United Kingdom.

Bourdillon's proposal was put to the test in Malta when Dominic Mintoff became prime minister of the island. Unlike his predecessor, he was in favour of closer integration with the United Kingdom. Negotiations started and the Cabinet agreed to grant integration and parliamentary representation at Westminster. In the end, however, both parties fell out over Mintoff's demands for financial assistance: these were much higher than anything the government was willing to concede.[158] A referendum held in Malta did not produce a clear majority in favour of integration, which led British officials to drop the project. Macmillan urged his colleagues to accept 'the voluntary and patriotic desire of Malta to join us'. But ministers were doubtful about the wisdom of any arrangement which would make Britain's social services available to the island's relatively poor population.[159] Since integration was not considered desirable, but full control over the island's defence facilities was still regarded as vital, Malta's future status was left in abeyance.

After their negative experience with Malta, policy-makers were reluctant to consider the integration of any other territory into the United Kingdom. Nor did they think it impossible to prolong colonial rule in territories where this seemed necessary. Cyprus was the best-known example, but there were others such as Somaliland, Aden and Singapore. The last of these is of special interest as it stood in stark contrast to Britain's liberal policy in Malaya at the same time. It illustrates well how important it was to Britain to trust local leaders and foster good relations with them. When Malaya's independence was negotiated early in 1956, Singapore's Prime Minister, David Saul Marshall, asked for similar concessions. The Governor, Robert Brown Black, urged the CO to make them: nationalism and anti-colonialism had too great a hold on the population to allow the government to deny constitutional advance without the gravest consequences.[160]

Lennox-Boyd acknowledged the force of the Governor's arguments, but pointed to the importance of Singapore as a logistic base for south-east Asia. Britain's military requirements were only secure if Singapore was part of the Federation of Malaya, a state Britain could count upon. Independence for Singapore was a 'delusion'. Neither economically nor militarily was the territory's survival secure. Singapore had a large population without any natural resources or industries, and 900,000 out of the territory's 1,300,000 inhabitants were Chinese.[161] Unless the city-state united with Malaya, it would become 'an independent Chinese outpost at the strategic heart of South-East Asia'. If Britain transferred power, it would have 'no more than paper safeguards', remaining in Singapore only so long as it suited the Chinese. Admittedly there was a danger of the colony becoming 'another "Cyprus" ... with our scattered defence facilities the targets for strikes and sabotage and our own people living behind barbed wire'.[162] But the stakes were so high that, whatever the consequences, Britain had to stand firm on its vital defence requirements. While Britain could make some nominal concessions, control of defence, foreign relations and internal security had to be retained.[163]

By far the most difficult of the smaller territories was Cyprus. Britain maintained that the issue of *enosis* was closed and tried its best to keep the island out of the news. A tough policy was thought necessary to convince Greeks and Cypriots that Britain meant to stay.[164] Once Britain promised self-determination, it would be under strong pressure to name a date for its exercise. But for the time being it was impossible to predict when Britain could risk a withdrawal. The Cypriots had to be cured of their 'mania' for self-government. Britain's strategic requirement could only be secured through control of the whole island.[165] The situation in the United Nations was worrying, but the best way to counter it was to reaffirm Britain's position and to expose links between the supporters of *enosis* and communists. The Cabinet accepted these recommendations and authorised Lyttelton to make a parliamentary statement affirming that Britain could not contemplate a change of sovereignty in Cyprus.[166]

On 1 April 1955 the Cypriot question received a new dimension: the Ethniki Organosis Kyrion Agoniston (EOKA – National Organisation of Cypriot Fighters) a Greek–Cypriot underground organisation, unleashed a terrorist campaign.[167] At the same time, Athens intensified its attempts to bring the Cyprus question before the United Nations. In 1954 Britain had managed to prevent a discussion in the United Nations by means of procedural devices. But policy-makers were aware that Britain would not be able to repeat this exploit. The only way of preventing a United Nations debate on Cyprus in 1955–56 was to show that Britain did not exclude the prospect of self-determination.[168] While ministers were looking for a political solution, the Chiefs of Staff continued to point to Cyprus's strategic importance. They acknowledged that on the whole there were no overriding strategic requirements which precluded 'a partial transfer of sovereignty' – provided the island was in the hands of a power which could be 'absolutely' relied upon to permit, in all circumstances, the use of bases (a condition Greece obviously did not fulfil).[169] Therefore, the military argued, it was difficult to see how sovereignty over Cyprus could be relinquished for at least 10–15 years.[170] At the outbreak of the Suez crisis, there was thus a certain willingness to move ahead – but no plan for total withdrawal.

Conclusion

Before taking office in October 1951, the Conservatives had tended to see Labour's colonial policy as a breach of Britain's trust. When they took office, they therefore intended at first slowing down the pace of change, but they were quickly persuaded by their officials as well as by the situation in the colonies not to do so. They also realised that, at least in the case of larger territories like Nigeria and the Gold Coast, it would not be possible to retain control over defence or foreign affairs after the end of formal rule; nevertheless they still hoped that Britain would be able to exert a guiding influence after independence.

From 1953 onwards the timetables were increasingly shortened. The former insistence on 'good government' and nation-building was all but scrapped. Most 'normal' colonies were now able to attain independence within a decade rather than after a generation or more. Policy-makers began to stress the importance of the locals learning *national* rather than *local* self-government. The speed of decolonisation can be explained by several interrelated factors. First, there was the presumed upsurge of nationalism. Like their predecessors, Conservative policy-makers considered it vital to retain the goodwill of Asian and African politicians. This was to secure British influence and provide protection for British interests. But policy-makers also feared that the refusal of concessions would open the way to more radical, anti-British forces as well as to communist subversion. The latter point, especially, gained importance as the Cold War was seen to spread to the Third World: self-government was Britain's 'constructive answer' to communism. While a progressive colonial policy could thus be considered part of a containment strategy, it also helped reduce the international pressure building up against the colonial powers.

Another reason for the acceleration of constitutional development was Britain's continuous lack of resources: it had neither the money nor the manpower to deal with any more emergencies than those it was already involved in. Given this weakness, it was difficult for Britain to let negotiations collapse. Last, but not least, colonial administrations were increasingly weakened by the loss of heart on the part of many white civil servants who saw no future in a dying service. Although the last two factors were not decisive for the basic decision to move towards self-government, they certainly increased Britain's readiness to move faster than originally planned.

The interplay between these factors is illustrated by developments in Malaya and the Gold Coast. In the former case, Britain began to contemplate an acceleration of constitutional development even before a strong nationalist movement had emerged. Once it did, independence was granted after the minimum possible delay, and without any strings attached. Policy-makers thought that the resulting goodwill was the best protection for Britain's economic and strategic stake. In the case of the Gold Coast, the transfer of power was more controversial. Policy-makers did not consider the country ready for independence. But a majority thought that despite the risks, it was better to go ahead in order to preserve local goodwill. Bad self-government was better than good colonial government. The Africans had to be allowed to make their own mistakes. Repression of the demands for independence would only lead to more radical forces taking over, while world opinion would be most critical.

While 'normal' colonies thus advanced at increasing speed to independence, the Churchill and Eden governments refrained from taking any radical measures with regard to East and Central Africa. White immigration continued, and the political rights of the Africans remained limited. In Central Africa, a federation was to ensure that Southern Rhodesia was kept out of South Africa's gravitational field. While the Central African Federation was scheduled to become independent in 1960, the situation in East Africa remained blocked. African resistance made it impossible to impose a federation, and the whites were not numerous enough to take over control of local affairs. Therefore Britain played for time, and hoped that multi-racialism would sooner or later become a reality. This was to allow African participation in political life while securing the future of the white minorities.

With regard to smaller territories, there was not much progress either: all attempts at finding a special status were unsuccessful, but it was still considered inappropriate to grant full independence. Britain doubted the territories' capacity to survive on their own, and did not want to dilute the Commonwealth with 'small fry'. In the case of the fortress territories, the problem was not only their lack of viability but also Britain's belief that the local population could be relied upon to let Britain use military installations after independence. Probably the toughest nut to crack in this context was Cyprus. The island was a symbol of Britain's presence in the Middle East as well as an important military stronghold. Independence, it was feared, would lead to union with Greece, provoke the loss of bases and prestige, and antagonise Turkey. All this was expected to have disastrous consequences for Britain's military position as well as her economic interests in the oil-producing countries. Therefore Britain decided to maintain the *status quo*, even against considerable local and international resistance.

In many respects, colonial policy under the Churchill and Eden governments continued on the lines laid down by their predecessors. The future of East and Central Africa as well as that of the smaller territories remained in abeyance, but in the case of 'normal' territories there was a clear move forward. Constitutional advance in these colonies was accelerated in order to retain the goodwill of indigenous nationalists. Any other course, it was feared, would impose a heavy burden on Britain and give the Soviet Union a decisive advantage in the Cold War. In the context of the Cold War decolonisation came to be seen as one political weapon among others – whereas formal rule came much less to be perceived as an appropriate means of protecting British interests or of preventing the spread of communism.

THE COMMONWEALTH

Under the Conservative governments of the early 1950s the Commonwealth continued to be exalted as an important factor for Britain's power and prestige. However, the economic, political and strategic links between its members grew increasingly weaker. To compensate for this, policy-makers began to favour closer links with

Europe without considering the two circles as mutually exclusive. On the contrary: the Commonwealth link was to help secure Britain a leading position in Europe, while the Continent was to serve as a market and provider of investment capital for the Dominions . It was still hoped that the club would help keep former colonies within Britain's sphere of influence and boost its standing *vis-à-vis* the United States.

The Commonwealth in the Early 1950s

When Churchill became Prime Minister for the second time, he declared the consolidation of the Commonwealth and 'what is left of the former British Empire' to be the first objective of his foreign policy. Even so, he was reluctant to deal with the question of Commonwealth membership 'on Tuesday morning when everyone will be thinking about the Budget and there are so many other matters pressing upon us'.[171] While the Prime Minister was strongly interested in close links with the United States and the white Dominions, the Commonwealth as a whole (like the colonial empire) was a low priority for him. For Churchill, the existence of the 'brown' Dominions defeated the Commonwealth's original purpose, i.e. being an association of (white) nations, which allowed effective political and strategic cooperation. Not so for other policy-makers. Foreign Secretary Eden, for example, thought that without the Commonwealth, 'we should be no more than some millions of people living on an island off the coast of Europe, in which nobody wants to take any particular interest'.[172] Many officials also continued to believe that the Commonwealth would help Britain to maintain its role as a world power. In the modern world, they argued, Britain could not hope to maintain the influence exercised by 'our small country of fifty million people' unless its succeeded in holding together in a new form of association those parts of its empire which attained self-government. In international affairs, Britain increasingly had to rely on its position as *primus inter pares* in the Commonwealth.[173] Admittedly, cooperation (especially in the defence sector) was not as close as before the war. While Britain had to concentrate a large part of its forces on the Rhine, the 'white' Dominions increasingly turned to the United States for their military needs. But policy-makers were confident that, with wise leadership, Britain might still be able to mobilise a considerable part of the Commonwealth's diplomatic and military resources in support of some causes. All members had legal, historical, linguistic and cultural ties, which were likely to lead to a 'broad similarity' in their approach to major international problems.

In the early 1950s, the United Kingdom's status as a world power was thus still said by many to depend on its position as head of the Commonwealth, not least because the United States was thought to have 'a healthy respect' for the association.[174] Of course, the CRO was the biggest champion of such arguments. Both the Secretary of State for Commonwealth Relations and his officials continually claimed that the United Kingdom's importance in international affairs would be 'immensely less' without the Commonwealth.[175] However, more and more officials, especially in the Treasury, began to question the CRO's dogma that the Commonwealth was 'a good thing in itself and that it must be a fundamental objective of policy to keep it in being, without enquiring why this should be so'. If this policy was carried too far, Britain would end up with nothing more than 'a glossy facade'.[176] In the mid-1950s, these voices were not yet very strong. It was only after the Suez débâcle had revealed how limited Commonwealth solidarity was, that a vigorous FO-led onslaught began.

While in the early 1950s it could still be assumed that the enlarged Commonwealth would sooner or later seek closer political and military links with Britain, no such hope could reasonably be entertained in the economic sphere. The government reaffirmed its belief in imperial preferences while acknowledging privately that no Dominion was likely to support an extension of the preferential system or any alteration in GATT.[177] The Board of Trade underlined that the advantages for British industry accruing from the Commonwealth were not so much due to imperial preferences as to cultural links, traditions of trade and the sterling area.[178] These did not depend on any formal regulations. Moreover, Britain was not able to import any more Commonwealth products, and the Dominions wanted to protect their nascent industries. This as well as the 'no new preference' rules of GATT were bound to further weaken the importance of imperial preferences. Discriminatory directives about giving preference to other Commonwealth countries would be open to attack by foreign governments and would conflict with Britain's own interests since they would weaken its attack upon the United States' 'Buy American' Act. Discrimination within the Commonwealth would contribute practically nothing to the objectives of other members and would therefore certainly not appeal to them.[179] Moreover, an artificial strengthening of Commonwealth trade would be costly for British consumers and taxpayers.[180]

The Commonwealth as an economic unit was thus bound to lose more of its coherence. After a while this was also acknowledged in the Conservative Party where a resolution or amendment had been carried at every party conference since 1945 urging the government to revise GATT in order to restore preferential freedom of action. The party's election programme for 1951 had declared the Conservative Party 'the Party of the Empire', pledged to 'retain Imperial Preferences'.[181] Three years later, Peter Thorneycroft stated frankly that Britain was in GATT 'because it pays us to be in it', which resulted in the Conservative Party conference voting against the amendment calling for an extension of imperial preferences. Conservative Party policy now emphasised the 'move towards a world-wide system of freer trade and freer payments'.[182] In the mid-1950s, the idea of developing an economic bloc based on the Empire-Commonwealth thus disappeared. Britain apparently had more to gain by liberalised world trade.

In the second half of the 1950s, the case for an economic system based on the Commonwealth and the sterling area had lost most of its partisans. But it was still hoped that the club might boost Britain's prestige and keep newly independent states in its sphere of influence. And despite the realisation that an imperial trade area was not feasible, economic links (like emotional and political ties) with the Dominions were still considered of primary importance to Britain. The following section will demonstrate how these expectations and habits of thought persisted and led to the opening up of the club to African states – while preventing any closer association of the Commonwealth with the emerging European Economic Community (EEC).

The Admission of African Members

Although India, Pakistan and Ceylon were nominally admitted to full membership, the new Dominions were not treated as equals of Australia, South Africa or Canada in all aspects. A distinction was drawn between old and new members. Consultation between Britain and members of the Commonwealth, especially with regard to defence questions, was often limited to the 'white' Dominions.[183] Effectively, though not officially, the club was run on a two-tier basis. The new members did not object, but policy-makers expected that any further enlargement would make it difficult to uphold this distinction forever. The admission of new (African) members was also problematic because of the resistance South Africa and, to a lesser extent, Australia and New Zealand, were expected to offer. The situation had to be clarified, not only for the sake of strategic and diplomatic cooperation, but also in order to maintain the Commonwealth's standing as an 'effective voice in world councils' – many feared that the club 'could not stand dilution indefinitely if it were to remain a force in world affairs'.[184] Policy-makers did not want to risk a confrontation with the old Dominions because of the African territories – but on the other hand, they did not want to see the latter depart either. Therefore they set out to find a status that would allow the retention of the African territories without losing the old Dominions.

The Sudan and the Gold Coast

In 1952 British officials began to discuss whether the Sudan should be admitted to the Commonwealth in case she applied for membership. There were not many in favour of such a move. For the Foreign Office, it would be an embarrassment in Anglo-Egyptian relations, and the CRO was moved by 'fear of anything' likely to cause awkwardness with South Africa.[185] Moreover, any increase in the number of 'small member countries' would weaken the Commonwealth's coherence.[186] The Sudan had no positive contribution to make on the political side. From the strategic point of view there would be no advantage either in having this 'quasi-foreign State' in the Commonwealth. The only major economic interest Britain had was the continued purchase of cotton in sterling – an interest which could be secured by a treaty. In addition, admission to full membership might encourage the Sudanese to expect help from the United Kingdom; given Britain's strained resources, this was not desirable.

Only in the CO was there some support for Sudanese membership. Officials admitted that the country would not be 'much of a source of strength', but pointed out that sooner or later there would be other relatively weak African units, asking for admission. Therefore not too much should be made of the argument that the Sudan was not a major power. In addition, there would be some advantage in having this large neighbour of Kenya and Uganda within the Commonwealth, rather than see it come under the domination of Egypt. Commonwealth membership would help to keep the Sudan in the British camp and prevent a destabilisation in East Africa.[187] Brown or black Dominions might not always be easy members, but they would be much more difficult if they were 'outside the fold'. After the decision to admit India, Pakistan and Ceylon, the United Kingdom was already committed to the policy of a multi-coloured Commonwealth. If the government had to choose between going back on that policy or losing South Africa, it had to face the latter.[188] The real difficulty, CO officials mused, seemed to be that nobody was really convinced that the Sudan was ripe for self-government, and this might cause embarrassment in the Commonwealth later on. In the end, the arguments of the FO and the CRO prevailed. Ministers decided that membership of the Sudan was not desirable and instead preferred to conclude a treaty covering Britain's specific interests.[189] The Sudan thus became independent outside the Commonwealth on 1 January 1956.

The Gold Coast was different from the Sudan, firstly because its leader clearly indicated a desire for Dominion status. Moreover the country had been connected to Britain for quite some time and had played an important role in the sterling area. In addition, it was always assumed that decolonisation in the Gold Coast would serve as an example for other African colonies. Britain had every incentive therefore to retain the country in the club. On the other hand, to admit the Gold Coast as a full member was bound to have repercussions on Britain's relations with the white Dominions, especially South Africa, which was likely to offer strong resistance to the admission of any black Dominion; other white Dominions might feel that it was not worth their while to maintain their close affiliation with Britain and turn to the United States instead. Policy-makers therefore searched for ways of having the best of both worlds: close cooperation with old *and* new Dominions.

The Commonwealth Secretary Swinton feared that Ghana's admission would do irreparable harm to the cooperation with the old Dominions (which had already been weakened through the admission of India, Pakistan and Ceylon). To enlarge the number of participants in the Commonwealth Prime Ministers' meetings too rapidly would lead to disastrous 'disparities of outlook'.[190] The association would become unwieldy in size, and be weakened by internal dissent. Its strength lay in the 'unity of purpose' of a small number of like-minded people. The power of its members to exercise 'a decisive influence in world affairs' depended to a large extent upon 'public demonstrations of solidarity' by the whole club. Any diminution in such manifestations of unity would be interpreted as a sign of disintegration and lead to a weakening of that influence. On the other hand, would a two-tier system be unacceptable to Africans? In the end, Britain would have to choose between the defection of the African and Asian peoples and the expansion of the Commonwealth to a point where its membership hardly conveyed any meaning. In that case, Britain should opt for the solidarity of the old Dominions rather than for new members. Swinton clearly preferred 'the realities of the old Commonwealth' to 'some new unreal evolution that would make the worst of both worlds'. The admission of the Gold Coast against the wishes of South Africa could lead to the withdrawal of the latter and the eventual disintegration of the association.[191] For the time being, though, British officials should use 'what period of grace we have to try to avoid being faced with such a choice' and work out a solution that would allow the retention of the Gold Coast without weakening the cohesion of the Commonwealth.

Swinton's doubts were shared by officials in the CO and the CRO. They speculated that local aspirations might be satisfied by creating 'HM Government in the Gold Coast' (HMGGC): HMGGC would be responsible solely for advising the Sovereign on Gold Coast affairs, but without international status, and therefore would not qualify for full membership.[192] Another proposal was the creation of a two-tier Commonwealth: a joint CO/CRO committee proposed the title of 'intermediate territory' that would exclude territories like the Gold Coast from participating in meetings of Commonwealth Prime Ministers (at least in principle), and thus reassure South Africa with whom the old intimacy could be maintained.[193] However, officials realised that Africans would not be satisfied by such a 'half-way house'. Therefore they continued to look for alternative solutions.

Percivale Liesching, Permanent Under-Secretary of State in the Commonwealth Relations Office (1949–55), proposed to make membership largely honorary. The United Kingdom should give up the traditional informal cooperation with all Dominions, and instead enter into a kind of treaty relationship on the lines of NATO with countries 'willing and qualified' to form an inner circle. Thus it would be possible, for example, to include Pakistan (which offered bases and a defence agreement), while excluding India (which wanted to remain neutral). Another proposal was that of a special treaty relationship with the United Kingdom; this would be 'more acceptable to national pride' than a two-tier system.[194] There would be two concentric circles: that of the Dominions and that of the treaty relationship countries, with Britain as the common centre – a solution that would allow close relations simultaneously with the old Dominions *and* the former colonies, without offending either of them.

None of these proposals was considered wholly satisfactory; therefore in April 1953 an official committee was appointed to investigate the possibility of independent countries remaining in the Commonwealth without enjoying the rights and privileges of full membership, i.e. strategic cooperation and participation in meetings of Commonwealth Prime Ministers. Practically, the committee was to advise whether it was feasible to develop a two-tier status. At first officials did not consider this inconceivable.[195] In 1953 policy-makers were still confident that territories like the Gold Coast would accept a lower status than Canada and Australia. Presumably they were principally interested in internal self-government and had no wish to conduct their own foreign affairs. Policy-makers also toyed with the idea of making a distinction between the position of a country within the Commonwealth that was fully responsible for its own affairs, but not a full member, and that of a country which was a full member.[196] Prime Minister's meetings would remain restricted to old members while African territories could become self-governing within the Commonwealth – thus at once satisfying their *'amour propre'* and proving Britain's liberal colonial credentials.

However, the committee soon concluded that a two-tier Commonwealth was a 'no-go'. Arden-Clarke played a crucial role in this change of mind. He warned that the Gold Coast wished, 'as a matter of status', to be recognised as a full member. Rather than accept a place in the second tier, the Gold Coast would assume independence outside the Commonwealth. This would deal a blow to British prestige and make it difficult to maintain close relations after independence. Once this occurred there was no hope of holding any of the other African territories within the club. On the other hand, as long as the Gold Coast was *formally* a full member it would probably be content that *informally* there should be 'an inner ring of the strongest and senior members capable of shouldering the burden of their own defence'.[197] The Governor's warning found expression in a report on 'The Future of Commonwealth Membership'. This report concluded that for several reasons, a two-tier system was not advisable. The Gold Coast, Nigeria, the Central African Federation, Malaya and the West Indian Federation should be admitted to full membership.[198] Even though this might be 'unpalatable', it was the only alternative to a 'Commonwealth of dwindling power'. To encourage colonial territories to secede from the Commonwealth was seen as 'tantamount to adopting a policy of deliberately weakening our own strength and authority in world councils by a series of self-inflicted wounds'.[199] There could be no test of suitability for full membership. In addition, newcomers would probably be discontented with a lower-class membership: their discontent would be exploited by India who had already shown 'dangerous tendencies' to foster African nationalism.[200] Officials were also apprehensive that the newly independent countries might 'go over to the Soviet camp' if Britain did not succeed in retaining their friendship.[201] Countries which maintained the connection with Britain, however, were less likely to pass under the influence of hostile powers 'in the period of their political immaturity'.

Retaining the new states in the Commonwealth, officials argued, would strengthen the United Kingdom's political influence throughout the world. Britain's prestige and international standing had been enhanced by its capacity to retain India, Pakistan and

Ceylon within the Commonwealth. Retaining the Gold Coast and others would have the same effect. Moreover, it would strengthen the United Kingdom's economic position by adding political cohesion to the sterling area. Britain's defence potential would also be strengthened; through 'wise political leadership' it might be able to mobilise a considerable part of the Commonwealth's military resources in support of some causes. It was important that newly independent countries should conduct their foreign affairs in conformity with British policies. The only way to achieve this was to bring them by stages into day-to-day consultations with other Dominions, to let them take part in meetings on foreign affairs, and to make sure that they embarked on their career as an independent country with goodwill towards the United Kingdom unimpaired – a course which would be greatly eased by full membership. There would still be certain distinctions. *Formally*, all members would be equal, but *informally* there was to be a differentiation between those countries willing and able to shoulder definite commitments, and those that were not. The latter would not be provided with the same amount of information and guidance on international affairs. Apart from general and regional meetings, there would also be meetings attended only by the more important members. In addition, there could be further groupings in defence, which would create special relationships. This discrimination between 'more' and 'less' important members was not considered a radical departure from existing practice. Variations in the treatment of the different members were already evident, and apparently such discrimination could be managed without adverse effects.[202] The best solution therefore seemed to be the development of 'practical methods of consultation', which permitted 'free and close cooperation' between those members who actually exercised an effective influence in world affairs. Thus, while an inner ring (or upper tier) of some members might emerge, constitutionally there would be no difference between their status and that of the other members.

The official committee's report proved a persuasive document, convincing both Lyttelton and Swinton that neither the two-tier system nor the exclusion of the Gold Coast were a 'starter'.[203] The Commonwealth Secretary admitted feeling uncomfortable at the thought of having African countries as full members but nevertheless recommended their admission.[204] Swinton was still worried about the reaction of South Africa, but 'much less anxious' about the response of other older members. Commonwealth cooperation had 'never been so close as during the past year'. Economic cooperation was growing steadily, complemented by 'a closeness in foreign affairs and defence which I have never seen surpassed in peace'.[205] It was reasonable to hope that Canada, Australia and New Zealand would support full membership for the Gold Coast, while South Africa might be persuaded to accept it. There was some resistance in Cabinet: Lord Salisbury argued that 'these small countries inhabited by primitive peoples', were not at present 'mentally equipped' to be responsible either for their foreign or defence policy. Were they to become full members of the club, they would 'rapidly destroy the Commonwealth and the whole influence for good which it exercises in the world'.[206] The admission of Asian members had already completely destroyed the atmosphere of confidence which previously existed. Britain might now definitely lose the white Dominions by admitting African members. But, although most ministers 'greatly regretted' the envisaged course, they acknowledged that it would be impracticable to develop a two-tier system. And since it was more advantageous to admit the Gold Coast than to exclude it, the African state was allowed entry as a full member on attaining independence in March 1957.

South Africa objected to Ghana's admission, and its Prime Minister, Henrik Verwoerd, sent Eden 'an offensive letter'. Eden sent a firm reply, stating angrily that Britain required no lesson 'in how to treat black people'.[207] South Africa gave in, but the CRO warned that it would be too rash to conclude that the principle of accepting former colonies into the Commonwealth had been 'swallowed' by the Union. There would be more difficulties in the future, and Britain may be moving towards a situation in which she would be content to see the Union outside.[208] Notwithstanding this warning, the admission of Malaya to the Commonwealth led to no controversies, neither in London nor with the other Dominions. Malaya's membership was generally considered desirable and necessary: it would facilitate defence assistance and help to keep the country in the sterling area. Malayan leaders seemed eager to maintain the British connection, and their country was neither as 'primitive' nor 'as awkward a customer' as the Gold Coast.[209] Since Malaya was not an African state, even South Africa could accept this new member without fear of any repercussions on its racial policies.

The Debate about New European Members and Plan G

In the mid-1950s the Commonwealth was opened to African members. At the same time, policy-makers debated whether it should also take in various European states. The idea itself was not new: it had been voiced repeatedly, for example, by Leo Amery, but was never taken very seriously by British officials. This changed during

1955–56: first, it was realised that the intake of 'brown' and 'black' Dominions would make it more difficult to preserve Britain's central position in the Commonwealth, and that the club's military, political and economic weight was diminishing. Second, the move of France, Germany, Italy and the Benelux countries towards closer union raised the prospect of a continental *bloc* from which Britain would be excluded, thus diminishing its international standing, in particular with the United States. A union with France, and possibly also the Benelux and the Scandinavian countries, was to prevent the emergence of such a bloc. An alternative proposal, which eventually gained the upper hand was the creation of a free-trade area, embracing the whole of non-communist Europe.

Plan G and the Commonwealth

In the immediate post-war period, the war-torn countries of Europe were only of secondary importance to Britain. When Jean Monnet, director of the French Planning Office, came to London in spring 1949 to sound out British officials on an Anglo-French economic union, he received a polite rebuke. Neither France nor any of the other continental countries seemed desirable partners. The sterling area took half of Britain's exports, while western Europe took only a quarter. In 1947 British exports equalled those of France, Germany, Italy, Benelux, Norway and Denmark combined.[210] A meeting of senior officials from the Treasury, FO, Board of Trade and CRO concluded that there was 'no attraction for us in long term economic co-operation with Europe. At best it will be a drain on our resources. At worst it can seriously damage our economy.'[211] Politically, the prospects were hardly any better. Militarily, the Continent was a burden: Britain had to maintain a rather large contingent of occupation troops in Germany, and no country appeared able to muster enough forces in order to resist a Soviet onslaught. Britain therefore had to concentrate its defence effort in Europe in order to protect itself.

Probably the most important factors in keeping British policy-makers from getting involved with Europe, however, were emotional. Economic, military and political considerations all played a role. None of them, however, was a real obstacle. What mattered was the *feeling* that Britain's place was not in Europe, but in the wider world, notably in the Commonwealth. Attlee, for example, confessed himself 'disturbed with the suggestion ... that we might somehow get closer to Europe than to our Commonwealth. The Commonwealth nations are our closest friends.'[212] Only in the FO were there some voices calling for closer association with Europe – even though officials insisted that this was not to be at the expense of links with the Empire-

Commonwealth or the United States, but rather to bolster them.[213] Britain's global position depended on three circles: Europe, the United States, and the Commonwealth. Moving too close to Europe would harm Britain's standing with the other two.[214]

Britain's approach to Europe did not change under the Conservative government of 1951–55. After the war Churchill had called for a United States of Europe and close defence cooperation but this had been motivated mainly by the view that isolationism would gain the upper hand in the United States. After the establishment of a satisfactory defence framework through NATO, European cooperation now seemed much less urgent. The Prime Minister underlined that, for historical, cultural and geographic reasons, Britain could not be regarded as an integral part of Europe: 'We help, we dedicate, we play a part, but we are not merged and do not forfeit our insular or Commonwealth-wide character.'[215] Because of its geographic position, the UK was closely attached to the Continent. However, if western Europe was moving towards a federation, Britain could never be a member of it; it could only act as a close but separate ally. To act differently would lead to Britain being treated by the United States on the same footing as other European states. The links with the Commonwealth would be weakened, and the Dominions would turn to the United States, which according to the Prime Minister and most other policy-makers would spell the end of Britain as a Great Power.

As in the 1940s, policy-makers feared anything which might lead to a loss of national sovereignty, at least in a European – as opposed to trans-Atlantic – context. When the six European Coal and Steel Community (ECSC) powers began their talks in June 1955 in Messina on a common market, Britain was reluctant to participate. The advice ministers received (and accepted) from their officials was consistent with British policy since the war: Britain had more to lose than to gain in most areas. Joining a European common market would not only weaken economic relations with the Commonwealth and the United States, but also expose Britain to damaging competition in textiles and chemicals and probably the engineering industries as well. Other Commonwealth countries would probably see no difficulty in a closer association between Britain and Europe. But the danger was that they would seize the opportunity to require a re-negotiation (or even abolition) of imperial preference, which they regarded as heavily biased in favour of the United Kingdom. Britain's best hope of retaining the advantages of imperial preference lay in refraining from raising any tariff question at all. In fact the end of imperial preference was the 'major risk in any initiative in Europe'.[216]

The debate about Europe was loaded with emotional as well as rational political and economic arguments. Even the Chancellor of the Exchequer, R.A. Butler, despite his constant warnings about the need to diminish overseas commitments, was clearly against it. For Butler, the Messina meetings were 'archaeological excavations', and like Eden he was simply 'bored' with the European question. For him and other ministers, the Organisation for European Economic Cooperation (OEEC) continued to be the preferred vehicle for cooperation among European states.[217] They were convinced that the Messina Plan would not succeed: it was seen as just another project on European unity, doomed to predictable failure. The government decided not to commit itself and sent only a 'representative', rather than a 'delegate' to the meetings of the preparatory committee in Brussels – a participation which in any case lasted only until November 1955.

In early 1956, some policy-makers, at least in the Treasury and the Board of Trade, began to change their mind. Despite predictions to the contrary, the negotiations between the Six appeared to have been successful, and officials began to worry about Britain being excluded from the new club: 'On a longer view the question might become, not whether we should go into Europe to save Europe, but whether we should not have to move closer to Europe in order to save ourselves.'[218] The aim now was to neutralise the whole project by promoting cooperation on OEEC lines, i.e. under British guidance and on a strictly intergovernmental level. This was to be achieved through Plan G, which envisaged an industrial free-trade area, comprising the major part of non-communist Europe, but without the political or economic union the 'Six' (France, Belgium, West Germany, Luxembourg, Netherlands, Italy) advocated.[219]

The plan's principal backers in Cabinet were the Chancellor of the Exchequer Macmillan and Peter Thorneycroft, President of the Board of Trade. They argued that Britain could no longer expect to enjoy 'the best of both worlds', i.e. to secure the advantages of liberal trade practices in the world at large while retaining the benefit of the preferential system within the Commonwealth. Plan G had been devised to turn developments in Europe to the advantage of the United Kingdom and of the Commonwealth as a whole. The plan provided a unique chance of gaining simultaneously the support of 'what might be described as … the European and the Imperial wings of the Conservative Party.'[220] The economic ties with the Commonwealth were disintegrating. Since the British market could no longer continue to absorb primary products from the former colonies, they would look increasingly for alternative markets. Both the growth of industry in the Commonwealth and the government-aided expansion of British agricultural production tended to make the United

Kingdom and Commonwealth economies 'less naturally complementary than heretofore':[221] any increase in the import of Commonwealth produce would be almost entirely at the expense of agriculture in Britain. Reducing domestic output sufficiently, however, appeared politically impossible. The Dominions realised this and were looking elsewhere for the expanding markets they needed. Another problem was the lack of investment capital in Britain: the Dominions increasingly turned to other sources of finance, thus weakening Britain's influence on them.

Powerful centrifugal tendencies were at work, Macmillan and Thorneycroft argued, and there was little prospect of basing a policy solely on the Commonwealth connection. On the other hand, the United Kingdom had become 'too small an economic unit' to resist US supremacy on its own. If it did not attach itself to Europe, it would inevitably be drawn, as a minor partner, into the United States' sphere of influence. Britain should enter into association with Europe, and do so with a determination to assume its leadership. This was the best means of ensuring the United Kingdom's continuing status as a Great Power.[222] Plan G would revitalise the Commonwealth and lead to 'a new period of British strength and power'.[223] The free-trade area would provide a market for those Commonwealth products which Britain could not absorb, and would also be a source of new funds for Commonwealth development – a factor of particular importance for Britain, since the capacity to invest was even more important than the ability to trade.[224]

Lord Home, Lord Salisbury and Lennox-Boyd did not share Macmillan's optimism about the revitalising effects on the Commonwealth of a *rapprochement* with Europe. If Britain tried to assume the leadership of a different association of nations, the links between metropole and Dominions would be weakened rather than strengthened. An increasing proportion of British trade would be carried on with Europe, and Britain's interests would increasingly be bound up with it. Its (alleged) natural vocation of being a *world* power with global links and interests would thus be dealt a heavy blow. Britain's status as a world power depended on the extent to which it was able to give 'effective and acceptable leadership' to the Commonwealth, not upon its economic treaties with Continental powers – Plan G, however, jeopardised its capacity of doing so.[225] While the Dominions were rapidly industrialising, Britain's association with Europe would mean that even less preferential treatment could be granted, pushing them to look for alternative markets. Therefore their loyalty – which was bound up with trade – would diminish in the future. By speculating on hypothetical gains in Europe, Britain might lose 'the more tangible benefits' of the Commonwealth connection.[226] In addition, government support in the Conservative Party would be diminished if the Cabinet appeared to abandon 'traditional policies based on maintaining the solidarity of the English-speaking peoples.[227]

For Lord Home, Lennox-Boyd and Lord Salisbury, the Continent could never gain a position comparable to the old empire. Macmillan, however, thought it necessary to modify Britain's approach to Europe – not because he was a Little Englander, but because he recognised the Common Market as an important future source of power. This view was shared by most other ministers. They decided to go ahead with Plan G. Britain's leadership of the Commonwealth would help to secure it a similar position in Europe, which in turn would allow Britain to maintain its close affiliation with the rest of the Commonwealth. The combination of these two spheres of influence was the best means of ensuring Britain's 'continuing status as a Great Power'. It was not feasible to build on the Commonwealth alone, since the Dominions were eager to divert their economic, strategic and diplomatic relations. The Commonwealth therefore had to be supplemented – not replaced – with Europe.

Plan G was announced in the House of Commons in November 1956, and a White Paper published in January 1957. Negotiations with the other European states dragged on over the following months. Macmillan even tried to blackmail France and Germany into accepting cooperation between the Six and the proposed free trade area by threatening to withdraw Britain's contribution to European defence, but with little success.[228] Germany and France knew too well that Britain could not afford to adopt a policy of isolationism, given the repercussions it would have had on Britain's standing *vis-à-vis* the United States. The project collapsed when the French President Charles de Gaulle declared in December 1958 that there would be no cooperation between the Treaty of Rome countries and the proposed Free Trade Area. As a result, negotiations between Britain and Norway, Sweden, Denmark, Austria, Portugal, Iceland and Switzerland went ahead, and the European Free Trade Area (EFTA) was established in 1960. This was only a partial success, since the countries Britain had managed to assemble were clearly less dynamic and attractive partners than the members of the EEC. Britain continued to hope, however, that an agreement with the Six could be reached, thus overcoming the 'economic division' of Europe.

A French Dominion?

Simultaneously with Plan G were various other proposals dealing with how Britain might prevent having to choose between Europe and the Commonwealth. The debate was launched by Anthony Nutting of the FO who proposed to bring Europe into the Commonwealth.[229] Most other policy-makers rejected the idea as unrealistic. They argued that it would disturb relations with the coloured Dominions who already regarded NATO as a white man's club. To attract western Europe into the Commonwealth, it would be necessary to offer imperial preference and a free hand in trading. This was not feasible, though, since some members of the Commonwealth were already dissatisfied with the imperial preference system and would not want to make concessions to new and industrialised members. Nor would the Europeans be willing to provide duty-free entry for Commonwealth goods.[230] This attitude also prevailed when, in October 1956, ministers discussed the 'tentative suggestion' by French Premier Guy Mollet, who proposed that France might become a member of the Commonwealth, possibly through common citizenship.[231] The FO feared that a union with France would lead to negative repercussions on 'the intimacy of Anglo-US cooperation in defence, intelligence and atomic matters'.[232] Apart from the damage it would inflict on the special relationship, the admission of France would also weaken the ties between the various members of the Commonwealth. This would impair the role it was expected to play in bringing together the West and the non-aligned states. Britain would saddle itself with a weak partner, inherit French unpopularity in the Middle and Far East and strengthen anti-colonial prejudices. The reality of the Commonwealth connection derived from 'the long historical association' between the United Kingdom and other members – all of which had at one time been parts of the British empire. The essence of the Commonwealth was that its members, though independent sovereign states, did not regard themselves as 'foreign' in relation to one another. The introduction of France would entirely change the basis of this association. The Asian members might leave the club, thus affecting the readiness of other colonies to remain within the Commonwealth once they achieved independence.[233]

The same attitude prevailed at ministerial level. Only Eden was inclined to accept the proposal, hoping that it would lend the Commonwealth more weight in international affairs. He acknowledged that it was difficult to introduce a foreign country, but argued that the additional strength which the adhesion of France and possibly some other European countries would give, had to be weighed against the weakness of the Asian members. Moreover, the proposal would be easier to 'sell' to government supporters than Plan G. Given attempts by the Six to create a common market, Britain had to react. A possible solution would be the creation of some special association between the United

Kingdom and France within the Commonwealth, short of political union. The two countries would then have joint diplomatic, defence and economic planning, but still enjoy an independent existence. The Scandinavians and the Benelux countries might accede in a like manner. The possible loss of India, Ceylon and perhaps South Africa could be more cheerfully borne if they were replaced by countries whose habits of thought and vital interests were closer to those of Britain. Other ministers were less optimistic than Eden. France, Belgium and the Netherlands had no 'heritage of law and custom' in common with Britain. The advantages of their admission had to be weighed against the changes in the character of the Commonwealth which such an extension would involve. A specially constituted committee of ministers and officials also saw 'very powerful deterrents', notably France's colonial policy, would be unpopular with the new members.[234] Nor would France's admission appeal to the old Commonwealth including Canada, Australia and New Zealand, which might be encouraged to lean even more closely towards the United States. It would arouse disquiet and opposition in Germany and the Scandinavian countries, and Britain would no longer be able to maintain the special relationship with the United States. On the economic side, Britain would become associated with a 'sluggish' bloc.[235]

Combining Plan G with a scheme to bring European states into the Commonwealth would have the economic advantage of linking Britain to 'dynamic' Germany and the political merit of closing ranks with France. But it would be 'hazardous' to attempt to combine both operations in one comprehensive policy. It might be wiser, in the first instance, to launch Plan G and to 'allow any desire for political association between Europe and the Commonwealth to emerge naturally from this movement towards closer economic unity'. This verdict was accepted by Eden, and the subsequent development of the Suez crisis as well as the political situation in France put paid to any further high-level discussions about a French Dominion.

Maitland and the 'Expanding Commonwealth'

The idea of transforming the Empire-Commonwealth into a 'Third World Power' had been dropped by the end of the 1940s. And as the debate on a French Dominion showed, in the mid-1950s hardly anybody still entertained hopes of transforming it into a political or strategic instrument at Britain's ready disposal. Only some imperial thinkers upheld the idea, for example, Leo Amery: he saw the Commonwealth as a nucleus around which 'the ultimate world order' would crystallise. The club was to be enlarged through the association of Norway, Iceland and other states like Thailand.[236] Amery's ideas did not have much success, but they did not go wholly unnoticed either. They were taken up by some Conservative MPs interested in developing the Commonwealth into a third force under British guidance. Patrick Maitland created the *Expanding Commonwealth Group* that comprised about 18 MPs.[237] The group advocated the expansion of the club to include 'foreign countries of similar outlook and interests to the present members' – such as Norway, the Sudan, Somalia or (former French colony) Guinea. Thus it was gradually to become the normal thing for foreign countries to feel that the Commonwealth rather than the United Nations contained 'the germ of the new order'.[238] The new Commonwealth was to be complemented with a single currency covering the sterling area, Europe and the colonies of other European countries.[239] It would furnish the sinews of defensive and diplomatic power, promote trade and help Britain to achieve a sound balance of payments – in short, it would allow the United Kingdom to maintain its position as a world power.

Maitland's proposals found little support among British officials. Even the CRO viewed the ideas of the *Expanding Commonwealth Group* – like those of several other (Conservative) groups lobbying for a strengthening of the Commonwealth – rather sceptically. The admission of foreign countries to associate membership seemed too difficult. Officials expected India especially to pose problems if it came to the extension of membership to a Scandinavian country. In addition, the imminent inclusion of the Gold Coast and Malaya would already exercise the 'digestive powers' of the club fairly fully without adding additional items to the menu.[240] On the economic side, the arguments against the admission of 'foreign' states or the creation of an autarkic bloc were even stronger. The revival of imperial preferences was not feasible: the political and economic interests of the other members denied such an approach any chance of success.[241] Moreover, Britain itself could substantially increase its imports of Commonwealth produce only at the expense of European or domestic produce or by excluding Argentinian meat and US wheat – a move which would lead to a storm of protest by consumers not willing to pay higher prices for Commonwealth products.[242] In any case it was not advisable to return to the concept of an 'introspective' Commonwealth. Trade between developed economies was growing much faster than trade with non-developed economies. Free-trade areas within the Commonwealth could not be established either since virtually all members were anxious to protect their own industries. The high level of trade with the Commonwealth should be maintained and expanded wherever possible, but without losing sight of Britain's 'broader economic aims'.[243] Because of this combination of political and economic arguments against it, the idea of closer Commonwealth integration met with only a very lukewarm reception among British officials in Whitehall, who listened politely to the arguments of Maitland and his partisans, but did their best to ignore them.

Conclusion

In the early 1950s, the Commonwealth lost much of its former coherence in the military and economic sphere. While the Dominions increasingly turned to the United States for their defence needs, Britain realised that trade liberalisation rather than imperial preferences were in its own interest. Nonetheless, many policy-makers continued to believe that the club enhanced Britain's international standing. Therefore the Gold Coast was offered full membership. Many feared that this would reduce the club's intimacy, but a majority of policy-makers believed that Ghana's departure would deal a blow to Britain's prestige and make it difficult to maintain close relations after independence. Ghana's admission to full membership, coupled with the creation of two informal tiers, policy-makers hoped, would make it possible to maintain the old resolve and at the same time reduce the impact of independence on Anglo-Ghanaian relations.

While the club was opened up to African states, the proposal to take in European members was rejected. Most policy-makers believed that such a step would make it impossible for the Commonwealth to serve as a bridge between the West and the non-aligned world. France's admission might lead to the departure of the 'new' Dominions, while the 'old' ones would turn to the United States. In addition, France was a 'foreign' country, while Ghana and India were not. Therefore France's entering the club would entirely change the basis of the association. The same arguments were used against the proposal of offering associate membership to Norway or Guinea.

Britain did not want to Europeanise the Commonwealth. Nor did it want any formal association with Europe on the lines of the Treaty of Rome. It feared the repercussions on Britain's wider economic and political interests: the Continent alone supposedly could not compensate for the expected economic losses to be sustained in overseas markets, or the political losses likely to be incurred in the special relationship with the United States. On the other hand, British officials realised that the Commonwealth was no longer sufficient to underpin its claim to Great Power status. Macmillan and Thorneycroft therefore proposed the creation of an industrial free-trade area, which comprised all of non-communist western Europe. This was to provide British industry with a huge unified market and undermine French attempts at creating a Continental union. It was hoped that Plan G would thus allow Britain to retain the best of both worlds: to remain at the centre of a powerful Commonwealth and assume the leadership of Europe – without obliging it to give up part of its sovereignty.

NOTES

1. Anthony Adamthwaite, 'Overstretched and Overstrung: Eden, the Foreign Office and the Making of Policy, 1951–5', *International Affairs*, 64 (1988), p. 248.
2. Robert Holland, *The Pursuit of Greatness: Britain and the World Role, 1900–1970* (London: Fontana, 1991), p. 272.
3. Memorandum, 'The Economic Position: Analysis and Remedies' (C (51) 1), Butler to Cabinet, 31 October 1951. CAB 129/48 (Goldsworthy, *Conservative Government*, III, 358).
4. Adamthwaite, 'Overstretched and Overstrung', p. 248.
5. Memorandum 'Defence and Economic Policy' (C (52) 320), Butler to Cabinet, 3 October 1952. CAB 129/55 (Goldsworthy, *Conservative Government*, I, 9).
6. Minute by L. Rowan, 13 February 1952. T 225/318 (Kent, *Egypt*, II, 268).
7. Memorandum 'Economic Policy' (C (52) 166), Butler to Cabinet, 17 May 1952. CAB 129/52 (Goldsworthy, *Conservative Government*, III, 367); memorandum, 'Defence Programme' (C (52) 393), Butler to Cabinet, 5 November 1952. CAB 129/56 (Goldsworthy, *Conservative Government*, I, 11).
8. Memorandum 'Economic Policy' (C (52) 196), Macmillan to Cabinet, 17 June 1952. CAB 129/52 (Goldsworthy, *Conservative Government*, III, 369).
9. Note, 'Middle East Oil' (CP (55) 152), Macmillan to Cabinet, 14 October 1955. CAB 129/78 (Goldsworthy, *Conservative Government*, I, 45).
10. Memorandum 'British Overseas Obligations' (C (52) 202), Eden to Cabinet, 18 June 1952. CAB 129/53 (Goldsworthy, *Conservative Government*, I, 3).
11. FO memorandum, 10 December 1951. FO 953/1051, quoted in Philip M. Taylor, 'Power, Propaganda and Public Opinion: The British Information Services and the Cold War, 1945–57', in Ennio Di Nolfo (ed.), *Power in Europe? II: Great Britain, France, Germany and Italy and the Origins of the EEC, 1952–1957* (Berlin: de Gruyter, 1992), p. 445.
12. Minute by P. Dixon, 23 January 1952. FO 371/96920 (Kent, *Egypt*, II, 263).
13. Memorandum, 'British Overseas Obligations' (C (52) 202), Eden to Cabinet, 18 June 1952. CAB 129/53 (Goldsworthy, *Conservative Government*, I, 13).
14. Kunz, *British Post-War Sterling Crises*, p. 12. Sterling transactions accounted for over 40 per cent of world trade in 1950.
15. Report, 'Defence Programme' (D (52) 45), COS to Cabinet defence committee, 31 October 1952. CAB 131/12 (Porter and Stockwell, *British Imperial Policy*, II, 14).
16. Report 'Defence Programme' (D (52) 45), COS to Cabinet defence committee, 31 October 1952. CAB 131/12 (Goldsworthy, *Conservative Government*, I, 10).
17. Minutes of a meeting of CO, FO, CRO and Treasury officials in Brook's room (GEN. 494/1), 15 April 1955. CAB 130/109 (PRO).
18. Joint memorandum by CO and War Office, (September) 1954. PREM 11/581 (Goldsworthy, *Conservative Government*, I, 75).
19. Minutes of a meeting of United Kingdom and Commonwealth ministers on

defence policy, 12 December 1952. PREM 11/23 (PRO).

20. Memorandum, 'Egypt: the Alternatives' (C (53) 65), Foreign Secretary to Cabinet, 16 February 1953. CAB 129/59 (Porter and Stockwell, *British Imperial Policy*, II, 19).

21. Minute by Kirkpatrick, 14 June 1954. FO 371/108378, quoted in Wm Roger Louis, 'American Anti-Colonialism and the Dissolution of the British Empire', in Wm Roger Louis and Hedley Bull (eds), *The 'Special Relationship'. Anglo-American Relations since 1945* (Oxford: Clarendon Press, 1986), p. 275.

22. Memorandum, 'Egypt', Selwyn Lloyd to Cabinet (C (54) 187), 3 June 1954. CAB 129/68 (Goldsworthy, *Conservative Government*, I, 39).

23. Churchill to Eden, 15 January 1953. FO 800/827 (PRO); Churchill to First Lord of Admiralty, Foreign Secretary, Minister of Defence, Commonwealth Secretary, 25 August 1954. FO 800/757 (PRO). In April 1951 the Persian government nationalised the Anglo-Iranian Oil Company. London applied to the International Court of Justice. On 5 July, the latter issued an interim ruling that the company should be allowed to carry on its operations for the time being. The Persian government under Mohammad Mussadiq rejected the order and expelled the British staff in Abadan. At its last meeting the Labour government decided not to use force to protect British interests, but to organise a boycott of Persian oil – a decision not questioned by Churchill once he took over as Prime Minister.

24. Minute, 'Negotiations with Egypt' by Field Marshall Slim, 10 March 1953. PREM 11/486, quoted in Wm Roger Louis, 'The Anglo-Egyptian Settlement of 1954', in Wm Roger Louis and Roger Owen (eds), *Suez 1956: The Crisis and its Consequences* (Oxford: Clarendon Press, 1989), p. 59.

25. Churchill to Minister of State FO, 19 August 1952. PREM 11/392 (PRO).

26. Julian Amery and Lord Hinchingbrooke denounced the Suez agreement as evidence that the government was lacking the will to keep Britain as 'an independent force in the world'. Twenty-six Conservatives voted against the agreement (John G. Darwin, 'The Fear of Falling: British Politics and Imperial Decline since 1900', *Transactions of the Royal Historical Society*, 5th series, 36 (1986), p. 37).

27. Macmillan diary, entry for 30 December 1955, quoted in John Turner, *Macmillan* (London: Longman, 1994), p. 196.

28. Joint memorandum (PR (56) 2), Macmillan and Monckton to Eden, 20 March 1956. CAB 134/1315 (Goldsworthy, *Conservative Government*, I, 20).

29. Memorandum, 'The Future of the UK in World Affairs' (PR (56) 3), Treasury, FO and MoD officials to Cabinet policy review committee, 1 June 1956. CAB 134/1315 (PRO).

30. Report, 'Expenditure in Asia' (GEN 570/1) by official working party, 4 February 1957. CAB 130/122 (Stockwell, *Malaya*, III, 440).

31. Memorandum, 'Review of United Kingdom Position in Jordan' (DC (56) 7), Chiefs of Staff to defence committee, 22 March 1956. CAB 131/17 (PRO).

32. Minutes of meeting of ministers, 16 May 1956 (GEN 527/1). CAB 130/115 (PRO).

33. Note, 'Assumptions for Future Planning' (PR (56) 11), Eden to Cabinet policy review committee, 15 June 1956. CAB 134/1315 (Goldsworthy, *Conservative Government*, I, 25).

34. Report, 'United Kingdom Requirements in the Middle East' (DC (56) 17), Chiefs of Staff to defence committee, 3 July 1956. CAB 131/17 (PRO).

35. Economic steering committee/sub-committee on closer economic association with Europe/working party on the colonies, 6 November 1956. CAB 134/1878 (PRO).

36. Darwin, *End of the British Empire*, p. 211.

37. E. Shuckburgh, *Descent to Suez: Diaries 1951–1956* (London: Weidenfeld & Nicholson, 1986), diary entry for 7 January 1953, p. 71.
38. Eden to Eisenhower, 5 March 1956. PREM 11/1177, quoted in Geoffrey Warner, 'Aspects of the Suez Crisis', in Ennio Di Nolfo (ed.), *Power in Europe? II: Great Britain, France, Germany and Italy and the Origins of the EEC, 1952–1957* (Berlin: de Gruyter, 1992), p. 48.
39. Memorandum, 'Sterling and the Suez Canal Situation' by G. Bolton (Executive Director, Bank of England), 1 August 1956, quoted in Diane B. Kunz, 'The Importance of Having Money: The Economic Diplomacy of the Suez Crisis', in Wm Roger Louis and Roger Owen (eds), *Suez 1956: The Crisis and its Consequences* (Oxford: Clarendon Press, 1989), p. 215; report 'United Kingdom requirements in the Middle East' (DC (56) 17), Chiefs of Staff to defence committee, 3 July 1956. CAB 131/17 (PRO).
40. Memorandum, 'Persia' (CP (51) 212), Foreign Secretary to Cabinet, 20 July 1951. CAB 129/46 (Hyam, *Labour Government*, I, 37).
41. Howard J. Dooley, 'Great Britain's 'Last Battle' in the Middle East: Notes on Cabinet Planning during the Suez Crisis of 1956', *International History Review*, 11 (1989), p. 516. As it turned out, the loss was $279 million.
42. Governor of the Bank of England to Chancellor of the Exchequer, 20 December 1956, quoted in John Fforde, *The Bank of England and Public Policy, 1941–1958* (Cambridge: Cambridge University Press, 1992), p. 544 and 562.
43. Despatch Charles Keightly, Commander-in-chief of the Anglo-French forces at Suez, to Chiefs of Staff, quoted in Peter Hennessy and Mark Laity, 'Suez – What the Papers Say', *Contemporary Record*, 1 (1987), p. 8.
44. D. Goldsworthy, 'Keeping Change Within Bounds: Aspects of Colonial Policy during the Churchill and Eden Governments, 1951–1957, *Journal of Imperial and Commonwealth History*, 13 (1990), pp. 81–108.
45. Salisbury to Swinton, 2 April 1949. SWIN III, 3/2 (CC).
46. Salisbury to Swinton, 1 January 1949. SWIN I, 4/2 (CC).
47. Montgomery to Lyttelton, 27 December 1951. PREM 11/121 (Stockwell, *Malaya*, II, 258).
48. Swinton to Salisbury, 4 April 1949. SWIN III, 3/2 (CC).
49. CM 83 (54), 7 December 1954. CAB 128/27 (2) (PRO).
50. Memorandum, 'Malaya' (C (51) 59), Lyttelton to Cabinet, 21 December 1951. CAB 129/48 (Stockwell, *Malaya*, II, 257).
51. Memorandum, 'British Honduras' (C (53) 329), Lyttelton to Cabinet, 21 November 1953. CAB 129/64 (PRO). However, it has to be pointed out that the Prime Minister declined to agree with the statement – he merely 'noted' it. (David Goldsworthy, 'Keeping Change Within Bounds: Aspects of Colonial Policy during the Churchill and Eden Governments, 1951–57', *Journal of Imperial and Commonwealth History*, XVIII (1990), p. 83).
52. Amery to Dorman-Smith, 15 April 1943. L/PO/9/6 (Tinker, *Burma*, I, 13).
53. Churchill to Minister of State FO and W. Strang, 1 May 1953. PREM 11/645 (PRO); record of Bermuda Conference (BC (P) (53) 6, 2), 7 December 1953, quoted in A.J. Stockwell, 'British Imperial Strategy and Decolonization in South-East Asia, 1947–57', in D.K. Bassett and V.T. King (eds), *Britain and South-East Asia: Occasional Papers of the Centre for South-East Asian Studies No. 13* (Hull: University of Hull, 1986), p. 79.
54. *The Times*, 21 November 1942, quoted in Henry Pelling, *The Labour Governments, 1945–51* (Basingstoke: Macmillan, 1984), p. 147.
55. Memorandum, 'The Colonial Territories and Commonwealth Membership' (C (53) 122), Commonwealth Secretary to Cabinet, 8 April 1953. CAB 129/60 (PRO); memorandum (CCM (53) 2) by Commonwealth Secretary, 5 May 1953. CAB 134/786 (PRO).

56. Memorandum, 'The Colonial Territories and Commonwealth Membership' (C (53) 122), Commonwealth Secretary to Cabinet, 8 April 1953. CAB 129/60 (PRO).

57. Minute, by Ivor Thomas, 30 May 1947. CO 847/36/1/9, quoted in Hyam, 'Africa and the Labour Government', fn. 15, p. 170.

58. Minute, by C. Jeffries, 9 February 1953. CO 554/254 (Goldsworthy, *Conservative Government*, II, 267).

59. Lyttelton to Lord Swinton, 2 July 1953. DO 35/5056 (Goldsworthy, *Conservative Government*, II, 183).

60. B. Reilly to committee of inquiry into constitutional development in the smaller territories (STC (50) 7), 23 February 1950. CO 537/6185 (Hyam, *Labour Government*, III, 268).

61. T. Lloyd to J. Macpherson (Nigeria), 5 March 1953. CO 554/254 (Rathbone, *Ghana*, II, 123).

62. Arden-Clarke to Gorell Barnes, 2 September 1954. CO 554/805 (Rathbone, *Ghana*, II, 153).

63. Minute, by C. Jeffries, 16 December 1955. CO 1032/55 (Goldsworthy, *Conservative Government*, II, 204).

64. Cohen to Mackintosh, 11 June 1951. CO 537/7181 (Rathbone, *Ghana*, I, 100).

65. Note, 'Education and Economic Development' by R. Harvey, 14 December 1953. CO 859/362 (Goldsworthy, *Conservative Government*, III, 492).

66. A. Cohen (Uganda) to T. Lloyd, 12 January 1954. CO 822/892 (Goldsworthy, *Conservative Government*, II, 295).

67. Cyprus is an example of the latter, British Guiana of the former: in April 1953, the Progressive People's Party (PPP), the only organised party in British Guiana, gained 18 out of 24 seats in the legislative council. The CO accepted that the colony would be governed by ministers who were suspected of being under communist influence, but it was hoped that the responsibilities of office would modify their views. Memorandum, 'British Guiana' (C (53) 261), Lyttelton to Cabinet, 30 September 1953. CAB 129/63 (Goldsworthy, *Conservative Government*, II, 336). Five months later, however, the Colonial Secretary advised his colleagues to suspend the constitution: the PPP still seemed determined to further the communist cause. On 9 October 1953, British troops landed in Georgetown to overthrow the government of Cheddi Jagan. Over the following years, the CO did its best to promote more moderate nationalists. Notwithstanding this effort, Jagan won the 1957 election. This time the British reaction was acquiescence. After all, the PPP seemed not to be such a tremendous political threat anymore: 'there are grounds for hope that even extremists are growing up politically' (P. Renison (Georgetown) to Colonial Secretary, 14 August 1957. FO 371/126078, quoted in Frank Furedi, 'Britain's Colonial Wars: Playing the Ethnic Card', *Journal of Commonwealth and Comparative Politics*, 8 (1990), p. 78).

68. Draft CO despatch to governors of all African colonies and Aden, May 1957. PREM 11/3239 (PRO).

69. Catherine R. Schenk, 'Finance and Empire: Confusion and Complexities. A Note', *International History Review*, 18 (1996), p. 870. In 1952–53, Malaya provided £61 million towards the net balance of payments with the dollar area, i.e. 35.26 per cent of the total.

70. Memorandum, 'Internal Security in the Colonies' (C (54) 402), Macmillan to Cabinet, 29 December 1954. CAB 129/72 (Goldsworthy, *Conservative Government*, I, 18).

71. Despatch, 'Communism and Africa', Selwyn Lloyd to Gladwyn Jebb, 21 April 1956. PREM 11/3239 (PRO).

72. Memorandum, 'Communist Prospects in East and Central Africa' by W.

Ingrams, April 1952. CO 537/7780, quoted in Susan L. Carruthers, *Winning Hearts and Minds: British Governments, the Media and Colonial Counter-Insurgency 1944–1960* (London: Leicester University Press, 1995), p. 161.

73. Gorell Barnes to Anderson, 16 February 1951. BARN 3/1 (CC).
74. Cary Fraser, 'Understanding American Policy towards the Decolonization of European Empires, 1945-64', *Diplomacy & Statecraft* 3,1 (1992), p. 109.
75. Note of a meeting held in T. Lloyd's room on 17 February 1949. CO 537/4261 (PRO).
76. 'Report of the Committee on the Conference of African Governors'. Appendices I–VIII, 22 May 1947. CO 847/36/1 (Hyam, *Labour Government*, I, 59).
77. Despatch, O. Franks (Washington) to Foreign Secretary, 14 January 1950. CO 537/7136 (Porter and Stockwell, *British Imperial Policy*, I, 55).
78. Notes by Gorell Barnes, January 1952. BARN 3/1 (CC).
79. Note, 'Smaller Colonial Territories' (GEN 518/6/11), Brook for Cabinet committee on Commonwealth Prime Ministers' meeting, 18 June 1956. CAB 130/113 (Goldsworthy, *Conservative Government*, II, 215).
80. CA (O) 4 (56), 1 June 1956. CAB 134/1203 (PRO).
81. G. Laithwaite to official committee on colonial policy, 3 February 1956. CAB 134/1203 (PRO).
82. CO despatch, 'The political objectives of British policy in the African dependent territories' to all governors of African colonies and Aden, n.d. (1957). FO 371/125293 (PRO).
83. W. Wilson to W. Mathieson, 6 October 1954. CO 936/369 (Goldsworthy, *Conservative Government*, I, 36).
84. Minute, by H. Bourdillon, 12 December 1956. CO 822/912 (Goldsworthy, *Conservative Government*, II, 299).
85. W. Mathieson to B. Gidden, 7 January 1957. CO 822/912 (Goldsworthy, *Conservative Government*, II, 301).
86. Memorandum, 'The Future of the UK in World Affairs', Treasury, FO and MoD officials to Cabinet policy review committee (PR (56) 3), 1 June 1956. CAB 134/1315 (PRO).
87. Minute, by S. Caine, 9 November 1947. CO 877/31/5 (Hyam, *Labour Government*, I, 69).
88. Stephen Ashton, 'British Official Documentary Perspectives on Decolonisation: A Case Study of the Gold Coast', in *Décolonisations européennes: Actes du colloque international 'Décolonisations comparées', Aix-en-Provence, 30 septembre–3 octobre 1993* (Aix-en-Provence: Université de Provence, 1995), p. 121.
89. Minute, 'Interview with Mr Nehru' by O. Lyttelton, 11 June 1953. PREM 11/459 (PRO).
90. CO minute of talk with Templer, 3 December 1952. CO 1022/86 (Goldsworthy, *Conservative Government*, II, 344).
91. Memorandum, 'Political Objectives in British Territories of South East Asia', CO to JPS, 10 March 1953. CO 1022/91 (Stockwell, *Malaya*, II, 293).
92. Memorandum, 'Political Effects That a Deterioration of the Situation in Indo-China Might Have in British Colonial and Protected Territories' (FE (O) (53) 6), CO to Far East (official) committee, 13 June 1953. CAB 134/898 (Stockwell, *Malaya*, II, 301).
93. C (54) 155, 27 April 1954. CAB 129/68 (PRO).
94. Eden to FO, 30 April 1954. PREM 11/649 (PRO).
95. Memorandum, 'Federation of Malaya: Constitutional Development' (CP (55) 81), Lennox-Boyd to Cabinet, 20 July 1955. CAB 129/76 (Stockwell, *Malaya*, III, 356).

96. Memorandum, 'The London Talks: Alliance Demands and the Extent to Which They Might Be Met' by D. Watherston, n.d. (November 1955). CO 1030/75 (Stockwell, *Malaya*, III, 384).

97. Speech by Malcolm MacDonald at the Rotary Club, Singapore, 24 August 1955, quoted in Nicholas J. White, 'Government and Business Divided: Malaya, 1945–58', *Journal of Imperial and Commonwealth History*, XXII, 2 (1994), p. 259.

98. Memorandum, 'Conference on Constitutional Advance in the Federation of Malaya' (CA (56) 3), Lennox-Boyd to Cabinet colonial policy committee, 7 January 1956. CAB 134/1202 (Stockwell, *Malaya*, III, 394).

99. Memorandum, 'Singapore' (CP (56) 85), Lennox-Boyd to Cabinet, 23 March 1956. CAB 129/80 (Goldsworthy, *Conservative Government*, II, 355).

100. Memorandum, 'Federation of Malaya' (CP (56) 47), Lennox-Boyd to Cabinet, 21 February 1956. CAB 129/79 (Stockwell, *Malaya*, III, 405).

101. Lennox-Boyd to Eden, 5 January 1956. PREM 11/1302 (PRO).

102. Minute, 'Federation of Malaya', Lennox-Boyd to Eden, 22 August 1956. PREM 11/2298 (Stockwell, *Malaya*, III, 425).

103. Memorandum, 'Conference on Constitutional Advance in the Federation of Malaya' (CA (56) 3), Lennox-Boyd to Cabinet colonial policy committee, 7 January 1956. CAB 134/1202 (Stockwell, *Malaya*, III, 394).

104. Memorandum, 'Singapore: Constitutional Crisis' (CP (55) 97) by Minister of State for Colonial Affairs, 10 August 1955. CAB 129/76 (PRO).

105. Salisbury to Eden, n.d. (August 1955). PREM 11/874 (PRO).

106. CM 4 (56) 3, 17 January 1956. CAB 128/30/1 (Stockwell, *Malaya*, III, 400).

107. Draft memorandum, 'Safeguarding UK Economic Interests in Malaya' by Lennox-Boyd, n.d. (February 1956). CO 1030/72 (Stockwell, *Malaya*, III, 403).

108. 'Negotiations on Defence with Malaya and Singapore', MoD minutes of an inter-departmental meeting, 8 November 1955 (NDMS/M (55) 2). DEFE 7/493 (Stockwell, *Malaya*, III, 383).

109. A. MacKintosh to J. Martin, 16 January 1956. CO 1030/70 (Stockwell, *Malaya*, III, 399).

110. Circular telegram, 'Discussions with Federation of Malaya, December – January 1956–57'. FO to HM representatives, 4 February 1957. CO 1030/494 (Stockwell, *Malaya*, III, 441).

111. Note, 'The Outlook in Malaya up to 1960' by commissioner-general's office, n.d. (May 1957). FO 371/129342 (Stockwell, *Malaya*, III, 454).

112. H. Bourdillon to Bennett, Seel, Poynton, 25 June 1947. CO 537/2568 (PRO).

113. M. Hogan to Lennox-Boyd, 12 March 1956. Lennox-Boyd papers, box 3463 (Bodleian Library).

114. Memorandum, 'Malaya' (C (59) 31), Commonwealth Secretary to Cabinet, 16 February 1959. CAB 129/96 (PRO).

115. Memorandum, 'Amendment of the Gold Coast Constitution' (C (52) 28), Lyttelton to Cabinet, 9 February 1952. PREM 11/1367, Rathbone (*Ghana*, I, 115); CM 16 (52) 6, 12 February 1952. CAB 128/24 (Goldsworthy, *Conservative Government*, II, 266).

116. Report, 'The Future of Commonwealth Membership' (CCM (54) 1) by official committee on Commonwealth membership, 21 January 1954. CAB 134/786 (PRO).

117. Memorandum, 'Constitutional Developments in the Gold Coast and Nigeria' (C (53) 154). Lyttelton to Cabinet, 13 May 1953. PREM 11/1367 (Rathbone, *Ghana*, II, 131).

118. T. Lloyd to J. Macpherson (Nigeria), 5 March 1953. CO 554/254 (Rathbone, *Ghana*, II, 123).

119. Cohen to A. Gaitskell, 31 August 1955. Cohen papers, quoted in Robinson, 'Andrew Cohen and the Transfer of Power', p. 62f.

120. Minute, by Gorell Barnes, 5 February 1953. CO 554/254, quoted in Porter and Stockwell, *British Imperial Policy*, II, p. 197.

121. J. Macpherson (Nigeria) to Colonial Secretary, 16 March 1953. CO 554/254 (Porter and Stockwell, *British Imperial Policy*, II, 22); J. Macpherson to T. Lloyd, 18 January 1952. CO 544/298 (Goldsworthy, *Conservative Government*, II, 263).

122. T. Lloyd to J. Macpherson (Nigeria), 5 March 1953. CO 554/254 (Rathbone, *Ghana*, II, 123).

123. Memorandum, 'The Africanisation Policy of the West African Governments' by M. Smith, March 1953. CO 554/400 (Rathbone, *Ghana*, II, 126).

124. T. Lloyd to Arden-Clarke, 4 January 1954. CO 554/371, (Rathbone, *Ghana*, II, 147).

125. Arden-Clarke to Gorell Barnes, 4 December 1953. CO 254/371, (Rathbone, *Ghana*, II, 146). These measures included a ban on communist literature, restrictions on passports and visas for locals who wanted to visit communist countries, and a number of expulsions of (alleged) leftists from the CPP.

126. Arden-Clarke to Gorell Barnes, 2 September 1954. CO 554/805 (Rathbone, *Ghana*, II, 153).

127. Despatch Arden-Clarke to Lennox-Boyd, 5 March 1957. CO 554/1162 (Rathbone, *Ghana*, II, 291).

128. Memorandum, 'Notes on the Future of the Gold Coast with Special Reference to External Relations after Independence' by Cumming-Bruce, 19 August 1955. PREM 11/1367 (Rathbone, *Ghana*, II, 181).

129. Memorandum, 'The Gold Coast: Constitutional Developments' (CP (55) 183), Lennox-Boyd to Cabinet, 26 November 1955. PREM 11/1367 (PRO).

130. Cumming-Bruce to Laithwaite, 21 July 1956. DO 35/6178 (Rathbone, *Ghana*, II, 240).

131. CM 64 (56) 2, 11 September 1956. CAB 128/30/2 (Rathbone, *Ghana*, II, 253).

132. Lennox-Boyd to Macmillan, 23 October 1956. CO 554/891 (Rathbone, *Ghana*, II, 262).

133. Galsworthy to Eastwood, 28 January 1957. DO 35/6127 (Rathbone, *Ghana*, II, 282).

134. Home to Macmillan, 29 January 1957. PREM 11/159 (Rathbone, *Ghana*, II, 284) (Macmillan replied: 'I agree'); Lennox-Boyd to Home, 18 July 1956. CO 554/1435 (Goldsworthy, *Conservative Government*, II, 277 introduction).

135. Memorandum, 'The Africanisation Policy of the West African Governments' by M. Smith, March 1953. CO 554/4000 (Rathbone, *Ghana*, II, 126).

136. Minute, by Galsworthy, 23 January 1957. CO 554/994 (Rathbone, *Ghana*, II, 279).

137. Minute, by W. Wilson, 28 June 1954. CO 936/369 (PRO).

138. Home to Lennox-Boyd, 6 December 1956. CO 852/1483 (Goldsworthy, *Conservative Government*, III, 465).

139. Memo, 'Ghana: A Policy for Anglo-Ghanaian Relations', High Commissioner in Ghana to Commonwealth Secretary, 22 November 1960. CO 936/712 (PRO).

140. Lennox-Boyd to Macmillan, 23 October 1956. CO 554/891 (*Rathborne*, II, 262). The debate about whether aid should be granted to independent Commonwealth countries continued over the following years. In the 1960s the necessity of such aid was finally accepted, but British contributions never reached the level set by France for her former colonies.

141. David Goldsworthy, 'Britain and the International Critics of British Colonialism, 1951–56', *Journal of Commonwealth and Comparative Politics*, 29 (1991), p. 20.

142. Notes by Gorell Barnes, January 1952. BARN 3/1 (CC).
143. Hargreaves, *Decolonization in Africa*, p. 78.
144. Robert Shepherd, *Iain Macleod: A Biography* (London: Pimlico, 1995), p. 154.
145. Memorandum (CP (51) 109), Gordon-Walker to Cabinet, 16 April 1951. CAB 129/45 (PRO); memorandum (CP (51) 122), Griffiths and Gordon-Walker to Cabinet, 3 May 1951. CAB 129/45 (PRO).
146. Minute, by G. Baxter and A. Cohen (CP (51) 122, annex 1), 31 March 1951. CAB 129/45 (PRO).
147. Note by Cohen, 18 April 1951. CO 537/7203/7, quoted in Hyam, 'Geopolitical Origins', p. 157; minute by A. Cohen, 12 October 1948. CO 537/3608 (Hyam, *Labour Government*, IV 417).
148. Joint memorandum (C (51) 11), Swinton and Lyttelton to Cabinet, 9 November 1951. CAB 129/48, Goldsworthy (*Conservative Government*, II, 302).
149. Record of governors' meeting held at Entebbe on 18 February 1953. CO 822/338 (Goldsworthy, *Conservative Government*, II, 288 fn. 3). Actually black opinion in Central Africa over the establishment of the Federation was not unanimous: Africans in Northern Rhodesia and Nyasaland were clearly opposed to it, since they feared domination by Southern Rhodesia's whites. In Southern Rhodesia, there was (at least initially) some African support since the CAF was considered preferable to integration into South Africa.
150. Baring (Kenya) to Lyttelton, 29 October 1953. CO 82/599 (Goldsworthy, *Conservative Government*, II, 292).
151. Minute, by Gorell Barnes, 30 September 1952, and minute by Colonial Secretary, n.d. (1952). CO 822/338 (Goldsworthy, *Conservative Government*, II, 286, introduction).
152. Gorell Barnes to J. Macpherson, 20 August 1957. CO 822/1430, quoted in Furedi, 'Creating a Breathing Space', p. 101.
153. E. Twining (Tanganyika) to Gorell Barnes, 12 November 1956. CO 822/912, (Goldsworthy, *Conservative Government*, II, 298); despatch, 'Tanganyika: Review of Political Developments', Twining to Colonial Secretary, 29 May 1957. CAB 134/1556 (PRO).
154. Minute, by Gorell Barnes, 12 September 1956. CO 822/859 (Goldsworthy, *Conservative Government*, II, 299, fn. 3).
155. W. Mathieson to E. Twining (Tanganyika), 28 December 1956 (Goldsworthy, *Conservative Government*, II, 300); minute by H. Bourdillon, 12 December 1956. CO 822/912 (Goldsworthy, *Conservative Government*, II, 299).
156. Note on 'Smaller Colonial Territories' (GEN 518/6/11), Brook for Cabinet committee on Commonwealth Prime Ministers' meeting, 18 June 1956. CAB 130/113 (Goldsworthy, *Conservative Government*, II, 206).
157. Minute, 'Destination of Smaller Territories', H. Bourdillon to T. Lloyd, 31 May 1956. CO 1032/55 (PRO).
158. Memorandum, 'Malta: Outcome of Financial Talks' (CP (56) 169), Lennox-Boyd to Cabinet, 13 July 1956. CAB 129/82 (Goldsworthy, *Conservative Government*, II, 320). Whereas Lennox-Boyd offered £1.5 million over a period of 18 months, Mintoff demanded £6.5 million.
159. Macmillan to Prime Minister, 2 July 1955. FO 800/679 (PRO); CM 29 (54) 6, 15 April 1954. CAB 128/27/1 (Goldsworthy, *Conservative Government*, II, 315).
160. Memorandum, (CP (56) 97), Lennox-Boyd to Cabinet, 14 April 1956. CAB 129/80 (Goldsworthy, *Conservative Government*, II, 356).
161. Memorandum, 'Singapore' (CP (56) 85), Lennox-Boyd to Cabinet, 23 March 1956. CAB 129/80 (Goldsworthy, *Conservative Government*, II, 355); minute by P. Dean, 9 March 1956. FO 371/123212, quoted in Tarling, *The Fall of Imperial Britain*, p. 184.

162. R. Scott to Eden, 23 October 1955. CO 1030, Stockwell (*Malaya*, III, 375).
163. It was only after the People's Action Party (which demanded independence through merger with Malaya) had won the 1959 elections that Britain was willing to consider the end of formal rule. In August 1961 Singapore and Malaya settled upon a merger subject to the inclusion of the Borneo states. The following November a conference brought an Anglo-Malayan agreement: in exchange for the unrestricted use of the Singapore base, Britain agreed to include the Borneo territories in the new federation, thus ensuring the non-Chinese majority sought by the Malayan government. For Britain, the right to use the Singapore base was crucial since it would apparently exclude communists from south-east Asia, and maintain British influence with Australia, New Zealand and the United States. Formal rule was no longer thought to be essential since Malaya was considered sufficiently reliable (contrary to Singapore with its huge Chinese majority). In September 1963 British rule ended and the city state became part of Greater Malaysia.
164. Joint memorandum, 'Cyprus' (C (54) 245), Lyttelton and Selwyn Lloyd to Cabinet, 21 July 1954. CAB 129/69 (PRO).
165. 'Progress Report', Cyprus committee to Cabinet (C (70) 297), 23 September 1954. CAB 129/70 (PRO).
166. On 28 July 1954, Henry Hopkinson, CO Minister of State, declared in the House of Commons that there were certain territories in the Commonwealth which 'owing to their particular circumstances', could never expect to be fully independent (*Hansard* 531, col. 508). This declaration led to fierce attacks by the opposition (in contrast to similar declarations made later about Malta and Aden – an indication that Labour's indignation was mostly due to domestic considerations).
167. Paper, 'Cyprus: Need for Action', FO/CO officials to Ministerial committee on Cyprus (GEN 497/1), 23 June 1955. CAB 130/109 (PRO).
168. Memorandum, Foreign Secretary to Cabinet, 5 April 1955. PREM 11/832 (PRO).
169. Report, 'Facilities Required by HM Forces in Cyprus in Peace and War', JPS to COS (COS 55 (56) 2, annex), 28 May 1956. DEFE 4/87 (Goldsworthy, *Conservative Government*, I, 49).
170. Report, 'United Kingdom Requirements in the Middle East' (DC (56) 17), COS to Cabinet defence committee, 3 July 1956. CAB 131/17 (Goldsworthy, *Conservative Government*, I, 51).
171. Note, 'United Europe', Churchill to Cabinet, 29 November 1951. CAB 129/48 (Goldsworthy, *Conservative Government*, I, 2); Churchill to Brook, 11 April 1953. PREM 11/1726F (PRO).
172. Anthony Eden, *Full Circle* (London: Cassell, 1960), p. 36.
173. Report, 'The Future of Commonwealth Membership' (CCM (54) 1) by official committee on Commonwealth membership, 21 January 1954. CAB 134/786 (PRO).
174. O. Franks (Washington) to W. Strang, 24 March 1950. PREM 8/1220 (PRO).
175. Minute, by P. Rogers, 28 October 1955. CO 1031/1718 (Goldsworthy, *Conservative Government*, II, 340).
176. Minute, by Armstrong, 28 June 1956. T 234/195, quoted in Sabine Lee, 'Staying in the Game? Coming into the Game?', in Richard Aldous and Sabine Lee (eds), *Harold Macmillan and Britain's World Role* (Basingstoke: Macmillan, 1996), footnote 19, p. 146).
177. Catherine R. Schenk, 'The Sterling Area and British Policy Alternatives in the 1950s', *Contemporary Record*, 6, 2 (1992), p. 277. At the Commonwealth Economic Conference held in December 1951, the members of the sterling

area had resolutely set their future on the liberalisation of trade and payments.

178. BoT memorandum, 18 August 1955. CAB 134/1044/12, quoted in Wolfram Kaiser, *Großbritannien und die Europäische Wirtschaftsgemeinschaft 1955–1961: Von Messina nach Canossa* (Berlin: Akademie Verlag, 1996), p. 35.

179. Report on external economic policy, 24 June 1952, and P. Liesching to Otto Clarke, 26 June 1952. DO 35/6488, quoted in Schenk, 'Sterling Area', p. 277.

180. When Amery proposed that Britain should try to obtain all her wheat, tobacco and sugar from non-dollar sources, even if this meant paying rather more than world prices, Churchill rejected the idea as unrealistic: 'I cannot ask for any more sacrifices from our people.' Quoted in John Barnes and David Nicholson (eds), *The Empire at Bay: The Leo Amery Diaries 1929–55* (London: Hutchinson, 1988), p. 1055.

181. Schenk, 'Sterling Area', p. 276.

182. Quoted in Barnes and Nicholson (eds), *Empire at Bay*, p. 1056.

183. Minutes of smaller territories committee, 2 January 1952. DO 35/2217 (PRO).

184. Commonwealth Secretary to Liesching, 16 February 1951. DO 35/2217 (PRO); memorandum, 'Cyprus and the Commonwealth' (CPC (60) 10) by Commonwealth and Colonial Secretaries, 22 April 1960. CAB 134/1559 (PRO).

185. Minute, by W. Morris, 20 November 1952. CO 1032/10 (PRO).

186. CM 93 (52) 4, 6 November 1952. CAB 128/25 (Goldsworthy, *Conservative Government*, II, 258); memorandum 'Membership of the Commonwealth: the Sudan' (C (52) 452), Swinton to Cabinet, 23 December 1952. CAB 129/57 (Goldsworthy, *Conservative Government*, II, 260).

187. Jeffries to Sedgwick, 22 November 1952. CO 1032/10 (PRO).

188. Minute, by Gorell Barnes, 20 November 1952. CO 1032/10 (PRO).

189. CCM 1 (53), 7 May 1953. CAB 134/786 (PRO).

190. Memorandum, 'The Colonial Territories and Commonwealth Membership' (C (53) 122), Commonwealth Secretary to Cabinet, 8 April 1953. CAB 129/60 (PRO).

191. Swinton to P. Liesching, 16 March 1953, and Swinton to Lyttelton, 8 July 1953. DO 35/5056, quoted in Porter and Stockwell, *British Imperial Policy*, II, p. 69f.

192. Minutes of smaller territories committee, 2 January 1952. DO 35/2217 (PRO).

193. Report by CO/CRO working party, 29 March 1951. CO 967/148 (PRO); CRO note of an interdepartmental meeting with the CO, 1 June 1951. DO 35/2218 (PRO).

194. Foster to Sedgwick, 26 February 1953. DO 35/5056 (PRO).

195. CCM 1 (53), 7 May 1953. CAB 134/786 (PRO). The Ministerial committee consisted of Lord Swinton (Commonwealth Secretary), Lord Salisbury (Lord President), Oliver Lyttelton (Colonial Secretary), Walter Monckton (Minister of Labour) and Selwyn Lloyd (FO Minister of State). The official committee consisted of N. Brook (Cabinet Secretary), T. Lloyd (CO), P. Liesching (CRO) and P. Dixon (FO).

196. CCM 2 (53), 23 September 1953. PREM 11/1367 (Rathbone, *Ghana*, II, 144).

197. Watt to J. Bennett, 17 February 1954. CO 1032/50 (PRO).

198. Report, 'The Future of Commonwealth Membership' (CCM (54) 1) by official committee on Commonwealth membership, 21 January 1954. CAB 134/786 (PRO).

199. Brief, 'Commonwealth Membership', Brook to Churchill, 1 December 1954. PREM 11/1726F (PRO).

200. Watt to Bourdillon, 28 June 1956. CO 1032/51 (PRO).
201. J. Garner to P. Liesching, 23 November 1953. DO 121/215 (PRO).
202. CCM 1 (54), 5 July 1954. CAB 134/786 (PRO).
203. T. Lloyd to Colonial Secretary, 3 September 1954. CO 1032/50 (PRO).
204. Draft memorandum, 'Commonwealth Membership' (CCM (54) 8) by Commonwealth Secretary, 21 September 1954. CAB 134/786 (PRO).
205. Memorandum, (CCM (54) 7) by Commonwealth Secretary, 16 June 1954. CAB 134/786 (PRO).
206. Minute, by Lord Salisbury, n.d. (February 1953). DO 35/5056 (Goldsworthy, *Conservative Government*, II, 177).
207. F. Bishop to H. Smedley (CRO), 7 July 1956. DO 35/6176 (Rathbone, *Ghana*, III, 234 introduction).
208. P. Liesching to H. Lintott, 14 March 1957. DO 35/6281 (Stockwell, *Malaya*, III, 445).
209. I. Watt to J. Johnston, 19 February 1957. CO 1030/437 (Stockwell, *Malaya*, III, 444).
210. David Reynolds, *Britannia Overruled: British Policy and World Power in the Twentieth Century* (London: Longman, 1991), p. 193.
211. Minutes of a meeting of Treasury, FO, BoT and CRO officials, 5 January 1949, quoted in Darwin, *Britain and Decolonisation*, p. 129.
212. Quoted in Christopher Andrew, 'L'Empire Britannique et le Commonwealth, facteurs de puissance mondiale de 1938 aux années 1960', in Jean-Claude Allain (ed.), *La Moyenne Puissance au XXe siècle: Recherche d'une définition* (Paris: Institut d'Histoire des conflits contemporains, 1988), pp. 254.
213. Geoffrey Warner, 'Britain and Europe in 1948: the View from the Cabinet', in Becker and Knipping (eds), *Power in Europe?*, p. 35.
214. Memorandum (CP (49) 208), Bevin to Cabinet, 18 October 1949. CAB 129/37 (1) (Hyam, *Labour Government*, II, 152).
215. Note, 'United Europe', Churchill to Cabinet, 29 November 1951. CAB 129/48 (Goldsworthy, *Conservative Government*, I, 2). See also John W. Young, 'Churchill's 'No' to Europe: The 'Rejection' of European Union by Churchill's Post-War Government, 1951–1952', *Historical Journal*, 28 (1985), p. 924.
216. 'Report of a Working Group of Officials on a United Kingdom Initiative in Europe', n.d. (June 1956). PREM 11/2136 (PRO).
217. Quoted in Lee 'Staying in the Game?', p. 135.
218. Treasury memorandum, 25 April 1956. T 234/101, quoted in Kaiser, *Großbritannien und die Europäische Wirtschaftsgemeinschaft*, p. 71.
219. CM 65 (56) 2, 14 September 1956. CAB 128/30 (2) (PRO).
220. Memorandum, 'United Kingdom Commercial Policy' by Chancellor of the Exchequer and President of the Board of Trade, 28 July 1956. CAB 129/82 (PRO).
221. Interim report (CP (56) 191) by officials of FO, Treasury, Board of Trade, Ministry of Agriculture, CRO, CO, Board of Customs and Excise and Bank of England, n.d. (July 1956). CAB 129/82 (Goldsworthy, *Conservative Government*, III, 387).
222. Memorandum, 'Plan G', Macmillan to Cabinet, 11 September 1956. CAB 129/83 (Goldsworthy, *Conservative Government*, III, 389).
223. Note, 'Political Association of the United Kingdom with Europe' (GEN 553/1) by officials, 9 October 1956. CAB 130/120 (PRO).
224. CM 44 (57) 1, 4 June 1957. CAB 128/31 (2) (PRO).
225. Memorandum, 'Plan G and the Commonwealth' (CP (56) 207), Home to Cabinet, 7 September 1956. CAB 129/83 (PRO); note, 'United Kingdom

Commercial Policy' by Lord Privy Seal, 9 August 1956. PREM 11/2136 (PRO).

226. CM 66 (56) 2, 18 September 1956. CAB 128/30 (2) (PRO).
227. Minutes of *ad hoc* group of the economic steering committee, 3 September 1956 (GEN 549/1st). CAB 130/120 (PRO).
228. Macmillan to Selwyn Lloyd, 24 June 1958. PREM 11/2315 (PRO).
229. A. Nutting to Foreign Secretary, 10 January 1956. FO 371/122023 (PRO).
230. Minute, 'Europe', Dodds-Parker to Nutting, 17 January 1956. FO 371/122023 (PRO); Wright to Nutting, 21 January 1956. FO 371/122023 (PRO).
231. Minutes of a meeting of ministers (GEN 551/2nd), 1 October 1956. CAB 130/120 (PRO).
232. FO memorandum, 'Franco-British Union' (GEN 551/2), 22 September 1956. CAB 130/120 (PRO).
233. Memorandum, 'Commonwealth Membership' (GEN 551/4) by Secretary of the Cabinet, 29 September 1956. CAB 130/120 (PRO).
234. Minutes of a meeting of ministers (GEN 551/1st), 24 September 1956. CAB 130/120 (PRO).
235. Correspondence between Treasury and Cabinet Office, 19–20 September 1956. T 234/90, quoted in Gustav Schmidt, 'Die politischen und die sicherheitspolitischen Dimensionen der britischen Europapolitik 1955/56–1963/64', in ditto (ed.), *Großbritannien und Europa – Großbritannien in Europa. Sicherheitsbelange und Wirtschaftfragen in der britischen Europapolitik nach dem Zweiten Weltkrieg* (Bochum: Brockmeyer, 1989), p. 175.
236. L. Amery to Churchill, 14 and 29 April 1949. Churchill papers, 2/44 (CC).
237. G. Cunningham to Chadwick, 17 January 1957. DO 35/5012 (PRO).
238. P. Maitland to Selwyn Lloyd, 27 November 1958. DO 35/7846 (PRO).
239. Minute by H. Rumbold, 28 June 1956. DO 35/5012 (PRO); 'Expanding Commonwealth. The Broad Concept', statement by Expanding Commonwealth Group, n.d. (June 1956). DO 35/5012 (PRO).
240. E. Sykes to R. Tenison (FO), 3 April 1956. DO 35/5012 (PRO).
241. Maudling to Prime Minister, 5 August 1958. PREM 11/2531 (PRO).
242. Report, 'Commonwealth Trade and Economic Conference' (ES (CE) (57) 27 final), sub-committee on Commonwealth trade and economic conference to economic steering committee, 6 January 1958. CAB 134/1841 (PRO).
243. Minute by D. Royee, 29 January 1958. FO 371/135623 (PRO).

— 4 —

The Empire-Commonwealth under the First Macmillan Government

THE INFORMAL EMPIRE

THE SUEZ CRISIS demonstrated how delicate Britain's financial situation had become – and how much Britain depended on US support. But contrary to the argument put forward by some authors, it certainly did not break Britain's 'will to rule'.[1] Macmillan, the new Prime Minister, announced his intention of reducing the nation's overwhelming burden in order to permit economic recovery. He therefore ordered several studies that were to review Britain's overseas commitments. But none of the studies, executed between 1957 and 1959, was able to establish where significant economies could be made. This was due to the fact that an overwhelming majority of policy-makers (including the Prime Minister) considered it vital not to appear weak in order to prevent repercussions on the sterling and Britain's special relationship with the United States, the alleged guarantors of Britain's survival as a Great Power in political and economic terms.

Macmillan as Prime Minister: A New Approach?

Like his predecessors, Macmillan faced the daunting task of revitalising the ailing British economy. The latter had been dealt a further blow by the Suez adventure: credit controls and a loan from the International Monetary Fund (IMF) were needed to cope with the economic aftermath of the crisis.[2] Resolving the country's manifold economic difficulties, Macmillan later wrote, was 'not a subject to be solved by mathematical formulae, or exact calculation. It was like bicycling along a tightrope.'[3] This was not a new insight. Attlee and Eden also strove to find the right balance between reducing the strain on Britain's resources while maintaining confidence in sterling. But Macmillan's task was rendered exceedingly difficult by the move to full convertibility in 1958. Sterling thus became increasingly vulnerable to speculative short-term capital movements. In the late 1950s and early 1960s there was a long-running series of 'runs on the pound'. In response to these crises, the Bank of England was obliged (under the Bretton Woods fixed parity arrangement) to intervene in the currency markets in order to support sterling – with each intervention constituting a drain on the country's gold and foreign currency reserves.

Like his predecessors, Macmillan also believed that a stable currency was the key to many other problems facing the country. In fact he was virtually obsessed with the stability of sterling. He feared that devaluation would destroy sterling's international position, both as a store of value and as a trading currency. One of his prime objectives throughout his premiership therefore was to maintain a strong pound – which, he supposed, depended more on international confidence than on a balanced budget. The Prime Minister was very keen to defend the British currency, but not at the price of austerity at home. Rather than fighting against the inflationary threat to the currency, he concentrated on more abstract issues, such as the projection of British power overseas – despite his earlier attacks on this role.

While he was Chancellor of the Exchequer, Macmillan had warned that Britain was spending a great deal of money to provide defences which were not effective and, in some important respects, 'little more than a facade'.[4] The burden this placed on the national economy was a cause of weakness rather than of strength. In order to strengthen Britain's financial and political position, the government had to nerve itself to 'bold decisions'. Britain's policy, at home and abroad, had to be based upon its real resources. These resources had to be increased by stimulating investment and production at home, and by increasing exports. Defences had to be kept 'in good order', but first of all the country's economic strength had to be renewed. To pursue the former without the latter was 'to chase a will o' the wisp': 'One might as well aim to be happy.'[5] Unless Britain was economically strong, it could not maintain a commanding position in the world.

As Prime Minister, Macmillan therefore seemed poised to achieve what his predecessors had not been willing or able to do: a radical reassessment of the nation's commitments. Talking informally to representatives in the Far East and the Pacific, he likened Britain to 'a great land-owner who, faced with high taxation and heavy death duties, declined to give up the old house even though he had to close some of the wings and cut down some of the trees'.[6] Britain was attempting to do more than it could easily do with the resources at its command. The empire had been acquired in an exceptional period that was not representative of the long perspective of British history: now that Britain had lost its pre-eminence in material strength, it would once more be living by its wits, as it had done in earlier periods of its history. The greatest moments of this history had not been those 'when we have conquered, but when we have led'.[7]

Macmillan seemed determined to restore Britain's position in the world by concentrating on essential commitments and by renewing the alliance with the United States. Like Attlee, he advocated (at least for a brief moment) a major reduction in British forces in the Middle and Far East. He acknowledged that this might involve certain risks for Britain's lines of communications, but argued that there might be other, cheaper, ways of attaining British ends, especially with help from the United States.[8] Once he had moved into 10 Downing Street, Macmillan accordingly set out to mend fences with US President Dwight D. Eisenhower and his Secretary of State, John Foster Dulles. The meeting in Bermuda in March 1957 was a first step, and a few months later Macmillan secured the restoration of full Anglo-American nuclear cooperation (which had ceased in 1946).[9] This allowed Britain to possess its own deterrent without being crippled by excessive research and development costs. The necessity of far-reaching cuts in British overseas commitments thus seemed less urgent – and less desirable: if the United States were to continue to pay particular attention to Britain's views while taking over some of its burden, Britain could not be seen to withdraw too quickly. Macmillan continued the review begun under the Eden administration. But despite his initially rather radical rhetoric, he refrained from taking any decisive measures. This gap between Macmillan's rhetoric and the policy actually implemented was to persist throughout his premiership. Indeed, he seemed, as a matter of principle, afraid of taking clear-cut, far-reaching decisions. His motto often was:

> In this strange new world in which we live there are so many uncertainties and so many conflicting arguments that it would be a bold man who would reach a final conclusion. Indeed, no one but a journalist would attempt it.[10]

Contrary to what is often assumed, there was thus no radical new approach to imperial affairs under Macmillan: accelerated transfers of powers were due to initiatives emanating from the CO rather than from the Prime Minister. And while the British presence overseas was constantly thinned out, no substantial military commitment was completely given up. Macmillan was no 'Little Englander'. What he had in mind was a partial shedding of Britain's burdens. Britain was to rid itself of unnecessary or overly expensive overseas commitments. However, as a matter of fact, not even the Prime Minister had an exact idea of what these dispensable commitments were. Furthermore, he considered it vital that the withdrawal was not to take place precipitously or without securing a succession favourable to British interests.

This gap between words and actions is not surprising if Macmillan's ideas about empire and its importance for Britain are examined more closely. Before becoming Prime Minister, he had shown great interest in imperial affairs, and nothing in his career suggests any willingness on his part to preside over the dismantling of the empire. While he was no imperialist of the Salisbury stamp, any large-scale withdrawal from overseas commitments was definitely not on his agenda. For Macmillan, Britain's economic survival largely depended upon world confidence in sterling, which in its turn depended upon Britain's ability to maintain itself as a Great Power with worldwide commitments. Therefore he condemned any action that would weaken this confidence. For example, when Herbert Morrison announced that there would be no military action against Iran after the appropriation of the Anglo-Iranian Oil Company, Macmillan fumed about this act of 'appeasement': 'I have heard nothing like it from a Foreign Secretary at such a moment. This dirty little cockney guttersnipe has at least revealed himself for what he is.'[11]

Although there was no radical departure from previous politics, Macmillan's premiership differed from that of his predecessors insofar as he authorised several reviews that sought to analyse, firstly, the nature of British interests and objectives, and, secondly, the manners in which these interest could be secured with the nation's reduced means. These reviews attempted not so much to reduce the imperial burden, as to provide the government with arguments as to why existing commitments had to be maintained, and how this could best be achieved with limited resources. The various official reports produced over the years rarely presented any radically new features, and in general confirmed traditional lines of policy. They reflected the inertia of the imperial idea in the official mind, and demonstrated that the informal empire in particular was still believed to have concrete financial, economic and geopolitical advantages for Britain.

The Middle Eastern Review

The joint memorandum of June 1956 had established certain guidelines along which British policy should develop in the future. One result of these guidelines was a new Defence White Paper, published in the spring of 1957. It announced that until 1962 forces were to be run down from 690,000 to 375,000 men, and that national service was to be abandoned. Defence expenditure was to be cut back from 10 per cent of GNP to 7 per cent. At the same time, the government committed itself to the development and maintenance of an independent nuclear deterrent. For the Chancellor of the Exchequer this was not enough. He called for bigger cuts in the defence budget (especially in overseas expenditure) in order to achieve the desperately needed overall surplus. This, he argued, was necessary not only to meet the country's debts and to provide investment, but also to maintain confidence in Britain as the banker of the sterling area.[12] Unless this happened, there was no reasonable chance of holding the present rate. And if the rate had to be abandoned, costs would soar and the value of a defence budget of about the present level might well have to be halved. Alarmed by these arguments, the Prime Minister appointed an official committee that was to consider the possibilities for reducing expenditure in an area where a major part of Britain's overseas defence effort was concentrated, that is, the Middle East.

The committee defined Britain's general objectives in the Middle East as the maintenance of access to oil and communications to the Far East. The free flow of oil especially was said to be essential. Much of the strength of sterling derived from Britain being the chief purveyor of oil to Europe. These objectives implied the continuation of Britain's 'historic policy of preventing the Middle East falling under the control of a hostile or potentially hostile power, which today meant in effect the USSR.'. The main aim should be to build up a vested interest in the transit countries in the continued flow of oil. While Britain (and western Europe) could not afford the interruption of any of these oil communications, neither could it hope to dominate the whole of the Middle East.[13] Refraining from doing so was particularly important in the context of the aftermath of the Suez crisis, which strained Anglo-American relations and triggered Arab hostility. The United States had agreed that the Western connection with the Middle East should be maintained, and that the Soviet Union had to be kept out. But the members of the committee believed that circumstances had made certain methods of doing this out of date. They were therefore interested in finding new formulae and techniques for the future.[14] In particular, they wanted Britain's relations with all Middle Eastern countries to be visibly based on independence and mutual respect, 'free from what our enemies call "colonialism" and "imperialism"'. This meant that political relationships should be formulated wherever possible in terms of treaties between equals, and an acceptance of neutrality elsewhere.

Another factor making a reorientation necessary was Arab nationalism. While the *presence* of British troops acted both as a stabilising factor and as a deterrent to Nasser, their *use* in actual fighting, even with the consent of the government concerned, would act as a provocation to nationalist opinion.[15] Moreover, pressure from world opinion would more often than not nullify the success British troops gained on the ground. In any case, military action might help to establish a more favourable climate for a short-term political settlement, but would not provide any solution in the long term.[16] Britain should therefore seek to maintain its position by political rather than military means. This meant *inter alia* the expansion of information and British Council work in the wealthier and more developed sheikhdoms, and the extension of economic and technical help to the poorer countries in the region.[17]

While officials argued for a new approach based on non-violence and cooperation, they were as yet not ready to do without the existing commitments in the Middle East – particularly not after a revolt had overthrown Iraq's pro-British monarchy. The new regime posed a direct threat to British interests in the region, especially in Kuwait, where British oil firms had a particularly large stake and where the regime was expected to come under increasing Iraqi pressure. The resulting determination to hold 'what we have' emerged clearly when the Governor of Aden, William Henry Tucker Luce, began to advocate a policy of gradual disengagement.[18] Britain should withdraw over a period of ten years. This was to undermine the growing support for anti-British movements in the area. Military force, or the threat of using it (for which Aden was needed), was no longer necessary or useful to maintain Britain's position in the Persian Gulf. Events at Abadan had shown that, if it came to a confrontation, pure military force was not in itself dissuasive. Policy-makers in London feared that to implement these proposals would have 'very serious' political and military implications. To end the colonial status of Aden would certainly carry some political advantage. But any goodwill gained would not outrun the likely loss of prestige. While it was clear that Britain could not stay on indefinitely, it was dangerous to announce that she would withdraw within ten years:

> If we once get into the state of mind that we shall be out in 10 years, then we are likely in fact to be out in 2 or 3; for, whatever their material interests, even the responsible people are not likely to back us once they think we are on the way out.[19]

The aim should rather be to stay as long as was possible without forfeiting the goodwill of the 'responsible elements'. If the Governor's proposals were accepted, the United Kingdom's ability to use Aden as a base, or even as a staging post, would become dependent on the goodwill of 'what must, in any case, be a weak Arab State inevitably subject to external influence'.[20] While it might be possible to retain defence facilities by treaty, experience showed that the treaty as well as the continued presence of British forces would soon become a source of great embarrassment to any independent government and 'a rallying cry for every political agitator'. Therefore it was considered better not to move – even at the risk of having to use force.[21] Officials thought it essential to retain full and unrestricted use of the military facilities in Aden. Britain had to retain the ability to honour its treaty obligations and to secure its oil supplies.

The committee was adamant that Britain's position in the Middle East was an integral whole, no part of which could be removed without affecting the rest. Withdrawal from any one of the territories for whose protection Britain was responsible would fundamentally weaken the whole system and lead to its collapse – thus totally eliminating British influence from the region. Therefore it was not possible to withdraw protection from Muscat or Oman in order to make some small-scale savings. It would not only affect Britain's prestige, but would also seriously endanger its economic interests.[22] There would be some saving, but this would be far outweighed by the serious effect upon Britain's balance of payments which would necessarily result from a deterioration in the position of the British oil companies. This in turn would react upon British trade. Instead of reducing the amount of money spent in the region, Britain should consider increasing it. Britain was managing to maintain its position on a shoestring, but this was no longer realistic.[23]

The committee was supported by military officials who insisted that they would continue to need a network of airfield facilities, overflying rights and weapon stockpiles to ensure the mobility of the strategic reserve. In order to meet the erosion of facilities in Africa and the progressive extension of the Middle Eastern air barrier, they were planning for longer-range transport aircraft. However, they would not be able to do without staging airfields or overflying rights. It was particularly important to enjoy full and unrestricted use of military facilities in Aden, 'for as far ahead as we can see', to support operations in the Persian Gulf and the Arabian Peninsula.[24] The security of defence facilities under treaty agreements was inadequate. Therefore Aden had to remain under British authority. The colony was 'absolutely crucial' to Britain's position in that part of the world: if it lost its base it would have to adopt 'an extremely costly mobile strategy', for which Britain was not ready.[25]

The advice given by the committee and military planners was thus clearly in favour of maintaining the *status quo*. While more weight should be laid on political and economic measures, Britain's military presence was to be maintained undiminished. The protection of British oil interests and the containment of Soviet encroachment were seen as directly linked to the various commitments in the region. As we will see, this result was far from definitive. The debate on Britain's position in the Middle East continued in other reviews executed over the following years.

The General Policy Review

Early in 1958 the Prime Minister commissioned the General Policy Review: it was to do for all overseas commitments what had been done earlier for the Middle East, i.e. analyse whether they should be maintained at their present levels and consider the alternatives. The review was the first occasion when senior officials started to question seriously the general principle and necessity of overseas commitments, not just their extent. The study group, consisting of FO, CO, CRO, Treasury and BoT officials actually split into two major factions: while all members agreed that it was crucial to remain on good terms with the United States and to ensure the latter's continued involvement in European defence, there was disagreement on how British influence *vis-à-vis* the United States could be best maintained. While one group gave priority to Britain maintaining its worldwide presence supported by the armed forces, the other laid greater emphasis on 'our being good Europeans ... pulling in our horns in the Middle and Far East'.[26] The latter group was led by Roger Makins of the Treasury, a keen Atlanticist and powerful proponent of free trade.[27]

In a preliminary discussion in February 1958 Makins and some other Treasury and BoT officials questioned the assumption that Britain had no alternative to retaining all its overseas commitments. In view of Britain's weak external financial position it was questionable whether overseas commitments really contributed to its well-being and importance. There was no clear link between the strength of sterling and Britain's overseas commitments. The latter might contribute to maintaining international confidence in sterling, but they could also be said to sap the country's economic basis. Other nations, for example, Switzerland and Sweden, had strong currencies without international commitments. The present economic position of Germany was not built on world power either. It might be better to go in with the nascent EEC and to abandon the attempts to synthesise cooperation with Europe on the one hand, and the Commonwealth and the United States on the other. Britain's place on the international scene would be better secured by building up its economic strength rather than by maintaining a worldwide military presence. What should be studied were areas where the government could best take the risk of disengagement from Britain's present commitments.[28]

These proposals met with strong resistance from the FO, the CO and the CRO whose views dominated the resulting report on the 'Position of the United Kingdom in World Affairs'.[29] The report acknowledged that Britain no longer enjoyed its former 'overwhelming strength' in the military, political and economic sectors. Nonetheless, it could still exercise 'a substantial influence in world affairs' – partly because of its position in Europe, partly because of its leadership of the Empire-Commonwealth and because of its special relationship with the United States. The task ahead was to preserve and strengthen the remaining substance. To achieve this, the government had to foster the cohesion of the Commonwealth, further British trading interests, maintain the sterling area and bolster the strength of the pound. In doing this, it was important to keep in mind that Britain's standing, the Commonwealth and the strength of sterling were all interdependent. The Commonwealth was an important link between the independent Afro-Asian countries and the West. It helped accommodate neutralist tendencies, and enhanced Britain's standing, especially in relation to the United States. Its cohesion thus ensured Britain's position as a world power, and bolstered sterling and the sterling area. The sterling area, in its turn, was vital for Britain: if, for any reason, sterling ceased to be a recognised international medium of exchange, the result would be devastating.[30] London would lose its position as a financial centre, the post-war system of multilateral trade could break down, and bilateralism with all its defects would return. All countries would suffer, but the less developed countries would be hit hardest. This would open unwelcome opportunities for the Soviet Union. Therefore it was crucial to inspire confidence abroad by showing that Britain believed in the economic and political value of the sterling area and that it had no intention of winding it up.[31]

The United Kingdom was part of three important groups: the Commonwealth, the 'Anglo-American nexus' and Europe. Giving priority to the last of these was impossible. Britain could not abandon the Commonwealth or its special relationship with the United States and still hope to maintain its worldwide trading position and the international status of sterling. The Commonwealth connection made Britain 'indispensable' to the United States – and without the United States, Britain's decline was inevitable. It must not therefore abandon its position as a power with worldwide interests, even if it could no longer hope to enjoy the imperial power it exercised in the nineteenth century – the gunboat had to be replaced by other, more appropriate and subtle means.[32] Enlarging the country's economic strength was essential to secure greater flexibility and room for manoeuvre. But revitalising the economy was impossible without an international belief in Britain's strength and standing – therefore disengagement was not advisable. Some small savings might be achieved by granting independence to a couple of territories, but it was not advisable to do so. Some colonies were a considerable drain on national resources, others had no strategic or economic value for Britain. But premature withdrawal from any of them would leave 'an undesirable vacuum' and lead to a general sense of instability in other colonies as well.

Both geography and history made it impossible for Britain to emulate the 'neutrality and comparative isolation of Sweden and Switzerland'. Disengagement would injure Britain's prestige unless it could achieve 'correct timing' and a transfer to acceptable partners, like India. Any reduction of overseas commitments based on domestic rather than local or international reasons would lead the Dominions to believe that Britain was no longer a power they could reckon with. Britain was already running down its overseas commitments as fast as circumstances safely allowed. But to do this wholesale would undermine the position of sterling and the sterling area. If the government had to make cuts in spending, these should be undertaken at home. The needs of foreign policy could not be subordinated totally to the need to build up reserves.

Britain's international position was bound to become increasingly expensive, and modifications had to be made. But to relinquish that position over-hastily would damage the country's future prospects, including its balance of payments and its reserves.[33] Britain had to achieve a larger surplus in overseas earnings. This surplus could partly be achieved by reductions in military expenditure. However, since this involved a loss of prestige, Britain had to intensify its foreign expenditure on aid and assistance. Otherwise it ran the risk of weakening its position in world affairs, thus making it even harder to maintain the strength of sterling. The Treasury was right in arguing that, if sterling weakened, the United Kingdom would not be able to maintain its present commitments either at home or overseas, and that savings had to be made to prevent this.[34] The big question was *where* these savings were to be made. Financial and foreign policies were interdependent and could not be treated separately. Ministers had the choice between making cuts in 'unproductive home expenditure' or causing severe damage to Britain's international position. Foreign confidence in sterling was of basic importance to Britain's economic aims. Equally important, however, was foreign confidence in her future as a power with worldwide influence and interests. Britain could not fulfil its tasks on its own. But it could not expect US cooperation unless it showed itself willing and able to contribute 'something, however small', to the costs of defending Western interests.

When ministers discussed the report, there was general agreement with its conclusions. Britain's military commitments should be gradually reduced, but some 'limited further expenditure', for example, in support of the Baghdad Pact or aid to the Horn of Africa, could be justified by the importance of safeguarding the very large financial interests at stake. Many friendly governments were clamouring for help. There were big dividends to be won at little cost by a 'modest but rightly directed response'. If Britain failed to respond, it risked being eclipsed as a Great Power. Because of budget cutbacks, the government had already been obliged to reject a substantial number of requests for assistance of all kind.[35] Ministers thought that as a result Britain had lost many opportunities for maintaining and extending its influence. Some countries were beginning to look to the Soviet Union or China. This was a dangerous trend. Friendly countries could be helped both effectively and cheaply by assistance in military training, but also by cultural measures. For example, it was proposed that officials should study the possibility of an expanded programme for the teaching of English overseas.[36]

The Future Policy Report

After the completion of the General Policy Review, official attention concentrated on the future of the colonies in East and Central Africa. This debate will be analysed later. Here we will continue our examination of the general discussion on the informal empire. This discussion revived in June 1959 when Macmillan called for a further study of the objectives, during the next decade, of Britain's foreign, colonial and strategic policies. Officials were to make a comprehensive review of overseas policy that was to show the best way of using the country's shrinking resources. The study was to provide an elaborate analysis of the nation's means, and the resources and probable intentions of other countries. Future policy was to be deduced from and follow the implications of this preliminary analysis. Officials were to consider to what extent Britain's interests in Africa, the Middle and the Far East should be reassessed, and by what means they could be best protected.[37] They were also to advise on the form of British commitment in these areas, and the degree to which conventional forms of control (through bases and formal rule) might be replaced by other means, for example, by making British commitments a collective interest (and responsibility) of the West as a whole.

As in 1958, there were some officials who criticised the outline of the review. This time they were to be found not only in the Treasury, but also in the CO. In order to be useful, these officials argued, the review should start from the very beginning and 'not somewhere along the road'.[38] Without a preliminary statement of Britain's general strategy, the study was bound to lack cogency: policy assumptions were bound to creep into the analysis and colour the implications to be drawn. This might lead to a policy which seemingly derived from an objective recital of facts, but in fact sprang from relatively unexamined policy assumptions which governed the choice and the presentation of the facts themselves. The papers prepared hitherto contained no clear statement, but only 'shirking platitudes' of what the objectives of a British government should be. It was possible that Britain had a much greater interest in the maintenance of the strength of sterling and the economic development of the Commonwealth than in meeting its present military commitments.[39] United Kingdom funds should be used to foster economic development: this would create assets of lasting value, help raise the standard of living of the colonial peoples and encourage the growth of world trade. As a result, there would be 'an appreciable economic gain of a direct nature' to the United Kingdom. The Ministry of Defence should think more carefully about the order of priority of Britain's commitments and in some cases about the actual nature of those commitments over the next ten years. Over-flying and staging rights in foreign countries could only be used effectively as long as British policies were not offensive to the countries concerned. Many policy-makers seemed not to understand this. They indulged in wishful thinking about the importance of these rights. Another shortcoming of traditional policy was the fixation on the special relationship. The alliance with the United States was important, but the FO tended to pamper it to such a degree as to neglect Britain's relations with others. Policy-makers should not forget that in any alliance one was the leader and the other the led. In the case of the special relationship Britain was quite manifestly not the leader. This pointed to

the desirability of not putting all our eggs in one basket; the more other groups we are happily involved with, the less wholly dependent we are on the United States and the more they must pay attention to what we have to say.[40]

These criticisms were but faintly reflected in the Future Policy Report which mainly represented FO, CRO and MoD views. The report stated that Britain's resources did not lie in material assets, but were rather to be found in its leadership of the Commonwealth, its special relationship with the United States, its European trade traditions, the 'legacy' of its imperial past and the reputation of its 'political and technical experts with influence in and knowledge of the world outside Europe'. All these factors provided invisible support for Britain's claim to a position amongst the leading powers.[41] The colonies played only a secondary role in Britain's economic well-being and its political importance. Some colonies were even a commercial and military liability, but had to be maintained on political and humanitarian grounds.[42] According to the report, Britain's physical security and economic well-being depended to a large extent on its international standing, and this in its turn depended on its links with the Commonwealth, the sterling area and the United States.

The special relationship was the most important source of power: Britain's status in the world depended increasingly upon the United States's readiness to treat it as its closest ally. It would be more ready to do this if Britain played its full part in international groups to which it belonged. As for sterling, it was Britain's 'first economic responsibility, and the necessary condition for maintaining our place in the world' to keep its currency strong. This meant keeping commitments within resources. In order to make the most effective contribution to the defence of British interests and of the free world, the government had to strike a balance between the risks of doing too little and of doing too much. In the first case it risked being eclipsed as the United States's privileged partner; in the second, it risked undermining its international influence and authority by a further series of sterling crises. There were occasions on which it would be more dangerous to refrain from spending than to spend. But the government had constantly to watch the state of the external financial position and the course of the balance of payments. These were likely to forbid any ambitious expansion of overseas or domestic spending.

The report went on to discuss possible courses for the future. At present Britain sustained a proportionately greater effort than others in the field of defence and international aid; therefore its balance of payments was suffering. It was important that 'a better parity of effort' be brought about. Britain's interests were 'inextricably linked' with those of the free world as a whole, and it could not defend them by itself. In the Middle East and North Africa, the general interests of the West were the containment of the Soviet Union, the fullest possible freedom of trade and movement, and the maintenance of peace and order. Britain should aim to win the support of its allies in achieving these objectives. Of special interest to the United Kingdom was the control of oil sources by British companies (especially in Kuwait), with consequential profits to the metropole. In order to secure this, Britain had to honour its treaty obligations towards local rulers and preserve its base in Aden. In sub-Saharan Africa the general interest of the West was to exclude Sino-Soviet infiltration, to keep local governments 'on our side', and to maintain access to raw materials. A prerequisite to this was the establishment of free societies throughout Africa. This included both the orderly progress towards independence of purely African colonies and a solution to the problem of multi-racial communities. The CO's insistence that time was needed to allow integrated societies to develop could lead to difficulties with 'impatient African nationalists'. This in its turn might lead to a conflict with the general interest of ensuring that the newly independent states retained their Western ties, or at least, remained benevolently neutral. This was a danger which Britain should avoid at all costs.

The government should increasingly think in terms of interdependence rather than individual effort. But it was unlikely that substantial economies could be made without undertaking a radical revision of the means by which Britain protected its interests. Even if a particular commitment was dropped, this would not necessarily lead to a reduction of one or other of the services. The size and organisation of the services was not directly related to the sum of particular commitments. Any partial withdrawal would allow only a small reduction. There was no direct relationship between particular commitments and the theoretical cost of maintaining them.[43] In any case, changes had to be made gradually. Suddenly to abandon any of Britain's commitments would start a chain reaction that would be impossible to stop. Furthermore, any such move would have to be co-ordinated with the United Kingdom's allies. Most (if not all) commitments could only be abandoned safely if they were taken over by another friendly power. The United Kingdom was 'much too important a part of the free world' to be able to retreat into a passive role like Sweden or Switzerland.

According to official opinion, there was no way of pin-pointing specific commitments outside Europe which could safely be shed. If the government were free to decide whether or not to station troops in the Middle and Far East, it might conclude that the balance of advantage was against doing so. However, as 'a legacy of our own history', British troops were already stationed in these areas. Their abrupt withdrawal would seriously affect Britain's position as a world power, weaken the West and provoke widespread instability. Any alteration in the military concept such as the development of self-sufficient sea-borne forces would be extremely costly. The United Kingdom should therefore maintain forces in Aden and Singapore so long as it could rely upon the cooperation of the locals. At the same time, it should discuss with the United States and principal members of the Commonwealth the means by which general Western interests defended by Britain could be more widely shared.[44] While the report thus struck a somewhat more prudent note than the General Policy Review, it was still in line with the principles laid down in earlier papers. There was to be no hasty reduction of overseas commitments, but only a slow scaling-down to avoid damage to Britain's international standing and the stability of sterling.

The Chancellor of the Exchequer thought the report was too optimistic: Britain could not continue to carry its present commitments, even with the help of its friends and allies.[45] But despite his objections, most ministers agreed with the conclusions drawn by the report. By the end of the 1950s, most policy-makers were still convinced that Britain had to maintain a worldwide military presence – and that it possessed the means to do so. As in the past, overseas commitments were considered an essential ingredient of Great Power status and a vital contribution to the strength of sterling. The burden was increasingly to be shared with the United States and other allies, although the United Kingdom still had to carry the major part of it. What became evident during the discussions was the CO's growing isolation within Whitehall. Not only were the colonies no longer regarded as military or economic assets, they were also considered an embarrassment on the international scene. According to many officials, as well as a growing number of ministers, Britain would gain rather than lose by granting independence (above all in Africa, less so in the fortress territories) as soon as possible. As will be seen, this stance did not fail to have repercussions on colonial policy.

Conclusion

In the early 1950s, Macmillan called on the government to base Britain's policy overseas on the country's real resources. Unprofitable commitments should be shed in order to strengthen sterling and the domestic economy. However, once he had become Prime Minister Macmillan did little to put this into practice: he considered it more important to repair the special relationship. Maintaining far-flung commitments was to convince the United States that Britain was still a worthy partner. Like his predecessors, he was convinced that the country's economic strength, the stability of sterling and the special relationship were all interdependent. Therefore he was reluctant to give up any part of the informal empire if there was no cogent reason for doing so.

As the various reviews executed under his first premiership demonstrate, Macmillan's reasoning was shared by most other policy-makers. The first of these studies, the Middle Eastern Review, concluded that it was necessary to prevent the Middle East from falling under the control of a hostile power. However, the means to control it should be political rather than military. But while officials were in favour of an approach based on cooperation with nationalist forces, they did not consider it feasible for Britain to maintain its position without troops and bases in the region. Fixing a date for withdrawal from Aden or any other commitment would make it impossible to remain in control of the situation. Britain's commitments were interdependent. To abandon any one of them would start an erosion of Britain's prestige and standing which would be impossible to stop. Rather than reduce the amount of money spent in the region, the government should increase it.

The same attitude prevailed in the General Policy Review of early 1958. Some officials argued that Britain's economic and political strength would be increased by withdrawal, not by a stubborn de-fence of inherited positions. But a majority of policy-makers thought that to abandon any of Britain's far-flung commitments would entail an enormous loss of prestige. It would lead the United States as well as the Dominions to conclude that Britain was a power they no longer needed to reckon with. These conclusions were repeated in the Future Policy Report. Despite some dissenting voices a majority of officials still thought that Britain was much too important to retreat into a passive role. If it attempted to do so, the United States would immediately withdraw its support. This would have fatal consequences for sterling and Britain's standing on the international scene. On the other hand, it was important not to overstrain national resources and trigger another sterling crisis and possible devaluation. Britain's allies should carry a larger part of the burden. Some military commitments could possibly be reduced. But none of those in the Middle or Far East could be abandoned without doing considerable harm to Britain's economic, strategic and diplomatic interests. This verdict was accepted by most ministers. They still considered overseas commitments an essential ingredient of Great Power status, and did not think it feasible for Britain to be without its informal empire.

THE FORMAL EMPIRE

During his first premiership, Macmillan also called for a review of colonial policy. The Central African emergency, the row over the death of detainees in Kenya and developments in the Belgian and French empires heightened the Prime Minister's awareness of the urgent need to find a solution to the outstanding colonial problems. He was not ready, though, to abandon white minorities in Africa or to confront the right wing of the Conservative Party. Despite the resolution of the Cyprus problem, Macmillan's first premiership was marked by continuity rather than any new approach. Contrary to the assumption made by Robert Holland, Macmillan's call for a cost–benefit analysis of the colonies was not due to any financial concerns about Britain becoming 'the milch-cow for the grant needs of underdeveloped economies';[46] the Prime Minister worried about the country's financial situation, but considered the colonies more of a political problem (which it was not possible to shed immediately) than a financial liability.

The Colonial Policy Review

The attempt to review Britain's manifold commitments was not limited to the informal empire. In January 1957 Macmillan invited the CO, the CRO, the FO, the Treasury and the Board of Trade to submit an estimate of the probable course of constitutional development in the colonies over the years ahead.[47] They were to deal with three points. First, they were to inform ministers which territories were likely to become ripe for independence over the next few years – or, even if they were not ready for it, would demand it so insistently that their claims could not be denied – and at what date that stage was likely to be reached. Second, they were to distinguish those colonies which would qualify for full Commonwealth membership, and indicate what constitutional future there was for the others, i.e. find a solution for the problem of the smaller territories. Finally, they were to draw up 'something like a profit and loss account' for each colony, so that the government was better able 'to gauge whether, from the financial and economic point of view, we are likely to gain or to lose by its departure'. Each territory's economic and financial importance was to be weighed against the political and strategic considerations involved and an attempt made to estimate the balance of advantage by taking all four factors into account, of losing or keeping each particular territory. There were presumably places, Macmillan mused, where it was in Britain's vital interest to maintain formal rule, and others where there was no such interest in resisting constitutional change. The report was to establish which territory belonged in which category.

According to Norman Brook, the whole purpose of the 'profit and loss' exercise was to enable ministers to know more about the relevant strategic, economic, financial and political factors when discussing constitutional developments in any particular territory.[48] He emphasised that the aim was *not* to 'write off' any of the colonies in order to save money. Nonetheless, many CO officials remained suspicious about the real purpose of the study. They suspected that a re-appraisal of the value of the colonies was one of the Prime Minister's objectives, leading him to withdraw from certain territories because they were no economic or strategic asset. Was this what Macmillan had in mind? According to Robert Holland (see p. 175 above), Macmillan's call for a cost–benefit analysis of the colonies was due to his fear of Britain's having to subsidise its dependencies for decades to come. Certainly, the Prime Minister was eager to lessen the strain on national resources, but his call for a cost–benefit analysis does not reveal any radical new approach. Contrary to what officials feared, Macmillan did not order the review in order to 'write off' some colonies. Rather he wanted to know where it would be advantageous to *delay* constitutional advance.

The Prime Minister was particularly worried about sterling balances. He feared that their sudden withdrawal by newly independent countries might make it impossible for the government to reach a stable balance of payments and to build up resources. The review was to ensure ministers knew the risks inherent in any transfer of power, allowing them to opt for a delay wherever this seemed in Britain's interest.[49] Apart from the sterling balances, Macmillan's readiness to end formal rule was conditional on several factors which had already been established by his predecessors: Britain's vital strategic interests were to remain secure, either through the retention of bases and enclaves, or the conclusion of defence agreements. In addition, there should be no strong external threat which might endanger the new states' independence. The withdrawal of formal rule was not to have negative consequences for Britain's standing and prestige: the transfer of power was not to appear as a scuttle, but as the result of a British initiative. And, finally, no substantial European minorities were to find themselves under indigenous rule without substantial safeguards for their privileged position. Whereas formal rule over West Africa or Cyprus was therefore dispensable provided the local nationalists proved cooperative, rapid withdrawal from East and Central Africa or the Middle East was definitely not on the agenda.

The official committee on colonial policy considered each territory under four main headings:[50] (1) After an assessment of the local political situation, officials made an estimate of the territory's strategic importance as well as of HMG's requirements. (2) This was followed by an estimate of the extent to which the retention of these strategic requirements depended upon formal rule. (3) The same procedure was applied to economic interests. (4) Under the headings 'obligations and repercussions' officials made an estimate of the effect that the end of British rule would have upon the political, economic and social development of the territory, including the effect upon racial and tribal minorities. They also considered the repercussions on British prestige and influence, and whether a 'premature withdrawal' would leave a vacuum which could be filled by a hostile country. The list of points officials took into consideration was much more comprehensive than that drawn up by Macmillan. Whereas the Prime Minister had called for a consideration of the costs and benefits to *Britain*, the committee's report on 'Future Constitutional Development in the Colonies' pondered extensively on the repercussions for the colonies themselves and continuously pointed to the dangers of any 'premature' withdrawal – an indication of the lingering doubts as to the true motives of Macmillan's call for a cost–benefit analysis.[51] The paper continuously pointed out that Britain would lose rather than gain by a premature transfer of power.

The report began by outlining those colonies likely to obtain independence within the next ten years. Officials expected Nigeria to become independent in 1960 or 1961, the West Indian Federation in 1963 and the Central African Federation (CAF) some time after 1960.[52] Formal rule over Singapore might also be ended within a decade, provided it joined the Federation of Malaya. Gambia, Gibraltar and Mauritius were not scheduled ever to reach independence, but contrary to other smaller territories, they would at least be allowed to control their internal affairs. In Aden British sovereignty was to be retained for the time being because its removal would greatly diminish Britain's prestige in the Middle East and render military operations in the area impossible. Cyprus, Kenya, Sierra Leone, Somaliland, Tanganyika and Uganda were not expected to reach internal self-government in the following decade. In these colonies, Britain had either a negative strategic interest, i.e. to deny the territory to a hostile power, or a moral obligation which made it necessary to maintain formal rule. In Uganda there would almost certainly be African pressure for rapid advance. But the territory had not yet acquired the 'skill in government' which would justify the United Kingdom relinquishing its authority. Britain would therefore be obliged to maintain formal rule in the face of opposition and criticism. The same applied to the CAF. There, pressure from the Europeans for early independence and pressure from the Africans in Northern Rhodesia and Nyasaland for their secession as African states outside the Federation would have to be resisted until the 'climate' of opinion had changed, and at any rate until 1960 – the date at which the Federation's constitution would be reviewed.[53] Self-government in Kenya and Tanganyika would come at some vague date in the future, presumably in the 1980s. In the other territories, there were 'no discernible signs' of pressure for a significant political advance within the next decade. They would probably be satisfied with the limited rights Britain intended to bestow on them.

The report went on to discuss the economic, strategic and political importance of the colonies to Britain and whether it was feasible – and desirable – to transfer power earlier than planned. It concluded that economic considerations tended to be 'evenly matched', and that Britain's interests were unlikely in themselves to be decisive in determining whether or not a territory should become independent.[54] Any premature withdrawal would seriously affect British trading and financial interests, but assuming an orderly transfer of power, independence would not necessarily affect the United Kingdom's trading position. British producers did not enjoy any formal advantages in the colonies, save to the extent that they benefited from imperial preferences. The preferences would not necessarily be affected by independence, provided the territory concerned remained a member of the Commonwealth (otherwise the preferences would have to be given up in favour of most-favoured-nation status). British firms undoubtedly enjoyed certain intangible advantages which might diminish after independence. However, even if the transfer of power did lead to the loss of an established market for British goods – as could be said to have happened with India – British traders could find 'other and perhaps more valuable markets' if they made sufficient effort. In any case the dangers to Britain in deferring independence for its own selfish interests would be far greater than any dangers resulting from a transfer of power negotiated in an atmosphere of goodwill.

For the authors of the report, a more relevant factor in considering the consequences of independence was the financial aspect, i.e. the question of whether the territory would stay in the sterling area. The chief danger was that a country would wish to convert its sterling balances into dollars. This would be 'a serious threat' to sterling. In the past, the colonies as a whole had contributed to the strength of the sterling area.[55] If any territory decided to leave, the consequences for the United Kingdom and the rest of the sterling area could be serious. A premature grant of independence, resulting in a serious deterioration in political and economic conditions, might easily cause a serious loss to the sterling area's dollar reserves. But postponement and any nationalist discontent resulting from it were even more likely to lead to an abandonment of sterling area connections. It was important to maintain the right balance between transferring power when a colony was ready for it and not waiting too long once it had reached that stage so as not to lose its goodwill.

The committee also discussed whether an early transfer of power would allow any significant savings. The cost of the colonies in terms of expenditure was put at about £51 million per annum. The further the process of ending colonial rule went, the greater therefore would be the reduction of the burden on the Exchequer. But the committee pointed out that the net saving of decolonisation would almost certainly be 'considerably less' than generally imagined. In general, the territories that were nearest independence tended to be least in need of Exchequer assistance. And if Britain granted independence before the territory concerned could hold its own financially, there were likely to be special reasons for this decision – reasons which would also lead the government to continue financial support after independence. Thus the Federation of Malaya would continue to need, and had been promised, considerable financial assistance in connection with the emergency.[56] It was clear that a grant of independence would not automatically reduce the strain on British resources – while withdrawal from a territory which was not yet economically viable would only lead to its subsequent collapse. The losses caused by such a development would far outweigh the savings.

The committee concluded that economic and financial considerations were fairly evenly balanced and unlikely to influence the timing of independence. The advantages colonial rule bestowed on the United Kingdom were relatively slight and largely outweighed by the financial burden it imposed on the metropole. Any premature end to formal rule would above all be to the detriment of the colonies themselves, not of Britain. While economic and financial considerations were thus discarded as secondary, political and strategic arguments led the committee to advise firmly against any premature withdrawal. Not only would it hurt the territories themselves, but it would also jeopardise Britain's strategic position as well as its international standing. The colonies made an essential contribution to the facilities required to maintain and control the United Kingdom's worldwide sea, air and wireless communications. In certain areas they also provided bases where forces could be stationed in support of

British interests. Any premature withdrawal of British authority would add to the 'areas of stress and discontent in the world', and deprive Britain of strategic assets. Even territories such as St Helena or British Guiana might, despite their low importance in the British defence system, became problematic were they to be integrated into the strategic system of the Soviet Union.[57] In many territories it was only British administration that allowed the peaceful co-existence of peoples of different racial or tribal loyalties. The United Kingdom bore 'some past responsibility' for encouraging the immigration of non-indigenous peoples. Therefore its present responsibility was to guide the races towards tolerance and cooperation. This was a slow process. Conditions in East Africa in particular were such that it would be irresponsible to remove control before the advance to self-government and multi-racialism had been carried 'well beyond the present stage'.[58]

Even in territories without racial problems British rule was still needed. There were some territories over which jurisdiction might be surrendered precipitately without prejudice to essential interests and at some modest savings to the Exchequer. But it was doubtful whether Britain would stand to gain by thus rewarding 'loyalty to the Crown': it had been too long connected with its colonial possessions to sever ties abruptly without creating a 'discreditable and dangerous' bewilderment. It was important not to be earmarked as a reactionary colonial power. But it was equally important to avoid the impression of betraying loyal supporters of the British connection.[59] These general arguments were followed by a detailed analysis of each territory. The conclusion of these country surveys inevitably was that colonial rule was vital as well as beneficial for the colonies, and that a premature withdrawal of metropolitan control would be detrimental to both colonial and British interests.

Although the report had been drafted by a joint committee, it represented to a large extent the CO's view of decolonisation. In the Colonial Office the resistance against 'precipitate' withdrawal was strongest. Other policy-makers, especially in the FO, began to have second thoughts about the advisability of maintaining formal rule (at least in Africa). But the CO continued to underline its importance and to proclaim Britain's responsibility and commitment to its colonies. It believed that Britain should continue to promote self-government within the Commonwealth, in conditions of political stability, rising standards of living and freedom for the individual.[60] The colonies should be taught gradually to stand on their own feet. To continue traditional policy was not only 'a moral obligation', it was also in Britain's interest. Independence, the CO argued repeatedly, had to be conceded sooner or later. But the problems of different territories varied widely. Although there had to be progress everywhere, it could not take place at a uniform rate. In each case, the government had to find a middle way between moving too fast (a course which was likely to lead to chaos and anarchy) or too slowly, thus driving local leaders into the arms of the Soviet Union.[61] For the time being, the CO's verdict was not openly contradicted. By the second half of the 1950s, even parts of the CO had come to believe that, given the scarcity of resources, the government would have to begin 'a deliberate policy of shedding some of our colonial burdens'.[62] However, under Macmillan's first government, this was an exception. Eventually local as well as international developments led slowly to a change of heart, first in other ministries, and finally within the CO itself – an evolution that became evident by 1959.

'Normal' Colonies

The results of the Colonial Policy Review demonstrate that by 1957 relatively little had changed in the attitude of British officials. However, under the surface there were important shifts. While the CO continued to stress the need to wait until the territories were ready for self-government, the FO began to favour a rapid dismantling of the remaining empire in Africa – not because it had 'served its purposes',[63] but because the international mood was increasingly against prolonged colonial rule. For the time being, this dispute was carried on mostly in Whitehall and as yet made little impression on the Cabinet. Admittedly the Prime Minister argued that Britain's external policy should 'in principle' be directed to reducing its commitments where this could be done safely; thus its resources could be concentrated on maintaining or strengthening its position in those territories which were more important to it.[64] For example, when it was suggested that Britain 'renounce' smaller territories without any significant value, thus acquiring '*kudos*' for its liberal stance, the Prime Minister thought this an 'extremely good' idea.[65] Lennox-Boyd, on the other hand, argued that concessions should only be made where there was sufficient local de-mand – and where the territories themselves were ready for such a step. A closer look at developments under the first Macmillan government, however, clearly suggests that actual policy followed neither the first nor the second course. The timing of colonial policy continued to depend on a delicate balance of Britain's local and wider interests. In some cases this led to an acceleration of constitutional development, while in others it prevented any significant advance.

Despite his insistence on Britain's responsibility for the colonies and the dangers of any premature withdrawal, Lennox-Boyd did not oppose constitutional advance where it seemed opportune. Whereas (like Macmillan) he tried to slow down advances in East Africa, he advocated bolder steps in other territories, for example, Nigeria. Until the mid-1950s it was argued that the pace set by the Gold Coast was more than Nigeria was able to take.[66] However, officials soon realised that the concessions made to Nkrumah made it difficult (and pointless) to deny similar development elsewhere. In the spring of 1957 the Nigerian parliament demanded independence within two years. Lennox-Boyd agreed, acknowledging that this could lead to an administrative breakdown or the country's disintegration. Although self-government would hardly be good government, it would be impractical to try to govern 'a discontented and possibly rebellious Nigeria': this would present insoluble administrative problems since in the domestic field, the transfer of power had already effectively taken place. Britain might even need substantial military forces.[67] Despite the risks involved, the arguments were therefore clearly in favour of an early transfer of power. A slow pace would lose Britain the goodwill it enjoyed at present and cause much friction. Like the Indians and the people of the Gold Coast, the Nigerians could 'only learn to govern well if allowed to govern badly and to reap the fruits of such misgovernment'.[68]

This view was shared by the Prime Minister. When visiting Nigeria in 1958, he asked the Governor-General whether the locals were fit for self-government. James Robertson replied: 'No, of course not.' They would be ready in 20 or 25 years. Nonetheless, self-government should be granted at once. If the Africans could be persuaded to learn administration within 20 years, it would be better to wait. However, this was unlikely to happen. 'All the most intelligent people' would become rebels and there would be violence, bitterness and hatred. Instead of having 20 years of repression, therefore, the Africans should learn to rule themselves at once. Macmillan thought this advice 'very sensible'. Self-government was to come too soon rather than too late.[69] The other ministers agreed: experience in the other colonies seemed to show that once the decision to hand over to an independent government had been made, it was best to go ahead at top speed. Thus no one could have second thoughts or suggest that Britain was 'giving something grudgingly'.[70] Self-government should be granted, and indeed Nigeria became a fully self-governing member of the Commonwealth in 1960.

During Lennox-Boyd's tenure of the Colonial Office, there was thus no attempt to delay the independence of territories without any strategic importance or white minorities. In Nigeria, the end of formal rule was even advanced considerably, in full agreement with moderate nationalists. Responsible for this were the various factors described in the chapter above on the colonial policies of the Churchill and Eden governments. All of them persisted, but one of them gained particular importance in the late 1950s: anti-colonialism. During Macmillan's first premiership, colonial issues became more of an international problem. The second half of the 1950s saw increased US (and Soviet) interest in African affairs. Suez had strengthened the United States's determination to prevent any further loss of face in Asia or Africa as a result of British or French actions. In November 1956 the US Secretary of State, John Foster Dulles, stated that the United States had for many years been

> walking a tightrope between the effort to maintain our old and valued relations with our British and French allies on the one hand, and on the other trying to assure ourselves of the friendship and understanding of the newly independent countries who have escaped from colonialism.[71]

The United States was determined not to be pushed from that tightrope by the rash actions of the European powers. The United States feared that unless it managed to maintain its leadership in championing the cause of the newly independent countries at the UN, they would turn to the Soviet Union. France and Britain were not to be forced to transfer power immediately. But they were no longer to be allowed to divert world opinion from the real threat, i.e. that originating in the Soviet bloc. This conclusion was reflected in Washington's increasingly hostile public stance towards colonialism.[72] The United States demonstrated clearly that it was interested in getting rid of 'colonialism' which was a welcome propaganda topic for the Soviet bloc.

   Thus by the late 1950s anti-colonialism had become more of an embarrassment to Britain. The heat was now turned on not only from Moscow, but also from Washington. At the same time, the composition of the United Nations General Assembly had changed markedly in favour of the Arab–Asian group and the Soviet bloc. Thus the chances of the colonial powers securing a blocking third in any UN vote diminished more and more. Lord Swinton complained that the United Nations had become 'a log-rolling institution where Asian, African and South American blocs combine to make mischief and draw cash' – and in which the colonial powers were ostracised because of their overseas possessions.[73] Ghana's arrival on the international scene had an especially galvanising effect on the anti-colonial lobby. Rather than moderating the criticism of other countries, the independence of the Gold Coast led to an increase in the attention devoted to colonial affairs in the UN and the Commonwealth.[74] This was actively promoted by Nkrumah. To the dismay of Britain, he became a leading voice in the choir denouncing Britain's status as a colonial power. He gave also strong support to other nationalist movements. In 1958 he convened two international conferences in Accra, the first in April of eight independent African governments, the second in December of radical nationalists from throughout the continent.[75] It became increasingly difficult for Britain to argue that some colonies had to wait much longer than others. Ghana was 'regarded by every African as having set the perfect pattern for constitutional development'.[76] This perception of Ghana as a model country had repercussions throughout Africa. Moreover, the French territories also began their advance towards independence. The 1958 referendum sent a warning shot of what might come in the future, alarming especially the FO.

East and Central Africa: Business as Usual or Preparation for Major Changes?

The attempt to evaluate the importance of the colonies and to develop a coherent policy continued after the various reviews executed in 1957 and 1958. In January 1959 the Africa committee began to examine British interests in the black continent, with special regard to future policy in East and Central Africa.[77] The study was generated by the belief that Africa was likely to be the next object of Soviet subversion. The committee was to clarify the interests of the United Kingdom and the means by which they could best be defended. In the following months, an acrimonious debate developed among British officials. The CO and the FO were at loggerheads over the speed at which independence was to be conceded. While the FO considered the prolongation of colonial rule to favour the spread of communism, the CO still argued (as the FO had done a few years earlier) that British rule was the very factor which prevented these territories from coming under Soviet influence.

Pressing for Change: the FO

By 1959 the FO disagreed openly with the pace of constitutional advance the CO envisaged for East and Central Africa. For the FO, the colonial empire was no longer an asset. Far from boosting Britain's power and prestige, it had become an embarrassment, threatening to make the country appear incapable of adapting to political change. France had indicated its readiness to end formal rule, and a change also seemed imminent in the Belgian Congo. Britain risked being classed as a reactionary colonial power, thus losing many points on the international scene. Its standing would also increasingly be affected by the divergence between the course of events in West Africa on the one hand, and policy in East and Central Africa on the other. Until now, the size of the continent, the poverty of its communications and the 'limited outlook of its peoples' had concealed the fact that Britain pursued a purely African policy in the West and a predominantly European policy in East and, above all, in Central Africa. Now, however, the divergence was widely noticed. Racial discrimination and the dismissal of nationalist demands for more political rights would turn African thoughts towards violence and communism.[78] The transfer of power in the remaining territories should be accelerated, rather than be spread over the next 15–20 years as recommended by the CO. Moreover, the white minorities should not be allowed to monopolise political power.[79]

According to the FO, evidence from foreign territories suggested that the government had to expect a rapidly rising tide of popular demand for self-government. By the end of 1960 virtually all colonies north of the Congo would either enjoy independence or be able to attain it by asking: independence would be 'the fashion'. The five African states that were independent in 1953 would be joined by over 20 others.[80] The inhabitants of Britain's remaining colonies would thus see independence come to neighbouring states which could not by 'any stretch of imagination' be regarded as more experienced politically than they themselves.[81] If these territories achieved independence, however, it would be difficult to offer less to Britain's colonies.[82] Very soon the period of 'British leadership of the advance towards independence of colonial territories' would be over. The tendency in the 1960s (despite Sierra Leone) would be for France and perhaps Belgium to share the position of leaders, Britain being classed – 'however wrongly, given our past record and the difficulties in East and Central Africa' – with Portugal as the main obstacles to further advance.[83] Lagging behind with the Portuguese, however, would create serious difficulties in a wide range of international affairs. The heat of the anti-colonial movement would be turned on to the remaining colonies.[84] The United Nations would take 'a lively and unfriendly interest' in the forcible suppression of popular movements in Africa. The United States might well try to prevent the Africans from looking to the Soviet Union by publicly campaigning for African freedom, especially if disorders on 'anything like the Algerian scale' developed. Britain was faced with a series of difficult and dangerous choices. If it took its hands off immediately, it risked chaos. On the other hand, if it failed to convince the Africans that the period of 'tutelage' was limited, Britain risked creating 'an emotional atmosphere comparable with that of the Middle East'.

The FO underlined that resolving the colonial question in Africa was important for Britain's influence, particularly in the United Nations. Britain's standing in the world community depended to a large extent on its success in handling its colonial problems.[85] If the government failed to maintain a good record, Britain would rapidly lose its influence, whatever other virtues she displayed. But if she *did* maintain a good record, her influence and prestige would increase. However, it was not only Britain's position in the United Nations that was at stake. The new 'battle for Africa' would largely turn on Britain's ability to solve the racial and constitutional problems of East and Central Africa – and on its success in providing economic assistance on terms acceptable to the self-consciousness of 'inexperienced and newly-awakened peoples'.[86] The 'struggle for the soul of Africa' would not be won by force, but by understanding. The strategic objective of the Soviet Union was to bring the continent within the communist system.[87] The Soviet Union would seize every opportunity to establish links with African political movements by supporting demands for an end to colonial rule. Britain had to counter this, if need be by supporting political groupings which fell short of those which would normally be regarded as ideal. Economic or strategic interests might to some extent have to be sacrificed in order to preserve stability. The prime objective had to be the erection of buffer states against 'the southward drive of Nasser and the Russians'.[88]

The FO acknowledged that the future of non-African minorities needed to be safeguarded: they generated much of the wealth of the territories they resided in. But officials thought that it would be impossible to wait as long as envisaged by the CO. Even the Belgians were now moving fairly rapidly towards self-government on the principle of 'one-man-one-vote'. Britain should follow this example. Deferring the independence of the East and Central African territories for 15 to 20 years would undoubtedly be interpreted by the Africans as a last-ditch attempt to perpetuate colonial rule and white supremacy. This would lead to difficulties with 'impatient' African nationalists, thus jeopardizing Britain's general interest of ensuring that the newly independent countries retained their Western ties.[89] In the short term, British (and Western) interests were secured as long as formal rule continued. But in the longer term, they depended upon political advancement that was fast enough to satisfy the Africans.[90] Britain had to move speedily towards independence while taking adequate steps to train future leaders. The aim had to be political stability in order to reduce the openings for communist interference and to establish the right climate for rapid economic advance. Only strong independent states – backed up by Western assistance – could form a 'strong, indigenous barrier' to the subversion of Africa.

In the Foreign Office, formal rule in Africa clearly was no longer considered essential to safeguard Western interests. The white settlers were now seen as an impediment obstructing a good understanding with the black majority. Colonial rule was considered as an obstacle to international relations. Economic, commercial and cultural links, and even a 'genuine emotional bond', were expected to remain intact after the end of formal rule. This would ensure the West a position of strength that could not be undermined easily by the East – provided independence was granted early enough.

Still in Search of Multi-Racialism: the CO and the CRO

Officials in the CO and the CRO acknowledged that Britain had to adapt to changing circumstances, but criticised the FO's 'newly found and perhaps hyper-sensitive African consciousness'.[91] Britain could either repress African demands for more political rights, or force the European settlers to accept the loss of their privileges. Neither of the two was ideal though, and would not lead to permanent peace and stability. As the French example in Algeria showed, it was extremely difficult to impose a multi-racial solution. Acquiescing in full adult suffrage, however, would

> sentence the European and Asian communities in East and Central Africa to dependence on the toleration of Africans in the same way as the less numerous European communities in most countries of Asia have, since 1947, depended on Asian toleration.[92]

This was hardly feasible, though, since the economic and social progress of these territories was essentially based on the Europeans' technical and political know-how, and the capital they contributed or could attract – and the whites would not stay on under African majority rule, at least if it was implemented in the near future. Transferring power without ensuring the continued presence of these minorities would therefore lessen, if not destroy, the territories' economic viability. The problem was to reconcile the Europeans to the idea that there would eventually be African majority governments, while educating the Africans to enable them to participate in political life and to make them realise the importance of the non-African communities. Until all races accepted 'fully and unreservedly the principle of racial equality', there had to be constitutional checks to preserve 'a proper balance'.[93]

The CRO was above all interested in the CAF. Officials warned that the whites would not accept being pressured into accepting African majority rule. If Britain tried to do so, the Federation would break up. At least Southern Rhodesia would drift into the Union's sphere of influence and perhaps amalgamate with it. This would extend Afrikaner racial policies to the Zambesi, damage Britain's international standing and destroy its influence in Africa. If Britain managed to maintain the Federation, however, a multi-racial society might develop in time. By 1964 the whites would still dominate Southern Rhodesia, while Nyasaland's legislature would be controlled by Africans. Black Africans would also make up a substantial part of the legislature of Northern Rhodesia. Five years later the Europeans would still dominate the federal government. But the franchise would have been enlarged, giving the Africans a greater share in power. Thus it might be possible to build up a multi-racial society. According to the CRO, events in neighbouring territories would not precipitate development in Central Africa.[94] If things went badly, they might even serve as a reminder of the beneficial effects of British rule.

These arguments received particular support from the Commonwealth Secretary. According to Lord Home, a predominantly black parliament would not be able to maintain competent administrative standards. Universal suffrage could not be introduced until a sense of responsibility developed that would discourage them from abusing the vast majorities they might control. 'Good government' was a condition for self-government. This meant 'tolerable standards of administration and of justice'. Britain had taken 600 years to achieve 'one-man, one-vote'. No one suggested such a lengthy apprenticeship for Africa; but until all its people were educated enough to accept the rights of minorities and individuals, there had to be qualifications on the vote.[95] Any attempt rapidly to extend majority rule to countries where there were 'strong minorities with what they regard as special interests', would only result in disaster. If Britain permitted the pace of constitutional advance to be set by African nationalist opinion, even in its more moderate forms, administrative chaos was inevitable. Few Africans could hold responsible posts (in Nyasaland there was allegedly no African at all fit for appointment as district officer) and the likely result of premature independence would be 'a reversal to tribalism'.[96]

While the CRO cared above all about Central Africa, the CO focused on East Africa. In the late 1950s, officials still recommended that the region's constitutional advance be extended over 15 to 20 years. At a conference held in October 1957 in Entebbe, it was agreed that Uganda would achieve independence in the early 1970s, followed by Tanganyika in the mid-1970s.[97] Kenya's independence was vaguely envisaged for the early 1980s. The Colonial Secretary even thought it possible to retain enclaves under British sovereignty. He had advised against this in Malaya, but argued that the situation in East Africa was different. However, the main reason for Lennox-Boyd's proposal was not to secure any strategic interests (as the Colonial Secretary claimed), but to reassure the whites that Britain was willing (and able) to intervene on their behalf if need be. For the time being, it seemed as if the CO would be able to remain in control of the timetables – East African nationalism was developing slowly and international interest was not as yet very strong. From 1958 onwards, however, African demands began to be voiced more strongly, undoubtedly encouraged by events in the French empire. Early in 1959 officials in the CO gradually began to realise that the timetables would have to be shortened if they wanted to maintain at least a façade of orderly transition. This insight took some time to set in. In January 1959 Lennox-Boyd presided over a conference at the Prime Minister's official country residence, Chequers, where it was decided that Tanganyika might achieve independence by 1970, Kenya by 1975, and Uganda somewhere between the two.[98]

Despite the still comparatively slow progress envisaged at Chequers, the Governor of Tanganyika concluded soon after his return that the need for rapid constitutional reform was urgent. For a time, Nyerere, leader of the Tanganyika African National Union (TANU), was able to hold off the extreme elements of his party; but the longer he took to bring home the bacon the less authority he could exert.[99] The Colonial Secretary accepted this in principle, but thought it necessary to hold back in order to remain in control of developments in Kenya. On the basis of experience elsewhere, it was evident that once the balance moved in favour of freely elected representatives, rapid progress to internal self-government would be difficult to check. It was unlikely that the state of internal self-government itself could be maintained intact for 'more than a very few years'.[100] Theoretically, Uganda and Tanganyika could become self-governing in the near future, under predominantly, if not wholly, African governments. In the case of Kenya, however, there was no prospect in the foreseeable future of a situation developing which would allow HMG to relinquish control. Once Kenya's neighbours achieved independence, this course would be difficult to maintain. Therefore constitutional development in all the three East African territories had to take place at about the same speed.

According to Lennox-Boyd, Britain had three choices. First, it could prepare a rapid withdrawal, meaning that it would be out of East Africa by 1965.[101] The consequences of such a policy ('quite apart from the probable loss of vital defence interests') were not difficult to imagine. Not only would it make the outbreak of violence in Kenya likely but Britain would also have to hand over power to governments incapable of standing on their own feet. Such a course would create 'a most dangerous political vacuum', which would seriously prejudice Britain's position in Central Africa. Britain's second choice would be to attempt to consolidate, as far as possible, its position and make clear that there was no prospect of it relinquishing control in the foreseeable future. The chief disadvantage of such a policy was that it could only be carried out if the government was prepared and able to hold the area by force, a prospect which could appeal only to 'extreme diehard opinion'. The third option, recommended by Lennox-Boyd, was a 'middle road' policy: over a period of ten years, Tanganyika and Uganda would gradually be prepared for self-government. Kenya would follow, though more slowly than the others. No timetable was to be made public so as to avoid pressure for accelerated change. The result would be a multi-racial society in which Africans, Asians and Europeans enjoyed equal rights, the social and economic position of each group being respected by the others.

In mid-April the Cabinet endorsed Lennox-Boyd's proposals. There was general agreement that the *status quo* in East Africa could not remain unchanged, but also that the United Kingdom should not surrender its responsibilities all of a sudden.[102] Uganda, Tanganyika and Kenya should advance step by step towards self-government. In early 1959 the CO obviously still had enough backing to reject the FO's demands. However, it is interesting to note that in his memorandum, the Colonial Secretary put the strategic interest first and the protection of minorities last. In reality, the CO's priorities had exactly the reverse order. Lennox-Boyd probably realised that his colleagues still backed his policy, but were not ready to run major risks only for the sake of 'kith and kin'. Highlighting the region's wider strategic importance for the Middle East and south-east Asia was to strengthen the CO's case.

On 22 April 1959 Lennox-Boyd stated in parliament that he could not foresee a date at which it would be possible for any British government to surrender 'their ultimate responsibilities for the destinies and well-being of Kenya'.[103] There was to be a constitutional conference, but no African majority in the Kenyan legislature. In his memorandum, the Colonial Secretary had spoken of a period of ten years. None of this was reflected in his statement. Lennox-Boyd and

Governor Evelyn Baring still hoped for the development of a multi-racial society. They placed great hopes in Michael Blundell, a long-standing member of Kenya's legislative council, who had just established the New Kenya Group (NKG) and who it was hoped would be able to build a multi-racial organisation, uniting Europeans, Asians and moderate Africans. Therefore there was no reference to African majority rule or any date for independence, lest it scare off potential European voters of the NKG. In the coming years, the Colonial Secretary and his successors did their best to bolster the prestige of Blundell and his party.[104] Indeed some ideas originally mooted by the CO were made to appear as if they had been proposed by Blundell. The intention was not only to boost the NKG's prestige but also to allay fears within the Conservative Party over the treatment of the Kenyan Europeans. The CO thus appeared to respond to pressure for constitutional advance coming from the settlers, not the Africans.

'The Next Ten Years in Africa'

In June 1959 the Africa committee presented its report titled, 'The Next Ten Years in Africa'.[105] The paper pretended to cover the whole of the continent, but the arguments brought forward applied almost exclusively to East and Central Africa – after all, Nigeria and Sierra Leone were already firmly set on the road to independence, and Gambia was considered a smaller territory which could never do without British rule. Although some of the concerns voiced by the FO were integrated, the results were overwhelmingly in favour of the position held by the CO and the CRO (as well as the Ministry of Defence). According to the report, the political objectives of preserving stability and keeping Africa in the Western camp were of primary importance. In comparison, economic and strategic interests were secondary. Moreover, they would be best met if the political objectives were reached. Africa's economic significance lay in its role as the producer of a number of raw materials, many of which could not easily be produced elsewhere. The continent also had a certain value as a market for British goods. Provided the break between metropole and colony occurred amicably, independence would make very little difference to economic relations between the United Kingdom and its African territories.[106] Britain's military interests in Africa consisted principally of the stationing of the strategic reserve in Kenya as well as over-flying and staging rights in other territories. Provided Aden was retained, British requirements for the safeguard of interests in the Persian Gulf and the Far East could be met by other means, although this would be 'extremely expensive'.[107] Last, but not least, there was the safety and welfare of white settlers and other minorities. The government had a particular responsibility to ensure that these people would be able to live in security and to contribute to the development and prosperity of 'their own part of Africa'.

The part dealing with general British interests was followed by a discussion of the question of whether these interests would best be served by the retention of formal rule or by early withdrawal. In accordance with the views predominating in the CO and CRO, the report duly underlined that an early transfer of power was not necessarily the best way of ensuring a pro-Western or politically neutral Africa. The pan-African concept promoted by Ghana, as well as developments in other colonies, had stimulated African demands for more political rights. Too rapid a retreat, however, meant running the risk of transferring power before the locals were able to maintain a stable and viable administration. There was 'as yet no reasonably educated middle class'; withdrawing too quickly would lead to a dangerous vacuum and open the way to anti-Western influences. There was the alternative danger that the whites, particularly in the CAF, would try to declare themselves independent. If, on the other hand, Britain was too intransigent in opposing indigenous aspirations, it ran the risk of being identified with the extreme racial doctrines of South Africa, of exacerbating African hostility towards the European minorities, and of provoking the Africans to turn towards the Soviet Union.

The aim therefore had to be to find a middle course between these two extremes, i.e. to stay long enough to build up an adequately educated middle class, and to promote measures such as the reform of land tenure. Britain had derived substantial credit from its colonial policy in West Africa, and it was important not to lose it by artificially delaying the transfer of power in the rest of the continent. But it also had to secure time to allow the Africans to develop and to foster the gradual evolution of 'the right kind of relationship' between the races. Power should not be transferred precipitately only to gain terrain in the Cold War. Political reform as well as social and economic development were to provide stability and African goodwill while securing the future of the white minorities. Officials were confident that there was still enough time to do so.

Macmillan and Africa in 1959

Macmillan's private secretary for foreign affairs, P. de Zulueta, condescendingly described the report as a not very good paper, which was 'permeated by the unimaginative spirit of colonial administration in decadence'.[108] The Prime Minister, however, liked the paper. In July 1959 he called for a further report on future policy in Africa. The continent would undoubtedly become more important in the next few years and young people of all parties were uneasy about Britain's moral basis. Something had to be done to lift Africa on to 'a more national plane, as a problem to the solution of which we must all contribute, not out of spite ... but by some really imaginative effort'.[109] The Prime Minister gave some rough indications how this was to be achieved: officials should consider how far British policies could be co-ordinated with those of other colonial powers, territorial adjustments included.[110] They should also examine the relative success of the various colonial powers in developing self-sufficient institutions that would be favourably disposed towards the West. More thought should be given to the role of Christianity in keeping the Africans orientated towards Western ideals. Finally, officials should investigate the possibilities of stronger economic cooperation between the colonial powers. Macmillan hoped that cooperation in Africa would help prevent 'the economic division in Europe' which seemed imminent with the creation of the EEC. The ministers' response to Macmillan's minute was mixed. Lennox-Boyd thought it difficult to co-ordinate Britain's policies with those of other colonial powers: it was 'fifty years too late' to indulge in the exercise of adjusting territorial boundaries. Foreign Secretary Selwyn Lloyd welcomed the proposed consultations with other colonial powers, but pointed out that it would not reduce Britain's difficult position on the international scene.[111] In the end, no new report was written. Developments in the colonies soon demonstrated that there was no time to be lost in lengthy debates about the future. However, it is important to ask what suddenly led Macmillan to accord such a high priority to African affairs.

The reason for Macmillan's heightened interest in the black continent was shaped in part by developments in the territories of other colonial powers as well as the rise of international anti-colonialism. In addition there were two particular incidents which undermined Britain's moral position in the colonies. In March 1959 it became known that 11 prisoners in a detention camp in Kenya had died after being beaten by warders. The news led to considerable alarm in parliament, including the Conservative benches, and received wide media coverage. Mau Mau prisoners were a sensitive topic, since earlier reports of mistreatment by the security forces had already led to public alarm in Britain.[112] An enquiry was called for, and a White Paper published in early June. Although Macmillan tried to play down the report's impact in public, he recorded in his diary: 'We are in a real jam.'[113] He feared that the affair might prove 'really difficult as well as politically damaging at home', possibly even leading to a serious split in Cabinet. When the White Paper was discussed in the House of Commons, Lennox-Boyd was severely criticised, even by some Conservative MPs. Enoch Powell attacked the government, arguing that the situation in Kenya was a disaster. Britain could not, 'in Africa of all places', give the impression of acting against the interests of other people.[114] Maintaining colonial rule under present conditions, Powell warned, was detrimental to British interests, especially in the Cold War context. The Colonial Secretary offered his resignation, but Macmillan rejected it – not only because of the repercussions this might have had on the government a short time before the elections, but also because he did not hold Lennox-Boyd responsible for events in Kenya.

The controversy coincided with the publication of an embarrassing report about the situation in Nyasaland. In 1958 there had been the first signs of impending trouble in Central Africa: the African parties of Nyasaland, Northern Rhodesia and Southern Rhodesia announced their intention to boycott the impending elections, preferring to demand self-government outright. At the same time the Southern Rhodesian 'Dominion Party' demanded independence under a white government and threatened a unilateral declaration of independence from both Britain and the CAF. At the beginning of 1959 the leader of Nyasaland's Congress Party, Hastings Banda, proclaimed that civil disobedience would be used to fight against the policies of the federal government. When serious riots broke out in March 1959, Governor Robert Armitage declared a state of emergency. More than 1,320 people were arrested, including Banda and more than 60 members of his party. In the ensuing disturbances, 48 Africans were killed by police. Similar repression followed in Northern Rhodesia, where Kaunda and some colleagues were arrested.

The so-called 'Devlin commission' (after Patrick Devlin) inquired into the circumstances of the emergency and came to the conclusion that Nyasaland was – 'no doubt temporarily' – a police state where it was not safe for anyone to advocate secession from the CAF.[115] There was no African support for membership of the CAF. Nor was there any evidence to support the assertion that Banda and his followers had been plotting 'massacre and assassination'. Britain – like all other colonial powers – had to choose between continuing with 'benevolent despotic rule' or transferring responsibility to the natives.[116] The report, released in July 1959, was highly embarrassing for the government: Macmillan thought it 'dynamite' which might 'well blow this Government out of office'. Having tried in vain to have the 'Fenian' Devlin omit several particularly drastic passages, he urged the Governor to write a refutation of the report.[117]

Macmillan's manoeuvring proved successful. The impact of the Devlin Report was less grave than feared. Nonetheless, it had become clear how dangerous developments in the colonies could become for the home government – and that even in Central Africa constitutional advance could not wait for much longer. In order to 'buy some time', Lord Home recommended sending a commission to review the CAF's constitution.[118] In the present circumstances it was likely that if any hint was given to Nyasaland that it would be possible to secede from the Federation it would take it, and Northern Rhodesia would be compelled to follow suit.[119] In this event Southern Rhodesia would be driven to join South Africa. Therefore it was best to play for time. Macmillan took up the proposal and sent an advisory commission which was to prepare the ground for a review of the CAF constitution. He thus managed to prevent Africa from becoming a controversial issue in the 1959 elections.

Although they did their best to play down Devlin's report, the Prime Minister and his entourage did not consider Armitage's handling of the situation (or that of the Kenya government) inappropriate. Norman Brook, for instance, commented that the need to enforce respect for law and order was 'infinitely greater' in places like Nyasaland, where a handful of white people were controlling 'hordes of primitive people'. If these hordes were once allowed to get out of control 'anything may happen'.[120] Lennox-Boyd fully shared Brook's point of view. Shortly after leaving the CO, he had a meeting with his successor, at which he handed him details of abuses carried out by the security forces in Kenya (which, unlike the Hola Camp events, had been successfully covered up). When Iain Macleod, Secretary of State for the Colonies since October 1959, expressed shock at these revelations, the former Colonial Secretary replied that he did not believe that one could 'apply the canons of a cloister to a battle in tribal Africa'. Moreover, admitting any wrongdoing in public would make the position of the colonial administration impossible.[121]

Macleod certainly did not want to apply the canons of a cloister either, but he feared that events in East and Central Africa threatened the electoral fortunes of the Conservatives: the area remained 'perhaps our most difficult problem' as far as the relationship with 'the vital middle voters' was concerned. The political rights of Africans were the only issue which led to severe criticism of the government's policies. The heart of the colonial problem lay in the multi-racial communities of East and Central Africa. If their problems could be resolved, everything would fall into place.[122] Macleod was not the only one who was worried about events in Africa. Even before the publication of the Devlin Report, there was considerable unease over the CAF within all sections of the Conservative Party. Its 'left' wing was also pleading for a reassessment of Britain's policy in Kenya. The mood of the party began to turn against the preservation of unre-formed colonial rule. The East Africa Sub-Group of the Conservative Commonwealth Council, a body known for its staunch defence of settler interests, made clear its support for accelerated constitutional advance: 'yet another limited constitution', imposed without the agreement of the African elected members, would only increase the risk of a serious breakdown in security.[123] Whilst in late 1959 and early 1960 even traditionalist Tories were apparently willing to accept accelerated constitutional change – not only in Tanganyika and Uganda, but also in Kenya – it was because they had miscalculated the speed with which this would culminate in independence under an African-majority government. But it has to be pointed out that at this moment even Macleod did not think Kenyan (or Tanganyikan) independence was likely to be granted in the near future.

The events in Kenya and Nyasaland as well as the reactions at home and abroad demonstrated two things: first, that the CAF could not be allowed to achieve independence under its present constitution, and second, that the East African territories had to be allowed a considerable measure of political advance. However, this did not mean that the Prime Minister or his entourage expected British rule to be swept aside by a 'wind of change'. Macmillan was not yet in favour of rapid decolonisation. He envisaged gradual change rather than sudden independence. He realised that the Africans had to be allowed some political advance, but not at the expense of the Europeans: 'the cruder concepts', whether of the left or of the right, were wrong. The Africans could not be dominated perma-nently, nor the Europeans be abandoned.[124] If Britain failed to devise a workable multi-racial state, Kenya would collapse into anarchy. Africa might turn out to be no longer 'a source of pride or profit', but 'a mael-strom of trouble into which all of us will be sucked'.

'Unfortunately', Macmillan thought, the Africans had come to consider universal suffrage as an essential ingredient of democracy. Recent discontent in the Gold Coast, however, had given pause to 'thinking men of all races'.[125] Perhaps it was possible to launch a new experiment, enabling 'the advanced & experienced elements in the population to play their part in democratic processes, whilst leaving the interests of backward tribes or individuals to continue for a time to be looked after by official or nominated members'. Britain's policy should be one of gradual constitutional advance. What exactly was to be the result of this advance, and at what time colonial rule would be end, was not stated. Macmillan aimed at 'some genuine system of fair partnership with fair representation of the different elements in an agreed system'[126] – without making clear exactly what this meant. Presumably he himself did not know.

Macmillan's 'genuine system of fair partnership' certainly did not mean African rule on a 'one-man, one-vote' basis, at least not in the foreseeable future. The Prime Minister doubted whether it was necessary (and desirable) for everyone to have a vote. After all, in Britain the franchise had been comparatively narrow until the early twentieth century, and yet people had not complained about this.[127] It did not necessarily matter that all had a vote, 'the important thing was what life people led'. In countries with significant European minorities, there might be advantages in a more indirect form of voting, designed to prevent the complete subjection of minority interests by the majority. If the British practice of a simple majority were to be adopted there would be 'the greatest instability'.[128] One day the black majority would make itself effective. Even then, however, the rights of the whites were to remain inalienable: the rules of the constitution would be imposed from outside, so that they could not be changed by a simple majority vote in the legislative assembly, i.e. any privileges bestowed on the Europeans could not be changed after independence without amending the constitution.

A limited extension of the franchise was to help bring about some form of stability, and give enfranchised Africans a vested interest in maintaining this system for some time. There was to be no public announcement of future policy nor any timetable. The government should rather strive 'to induce the Europeans to accept something that was going to happen anyhow, and to assure the Africans that progress would be made towards the inevitable, the timing depending entirely upon a proper situation having been achieved'.[129] Clearly, the Prime Minister had no precise idea of when and how power was to be transferred. Macmillan knew that it was not possible to maintain white supremacy indefinitely but he was determined that the change should be as gradual as possible. He was aware of the need of change, but was reluctant to weather open resistance from the European settlers and their allies in the Conservative Party. As he said in a letter to Brook: 'Africans are not the problem in Africa, it is the Europeans.'[130]

At the end of Macmillan's first premiership there was an awareness that things in Africa had to change, but also perplexity about the appropriate course. Policy-makers knew that they approached a turning-point, but did not yet know in which direction it was best to go. As will be seen in the following section, the same helplessness prevailed with regard to the smaller territories.

Smaller Territories

Despite several attempts to develop a satisfactory status for the so-called 'smaller territories', no progress had been made by 1957. It was still assumed that territories like Aden or the Gambia could never be fully self-governing. On the other hand, it became increasingly difficult to defend this in public or in the territories. Therefore E. Larmour of the CRO urged his colleagues to take 'an imaginative line': in the age of nuclear warfare, the value of the strategic territories became more problematic every day. And in a limited conventional war it would be difficult to use them without the goodwill of the local population, which was constantly undermined by Britain's refusal to make any concessions. It also had repercussions on Britain's relations with the Afro-Asian group in the United Nations. Britain should accept that it was 'not justified on any grounds including that of expediency in clinging on to so-called strategic Colonies as bases without the consent of the people concerned'. All smaller territories should be offered self-government or other options such as federation with the United Kingdom.[131] Larmour's arguments fell on deaf ears. The CRO was reluctant to 'dilute' the Commonwealth by admitting 'small fry' which was bound to diminish the club's international standing.[132] Also Lennox-Boyd and his officials continued to argue that control over the smaller territories had to be maintained. Since there was no intermediate status between dependence and independence which could be defined as the final goal for these territories, they had to remain under British tutelage. Unless the territories that were not viable linked up with their neighbours, Britain had to retain responsibility for defence and external affairs. This was not only in the territories' own interest, but corresponded also to their feelings about British rule: Lennox-Boyd was confident that in most of the smaller territories there was 'no widespread desire to escape from dependence upon us'.[133]

Lennox-Boyd's optimism was not shared by all of his colleagues. Several ministers saw the danger that, from the point of view of domestic and world opinion, the strategic territories were becoming a liability.[134] The government had not done enough to demonstrate that the bases served the whole of the free world and were not being used against the will of the inhabitants of these territories. Because of these anxieties, officials continued their quest for a status which would, on the one hand, satisfy the political aspirations of the locals, and, on the other, guarantee British control over defence and foreign affairs. The CO proposed the status of 'Commonwealth State'. The territories would be internally self-governing, but foreign relations with other countries would continue to be mediated through Britain.[135] They would be allowed to participate in some Commonwealth activities, but not in the Prime Ministers' meetings. It was hoped that this 'enlargement of their international personality' (added to the material advantages attached to the status, for example, grants or balancing budget deficits), would give enough satisfaction to the smaller territories' ambitions, doing for them what the Balfour formula had done for the Dominions, that is, satisfy their political demands while retaining them in the empire. In exchange for renouncing their claim to the 'worthless … ornament of independence', the smaller territories would have control of their domestic affairs, while enjoying British protection and safeguards against economic ruin. But above all they would have 'an honourable and even perhaps an influential place' in the Commonwealth.[136]

The CRO dismissed the CO's proposal as 'muddled thinking': a diarchy was not an attractive solution. It was either the last station but one before the terminus, thereby implying a further stage of advance. Or a *pis aller* as in the case of Malta, where it was all the locals could hope for, 'given their unwanted strategic importance'.[137] The FO, however, thought Commonwealth Statehood 'a very interesting attempt' to devise an acceptable status short of independence. After all, Commonwealth States would remain eligible for financial assistance. It was probable that non-viable territories would accept a limitation on their freedom in return for such assistance. The real difficulty was to find a territory 'willing to be the guinea pig'. Once the territories in French Africa achieved some form of independence, it would be difficult to offer something less to Britain's other African colonies.[138] Commonwealth statehood might still be applicable to territories in the Caribbean or the Pacific, though. Norman Brook, who had been charged with examining the idea, concluded that statehood was no alternative to full Commonwealth membership. Since there was hardly anything to distinguish it from the penultimate stage of constitutional development towards self-government, it would probably not be accepted by the territories concerned.[139] While he rejected the idea of statehood, Brook recommended that the search for an appropriate constitutional status continue. The smaller territories should not be given full Commonwealth membership. If any one of them were to be admitted, many others would demand a similar treatment. This would change the whole character of the Commonwealth and lead to its dilution.[140]

A solution to the problem of smaller territories was all the more urgent since Cyprus kept occupying the minds of British policy-makers. In October 1956 the island saw a new upsurge in terrorism and violence. At the same time, Britain had to face the Suez débâcle. Policy-makers feared that the Cyprus issue might inflict on them another defeat in the international arena. When Macmillan took over as Prime Minister in January 1957, he therefore immediately began to look for an honourable way out. Getting rid of the Cyprus question before new elections, he argued, would be 'of immense advantage' for the government.[141] Cyprus attracted a lot of international attention, was the object of constant criticism by the opposition and committed valuable forces to a tedious guerrilla campaign. The island was clearly 'an appalling burden' on British resources. The Prime Minister did not think it consonant with Britain's duty to 'walk out of the island', but hoped for a settlement which would reduce Britain's burden while allowing it to maintain its 'comparatively small' strategic interest.

Following instructions given by the Prime Minister, the official committee on colonial policy discussed the costs and benefits of a continued British presence in Cyprus. It concluded that the political damage of withdrawal would probably be heavier than the relatively modest financial gains: withdrawal would injure Britain's standing throughout the Middle East, especially in Turkey.[142] Ministers shared these reservations but acknowledged a certain urgency in finding a solution: the Cyprus conflict was costly in terms of both money and publicity. And in view of the reduction of defence resources over the next two years, the establishment of troops in Cyprus would have to be reduced sooner rather than later.[143] On the other hand, nobody wanted to appear to withdraw under pressure. The problem was to find a solution which would satisfy the various conflicting interests. Partition was rejected as an 'extremely unsatisfactory solution'. It would be interpreted as a unique surrender of a colonial possession and would have political repercussions both in Britain and throughout the Middle East.[144] Apparently, the conflict could only be resolved through negotiation.

Ministers decided to release the Greek–Cypriot leader, Archbishop Makarios from his exile on the Seychelles, but at first things did not improve. The guerrilla campaign continued, and Makarios still insisted on *enosis*. In July 1957 Macmillan proposed a fresh initiative to break the deadlock: Britain's interest was to secure its essential military needs and to reduce its colonial commitment. Control of the whole island was not necessary to satisfy its strategic requirements as long as *enosis* could be prevented.[145] Britain should retain certain strategically essential enclaves under its sovereignty and surrender the rest (after a transitory period of seven years) to a condominium of Britain, Greece and Turkey.[146] The Chiefs of Staff and the Cabinet regarded this proposal as rather promising.[147] Retaining sovereignty would involve intolerable political and economic burdens, and partition was bound to do irreparable harm to Britain's international reputation. A gradual withdrawal, however, seemed to offer an honourable way out.

When Cyprus was shaken by Turkish-instigated violence in January 1958, ministers realised that it was not realistic to suppose that a final settlement could be postponed for as long as seven years. The burden of controlling what appeared likely to be an escalating pattern of inter-communal violence was calculated to be much greater than the already considerable burden of dealing with the EOKA.[148] A similar process of rethinking seems to have taken place on the Greek-Cypriot side: Makarios abandoned *enosis* in September 1958. He chose independence instead of partition, which was beginning to loom on the horizon as a consequence either of British action or Turkish intervention. This renunciation of union with Greece was the decisive signal Britain had waited for. It allowed them to transfer power, retaining only two bases. The determination to withdraw as soon as possible was enhanced by the warning from the military planners that Britain could simply not afford to maintain current levels of troop deployments on the island. Since the total strength of the armed forces was expected to decline, Britain had to find a political solution by the end of 1959 – 'or give this place up'.[149]

Alarmed by the spectre of escalating communal violence, Greece and Turkey also endeavoured to find a solution. In February 1959 they agreed to the so-called Zurich proposals: Cyprus was to become independent under a Greek president and a Turkish vice-president, with the two communities having almost complete autonomy. Policy-makers in Britain were happy with the settlement and signalled their readiness to accept it, provided two bases remained sovereign British territory. Greece and Turkey agreed, and in March 1959 a cease-fire came into operation. Ministers were relieved and ordered that the arrangements for Cyprus' independence be put into effect quickly because of the continuing costs of maintaining sovereignty.[150] The transfer of power was delayed for several months, though, because of discussions about the amount of financial assistance to be granted in exchange for the bases.

Makarios demanded £10 million over the following five years. Ministers were reluctant to grant that much since it might create 'an embarrassing precedent' in negotiations with other territories.[151] The government had to insist on a tough line. Bargaining with Makarios was 'a bottomless pit', and the government would end up 'getting nothing of value at a very high price'.[152] The Cypriot bases would be more of a strategic liability than an asset. The figures under discussion were alarming and might lead other colonies to expect continuing financial support from the United Kingdom on a similar scale. Macleod was somewhat more conciliatory. The amount of aid envisaged was very high, but in the last resort, failure to secure an agreement would pose incalculably greater risks than a generous financial settlement.[153] The point made by the Colonial Secretary was accepted by other ministers, and in the end Makarios got the amount of aid he had asked for. This indicated how desperate policy-makers were to end formal rule while maintaining sovereignty over the bases. In the final agreement signed in the summer of 1960 Britain, Greece and Turkey jointly guaranteed the independence and integrity of Cyprus, which was to become a member of the Commonwealth. British sovereignty over the base areas was recognised in perpetuity. While the Cyprus problem had thus been largely resolved by the end of Macmillan's first premiership, that of other smaller territories still remained.

Conclusion

Macmillan ordered not only reviews of Britain's informal empire, but also of its formal colonies. The Colonial Policy Review was to provide ministers with an assessment of the advantages of losing or keeping specific colonies. Many officials (especially in the CO) feared that the Prime Minister's aim was to withdraw from certain territories because they were no longer economic or strategic assets. As a result they continuously pointed to the dangers of a 'premature' withdrawal, both for the colonies and for Britain itself. Britain stood to gain very little by withdrawing before the territories under its protection were ready for independence. There would be some modest savings for the Exchequer, but also an enormous loss of prestige and standing.

The Colonial Policy Review was mainly a reflection of CO views. The CO was willing to accelerate constitutional development in territories without white minorities, provided this could be justified by indigenous demands for self-government, for example, in Nigeria. But officials were strongly opposed to any suggestion of forcing the pace in East or Central Africa. Other ministries did not yet openly contradict this policy. However, under the surface a sea change was in progress, particularly with regard to East Africa. The rapidly growing strength of international anti-colonialism, linked with developments in the French empire, led the FO to conclude that it was best to transfer power as soon as possible. This divergence of opinion clearly emerged when officials drew up another report entitled, 'The Next Ten Years in Africa'. But despite some acrimonious debate between the participating ministries, the final report was dominated by the views prevailing in the CO and the CRO. A transfer of power was not to take place before 'the right kind of relationship' had developed between the various races in East and Central Africa.

Macmillan liked the report, which coincided largely with his own views. He realised that he had to move, but was uncertain about the direction. While more political rights had to be conceded to the Africans, the whites were not to be forced into accepting black majority-rule. During Macmillan's first premiership, there was a considerable amount of discussion about the future course in Africa, but few concrete ideas about the steps to be taken. The same applied to the smaller territories. Policy-makers realised that the rapidly growing international hostility against any form of colonial rule made it urgently necessary to find a solution. However, self-government was still considered out of the question. It was generally thought that the territories would not be able to survive on their own. Moreover, their admission to the Commonwealth would destroy the club's standing in the world.

THE COMMONWEALTH

Cyprus's accession to the Commonwealth was a significant milestone in the development of the club. It paved the way for many other smaller territories that were to follow in the future. It also signalled the change the association had undergone by the late 1950s. The Commonwealth now mattered mostly because of its presumed ability to retain newly-independent countries in the Western camp. But the club was still considered an important political instrument enhancing Britain's standing, particularly in the United States. Far from being considered 'the ghost of the Empire',[154] policy-makers continued to attribute great importance to the Commonwealth link.

The Commonwealth in the Late 1950s

During Macmillan's first premiership, the role of the Commonwealth continued to change. But it did not diminish as drastically as maintained by some authors. In the economic sphere, it was increasingly realised that the links between Britain and the Dominions were likely to weaken in the future: the United Kingdom could not import any more Commonwealth products, while other members of the Commonwealth were eager to protect their nascent industries. However, an impressive amount of trade was still done with the

Commonwealth, even though its relative importance declined: in 1950, 47.7 per cent of British exports were shipped to the Commonwealth. By 1960 it still absorbed 40.2 per cent.[155] British imports from the Commonwealth amounted to 41.9 per cent of all imports in 1950. Ten years later they accounted for 34.6 per cent. The United States held the premier position among Britain's overseas suppliers and markets. But Commonwealth countries held the next five places among overseas suppliers, and the next four among overseas markets.[156] Of Britain's capital exports, 65 per cent went to the Empire-Commonwealth between 1950 and 1954, and still stood at around 60 per cent between 1958 and 1960.[157] A certain downward trend was discernible and it was expected to continue. Few, however, expected the dramatic slump of Commonwealth trade that was to take place in the 1960s, when Europe became Britain's major market. And even though its economic importance declined, the Commonwealth's political role was still seen as valuable by many policy-makers. Faced with predictions about the diminishing economic and financial weight of the United Kingdom, they believed their country's diplomatic weight could be enhanced by its position in the club.

Admittedly, there were two major disappointments. The first one concerned the Suez crisis. The lack of support from the old Dominions and the harsh criticism Britain had to face from the Commonwealth's newer members, in particular India, demonstrated painfully that Britain could not automatically count on the Commonwealth to sustain its actions – and that it could even become a forum where it could be openly chastised.[158] The second disappointment was Ghana. Policy-makers had hoped that Commonwealth membership would help to keep the country in the British orbit, but Nkrumah showed no signs of becoming more malleable. His support for African nationalist movements and his criticism of Britain's status as a colonial power proved constant embarrassments. But despite these two disappointments, policy-makers continued to attach considerable importance to the Commonwealth link. The CRO, in particular, defended the club as the basis of Britain's power and its principal source of influence. If it disintegrated, the United Kingdom would decline to the status of a continental European power.[159] The links with the Commonwealth enhanced Britain's influence with its allies, especially the United States, as well as its worldwide standing. It acted as a steadying influence and helped accommodate neutralist tendencies by allowing emerging countries to maintain a close relationship with Britain 'without necessarily being obliged to adopt a policy of alignment in the cold war'.[160] The club greatly facilitated trade and the provision of technical and financial aid.[161] Last but not least it was a measure of Britain's inherent well-being underlining the particularity of the British way of life: it was 'something which is as yet non-American, something which the Americans with all their push and power and dollar-imperialism can't achieve'.[162]

In the CRO, the Commonwealth was considered an integral part of Britain's world-power status, necessary to maintain the strength of sterling, the special relationship with the United States and the United Kingdom's prosperity. Losing the Commonwealth meant losing Great Power status, and *vice versa*. Without the Commonwealth, there could be no strong pound, while a weak pound would certainly involve the defection of most members. The financial and commercial links with the Commonwealth enabled Britain to maintain sterling as an international currency. If the other members thought that Britain was no longer a worthwhile partner, they would inevitably turn to the United States, the Soviet Union, or Germany.[163] Commonwealth economic (and consequently political) relations would disintegrate, a development which would certainly do fatal damage to Britain's international position. Therefore everything possible should be done to maintain Britain's close links with the Dominions. This verdict was not yet openly challenged by any department. But there were subtle changes. Policy-makers spoke less often of the Commonwealth as a source of *power*. What now became increasingly important was its role in the context of Cold War, a fact that clearly emerged in the debate about the admission of Cyprus.

The Idea of 'Statehood' and Cyprus's Admission as a Full Member

While policy-makers opted against the admission of 'foreign' countries into the Commonwealth, they opened the Commonwealth to smaller territories such as Cyprus. This was rather astonishing given official attitudes until then. In the mid-1950s, some CO officials considered Commonwealth membership to be the 'ultimate solution of the problem of what to do' with Cyprus, Somaliland and Malta. But the CRO, fearing a whole series of demands by other smaller territories, argued that these cases could not be treated as unique.[164] Having admitted anyone of the 'small fry' to full membership, the CRO feared, it would become very difficult to withstand the admission of other smaller territories.[165] Colonies like Southern Rhodesia or Jamaica would also demand independent membership. Until now they had always been told that they could aspire to membership only in larger federations, in the first case in order to protect the Africans and to prevent a drift towards South Africa, and in the second because it would make it impossible to find a solution for the other West Indian territories. Admitting any smaller territory would thus lead to a break-up of the two federations. It was important to retain a criterion for admission – 'the capacity to stand on your own feet and cut some ice in international affairs'.[166] Otherwise it would be impossible to exclude the smaller territories, and the Commonwealth would become nothing but a 'talking-shop' not taken seriously by anybody.

In the late 1950s, an increasing number of policy-makers came to consider Commonwealth membership for Cyprus as a welcome means that would allow an honourable withdrawal as well as the maintenance of Cypriot goodwill. This did not mean, however, that Cyprus was to be admitted as a full member. Lord Home warned that because of the precedent set for 'a host of other smaller Colonies' it would be 'extremely dangerous' to suggest that the island could aspire to full membership.[167] Cyprus was a doubtful political entity with close relations to Greece, which had gained its independence after terrorism and bloodshed. If Cyprus with a population of 500,000, devoid of a sense of British heritage and a doubtful record of political and financial viability were admitted without any reservation, 'our previous tacit criteria for Membership' would no longer stand the test.[168] A kind of association, comprising some, but not all, of the advantages and responsibilities of Commonwealth membership seemed feasible, though.[169] These proposals led Macmillan to instruct officials to examine a form of association short of full membership.[170] What the Prime Minister had in mind was a general formula that would embrace Cyprus as well as other colonies, including Singapore and Malta, thus finally resolving the problem of the smaller territories.

A working party of CO, CRO and FO officials proposed that, in order to satisfy the aspirations of smaller territories for independence, they should be allowed to broaden their existing exclusive relationship with the United Kingdom into a relationship with the Commonwealth as a whole. Foreign relations with non-Commonwealth countries would continue to run through United Kingdom. It was hoped that this 'enlargement of their international personality', added to the material advantages attached to it, would give sufficient satisfaction to these territories' ambitions for independence – a status they could not sustain and which, in a number of cases, Britain would not be willing to grant.[171] When Makarios insisted on 'full membership or nothing', policy-makers had to choose whether to exclude Cyprus or not.[172] Macleod argued that the object of the Commonwealth was to persuade all members 'to adopt the Western approach to life and not the Russian'. Therefore the United Kingdom would gain by having the doors 'wide open'. The Commonwealth was no longer significant in power terms, but it was still of great importance in the crucial relationship between the West and the underdeveloped countries. This role would not be helped by thinking of the club as an exclusive or discriminatory bloc.[173] The smaller territories would become independent one at a time and might be absorbed gradually. Thus the organisation could adapt itself slowly to changing circumstances. In any case, only three countries, that is, Nigeria, the CAF and the West Indian Federation, would attain independence until 1970, so that the Commonwealth Prime Ministers' meetings would still be smaller than the British Cabinet. After that date, meetings could be organised on a regional or group basis. Thus it would be possible to maintain at least some of the old 'unanimity of resolve'. Any failure by an emergent territory to seek membership (or its rejection as a candidate) would be regarded by the world at large as a sign that Britain and the Commonwealth were unable to adapt to modern conditions.[174]

According to the Colonial Secretary, Britain might even be charged with 'betraying her trust' if any of its former dependencies was excluded from the Commonwealth against its will. The United Kingdom, and possibly the Commonwealth as a whole, would be blamed for the disintegration in such a state (much as Belgium was blamed for the chaos in the Congo). Furthermore, the country concerned would almost certainly feel a deep and enduring resentment towards the Commonwealth for rejecting it. The repercussions on British interests would be 'wide and damaging'.[175] But by accepting the island as a full member, HMG would underline the Commonwealth's 'dynamic and constantly evolving character'. It would also ensure that the Commonwealth's collective influence would work for the long-term good of Cyprus.[176]

Macleod received support from other ministers: Butler thought that the importance of Cyprus joining the Commonwealth was 'overriding'. 'Little embarrassments' about Makarios coming to the next meeting should not be allowed to jeopardise the prize.[177] Selwyn Lloyd advised that there was no alternative to full membership; Cypriot leaders would not accept any other status and would regard a refusal as a rebuff. This would undo all the efforts that had been made during the recent negotiations to build up the goodwill needed to operate the bases in Cyprus smoothly and successfully.[178] The island's admission need not of itself change the character of the Commonwealth. A two-tier structure was still feasible. In the past it had been considered undesirable because it had arisen in the context of a division between 'white' and 'black' countries. But considered as a division between larger and more important countries on the one hand, and smaller and less important ones on the other, regardless of colour, it might be open to less objection.

Norman Brook and some of his 'more robust colleagues' in the FO, the CO and the CRO were against the concession of full membership to Cyprus – 'both because it is an unsuitable member and, even more, because its admission is bound to disrupt the Commonwealth association as we know it'. The club would be turned into a minor United Nations, containing many states that would never be able to fend for themselves.[179] The special character of the Prime Ministers' meetings – 'their informality and intimacy and the freedom of discussion' – could certainly not be preserved for long if they were attended by the President of the Republic of Cyprus. These meetings, however, were the most important aspect of the Commonwealth. They enabled the participants to meet at intervals to talk about current world problems against a background of shared experience and history, thus getting to know one another's minds and moods.[180] Makarios did not fit into this picture. His presence would destroy the special atmosphere of the meetings. Moreover, if Cyprus's admission were followed by that of other smaller territories, the prime ministers of larger countries might no longer find it worthwhile to attend meetings. In order to avoid such an unpleasant development, it was important to draw 'a sharp and final distinction' between territories that could hope to enjoy the full range of privileges that went with membership, and others that could not attain more than 'full internal autonomy'.[181] This would mean a two-tier Commonwealth. The upper tier would be composed of 18 sovereign (and more or less important) countries, while the lower tier would consist of smaller territories. These could attain the status of 'Commonwealth State' or 'Commonwealth Treaty State'.[182]

Lord Home also argued against Cyprus's admission.[183] But after some heart-searching he had to accept the advice given by his own officials as well as that of other ministries: since Cyprus would not accept a place in the second league, it was better, on the whole, to admit it to full membership. He informed the Prime Minister that he himself was not keen to see this come about, both because Cyprus would almost certainly be 'a nuisance' and because it would open the door to other territories which did not really qualify: 'If it were not for Cyprus knocking at the door, we could hold the shape of the Commonwealth prime ministers' meetings for some time to come.' But to refuse an application would be politically difficult.[184] On 27 April 1960 ministers therefore decided to agree, without delay, to Cypriot application for full Commonwealth membership. Britain, they calculated, would thus retain Cypriot goodwill and secure its influence. There were even some who hoped that the admission of Cyprus would not automatically open the door to other smaller territories since the island was a case *sui generis* – as will be seen later, a hope that was soon to be disappointed.

Conclusion

During Macmillan's first premiership the Commonwealth's economic and political importance continued to decline. There was some disappointment about the behaviour of the new Dominions, in particular during the Suez crisis. But policy-makers continued to believe in the association's importance, at least for the special relationship, Britain's international standing, and a strong pound. A growing number of policy-makers were sceptical as to whether the club really fulfilled all the functions attributed to it by the CRO, but the majority still believed that the Commonwealth had an important role to play, at least in the Cold War. This is demonstrated by the discussion about the admission of Cyprus as a full member.

Lord Home as well as many CRO officials at first objected to the island's admission, since it would open the door to many other potential candidates. The Commonwealth would thus become a sort of minor United Nations, i.e. an organisation without much influence, representing too many disparate opinions. At best the island should be offered some other kind of second-rate membership. Since the Cypriots insisted on 'full membership or nothing', policy-makers finally abandoned the idea of a second tier and admitted Cyprus as a full member. This was to ensure that the island remained in the Western camp and subject to British influence. It was acknowledged that it might be difficult to maintain the club's old 'unanimity of resolve'. But the Commonwealth's main objective was said to be to persuade all present and potential members that the Western approach to life was preferable to the Russian one. Therefore it was considered better to open the doors than to exclude anyone.

NOTES

1. David Throup, 'The Historiography of Decolonization' (unpublished paper given at the Institute of Commonwealth Studies on 31 January 1991), p. 1.
2. John W. Young, *Cold War Europe 1945–1991: A Political History* (London: Arnold, 1991, 2nd edn), p. 132.
3. Quoted in Alistair Horne, *Macmillan, 1957–1986. Volume II of the Official Biography* (Basingstoke: Macmillan, 1989), p. 65.
4. Joint memorandum, Macmillan and Monckton to Eden (PR (56) 2), 20 March 1956. CAB 134/1315 (Goldsworthy, *Conservative Government*, I, 20).

5. Memorandum, 'The State of the Economy' (CP (57) 4), Chancellor of the Exchequer to Cabinet, 4 January 1957. CAB 129/84 (PRO); minute by P. Markell, 28 January 1958. FO 371/135623 (PRO).

6. Note by Brook, 20 January 1958. PREM 11/2219 (PRO).

7. Nigel Nicolson reporting a speech by Macmillan to the 1922 Committee, quoted in Horne, *Macmillan*, p. 18.

8. Memo by Macmillan, 24 November 1956. Macmillan Archives, quoted in Horne, *Macmillan*, p. 47.

9. Jeffrey Pickering, *Britain's Withdrawal from East of Suez: The Politics of Retrenchment* (Basingstoke: Macmillan, 1998), p. 95.

10. Memorandum, 'Defence Policy: Heavy Aircraft Carriers' (D (55) 1) by Minister of Defence, 7 January 1955. CAB 131/15 (PRO).

11. Quoted in Holland, *Pursuit of Greatness*, p. 238.

12. D (57) 2nd meeting, 27 February 1957. CAB 131/18 (PRO).

13. OME (57) 3rd meeting, 1 February 1957. CAB 134/2338 (PRO); paper, 'Middle East Policy' (OME (57) 7 (final)) by official committee on the Middle East, 6 February 1957. CAB 134/2339 (PRO).

14. Memorandum, 'Anglo-American Co-operation in the Middle East' (OME (57) 14 (revise) addendum) by official committee on the Middle East, 13 March 1957. CAB 134/2339 (PRO).

15. Paper, 'Points for a Middle East Policy – Part II' (OME (58) 46) by FO, 19 November 1958. CAB 134/2342 (PRO).

16. Minutes of a meeting of officials (GEN 658/1st meeting), 22 July 1958. CAB 130/153 (PRO).

17. Paper 'United Kingdom Policy in the Persian Gulf' (OME (57) 31), FO to official committee on the Middle East, 2 May 1957. CAB 134/2339 (PRO).

18. OME (58) 6th meeting, minute 3, confidential annex; 10 April 1958. CAB 134/2341 (PRO).

19. Gorell Barnes to Governor of Aden, 14 April 1958. CO 1015/191 (PRO).

20. Report, 'Policy in South-West Arabia' (OME (58) 35 annex A) by official committee on the Middle East, 10 June 1958. CAB 134/2342 (PRO).

21. COS (58) 287 annex, 17 December 1958. CO 1015/191 (PRO).

22. OME (57) 32nd meeting, minute 1, confidential annex; 9 December 1957. CAB 134/2338 (PRO).

23. Minute, by W. Hayter, 3 March 1958. PREM 11/2418 (PRO).

24. Minute 'Long-term Policy in Aden', Parliamentary Under-Secretary of State to Colonial Secretary, 10 March 1959. CO 1015/1910 (PRO).

25. CPC (61) 13, 20 December 1961. CAB 134/1560 (PRO).

26. M. Carver, *Out of Step: Memoirs of Field Marshal Lord Carver* (London: Hutchinson, 1969), p. 288–89, quoted in Simon J. Ball, 'Macmillan and British Defence Policy', in Aldous and Lee (eds), *Harold Macmillan*, p. 74.

27. Saul Kelly, 'Transatlantic Diplomat: Sir Roger Makins, Ambassador to Washington and Joint Permanent Secretary to the Treasury', *Contemporary British History*, 13, 2 (1999), pp. 175.

28. Minutes of a meeting held in R. Makins' room, 4 February 1958 (GEN 624/2nd). CAB 130/139 (PRO); minutes of a meeting held in R. Makins' room, 18 February 1958 (GEN 624/3rd). CAB 130/139 (PRO)

29. Official report, 'The Position of the United Kingdom in World Affairs' (GEN 659), 9 June 1958. CAB 130/153 (PRO).

30. Draft, 'The Advantages of Membership of the Sterling Area' by T. Rowan, 2 October 1958. T 236/5362 (PRO).

31. Treasury paper, 'External Economic Aims' (GEN 624/3), n.d. (January 1958). CAB 130/139 (PRO).

32. Minutes of a meeting held in Brook's room, 3 March 1958 (GEN 624/4th).

CAB 130/139 (PRO).

33. Minute by P. Ramsbotham, 24 January 1958. FO 371/135623 (PRO).
34. Brief, 'Future Policy' by P. Ramsbotham, 3 February 1958. FO 371/135624 (PRO).
35. Memorandum, 'Report on Political, Economic and Information Measures in Eastern Asia' (GEN 538/10), official committee on eastern Asia to Cabinet policy review committee, 23 July 1956. CAB 130/118 (Stockwell, *Malaya*, III, 421).
36. Minutes of Ministerial meeting, 7 July 1958 (GEN 659). CAB 130/153 (PRO).
37. Macmillan to Foreign Secretary, 10 June 1959. FO 371/143702 (PRO). The group consisted of officials of the CO, the CRO, the FO, the Treasury and the MoD.
38. G. Carstairs to H. Poynton, 20 October 1959. CO 1032/171 (PRO).
39. R. Vile to Carstairs, 5 November 1959. CO 1032/172 (PRO).
40. Carstairs to Eastwood, 12 November 1959. CO 1032/172 (PRO).
41. FP (A) (59) 5 & 7, 10 & 20 November 1959. CAB 134/1930 (PRO); FP (A) (59) 7th, 4 December 1959. CAB 134/1930 (PRO).
42. FP (A) (59) 2nd, 20 October 1959. CAB 134/1930 (PRO).
43. Memorandum, 'The Cost of the UK Defence Effort' (FP (A) (59) 9), R. Powell to steering committee, 17 December 1959. CAB 134/1930 (PRO).
44. FP (A) (59) 10, 21 December 1959. CAB 134/1930 (PRO).
45. FP (60) 1st, 23 March 1960. CAB 134/1929 (PRO).
46. Holland, 'The Imperial Factor', p. 180.
47 Prime Minister to Lord President, 28 January 1957. CAB 134/1555 (PRO).
48. I. Watt to H. Poynton, 11 June and 1 August 1957. CO 1032/146 (PRO).
49. Brook to Macpherson, 9 March 1957. CO 1032/144 (PRO).
50. 'Skeleton Plan (To Be Followed in the Consideration of Each Territory or Area)', n.d. (first half of 1957). CO 1032/144 (PRO).
51. Report 'Future Constitutional Development in the Colonies' by official committee on colonial policy (CPC (57) 30 (revise)), 6 September 1957. CAB 134/1556 (PRO).
52. Official report, 'Constitutional Development in the Colonies' (GEN 174/012), September 1957. CO 1032/147 (PRO).
53. 'Draft paragraphs for "Profit and Loss" Survey – Federation of Rhodesia and Nyasaland' by D. Hunt (CRO), 29 March 1957. CO 1032/144 (PRO).
54. Board of Trade paper, 30 November 1956. T 234/223, quoted in Catherine R. Schenk, 'Decolonization and European Economic Integration: The Free Trade Area Negotiations, 1956–58', *Journal of Imperial and Commonwealth History*, XXIV (1996), p. 446.
55. 'Future Policy: Summary of a Memorandum by Colonial Office', January–February 1958. FO 371/135624 (PRO).
56. Note, 'Future Constitutional Development in the Colonies' (CP (O) (57) 6) by official committee on colonial policy, 4 July 1957. CAB 134/1551 (PRO).
57. CRO brief, 'The Soviet Threat to Tropical Africa', n.d. (1957). DO 35/7702 (PRO).
58. Report, 'Future Constitutional Development in the Colonies' by official committee on colonial policy (CPC (57) 30 (revise)), 6 September 1957. CAB 134/1556 (PRO).
59. AF (57) 7, 23 October 1957. CAB 134/1351 (PRO).
60. Lennox-Boyd to Prime Minister, 17 March 1957. PREM 11/3239 (PRO).
61. Draft CO despatch to Governors of all African colonies and Aden, May 1957. PREM 11/3239 (PRO).
62. Poynton to Lennox-Boyd, 5 July 1956. CO 1025/76 (Goldsworthy, *Conservative Government*, III, 438).

63. Tony Hopkins, 'Macmillan's Audit of Empire, 1957', in Peter Clarke and Clive Trebilcock (eds), *Understanding Decline: Perceptions and Realities of British Economic Performance* (Cambridge: Cambridge University Press, 1997), p. 252.
64. CPC 15 (58), 15 December 1958. CAB 134/1557 (PRO).
65. Minutes of steering committee of the Conservative Party, 28 May 1958. CRD 2/53/34, quoted in Murphy, *Party Politics and Decolonization*, p. 164.
66. CO memorandum, 'Nigeria', n.d. (1957). CO 1032/147 (PRO).
67. CM 42 (57) 4, 22 May 1957. CAB 128/31/2 (PRO); note, 'Nigeria' (C (58) 213), Colonial Secretary to Cabinet, 20 October 1958. CAB 129/95 (PRO).
68. Horace Alexander to Pethick Lawrence, 22 August 1946. L/P&J/7/5935 (*TOP*, VIII, 194).
69. Quoted in Horne, *Macmillan*, p. 190.
70. H. Foot to Higham, 6 February 1959. CO 926/721 (PRO).
71. National Security Council, 302nd meeting, 1 November 1956. Eisenhower papers, quoted in Louis, 'American Anti-Colonialism', p. 277.
72. Brian Lapping, 'Did Suez Hasten the End of Empire?', *Contemporary Record*, 1, 2 (1987), p. 32.
73. Swinton to Bögholm, 10 January 1959. SWIN I 7/4 (CC).
74. Memorandum, 'The Commonwealth 1960–1970' by the CRO, the CO and the Treasury, 30 July 1959. CAB 134/1935 (PRO).
75. Hargreaves, *Decolonization in Africa*, p. 161.
76. Governor of Tanganyika to Macleod, 2 March 1961. CO 822/2301 (PRO).
77. AF (59) 1, 14 January 1959. CAB 134/1353 (PRO). The committee consisted of officials of the CO, the CRO, the FO, the MoD and the Treasury.
78. Note, 'The Political Scene in Tropical Africa' (AF (59) 8), FO to Africa (official) committee, 20 January 1959. CAB 134/1354 (PRO).
79. Note, 'Prospects for the African Territories for Which the Colonial Office is Responsible' (AF (59) 22), FO to Africa (official) committee, 26 February 1959. CAB 134/1354 (PRO).
80. FO note, 'Africa South of the Sahara: The Future of the Foreign Territories' (AF (59) 3), 12 January 1959. CAB 134/1353 (PRO).
81. Report of the Advisory (Monckton) Commission on the Review of the Constitution of Rhodesia and Nyasaland, Cmnd. 1148, October 1960. PP (1959–60) XI, 21 (Porter and Stockwell, *British Imperial Policy*, II, 79).
82. Minute by P. Ramsbotham, 20 November 1959. FO 371/143700 (PRO).
83. Note, 'Africa South of the Sahara: The French and Belgian Territories' (AF (59) 7), FO to Africa (official) committee, 16 January 1959. CAB 134/1354 (PRO).
84. FP (A) (60) 5, 15 January 1960. CAB 134/1930 (PRO).
85. FO memorandum, 'Development of the United Nations and Other International Organisations and the Influence of World Opinion', n.d. (July 1959). CAB 134/1935 (PRO).
86. FO memorandum, 'Main Trends of Development in Africa', n.d. (July 1959). CAB 134/1935 (PRO).
87. Report, 'The Next Ten Years in Africa' (AF (59) 28 (final)) by Africa (official) committee, 3 June 1959. CAB 134/1555 (PRO).
88. Minute by Burke Trend, 1 March 1957. PREM 11/12582 (PRO).
89. FP (A) (59) 5, 10 November 1959. CAB 134/1930 (PRO).
90. FO draft, 'Africa South of the Sahara. The Nature of the British Interest in the Foreign Territories', 9 January 1959. FO 371/137951 (PRO).
91. Minute by H. Bourdillon, 19 October 1956. CO 936/337, quoted in John Kent, *The Internationalization of Colonialism: Britain, France, and Black Africa, 1939–1956* (Oxford: Clarendon Press, 1992), p. 308.

92. CRO draft, 'British Colonial Policy in Africa', n.d. (May 1959). DO 35/8039 (PRO).
93. Ibid.
94. CRO note, 'The Next Ten Years in Africa' (AF (59) 6), 9 January 1959. CAB 134/1353 (PRO).
95. Memorandum by Douglas-Home, 25 June 1959 (GEN 688/5). CAB 130/164 (PRO).
96. CRO note, n.d. (second half of 1956). DO 35/5012 (PRO); note of a meeting between Macmillan, Douglas-Home and Stirling, 11 June 1959. PREM 11/2583 (PRO).
97. Record of a conference of East African governors and the Colonial Secretary held at Entebbe on 7/8 October 1957. CO 822/1807 (PRO).
98. Lamb, *Macmillan Years, 1957–1963*, p. 223.
99. Turnbull (Tanganyika) to Gorell-Barnes, 13 July 1959. CO 822/1450 (PRO).
100. Memorandum, 'Future Policy in East Africa' (CPC (59) 2), Colonial Secretary to colonial policy committee, 10 April 1959. CAB 134/1558 (PRO).
101. Note, 'Policy in East Africa' (AF (59) 23), CO to Africa (official) committee, 4 March 1959. CAB 134/1354 (PRO).
102. CPC (59) 1, 17 April 1959. CAB 134/1558 (PRO).
103. *Hansard* (House of Commons Debates) 604, col. 563.
104. Murphy, *Party Politics and Decolonization*, p. 64.
105. Report, 'The Next Ten Years in Africa' (AF (59) 28 (Final)) by Africa (official) committee, 3 June 1959. CAB 134/1555 (PRO).
106. Record of a meeting between Canadian and British officials, 26 November 1959. DO 35/8804 (PRO).
107. The CO had proposed to safeguard Britain's strategic interests in Eastern Africa (notably in Kenya) by keeping enclaves as part of British territory. Similar proposals by the Ministry of Defence for India, Malaya and West Africa had been rejected on the ground that the retention of bases would alienate the new governments. With regard to Kenya, however, the CO considered it attractive since it would reassure the whites. The FO opposed the idea, arguing that such a step was certain to poison future relations with Africa as a whole. This time the FO's stance prevailed: the report stated that in the long term, Britain would gain the sympathy and support of newly independent states if it refrained from seeking to acquire, retain or use facilities. Record of a conference of East African Governors and the Colonial Secretary held at Entebbe on 7/8 October 1957. CO 822/1807 (PRO); note, 'Policy in East Africa' (AF (59) 23), CO to Africa (official) committee, 4 March 1959. CAB 134/1354 (PRO).
108. P. de Zulueta to Bligh, 1 July 1959. PREM 11/2587 (PRO).
109. Macmillan to Brook, 1 November 1959. Macmillan Archives, quoted in Horne, *Macmillan*, p. 185.
110. Prime Minister to Foreign Secretary, 3 July 1959. PREM 11/2587 (PRO).
111. Lennox-Boyd to Prime Minister, 30 July 1959. PREM 11/2587 (PRO); Selwyn Lloyd to Prime Minister, 28 July 1959. PREM 11/2587 (PRO).
112. Lyttelton to Twining (Tanganyika) and Baring (Kenya), 20 November 1953. CO 822/503, quoted in Carruthers, *Winning Hearts and Minds*, p. 173.
113. Macmillan diary, entry for 9 June 1959, quoted in Horne, *Macmillan*, p. 174.
114. *Hansard* (House of Commons Debates) 610, col. 237, 27 July 1959.
115. Quoted in Lamb, *Macmillan Years*, p. 235.
116. Note of a meeting between Macmillan, Lennox-Boyd, Perth and Brook on 13 July 1959. PREM 11/2783 (PRO).
117. Macmillan diary, entry for 13 July 1959, quoted in Horne, *Macmillan*, p. 181.
118. Home to Prime Minister, 29 May 1959. PREM 11/2588 (PRO).

119. Minutes of a meeting of ministers (GEN 680/6th meeting), 6 April 1959. CAB 130/160 (PRO).
120. Minute, 'Nyasaland', Brook to Prime Minister, n.d. (19 July 1959). PREM 11/2783 (PRO).
121. Interview of Lord Boyd by Alison Smith, 13 December 1974. Boyd papers Mss.Eng.c.3433, f. 264, quoted in Murphy, '"Holding Back the Tides?" Alan Lennox-Boyd at the Colonial Office 1954–57', unpublished paper given at the Institute of Commonwealth Studies, 28.3.96, p. 1f.; note of a meeting with Lennox-Boyd, 5 November 1958. Hetherington papers (LSE).
122. Report (PM (60) 33) Macleod to Macmillan, 1 June 1960. PREM 11/3240 (PRO); Macleod to Macmillan, 25 May 1959. PREM 11/2583 (PRO). It is questionable to what extent the letter expressed a real concern about the electoral fortunes of the Conservatives – it might also have been a means of capturing Macmillan's attention.
123. CCOC papers, vol. 2, CCC 174, 'The Revolution in East Africa' (1960), quoted in Murphy, *Party Politics and Decolonization*, p. 180.
124. Macmillan to Monckton, 22 August 1959. Macmillan Archives, quoted in Horne, *Macmillan*, p. 182f.
125. Draft memorandum, 'The Franchise in East and Central Africa' by Gorell Barnes, 15 October 1955. CO 822/929 (Porter and Stockwell, *British Imperial Policy*, II, 62).
126. Quoted in Horne, *Macmillan*, p. 192.
127. Note of a meeting between Macmillan, Home and Stirling, 11 June 1959. PREM 11/2583 (PRO).
128. CPC (60) 2, 18 March 1960. CAB 134/1559 (PRO).
129. Note of meeting between Macmillan, Home and Stirling, 11 June 1959. RPREM 11/2583 (PRO).
130. Macmillan to Brook, 28 December 1959. Macmillan Archives, quoted in Horne, *Macmillan*, p. 188.
131. E. Larmour to Snelling, 11 December 1958. DO 35/7873 (PRO).
132. Snelling to Chadwick, Allen and Larmour, 10 December 1958. DO 35/7873 (PRO).
133. Lennox-Boyd to Butler, 14 February 1958. CO 1032/129 (PRO).
134. Paper summarising views of ministers, Butler to Prime Minister, 25 February 1958. PREM 11/2248 (PRO).
135. Memorandum, 'A Suggested Form of Association of the Smaller Colonies with the Commonwealth' by working party on smaller colonial territories (SCT (59) 3), 9 March 1959. CAB 134/2505 (PRO); memorandum, 'Future of the Smaller Territories', CO to working party on smaller colonial territories, 20 March 1959. CAB 134/2505 (PRO). Even the promise of internal self-government was qualified though: officials thought it necessary to retain the right to suspend the constitution in order to prevent the emergence of a communist regime or any other threat to internal security. Public opinion, it was argued, would hold HMG responsible for the States' political and economic well-being.
136. STC (59) 2nd meeting, 24 March 1959, quoted in McIntyre, 'The Admission of Small States', p. 263.
137. Minute by Chadwick, 23 March 1959, DO 35/7870 (PRO).
138. Minute by K. Wilford, 7 August 1959. FO 371/143700 (PRO); minute by P. Ramsbotham, 20 November 1959. FO 371/143700 (PRO).
139. Note on 'Smaller Colonial Territories' (GEN 518/6/11), Brook for Cabinet committee on Commonwealth prime ministers' meeting, 18 June 1956. CAB 130/113 (Goldsworthy, *Conservative Government*, II, 206).
140. Report, 'The Future of Smaller Colonial Territories' (CP (O) (59) 1) by official

working party, June 1959. CAB 134/1552 (PRO).

141. Macmillan to Foreign Secretary, 27 January 1957. PREM 11/1757A (PRO).

142. Note, 'Future Constitutional Development in the Colonies' (CP (O) (57) 5) by official committee on colonial policy, 30 May 1957. CAB 134/1551 (PRO).

143. CPC 9 (57); 29 May 1957. CAB 134/1555 (PRO).

144. Note of a meeting of ministers (GEN 582/2), 2 May 1957. CAB 130/125 (PRO).

145. Memorandum, 'Cyprus', Prime Minister to Cabinet (C (57) 161), 9 July 1957. CAB 129/88 (PRO).

146. CM 51 (57) 6, 11 July 1957. CAB 128/31 (PRO); note 'External Defence of Cyprus', Minister of Defence to Cabinet (C (57) 184), 29 July 1957. CAB 129/88 (PRO).

147. Memorandum, 'Cyprus' (C (57) 265), Minister of Defence to Cabinet, 12 November 1957. CAB 129/90 (PRO).

148. CM 17 (58) 4, 18 February 1958. CAB 128/32 (PRO).

149. Campbell to Higham, 3 February 1959. CO 926/721 (PRO); Tock to Gorell Barnes, 2 January 1959. BARN 3/1 (CC)

150. Memorandum, 'Practical Problems Which Would Have to be Overcome in the Event of Authority Being Handed Over from the United Kingdom to a New Cyprus State' by official Cyprus committee (CY (O) (59) 1) 1 January 1959. CAB 134/1592 (PRO).

151. CM 3 (60) 2, 26 January 1960. CAB 128/34 (PRO).

152. Chancellor of the Exchequer to Prime Minister, 16 February 1960. PREM 11/2923 (PRO).

153. Colonial Secretary to Foreign Secretary, 6 April 1960. CO 926/1327 (PRO).

154. D.A. Low, 'Little Britain and Large Commonwealth', *Round Table*, 298 (1986), p. 111.

155. Darwin, *Britain and Decolonisation*, p. 304.

156. CRO memorandum, 'Commonwealth Aspect: Regional Analysis' (GEN 624/7), n.d. (January 1958). CAB 130/139 (PRO). In 1958, the EEC had a share of only around 20 per cent in British imports and exports (roughly the same as EFTA) (Roland Marx, 'Le Commonwealth et les choix européens de la Grande-Bretagne de 1948 à 1975', *Relations internationales*, 55 (1988), p. 366).

157. Porter, *The Lion's Share*, p. 327. These figures comprise Dominions *and* colonies, but the major part of British investments went to the 'old' Commonwealth.

158. Peter Lyon, 'The Commonwealth and the Suez Crisis', in Wm Roger Louis and Roger Owen (eds), *Suez 1956: The Crisis and its Consequences* (Oxford: Clarendon Press, 1989), pp. 257–73.

159. CSG (60) 2, 31 May 1960. CAB 133/200 (PRO).

160. Official report, 'The Position of the United Kingdom in World Affairs' (GEN 659), 9 June 1958. CAB 130/153 (PRO); Home to Lloyd, 21 May 1958. PREM 11/2689 (PRO).

161. CRO note, 'Future Policy – Commonwealth Aspect' (GEN 624/2), January 1958. CAB 130/139 (PRO).

162. Minute, 'Commonwealth Publicity' by P. Noakes, 1 January 1959. CO 1027/168 (PRO).

163. CRO memorandum, 'Commonwealth Aspect: Regional Analysis' (GEN 624/7), n.d. (January 1958). CAB 130/139 (PRO).

164. A.W.S. to H. Lintott, 19 December 1958. DO 35/7873 (PRO).

165. Snelling to Chadwick, Allen and Larmour, 10 December 1958. DO 35/7873 (PRO).

166. Brook to Prime Minister, 5 October 1955. PREM 11/1726F (PRO).

167. Home to Prime Minister, 17 February 1959. DEFE 13/96 (PRO).
168. CP (O)(60) 1, annex A, 30 March 1960. CAB 134/1552 (PRO).
169. Brook to Prime Minister, 17 February 1959. PREM 11/2910 (PRO).
170. Ian Watt to Higham, 17 February 1959. CO 926/744 (PRO); Macmillan to Commonwealth Secretary, 18 February 1959. FO 371/143699 (PRO).
171. Memorandum, 'A Suggested Form of Association of the Smaller Colonies with the Commonwealth' by working party on smaller colonial territories (SCT (59) 3), 9 March 1959. CAB 134/2505 (PRO).
172. Home to Prime Minister, 14 March 1960. PREM 11/3220 (PRO).
173. Note of a meeting between the Prime Minister, the Commonwealth Secretary, the Colonial Secretary and Brook, 13 July 1960. PREM 11/3220 (PRO); R. Clarke (Treasury) to P. Dean (FO), 4 August 1959. FO 371/143705 (PRO).
174. Macleod to Prime Minister, 24 April 1960. PREM 11/483 (PRO).
175. Note, 'General Factors Relating to the Admission of New Members to the Commonwealth' by A. Mackintosh, 9 February 1962. CAB 130/180 (PRO).
176. Memorandum, 'Cyprus and the Commonwealth' (CPC (60) 10) by Commonwealth and Colonial Secretaries, 22 April 1960. CAB 134/1559 (PRO).
177. P. de Zulueta to Prime Minister, 21 December 1960. PREM 11/3220 (PRO).
178. Foreign Secretary to Prime Minister, 21 July 1960. PREM 11/3220 (PRO).
179. Minute, 'The Future Development of the Commonwealth', Brook to Prime Minister, 26 April 1960. PREM 11/3220 (PRO); note, 'Cyprus and the Commonwealth' (CP (O) (60) 2), Brook to Cabinet and official committee on colonial policy, 27 March 1960. CAB 134/1552 (PRO).
180. Minute, 'Future of the Commonwealth', Brook to Prime Minister, 28 April 1960. PREM 11/3220 (PRO).
181. CRO memorandum, 'The Future of the Smaller Colonial Territories' (CP (O) (60) 1, annex A), March 1960. CAB 134/1552 (PRO).
182. Joint memorandum, 'The Smaller Colonial Territories. Relationship with the Commonwealth' (CPC (60) 9), Commonwealth Secretary and Minister of State for Colonial Affairs to colonial policy committee, 19 April 1960. CAB 134/1559 (PRO).
183. Memorandum, 'Cyprus and the Commonwealth' (CPC (60) 10) by Commonwealth and Colonial Secretaries, 22 April 1960. CAB 134/1559 (PRO).
184. Home to Prime Minister, 8 July 1960. PREM 11/3220 (PRO).

The Empire-Commonwealth under the Second Macmillan Government

THE INFORMAL EMPIRE

DURING MACMILLAN'S second term as Prime Minister, the informal empire continued to exercise an important hold on the minds of policy-makers. Despite strong Treasury pressure, ministers decided to maintain overseas commitments – even at the price of rising defence expenditure. Like most of their predecessors since 1945, they considered it vital to maintain a firm stand in order to secure Britain's oil supplies and its special relationship with the United States as well as international confidence in sterling. The plan to withdraw from south-east Asia (Malaysia) has to be seen in this perspective: it was part of Britain's move towards greater mobility, not an imperial disengagement. Aircraft carriers were to replace land bases. Although the stress was increasingly on non-military measures to preserve British influence and to protect British interests, overseas commitments were still seen as indispensable.

The Debate in the Early 1960s

The general election of October 1959 raised the Conservative majority to 100, but Macmillan still had to fight a multitude of problems. On the political side, the failure of the 1960 Paris meeting shattered his hopes of increasing Britain's international importance through his summit diplomacy. On the economic side, things were hardly any better. In 1958 there was a trade surplus, but the following year saw a deterioration in the balance of payments: the combined surplus on both visible and invisible account fell to £145 million and failed by a large margin to cover the capital outflow. Things were to get even worse: the modest surplus of 1959 gave way to a £273 million deficit in 1960.[1] Pressure on sterling led the Chancellor of the Exchequer to introduce emergency measures, combining orthodox deflationary measures with a public sector 'pay pause' (a highly unpopular decision). In 1962, a survey by the Organisation of European Corporation and Development (OECD) painted a pessimistic picture of Britain's economic performance over the previous decade, which had been marked by stop-go and a relatively large burden of defence expenditure overseas.[2] While the gap between Britain's economic performance and that of other developed nations increasingly widened, the debate about ways of resolving the crisis intensified, with pressure from the Treasury becoming ever stronger. Of particular importance in this context was the question whether Britain's numerous overseas commitments were necessary to safeguard its strategic, economic and political interests in the world.

The Treasury pointed out that the corpus of defence, economic aid and other related expenditure amounted to 8.5 per cent of GNP. These claims were in direct competition with other national objectives such as a higher standard of living through increased consumption, better social services, more leisure and lower taxes. If the amount spent on defence and economic aid was not reduced, a cut in the other programmes would be inevitable.[3] Given the persistently bad balance of payments, it was imperative that the external accounts be brought into balance quickly. Otherwise the deficit would continue to be met from the reserves – or by short-term credit from foreign lenders. However, the holdings of short-term sterling assets had already risen substantially in recent years, and their holders were becoming uneasy about Britain's ability to maintain the value of these liabilities. They were seeking to reduce them in ways which caused pressure on the reserves; unless the government could convince the overseas holders of sterling that it was determined to bring its accounts into balance, the pressure would increase.[4] It was essential to make cuts: the reserves were dangerously low. Trying to take up more short-term credits would further destabilise the already shaky international confidence in sterling.

When ministers discussed the issue, the Minister of Defence pointed out that substantial savings could be achieved only if forces were totally withdrawn from certain overseas establishments.[5] On military grounds, this was not justifiable. It might be possible, however, to make partial reductions in several overseas bases if there was a re-shaping of strategic policy so as to increase the mobility of British forces. This might save expenditure overseas, but would involve some addition to the total defence budget. The Foreign Secretary supported this, arguing that an adjustment was preferable to withdrawing completely from any area. The government should consider building up in the Persian Gulf a smaller edition of what the United States had in the Mediterranean in the shape of the 6th Fleet. Such a force would be capable of deploying its striking power in a few hours, thus avoiding a confrontation with Arab nationalists resentful of the presence of troops on the mainland. The changed military requirements of the West meant that Britain had far less need to cajole its allies into close association so as to secure rights upon their territories. But it was not (yet) able to do without some military presence in those regions of vital British interest.[6]

An official working party examined the issue and confirmed the arguments of the Minister of Defence: the only way in which overseas military expenditure could be reduced to the extent suggested by the Treasury was by cutting commitments and completely withdrawing troops from certain areas.[7] It was not possible to save £34 million merely by withdrawing a small proportion of the units engaged in a number of theatres in the hope that those remaining could continue to meet the commitment. If an attempt was made to retain a capability to intervene promptly in an area from which British troops had been withdrawn, very substantial expenditure would be required, for example, to expand transport aircraft, floating stockpiles and seaborne support. This additional expenditure would have an extremely adverse effect on the economy and thus on the balance of payments. On the other hand, if it was intended to station in the United Kingdom troops which were currently abroad, this would also involve additional expenditure such as new permanent accommodation and married quarters. In certain territories – for instance Hong Kong, Cyprus and Malta – a major reduction in overseas military expenditure might produce grave difficulties for the local economies, and it would be difficult to refuse some measures of compensatory aid. The government thus had the choice between giving up Britain's world role by completely withdrawing from certain areas (a course which would not necessarily have produced very large savings, as MoD officials were eager to point out), or deciding to maintain present commitments, even at the price of cuts in other sectors of government expenditure.

Macmillan was still convinced that it would be possible to have his cake and eat it. While he was determined not to give up Britain's world role, he was fully aware of the need to reduce overseas expenditure. This, he thought, might be possible by finding alternative means of maintaining Britain's influence and of protecting British interests. A reduction or even withdrawal of the forces stationed in Germany seemed not to be feasible because of the repercussions on Britain's standing in NATO and its special relationship with the United States. If cutbacks could be made, they would unavoidably have to be in the Persian Gulf or the Far East. Officials were therefore instructed to reassess Britain's defence requirements in these two areas. They were to study how Britain's defence and foreign policy could be restructured in line with Treasury demands, which required overseas defence expenditure to be reduced from £234 million per annum to £200 million – without, however, making it necessary to withdraw completely from any region.[8] To achieve this, officials were to define vital interests in each area and make an assessment of those which could be defended by military means. If the troops maintained at considerable cost in the Middle or Far East could not be used to guarantee a permanent protection of British interests, Britain had to find other means of achieving its aims. Officials were therefore instructed to pay particular attention to the practicability of meeting Britain's commitments by a strategy based on greater air and sea mobility – and less dependent on military measures.[9]

While Macmillan looked for alternative means to protect British interests, he in no way doubted the usefulness of informal empire. He believed that Britain's main interest in the Middle East lay in its continued access to Kuwait's oil on the present favourable terms. For this, Kuwait's independence (which depended on British support against Iraqi and Saudi encroachments) provided the best assurance. The question was how best to secure this independence. If Kuwait could be protected by a combination of political and military arrangements, with increasing emphasis on the former, it might be possible to reduce the number of troops stationed in the area. In south-east Asia, Britain's commitments stemmed mainly from a combination of its desire to prevent the expansion of Chinese and Soviet influence, and her responsibility for the defence of Malaya and the remaining colonial territories. Mingled with these aims was the wish to keep Australia and New Zealand in the Commonwealth, as well as to maintain Britain's standing in relation to the United States. Here the creation of a Greater Malaysia, i.e. a merger of Malaya, Singapore and the Borneo territories, seemed to offer the best hope for the future. The use of Singapore might not be guaranteed, but at least it would be possible to dispose of some obligations without undue risk. In the long run Singapore was to be replaced with large-scale forward bases in Australia. This would allow Britain to continue to play a substantial role in the region, but with less onerous military commitments.

In the ensuing discussions, official attention focused on the Middle East – not least because there was no prospect of a solution along the lines of Greater Malaysia which would allow for a graceful exit. The FO warned that in present international circumstances a reduction of Britain's military effort overseas would disproportionately affect its ability to fulfil its existing commitments. It would have far-reaching effects on Britain's prestige and influence as a world power and would involve a significant change in its overseas policy generally. Cuts in the Middle East would be particularly disastrous. Instead of attempting to make savings by limiting Britain's ability to meet its international obligations, the government should concentrate on 'positive policies' to improve overseas earnings.[10] The United Kingdom had to retain, for some time to come, the ability to intervene in Kuwait with military means. Oil from other sources would be dearer and an item of dollar expenditure. In addition, Kuwaiti oil was at the very heart of the trade of British companies like Shell and British Petroleum (BP), the profits of which were vital for the United Kingdom's balance of payments. If these companies were excluded from the Middle East, the additional cost to Britain's balance of payments would probably be around £200 million per annum and possibly much more.[11] British defence costs in the region, amounting to £30 million–£40 million, could therefore be considered money well spent.

According to the FO, the best chance of protecting the United Kingdom's economic interests lay in the preservation of an independent Kuwait and the continuation of its cooperation with HMG. This made changes in the present financial arrangements connected with the oil operations less likely to be to Britain's disadvantage, not only in Kuwait itself but also in the other oil-producing countries around the Persian Gulf. To achieve this, it was essential to maintain the confidence, not only of the Emir of Kuwait, but also of the region's other rulers – and this could only be done by a visible military presence. Nevertheless, in the long run, it was likely that the oil companies would be disadvantaged by the changes. Oil-producing states throughout the world made efforts to co-ordinate their policies with the object of gaining a larger share of the profits and some control of the industry. Although the possibility of preserving the present position by military means would thus steadily diminish over the next decade, the essential thing was to buy time. As long as Kuwait and the other Gulf sheikhdoms depended on the United Kingdom for protection and were 'reasonably assured that we are in a position to protect them', they were likely to follow rather than lead demands for an increased share in revenues.[12]

FO and MoD officials, as well as the military, argued that satisfactory insurance for British oil interests could not be obtained without the considerable military and financial effort Britain made at present. It was unrealistic to assume that Kuwait's membership of the Arab League would give it sufficient security. A United Nations force might help, but it was unlikely to be effective because its operations would be subject to veto by the Soviet Union. A considerable increase in the size and efficiency of Kuwait's own forces might reduce its dependence on British troops, but that would take some time. Moreover, when trying to revise the defence arrangements, Britain had to take care not to antagonise Kuwait's ruler. It was important to retain his confidence to ensure that he continued to keep his substantial financial reserves in sterling. That is why it was not feasible, at least for the time being, to consider even a partial withdrawal. Britain had to maintain a military presence in the area that was sufficient both to deter Iraq and, failing deterrence, to intervene in time to hold Kuwait itself in the face of an Iraqi attack.[13]

In reply Treasury officials pointed out that, since the economies of the region's oil-producing states depended on the sale of petroleum, even a communist-controlled regime would be reluctant to stop sales. Physical access to Middle East oil therefore did not depend on Britain maintaining a military presence in the area or on its sustaining any particular regime. The cost of the oil, and the size of the profits which accrued to British firms engaged in oil production, would be determined ultimately by commercial considerations. It was not likely that Britain could maintain for long a position in which states friendly to it received a smaller share in the profits of their oil production than those inclined to be hostile. Moreover, it was uncertain how useful military means really were to protect British interests. If Britain was presented with a successful revolution, it might well be that it would put its interests at risk if it tried to reverse it by force of arms. Equally, Saudi Arabia or another Arab state might establish an influence over Kuwait, which, while impairing its independence, would make a military remedy inappropriate.[14] For all these reasons, Treasury officials concluded, it was clear that a reduction of overseas commitments in the Middle East would not imperil any vital British interests – while their maintenance implied pointless expenditure which could jeopardise Britain's balance of payments and thus, at least indirectly, the stability of sterling.

The report written after these discussions, while acknowledging the reservations made of the Treasury, was overwhelmingly a reflection of FO and MoD views. It underlined that an effective military presence was necessary to protect British interests in the Middle East: Kuwait would continue to depend on British support for a considerable time to come. As concerned south-east Asia, officials concluded that at least throughout the 1960s it would be necessary to maintain a military presence in order to achieve the United Kingdom's general aims, i.e. the containment of communism, the maintenance of British influence and the promotion of trade. The long-term trend should be towards a reduction of the capacity to intervene in operations on the Asian mainland, while maintaining a visible military presence in Singapore and Malaya. British strategy in the area should increasingly rely on air-borne and sea-borne forces operating from Australia and New Zealand, 'the only permanent and reliable Western bases in the Eastern hemisphere'.

Britain's military presence in south-east Asia itself should be scaled back by 1970 – not because Britain's interests and obligations would have diminished, but because man-power and financial difficulties, coupled with uncertainties about bases, would make it necessary. It was not feasible, though, to contemplate the total withdrawal of forces without abandoning Britain's remaining colonial responsibilities, the obligations to Malaya and the South-East Asia Treaty Organisation (SEATO), and its part in containing China. It would also damage Britain's relations with Australia, New Zealand and the United States. Instead, more stress should be laid on economic programmes, information work, broadcasting and other cultural activities such as English-language teaching. Furthermore, Britain should do all it could to help the countries of the area to become militarily independent so as to lessen the need for intervention. Britain should also try to share with friends and allies commitments which, in many cases, were more vital to them than to Britain.[15] These deliberations also applied to the Middle East, even though as yet it was not feasible to move forces out of the area.

When ministers discussed the official findings, they agreed that a withdrawal of British forces from any area would have major repercussions. If withdrawals were contemplated, their timing would require careful study, and some 'acceptable substitute' for the presence of British forces would have to be made available.[16] While the commitment in the Middle East had to be maintained unchanged, it might be appropriate to begin planning for a change in Britain's military presence in the Far East. Instead of relying on cantonments in Malaya and Singapore, Britain should consider building a main base in Australia, with forward operating facilities in strategically located places such as the Addu Atoll, supported by aircraft carriers which could be used as floating airfields.[17] An air-borne and sea-borne capacity could then be used to intervene in south-east Asia. It was essential to reduce the strain on British resources, not only for financial reasons, but also because of the pressing need to find additional man-power to fill the serious gaps in troop numbers in Germany without recourse to some form of national service. Therefore everything should be done to merge Malaya, Singapore and the

Borneo territories into a Greater Malaysia. This would relieve HMG of its 'most invidious and burdensome responsibilities' in the area, and would resolve the problem of Singapore, which faced the danger of popular revolt because Britain had consistently denied constitutional advance.[18]

Ministers agreed that the most desirable strategy for the next decade would be a double stance: while trying to retain its bases as long as possible, Britain should also start building up, as an 'insurance' against their loss, large amphibious task forces capable in themselves of mounting operations in defence of metropolitan interests. Until the necessary preparations had been made, however, i.e. until the end of the decade, it was essential to retain facilities in Aden and Singapore. At the end of this period it might be possible to do without them.[19] In no case was it possible to accept that abandoning a base, at whatever date, would be followed by the total withdrawal of British troops (and influence) from the area affected. To do so would prejudice Britain's relations with NATO, CENTO and SEATO, i.e. all the major alliances of which it was a member. Ministers were still convinced that, without its informal empire, Britain would lose its standing as a world power as well as the special relationship, while also putting at risk its balance of payments and the stability of sterling.

1963: Planning for the Next Decade

Yet Another Review? The Oversea Co-ordinating Committee

The debate about informal empire continued in 1963, when the Chancellor of the Exchequer, Reginald Maudling, called for a radical reassessment of Britain's role east of Suez: the military commitments in the Middle and Far East should be given up by 1970 because they were not worth the money they cost.[20] No sensible policy could be based on the idea of total and immediate withdrawal. At the same time, the government should consider the possibility of taking decisions which would lead to major reductions by the end of the decade. The value of the Middle Eastern commitment was particularly questionable, not least because commitments in Africa had substantially contracted. The only military operation in Africa which British forces might be required to undertake would be to protect the settlers in Kenya. Once the colony was independent, such an operation (if it could be mounted at all) would not of itself justify the maintenance of substantial forces in Aden. The defence of Britain's oil interests, particularly those in Kuwait, was therefore the main argument in favour of retaining military bases in the area. But the economic validity of this justification was questionable. If analysed correctly, the economic benefits, both direct and indirect, that Britain derived from its interests in the area would be found to be less than the cost of maintaining its forces. A detailed study of this aspect should be made.

A withdrawal from Aden would not necessarily lead to the severance of communications or an interruption of trade. British ships still passed freely through the Suez Canal, although the bases in Egypt had gone. Britain still traded with Africa, although its military presence in the region had been substantially reduced. The same applied to the Middle East: the oil-exporting countries would still have to sell their petroleum, whether or not Britain maintained troops in Aden. Some kind of reassessment was also required with regard to British commitments in Singapore, which, according to the Chancellor of the Exchequer, derived solely from the need to safeguard Britain's position in India. Now that the Raj no longer existed, and with the total cost of maintaining forces east of Suez rising towards some £600 million per annum, the government should reconsider the economic and political consequences of a withdrawal. In the last resort the defence of Australia and New Zealand might be the only commitment to which it would be essential to make a contribution; and that by itself would require a wholly different military posture.

The Foreign and Commonwealth Secretaries replied that, notwithstanding its arguable economic value, the military presence in Aden was above all politically significant: it exerted a stabilising influence in the Middle East and sustained Britain's standing as a world power. Britain's prestige would decline if it was thought to have withdrawn its forces because it could no longer afford them. Aden was also 'a stepping stone' in communications to the Far East.[21] Therefore it was necessary to maintain an effective military presence; it might be desirable, however, to re-adjust British policy towards an accommodation of Arab nationalism instead of continuing support for autocratic regimes in whose hands many of Britain's economic interests were still concentrated. Special regard should be paid to alternative means of discharging treaty obligations towards Kuwait. The most effective course might be to encourage Kuwait to raise its own national forces on a scale large enough to hold a bridgehead against attack until the arrival of reinforcements from the United Kingdom. As regards the position in the Far East, it was not a relic once needed to protect the Raj. The forces based in Singapore had four important tasks: to meet Britain's commitment towards the external defence of Malaysia; to discharge its obligations to SEATO; to discourage the 'aggressive designs' of Indonesia; and to provide reinforcements for Hong Kong. With the possible exception of Hong Kong, it did not appear that any of these tasks could be abandoned without a fundamental change of policy. Moreover, the removal of British forces from the Far East would be regarded as a major political defeat and would (quite apart from its serious effect on relations with Australia, New Zealand and the United States), encourage the spread of communism.

In order to clarify the issue, the Prime Minister arranged for studies to be prepared on the cost of maintaining the base at Aden in relation to the value of the interests it was designed to protect. Officials were also to study the economic and political consequences of a withdrawal or substantial reduction of the forces based in Hong Kong and Singapore.[22] The overseas co-ordinating committee that was charged with the task consisted of FO, MoD, Ministry of Power and Treasury officials. As we have seen, the first three ministries were in favour of keeping British forces in the Middle East for as long as possible. Withdrawal would not merely remove the deterrent against foreign encroachment on Kuwait's independence, but would even provoke it by causing instability. Moreover, it would cause 'a great shock' in Iran and the Arabian Peninsula, where both Britain and the United States were doing their utmost to preserve stability. The United Kingdom had a clear economic interest in maintaining supplies of relatively cheap oil. But given Europe's dependence on oil and the inadequacy of alternative supplies, the security of Middle Eastern oil supplies was even more important than their low cost. Soviet influence or a unification of several Arab countries would be most damaging to Western interests. Both scenarios were for the time being excluded by Britain's commitment. The situation might change quickly, though, if troops were withdrawn.[23]

The Treasury replied that the forces stationed in the Middle East should be regarded as an insurance premium: their annual cost of about £125 million was too high in relation to their effect on the likelihood of damage and to the probable extent of that damage. In fact, Britain was paying a 100 per cent premium. The pressure for an increase in oil prices would rise in any case, and the cost of retaining the capacity to intervene would also mount. In addition, it was doubtful whether British forces would have any real bearing on the stability of the area or on the likelihood of Soviet penetration. These considerations apart, it was not feasible to maintain the present posture in Aden indefinitely. The increasing spread of Arab nationalism and growing international pressure would sooner or later impose a deadline on the maintenance of a major base in Aden along present lines. And whatever the present balance of economic advantage between the cost of the forces and the risk to Britain's oil interests, it was likely to worsen if the government adopted costly alternatives to Aden. Since Britain had to leave sooner or later, it ought to begin to plan for withdrawal: this alone would enable Britain to control the timing and the modalities of its action, and to leave with the maximum of goodwill and political stability. An essential element in any such plan would be the development of friendly relationships with Arab nationalists. Arab nationalism was the most effective antidote to communism, even if took an anti-Western form. Therefore British forces should be scaled back as fast as possible. The withdrawal should be completed by 1968 and 1970.

In May 1963 the overseas co-ordinating committee reported to ministers. Like its predecessor two years earlier, the committee was heavily influenced by the views of the FO and MoD. Apparently, the financial constraints were not (yet) strong enough to force any radical changes on policy-makers. The problem clearly centred on uncertainty over the precise effect of Britain's military presence; a withdrawal may not have the catastrophic consequences predicted by FO and MoD; but the Treasury could be over-optimistic. A majority of officials considered the assets at stake too important to put them at risk.[24] According to the official report, the United States welcomed Britain's military presence in the area and was ready to give full diplomatic support. But the United States had made it clear that it would be unable to replace Britain and therefore wished it to retain primary responsibility. If the United States was not in a position to take Britain's place, no other Western power could be expected to do so. Any widespread withdrawal could thus damage Britain's standing and influence in the United States and in NATO. Economies had to be made, and the object should be to produce substantial savings by 1970, when projections of defence costs showed a sharp increase. But the government should work towards a gradual reduction of forces, rather than a deliberate withdrawal – provided circumstances in the Middle East permitted this. Thus it would be possible to make adjustments in accordance with changes in the world oil supply position, as well as the relative position of oil-producing countries and companies. The political trends in the area made it possible that regimes to which Britain's oil and military policies were adjusted would have disappeared by the end of the decade. Though it was not possible to prevent this, British forces could at least slow down developments which could reduce the profitability of British oil interests.

Furthermore, the report argued, Britain's military presence in the Far East had to be considered against the background of global Anglo-American defence relations. The United States had repeatedly stressed that it attached great importance to secure the tenure of the Singapore base. Any reduction of Britain's defence contribution in the area could therefore cause the United States to revise its opinion of the United Kingdom as an effective partner in the defence of the free world. US support for British strategic interests might be diminished or even withdrawn. The United States could increase its pressure on Britain to raise its military expenditure in Europe. Thus the savings made in south-east Asia would be lost, and expenditure would have to be increased in an area where there were no vital economic interests to be defended.[25] This trans-Atlantic consideration apart, Britain also had a general interest in preserving the region's stability against communist penetration and Indonesian aggression. Malaya was still an important member of the sterling area, and it was important to protect its independence. Last, but not least, the maintenance of close relations with Australia and New Zealand depended to a considerable extent on the two countries' belief in Britain's continuing commitment to their defence.

The Debate About New Aircraft Carriers

As would be expected, the debate about Britain's overseas commitments was far from over once officials had reported their findings. In fact, it continued with even more vehemence. The reason for this was the MoD's request to plan for the construction of a replacement aircraft carrier which could take over from HMS *Ark Royal* in the 1970s, thus maintaining the carrier fleet's present strength of three. If no replacement carrier was provided, the Minister of Defence argued, Britain would have to rely on an island base solution, even though a panel of scientists had advised that this would be much less effective than a strategy based on aircraft carriers. If, in the 1970s, Britain wanted to be able to apply force overseas in the pursuit of political aims and for the protection of economic interests (as ministers had decided it should), it had to opt for the carrier replacement programme, since it was not clear how long bases in Aden or Singapore would remain available.[26] The Chancellor of the Exchequer, however, argued that the replacement carrier was beyond the Britain's means: the United Kingdom could no longer afford the burden that overseas defence expenditure put on its resources. The strength of the national economy depended upon the maintenance of Britain's position in a competitive world. If the government accepted burdens that were not carried by its main European competitors, it would subject the country to a handicap that might prove to be intolerable:

How can we rationally as a country plan to continue a situation in which we alone of the European powers maintain both our full contribution to European defence and massive external commitments that other European countries do not share [?].[27]

Britain's strategy assumed that it needed to fulfil three main roles, namely, to retain an independent nuclear deterrent, to contribute forces to the defence of Europe and to maintain a military presence east of Suez. In the present circumstances it was not possible to abandon either of the first two. The future of the aircraft carriers therefore had to be examined in the context of the third role, i.e. in terms of Britain's ability to deter limited aggression on a worldwide scale.[28] The levels of defence expenditure forecast would present the government with very serious economic problems; they would make it necessary to reduce public expenditure in other areas, for example, on housing and education, or dampen public consumption by raising the level of taxation. Either course would have profound effects which would do more damage to Britain's long-term prosperity, and therefore its international standing, than would a reduction in military capability. Moreover, given the degree to which defence expenditure had increased over comparatively short periods of time, it was doubtful how realistic the present forecasts were. The defence estimates for 1964/65 had risen by £164 million, while the target figure for 1965/66 would presumably exceed £170 million.[29] The same would happen in the future. Even though the Minister of Defence was only making a request for one ship, nobody doubted that this would inevitably lead in the 1970s to a substantial carrier fleet with the immense expenditure that would entail. If defence expenditure was to be brought down to tolerable limits, a major strategic decision had to be taken – that is, not to replace HMS *Ark Royal* and to withdraw the troops from east of Suez by the end of the decade.

The Chancellor of the Exchequer did not accept that the need for such a strategic decision had been obviated by the report of the overseas co-ordinating committee: the report merely took existing commitments in turn and noted the difficulties any change in present policy would engender. There had been no discussion of whether, for wider political reasons, the commitments should not be ended despite the difficulties existing in each case. The government had not yet taken any firm decision to maintain unchanged Britain's present worldwide strategy unchanged and to accept the economic consequences: the arguments had not yet been fully deployed. There was no question of an immediate withdrawal from commitments in the Middle or Far East. But it had yet to be shown that future plans were not be based on the assumption that by the early 1970s overseas commitments would have decisively contracted. By 1970 it might no longer be necessary to maintain forces in the Middle East for the protection of Kuwait, while in the Far East, Malaya might reach a political understanding with Indonesia which would reduce the risk of war. Moreover, no circumstances could now be foreseen in which Britain would be required to mount, unaided by the United States or its other allies, a military intervention in any part of the world. Under such circumstances there would be no need for carriers.

The government was advised in particular to re-think its decision to maintain a military presence in Aden, which was needed presumably to protect the region's essential oil supplies. But in reality it enabled Britain to deal with only one possible development out of many. While the military occupation of Kuwait by the Iraqis could be prevented by moving forces into the area first, it would not be feasible to use force to eject the Iraqis. Nor was it possible to prevent political developments which might, in commercial terms, be disadvantageous to Britain. As had been shown at the time of the Abadan crisis and subsequently in Indonesia, the economic interest of the producer countries rather than the threat of military intervention often proved to be the decisive factor inducing them to reach a satisfactory settlement. No hard and fast equation could be drawn between the cost of maintaining forces at Aden and the value of the interests thus safeguarded. Rather it was a matter of striking a balance between the likelihood and the disadvantage of various possible developments and assessing the degree to which the insurance against one particular risk (which the present forces at Aden represented) would in future years be likely to justify the cost of the premium.[30]

Maudling was supported by the Cabinet Secretary, Burke Trend, who argued that the government should concentrate on the essential: 'a reasonable contribution to Europe, the maintenance of some deterrent capability, no standing garrisons overseas, but a really efficient strategic reserve able to respond effectively to calls for help from any friendly power'.[31] Aircraft carriers would not necessarily have a part to play in such a concept and therefore needed no replacement. The forces in Aden protected Kuwait against a military take-over and so long as Kuwait remained independent, Britain would be assured of cheap oil. But military forces in Aden could do nothing to preserve oil supplies as such; if the Middle East countries found other customers prepared to pay a higher price, military pressure would be useless. Nor could military forces do anything against Soviet subversion.

What, in the last resort, would protect Britain's oil supplies was the

Middle Eastern countries' willingness to sell oil. The need to maintain commitments in the Far East was equally debatable.[32] If their object was to provide military help to friendly powers on invitation, then the question was whether this help should be provided by the United Kingdom. As concerned the protection of trade, it had to be kept in mind that other nations with extensive commercial interests did not maintain navies for their protection without suffering any substantial harm. There were two ways of seeking economies in defence expenditure: the government could either further reduce the forces stationed overseas without purporting to disavow any of its obligations or jettison its interests or it could explicitly shed obligations and interests in some parts of the world and tailor the defence effort accordingly. The first course was hardly practicable. It would not be possible for long to hide the reduction in military strength. Britain would thus merely invite the attack which its defence policy was designed to avert. If the second course was adopted, then cuts would have to be made overseas. For wider political reasons (in particular the special relationship), the effort in Europe could not be curtailed. Savings were therefore limited to the Middle and Far East. Britain had important interests, especially in the Middle East. It was relevant to ask what would happen if Britain withdrew its military presence. But it was also relevant to ask whether, even if Britain tried to retain its commitments, it would in fact be able to pursue, indefinitely, the type of strategy by which it had hitherto sought to protect its interests. Current indications in this respect were not encouraging.

According to Trend, it would be more realistic to opt for an alternative policy. So long as the government tried to discharge the full range of Britain's existing commitments, there was no doubt that the defence budget would account for more than 7 per cent of GNP, with further rises in future. Therefore reductions were necessary. First, the government could declare that Britain would never try to land ground forces in distant parts of the world without allies – thus being absolved of the necessity to build a replacement carrier. Second, it could seek to persuade others to carry a larger share of the defence burden. Finally, HMG should try to come to terms politically with Britain's potential enemies both in the Middle and in the Far East instead of trying to contain them by the threat of military force. This would imply disengaging honourably from commitments to individual rulers and governments as rapidly as possible, and seeking to substitute for them strong and stable anti-communist regimes which satisfied nationalist aspirations.

Maudling and Burke Trend were vehemently opposed by the

Minister of Defence Peter Thorneycroft, who acknowledged the strength of the economic arguments in favour of withdrawal, but insisted that the political difficulties and dangers involved in securing major reductions were no less powerful. He argued that the carriers were not only needed to protect British trade or to support the army. The uncertainty of the availability of bases east of Suez and the possibility of threats to British interests made it essential to have a flexible air base which could only be provided by aircraft carriers.[33] Without the carriers it would not be possible to maintain the commitments east of Suez. And since Britain could not afford to abandon its position in Europe, an independent deterrent, or its commitments east of Suez, defence expenditure would have to rise, possibly to about 7.5 per cent of GNP.

Thorneycroft was supported by the Foreign and the Commonwealth Secretaries. According to Lord Home and Duncan Sandys, the land bases east of Suez would probably have to be given up in the 1970s. Therefore it was understandable that the Chancellor of the Exchequer did not want to waste desperately needed resources on them. But expenditure on carriers would continue to show returns in the shape of the ability to maintain a military presence and to bring force to bear in any region of the world. The United Kingdom had worldwide interests and therefore needed a worldwide presence to protect them. As circumstances changed, the nature of Britain's commitments would change too: in the future, there would be fewer territories for whose security the United Kingdom was directly responsible, or where it had to maintain a direct physical presence. But it was absolutely essential to secure the sources of industrial power, in particular oil.[34] The British presence in the Middle East ensured the independence of the oil-producing states. This guaranteed as far as possible that oil was available not merely in terms of supply but above all on profitable commercial terms. Britain would certainly not gain 'anything very solid' in terms of either goodwill or commerce by dismantling its position in the Middle East. The little it would gain would not offset the advantages it derived from its presence in the region which, apart from oil, included a 'very flourishing trade' with the Gulf states.[35] As concerned the commitment in south-east Asia, it served to protect Malaya from Indonesian aggression and guaranteed that Britain could maintain its close relationship with Australia, New Zealand and the United States. Therefore it was indispensable for Britain's financial and political interests.

Macmillan acknowledged the reservations made by the Chancellor of the Exchequer: if Britain attempted to maintain a military role it could not afford, the economy could suffer substantial damage. On the other hand, what was at issue was the structure and capability of the navy not only over the next few years, but in the decades after 1970. The relative importance of Europe in the Cold War would progressively diminish, particularly if an agreement on the prohibition of nuclear tests led to some more general relaxation of political and military tension. But no similar prospect had as yet presented itself in the Far East. Indeed, the situation in that area of the world might develop in the opposite direction. As for the Middle East, there was no prospect that the threat to Kuwait's independence would diminish. Therefore the government could not afford to weaken its defences east of Suez. A majority of ministers felt the same way: on 30 July 1963 the Cabinet decided to maintain the aircraft carrier fleet at a level of three ships during the 1970s and to build a new aircraft carrier to replace HMS *Ark Royal* – even at the price of allowing defence expenditure to exceed 7 per cent of GNP. The informal empire was still considered essential for Britain's economic and political interests, and policy-makers were ready to pay a high price for it.

Outlook: The Wilson Government and the Commitments East of Suez

The elections in October 1964 did not bring about any decisive change in British strategy. The new Labour government under Harold Wilson was as determined as its Conservative predecessors to maintain Britain's world role and the still considerable commitments east of Suez: in the first two years of the Wilson government, the debate over savings concentrated largely on the question of how Britain was to fulfil its military commitments, rather than the scope of those commitments.[36] On financial grounds, the new Labour government under Wilson was anxious to avoid an open-ended commitment to the defence of Malaysia (i.e. the state created out of Malaya, Singapore and Borneo territories in September 1963) against renewed Indonesian aggression. But it thought it in Britain's interests to retain a military presence which would be considered worthwhile by its allies. Attempting to move out completely, it feared, would cause 'great offence' and prejudice the prospect of future collaboration – which was particularly relevant to US support for sterling.[37] It was essential to convince Australia, New Zealand and the United States that if Britain planned to withdraw some time in the future from Malaysia, this was not simply to save money. It would happen because the political situation there made retention of bases politically and militarily disadvantageous.[38] After the withdrawal, British forces should be stationed in Australia and the Indian Ocean islands. Despite redeployment and reduction, Britain would still therefore maintain forces in areas that were sufficiently powerful to make an effective contribution to the containment of China and the preservation of stability in south-east Asia – and thereby to preserve the special relationship with the United States, Australia and New Zealand.

The commitment in the Middle East was equally to be maintained, although the military presence in Aden should be strongly reduced. Local hostility was likely to weaken the base's value in the future. In order to lessen the political disadvantages the base entailed, the military presence in Aden was to be reduced to the minimum level needed to discharge Britain's treaty obligations. A military presence on a much reduced scale, coupled with some additional economic aid (facilitated by a substantial reduction in military expenditure) was expected to fill the gap comparatively cheaply and at much less cost in terms of Arab goodwill. Britain would thus be able to intervene in Africa, the Middle East and the Indian Ocean without appearing to threaten an area of predominantly Arab interest.[39]

The defence review of February 1966 reiterated the government's intention to retain the naval presence in Singapore (which left the federation in 1965) and Malaysia as well as the troops in Aden and the Persian Gulf, while also placing great emphasis on the 'overstretch' of Britain's defence capabilities. This overstretch was to be eliminated, and the defence budget was to be cut to 6 per cent of GNP. At the same time, overseas expenditure was to be reduced by £100 million in 1967/68.[40] Such a reduction, however, would be possible only if no new aircraft carriers were constructed and if commitments east of Suez were ended. For some time, policy-makers hoped that it was possible to avoid this. But in the end they had to acknowledge that it was no longer feasible to go on pretending that existing commitments could be met with the available resources. In July 1967 it was announced that Britain would withdraw all its forces from east of Suez by the mid-1970s. A further sterling crisis, leading to devaluation in November 1967, led the Cabinet to accelerate the withdrawal even further: the last British troops were now to leave Malaysia, Singapore and the Persian Gulf by the end of 1971. The fleet of F-111 aircraft, originally intended to provide an air power replacement for the obsolete carriers, was cancelled.[41]

Contrary to a widespread assumption, however, this decision did not by any means signal the end of Britain's determination to remain a major world power able to defend its interest all over the world. Thus even while troop withdrawals were being ordered, Britain still remained actively involved in the affairs of the Middle East and south-east Asia. The two aircraft carriers that had been due to be phased out in the early 1970s remained in service until 1978 and the early 1980s respectively (after they had undergone expensive refits), and, contrary to the decision taken in 1967, orders for new carriers were placed in 1973 and 1975. In Singapore and Malaysia, British forces were retained until the end of the 1970s. Hong Kong remained a colony until 1997, and the Gulf War of 1991 saw a massive British contribution to the effort of evicting Iraq from Kuwait. The objective of British defence policy still remains the capacity to project military power and to intervene in distant regions of the world. Aircraft carriers continue to play an important role in this context. The 1998 defence review announced that the government would spend up to £8 billion on two new large aircraft carriers to replace the navy's three smaller ones – as in 1962, the decision was vehemently questioned by the Treasury, but supported by the Prime Minister.[42]

Conclusion

During Macmillan's second term in office the Treasury continued to call for a cut-back in defence and overseas commitments. The military and the FO were ready to reduce certain commitments if there was some compensation in the form of aircraft carriers and rapid-intervention forces which would allow Britain to maintain a worldwide presence. This would reduce overseas expenditure, but involve some addition to the total defence budget – a course strongly resisted by the Treasury. In order to get an assessment of where money could be saved without doing damage to vital interests, Macmillan ordered another review.

In the ensuing discussion, Treasury officials stressed that overseas commitments were not needed to ensure that Middle Eastern countries continued to sell their oil to the West. As concerned the equally important question of the cost of oil and the share of profits, the presence of British troops could at best provide a short delay before regional developments would force a change. These short-term gains did not justify the relatively high expenditure incurred. FO and MoD officials, on the other hand, were adamant that any withdrawal from the region would do disproportionate damage to Britain's influence and international standing as well as to its economic interests. For them, the profits of informal empire far outweighed the amount of money spent on troops and bases. The commitments in south-east Asia also had to be maintained: they contained communism, preserved British influence, fostered trade – and made sure Australia, New Zealand and the United States continued to consider Britain a Great Power. This was crucial, not only for political reasons: without foreign confidence it would become impossible to maintain a strong pound sterling. In the long run, the presence of troops in the region might be reduced. But the capacity to intervene rapidly had to be maintained by the build-up of air-borne and sea-borne forces based in Australia. These views were fully endorsed by ministers. Wherever possible, reductions were to be made in order to save money and manpower. Under no circumstances, however, was the informal empire to be abandoned.

After a brief respite, the debate about Britain's overseas commitments continued in 1963. Again it was the Chancellor of the Exchequer who called for a reassessment. Given Britain's enormous financial difficulties, the government should prepare for withdrawal by 1970. Macmillan reacted by charging the overseas co-ordinating committee with drawing up a cost–benefit analysis of the British presence east of Suez. The arguments put forward by the officials were basically the same as those used two years earlier. The Treasury claimed that the insurance premium paid to protect British interests was far too high. Instead of opposing changes which had to come about sooner or later, Britain should begin to scale back its forces. The FO and the MoD replied that a withdrawal would destabilise the whole of the Middle East, lead to drastic increases in the oil price, and even jeopardise the supply of oil to the West. Furthermore, a withdrawal would lead the United States to revise its opinion of the United Kingdom as a worthy partner. As a result, it would no longer grant the necessary military, diplomatic and financial support, needed to maintain Britain's international position.

As in 1961, it was the views of the FO and the MoD which prevailed and were embraced by most ministers. However, the Chancellor of the Exchequer did not lose heart. When the MoD requested the building of a replacement air carrier, he strongly objected. The commitments east of Suez should be scrapped since they were neither a guarantee for stability nor vital for the protection of trade. The Minister of Defence, as well as the Foreign and Commonwealth Secretaries, defended the call for a replacement carrier as a necessary condition of maintaining a worldwide presence. It was also necessary to contain Soviet expansionism and protect British assets – in short, to demonstrate that the United Kingdom was still a Great Power. Macmillan and most other ministers agreed that it was vital to maintain a worldwide presence (particularly in the Middle East), and that the carriers were needed to defend it – even at the price of defence expenditure exceeding 7 per cent of GNP.

Initially, the Wilson Labour government followed policy along lines laid down by its predecessors. Ministers were anxious to reduce the pressure on Britain's balance of payments, but feared that complete withdrawal would antagonise its allies and have disastrous repercussions on its international position, its economic interests and the stability of sterling. Overwhelming financial difficulties finally led the government to announce that all forces would be withdrawn from east of Suez by the mid-1970s. A further sterling crisis coupled with devaluation further accelerated the end of informal empire. However, this did not signal the end of Britain's determination to play a leading role in international affairs. Rapid reaction forces remained an important part of the army, new aircraft carriers were built and British forces repeatedly intervened in the Middle and Far East. The belief that overseas commitments were vital for Britain's role as a Great Power never entirely disappeared from the official mind.

THE FORMAL EMPIRE

While the informal empire continued to exercise a strong hold on the mind of policy-makers in the early 1960s, the formal empire was dismantled with surprising speed. The following chapter will analyse how this came about, and the role of the two people who are often held to be mainly responsible for it, that is, Macmillan and Macleod. Contrary to the explanation given by a number of historians, we will not argue that the speed of decolonisation in Africa was due to a 'downward' reassessment by British officials of the capacity of white settler communities after 1959. Policy-makers were disappointed at the performance of the Europeans with regard to the acceptance of multi-racialism.[43] But what mattered far more (particularly in Kenya) was the insight that it was no longer possible to ignore the black majorities.

The following chapter will disprove Macleod's questionable claim that a rapid dismantling of the remaining colonial empire had been his aim from the very beginning. He certainly intended to accelerate Tanganyika's and Uganda's advance to independence and to announce this publicly. Unlike his predecessors, Macleod thought that in East Africa as in the rest of the empire, there was 'probably greater safety in going too fast than in going slow'. But he did not intend to be a 'gale of change man'.[44] As will be seen, even Tanganyika was at first still expected to become independent in 1968 (while Lennox-Boyd had spoken of 1970 as the likely target date). The following chapter will analyse what finally led Macleod to accept a substantial acceleration of the process. It was definitely not his belief that decolonisation could be used 'to maintain Britain's status as a great power'.[45] The reluctant decision to withdraw rapidly was due to the insight that, given developments on the spot and on the international scene, it was not possible to proceed as planned.

'Decolonisation is an Obvious Necessity': Colonial Policy in the Early 1960s

At the beginning of the 1960s, most 'normal' colonies had either become independent or were about to achieve self-government in the near future. What remained were the difficult cases of East and Central Africa as well as the smaller territories. Resolving these problems became all the more urgent because of local and international developments. The Africans of the CAF increasingly voiced their discontent at being under the sway of white officials in Salisbury. Furthermore, in East Africa demands for constitutional advance had grown stronger. This development coincided with events in the colonies of other European powers. Most French colonies in sub-Saharan Africa had been conceded a limited amount of self-government in 1958, and achieved independence (at least formally) by 1960. The bloody war in Algeria continued, with the *pieds-noirs* employing terrorist methods and parts of the army openly revolting in April 1961. While developments in French black Africa were likely to accelerate demands in the remaining British territories, events in Algeria served as a reminder of what might happen if Britain lost control over the policy-making process in Central Africa. Another warning was the cataclysm that devastated the Belgian Congo from the mid-1960 onwards, after the precipitate ending of colonial rule. These events attracted much international attention, and Belgium was widely blamed for the chaotic situation. At the same time, international criticism of the remaining colonial powers grew stronger, particularly in 1960, with 16 new members (most of them former French colonies) entering the United Nations.

Anti-colonialism reached its formal apotheosis when the United Nations General Assembly adopted a resolution calling for general and total decolonisation. International criticism also focused increasingly on South Africa and its racial policies. After South Africa's withdrawal from the Commonwealth in 1961 it was clear that it was hardly feasible anymore to admit a white-governed CAF (or Kenya) to the Commonwealth if Britain did not want to alienate its other members. Thus in the early 1960s, everything pointed to the need to find a speedy solution to Britain's African problems if it was to avoid a Congo-like break-down, widespread unrest or public chastisement as a reactionary colonial power, which could lead to its international isolation and a break-up of the Commonwealth.

The colonial policy of the second Macmillan government was

determined by the various factors mentioned in earlier chapters: international anti-colonialism, rising discontent in the colonies, fear of communist penetration, a determination to prevent costly counter-insurgency campaigns and maintain local goodwill, as well as developments in other dependent territories. But it was the state of world opinion which now came to have the strongest influence on policy-makers, in particular with regard to 'normal' colonies and smaller territories. The FO concluded by 1959 that colonial rule in Africa had to be ended as soon as possible in order to avoid major damage to Britain's international position. For the FO, maintaining the US alliance and Britain's role as an active and influential member of the United Nations were of paramount concern. Colonialism, however, was a word and an issue which aroused 'the most emotional reaction' among policy-makers in Washington and New York.[46] The FO hoped that by 1962 most of the bigger territories would have become independent, and that then 'our major potential source of embarrassment' would no longer exist. It would be a further advantage if at least some of the smaller territories could be taken outside the purview of the United Nations through association with the United Kingdom.

Increasingly, the need to heed world opinion was also recognised in the CRO. A note written in March 1960 warned that Britain was fast approaching a stage when 'the pressures, both internal and international, for the "ending of Imperialism"' were so strong that independence would have to be conceded before the colonies were ready for it.[47] Similar conclusions were reached by officials in the CO. A letter to various governors, written in September 1960, following the fateful developments in the Belgian Congo and the international condemnation of South Africa's apartheid politics, underlined the new role of the United Nations in relation to British territories, especially in Africa.[48] Events in South Africa and the Congo as well as international reactions to them were 'clearly a turning point of great importance'. The international climate in which Britain had to deal with the problems of its territories had changed – it was essential to find a speedy solution. The United Nations was increasingly dominated by the Afro-Asian group, particularly on colonial issues. With the accession of new members in 1960 it would 'almost certainly' become impossible for Britain to achieve a veto on any important issues. In addition, there was a rising tendency of the United Nations to intervene in the internal affairs of member states, especially where there were problems of a racial character.[49] Good relations with the leading African and Asian states and 'respect' for British policies were the best safeguards against unwelcome interference.[50] It was not feasible, though, to fend off intervention indeterminately. The object of British policy therefore had to be to buy time by making 'concessions on matters which we do not regard as of first importance in the hope of preventing actual interference by the UN while we are still engaged in the difficult problems of East and Central Africa'. In other words, Britain had to get 'off the hook' as soon as possible while struggling to prevent United Nations intervention from upsetting the remaining territories' advance to independence.[51]

What distinguished Macleod's tenure at the CO from that of his predecessors are two factors, both of which are closely linked to the increasing international hostility towards colonialism. Firstly, significant constitutional advance was allowed in East and Central Africa (a development described below), and secondly, for the first time a colony was given independence although there was no cogent internal or international demand for doing so – a sign that formal rule was no longer considered a responsibility or an asset, but rather a burden, even in the CO. The decision to grant Sierra Leone independence had been taken before Macleod took over as Colonial Secretary. What he did in the spring of 1960 was to advise his colleagues to transfer power much earlier than planned although there was no strong indigenous demand for such a step. According to Macleod, such a step would have a double advantage: it would underline Britain's image as a benevolent colonial power which granted independence voluntarily and without reservations.[52] At the same time it would reduce the burden on the Exchequer through the elimination of administrative costs. The Prime Minister and his colleagues agreed. They thought it more advantageous for Britain's image to concede independence than to maintain control over a territory that was of only marginal importance to the United Kingdom and to which assistance could also be granted after the end of formal rule. Once the necessary preparatory steps had been taken, Sierra Leone became an independent member of the Commonwealth in 1961.

Uganda was also set on the road to independence without any strong local demand for it. Until the late 1950s, British concerns about repercussions on neighbouring colonies and about the territory's economic and political viability, as well as Bugandan pressure to retain the kingdom's privileged status within the country, had prevented any significant advance.[53] In late 1959 these concerns were less strong than the desire to free Britain of colonial responsibilities wherever possible. Macleod announced in February 1960 that direct elections, followed by a constitutional conference, would be held the following year. The Bugandan parliament made an abortive declaration of independence, and only 3 per cent of the kingdom's electorate turned out to vote in the election of March 1961. Undisturbed by these developments, Macleod persuaded the Bugandans to attend the constitutional conference in September 1961. In exchange they secured a federal constitution which entrenched particular rights for Buganda. This was a drastic reversal of the centralising policy followed after 1945, which shows how desperate British officials were to reach a settlement that would allow Britain a graceful exit. Internal self-government was reached in March 1962, and in October of that year, Uganda became independent. The country was insufficiently prepared for self-government, and internal divisions were still strong. However, Britain had 'come out with honour' and could now concentrate on the remaining problems: Kenya and the CAF.

The transfer of power in territories which until then had been considered unviable, or which had not yet voiced a strong demand for independence, continued under Macleod's successor and culminated in the mid-1960s. Before describing these events we will first turn to developments in the remaining territories in East and Central Africa.

East and Central Africa

Macleod's First Moves as Colonial Secretary

In the months before the elections of October 1959, Macmillan had repeatedly expressed his concern about the situation in British Africa. He was relieved that, despite the Hola camp incident and the Devlin report, Africa was not a major issue in the elections. In the Prime Minister's view, the Conservatives had 'just succeeded ... in "getting by" on this'. Nonetheless, Kenya and the CAF were still 'the biggest problem looming for us here at home', and the government had to find a way of avoiding future embarrassments.[54] When Lennox-Boyd resigned for personal reasons, Macmillan appointed Macleod as his new Colonial Secretary – an astonishing move, since Macleod had barely any experience in colonial affairs. The explanation is that Macmillan was worried about developments in Africa and wanted to give a new impetus to colonial policy. On the other hand, he was aware of the resistance that might build up in the party, the government or among the white settlers. Therefore he chose Macleod, who, since spring 1959, had repeatedly tried to attract Macmillan's attention over Africa. Although not steeped in imperial affairs, Macleod was brilliant and persuasive. His appointment was a move designed to bring about a change while leaving open the possibility of the Prime Minister using him as scapegoat in case things went wrong.

Macmillan's calculation seems to have been correct: the new

Colonial Secretary immediately set out to cut Britain's Gordian knot in East Africa. Constitutional advance in Tanganyika was to reduce the pressure and allow policy-makers more time to resolve outstanding problems. In November 1959 Macleod informed the Cabinet that there ought to be a substantial step forward and there was 'everything to be gained by making it as quickly as possible'.[55] There was a 'great upsurge of nationalism' in the Belgian Congo; Rwanda and Burundi were in 'a state of turmoil', and there was trouble of a rather similar kind in Nyasaland. Unless British officials came up with an acceptable answer, Tanganyika would be shaken by turmoil as well. The colony's status as a trust territory meant that Britain was already being continuously asked in the United Nations about its plans for constitutional reform. Failing to take the opportunity to initiate a peaceful advance to self-government would be difficult to justify. It might lead the Africans to adopt a policy of non-cooperation and violence. The administrative breakdown and open hostility in the United Nations which would inevitably follow made it desirable to act while Britain was still in control of events.[56]

According to Macleod there was general support for Nyerere's Tanganyika African National Union (TANU), which had won all the African seats in the two-stage elections of 1958–59.[57] Even the European settlers supported it, since they felt they had to act in accordance with the Africans 'lest they find themselves on the shelf in the future'.[58] After the elections of 1960, the majority of both the council of ministers and the legislative council should consist of elected members instead of non-elected officials. Moreover, the elections should be conducted on the basis of a widened franchise – leading with all probability to an African majority government. The precise arrangements were to be settled at a conference in February 1960. Independence would be granted by 1968. Having yielded to the demand of constitutional advance, the government would be on much firmer ground to resist further premature changes. Now, however, it was important to make a gesture in favour of Nyerere because he had become the target of extremists – the 'sad fate' awaiting almost every African leader prepared to cooperate with Britain.[59] If Britain did not support him now, it would either lose Nyerere's goodwill or have to deal with more radical and uncompromising politicians later. If there was a conflict in a territory which hitherto had been regarded as a model for orderly and rapid development towards independence, this would be most damaging to Britain's standing in Africa and elsewhere. It was essential that any constitutional announcement should be seen to flow from HMG 'in the spirit of magnanimity and not as a result of pressure from local politicians'.[60] A well-disposed Nyerere could play an important moderating role in East Africa, ill-disposed, he could become 'an East African Nkrumah'. The government should seize the chance to score points in a territory where there were no major problems with European settlers, thus reducing the pressure in other territories.

Unlike his predecessor, Lennox-Boyd, Macleod advocated a public announcement of the advance in Tanganyika. He argued that this would not create any serious difficulties in Kenya. Sooner or later there would be pressure for self-government in Kenya as well, whatever happened in neighbouring territories. Concessions to Nyerere might slightly accelerate these demands, but in the long run Kenya's interests were better served by securing political stability in Tanganyika than by inducing a 'state of grievous instability'.[61]

In Kenya, there could be no simple or quick solution. But it was vital to reach a settlement lest the situation become more radicalised. Macleod acknowledged that it was important to include protection for property rights in the constitution (as advocated by Macmillan). This was the only way to maintain the settlers' confidence, and to encourage development and investment.[62] But what really mattered in the end was African goodwill: wherever the majority demanded self-government, the prospects of stability and happiness for the minority groups would be determined 'as much by the avoidance of unreasonable delays in the transfer of power as by the specific terms of the constitution'.[63] The important thing was not to lose the Africans' goodwill by delaying constitutional advance too long:

> Although there is much to be said for entrenching property rights deeply in the constitution, although there is much to be said for human rights and Bills of Rights, although, above all, you should do everything you can to ensure an impartial judiciary, yet you must realize that the only final safeguard is the goodwill of the people who live in that country.[64]

The first step to achieve this goodwill in Kenya, Macleod proposed, would be to lift the emergency in force since 1952. This proposal was approved by Cabinet, which announced an end to the emergency on 10 November 1959. Ministers also accepted Macleod's proposal concerning Tanganyika, although some feared that early independence would lead to chaos and have ramifications for the CAF. However, the Cabinet only accepted Macleod's proposal in exchange for some modest concessions – a postponement of the proposed Tanganyika conference from February to April or May 1960, and a limitation on the extension of the franchise, i.e. modifications that would not decisively slow down Tanganyika's advance to black-majority rule.

In the press the announcement of rapid advance in Tanganyika and the lifting of the emergency in Kenya were received very favourably. Macleod concluded that constitutional advance should also be permitted in Nyasaland. The continuation of the emergency could not justified for much longer: the government stood no chance of defending its action if it was brought before the United Nation's Human Rights Commission. The Colonial Secretary therefore pleaded for the release of Hastings Banda and most other detainees.[65] Experience in many other territories showed that more moderate men did not emerge to take the place of leaders who were detained – and in any case there were no more moderate leaders likely to emerge than Banda himself. Advance in Nyasaland was not to signal the end of the CAF. Although a federation was 'the best, indeed at the moment the only real solution for these territories', the government should not underestimate the strength of African opposition against it. The problem was that the governments of Southern Rhodesia and the Federation were 'too stubborn' to appreciate the resentment building up against them. Whether politicians in Salisbury liked it or not, concessions to Banda and his followers were the best, and perhaps the only, hope of holding the position.[66] The CAF could only be preserved if Britain demonstrated that the Africans in Nyasaland (and Northern Rhodesia) did not have to fear the unbridled hegemony of Southern Rhodesia. Once they were assured of this they would certainly recognise the advantages federation held for them.

At a meeting January 1960, Macmillan and Macleod agreed that Banda should be released in March. Thus he would be able, as a free man, to give evidence to the Monckton Commission which was preparing a review of the CAF. Governor Armitage, however, argued in favour of a delay: the emergency might have to continue for some time, and to release Banda while Monckton was still in Nyasaland would pose an unacceptable security risk. Roy Welensky and Edgar Whitehead, the prime ministers of the CAF and Southern Rhodesia respectively, also resisted the proposal. Their stance found some support among British officials. Some ministers argued that recent developments in Africa had given rise to 'widespread anxiety' among white settlers. The government was 'always led by circumstances into negotiating with the extreme African nationalists', making it impossible for the position of the settlers to be adequately safeguarded.[67] It was better to wait so as to reassure the whites. Faced with this opposition, Macmillan wanted to postpone Banda's release. Macleod, however, threatened to resign unless Banda was allowed to give evidence to the Monckton Commission. The Prime Minister yielded and the Colonial Secretary accepted a compromise according to which Banda would be released later than originally planned, but still some days before the departure of the Monckton Commission.

Onset of the 'Wind of Change'?

Despite these first steps taken in late 1959, the Prime Minister had as yet no intention to hand over power precipitately to the African majorities. It is often assumed that Macmillan's famous 'wind of change' speech, made in February 1960, signalled such an intention. This, however, is an erroneous interpretation. Macmillan certainly urged the whites of South Africa to face the reality of African nationalism. He explained that in the past few decades, the process which had given birth to the nation-states of Europe had been repeated all over the world. Fifteen years ago a wave of nationalism had spread through Asia; now the same thing was happening in Africa. In different places it took different forms but it was happening everywhere. The West had to come to terms with it. If it did not manage to do so, it might imperil the 'precarious balance' between the West, the communist bloc and those parts of the world whose people were at present uncommitted either to communism or to Western ideas. The great issue in the second half of the twentieth century was whether the uncommitted peoples of Asia and Africa would swing to the East or to the West. What was on trial was more than the West's military strength or its administrative skill: 'It is our way of life. The uncommitted nations want to see before they choose.'[68]

However, nowhere in his speech did Macmillan call for a rapid dismantling of the remaining formal empire in Africa. He dwelt on the need to come to terms with African nationalism, partly in order to persuade the whites in Africa to accept more rights for non-Europeans, but partly also to impress his post-imperialist credentials upon the United States. The Prime Minister was far more guided by the desire to achieve multi-racial cooperation than by the desire for precipitate de-colonisation. He realised that it was important to moderate the racial policy of South Africa and to prevent it from taking root among Britain's settler colonies. The key passage therefore was not about the 'wind of change', but rather about the South African idea of superior and inferior races. Macmillan warned his audience that there were

> some aspects of your policies which make it impossible [to support you] without being false to our own deep convictions about the political destinies of free men, to which in our territories we are trying to give effect.[69]

Rather than a new approach to colonial questions, the speech reflected a turn in Britain's stance *vis-à-vis* South Africa. By November 1959 officials had concluded that the balance of advantage between maintaining good relations with the Union of South Africa and securing Britain's international reputation had swung in favour of the latter. In a Cabinet paper Home argued that the insistence of South Africa on extreme policies of racial discrimination was a source of weakness for the Commonwealth. The goodwill of 'the emerging masses of Asia and Africa' was of vital importance to Britain, and public support for South Africa, for example, in the United Nations, tended to damage their confidence.[70] Thus, in the wider context of the 'battle against Communism for men's minds', South Africa was a liability to the West. Britain's wider interests and its relations with the newly independent states, in particular Nigeria, were at stake. Britain should warn South Africa that it would no longer support it in public. It was this insight which lay at the heart of Macmillan's 'wind of change' speech.

To a certain extent this public dissociation from doctrines of white superiority also applied to the British settler communities in the rest of the continent. However, for various reasons it was not as easy to cut loose from them as it was in the case of South Africa. Macmillan considered that Central Africa and Kenya were 'really our Algeria, on a smaller scale'[71] – and like the French, he was at a loss what to do. He was reluctant to leave even though he realised how difficult and dangerous it was to stay. On the one hand, he wanted to prevent another 'Boston Tea Party' (in the case of the CAF) or another 'Congo' (in the case of Kenya), on the other, he was afraid of 'an African blood bath'. The Prime Minister feared that if the government pressed on too fast with the extension of the franchise to Africans, 'the more reactionary white people' in Central Africa would try to join the Union, or unilaterally declare their independence. In Kenya the whites might panic and leave, leading to a total breakdown of the country's economy and administration. Britain would have to bear the international blame, but also the financial consequences, that is, the indemnification of the white settlers. In addition, chaos in Kenya would open yet another door to Soviet subversion. But Macmillan was also worried about domestic consequences. Looming very large in his mind were the repercussions on his own government which an open conflict with Lord Home, Salisbury and their supporters might have. Speaking to Lord Swinton on the need to heal the wounds inflicted by Suez on the Conservative Party he remarked: 'Our first objective must be to keep the party together, at all costs united.'[72]

Macmillan was convinced that open strife with the settlers or the party's empire loyalists would be fatal for his premiership. On the other hand, he feared that if Britain did not move fast enough the Africans would start disturbances. This would mean 'a long and cruel campaign – Mau Mau and all that'.[73] It would also be used by Britain's detractors in the United Nations to inflict further damage on its international standing. This was one of Macmillan's constant fears: after the Sharpeville massacre in South Africa, for example, he had predicted 'a tremendous effort to stoke up similar riots in Rhodesia or Nyasaland or Kenya, in order to put the United Kingdom in the dock'.[74] Macmillan felt the government was in a dilemma: whenever it would have to use troops – either against 'kith and kin' or against Africans – it would be condemned by the British public or world opinion. He was determined not to send British troops to fight British settlers. There would be 'no battle of Bunker's Hill',[75] but neither did he want to employ them against African nationalists. Therefore he tried to muddle through somehow, hoping both sides could be coaxed to accept a compromise which would allow Britain an honourable withdrawal.

While Macmillan was still trying to find a way of reconciling the various opposing interests centred on Africa, events on the spot led Macleod to speed up constitutional development in Northern Rhodesia and Nyasaland. At first Macleod had agreed with the traditional line which held that there could be no further change until Monckton's review of the Federation, begun in February 1960, had been completed. Macleod's first visit to the territories at the end of March 1960, however, led him to conclude that this position was no longer tenable: the situation on the spot was 'puzzling and worrying'. The independence of the Belgian Congo, announced for June 1960, would be 'a major disruptive element' and made it important to promise some form of constitutional advance, especially in the hitherto neglected Northern Rhodesia. Otherwise Kenneth Kaunda, leader of the United National Independence Party (UNIP), would not be able to hold his place, and 'worse men like Sipalo, ... a trained Communist', would take over. For the time being, Kaunda had 'some control' over the party and could be persuaded to advocate non-violence.[76] However, this might soon change. In order to make sure that Britain would negotiate with him, and not with more radical forces, it was advisable to promise constitutional talks for 1961, even though the federal review had not yet been published. The CAF could only be preserved (albeit in a somewhat looser form) if African opinion was won over to it – and this would only happen if the government demonstrated that Northern Rhodesia and Nyasaland did not have to fear amalgamation with Southern Rhodesia. Welensky and Home opposed Macleod's proposal, realising the threat it posed to white hegemony. They argued that constitutional talks in 1962 would be early enough. Over-hasty advance would only destroy the Federation. Nyasaland and Northern Rhodesia should not be granted independence before 1970: otherwise Southern Rhodesia would unilaterally declare its independence.[77] The threat proved effective. This time Macmillan abstained from backing Macleod, thus preventing him from promising early constitutional advance. At the same time, though, progress was made in the smallest territory of the Federation, Nyasaland.

Banda was released on 1 April 1960. Contrary to the predictions made by the opponents of such a move, there was no violence, and Macleod got on quite well with the leader of the Nyasaland Congress. The Colonial Secretary informed Macmillan that it was a great relief to have 'the little man' out of jail because it would reduce the pressure in Nyasaland. Unless he proved to be an effective leader, Banda's authority would diminish rather than increase. While he had been in jail, his authority had been strong no matter what his actions or capacities. Out of prison Banda would exhaust his appeal pretty quickly for he was 'a vain and ignorant man', and his ideas about constitutions were 'hopelessly inadequate and naive'. Presumably, the British government would have to impose a constitution at some later point.[78] Whether Macleod's denigration of Banda was meant to reassure Macmillan or whether it was simply an erroneous assessment remains open to doubt. What can be said for sure is that 'the little man' in no way quickly exhausted his appeal. After a two-week conference at Lancaster House in London in August 1960, which united Macleod, Banda and the territory's Europeans, a new constitution was agreed upon. This prepared the transition to African majority rule in Nyasaland and had profound implications for Northern Rhodesia and the CAF. Macmillan was highly satisfied with the result. Even though there would be difficulties in the future, the agreement was 'a splendid start and a great relief to us all'. Banda, 'like all these people' would be 'a demagogue one day and something like a statesman another'; but this was in the African's nature and Britain had to live with it.[79] What mattered most for the Prime Minister was the fact that Southern Rhodesia and the Federal government had accepted the results of the conference. They probably calculated that Nyasaland was not important enough to risk an open confrontation.

Now Macleod once again argued in favour of a constitutional conference for Northern Rhodesia in 1961, warning that UNIP would resort to civil disobedience and maybe even violence if no concessions were made. Although it was understandable that the whites in the

Federation were frightened, concessions were the only policy that could save the Europeans. The Colonial Secretary received support from the Monckton Commission which recommended rapid constitutional advance.[80] Reforms should be implemented as soon as possible. By the end of 1960 there would be more than 25 independent states in Africa. The inhabitants of the remaining colonies would see independence come to neighbouring states which could not 'by any stretch of imagination' be regarded as more politically experienced than they themselves. It would be difficult to offer something less to Britain's colonies.[81] But in order to maintain the CAF, there had to be 'drastic and fundamental changes' both in the structure of the association itself and in the racial policies of Southern Rhodesia. Otherwise it would be impossible to overcome the strong African opposition in the northern territories. Having read the report and determined to avoid 'an Algeria' in Central Africa, the Prime Minister finally agreed to hold a constitutional conference for Northern Rhodesia in February 1961.[82] The protests of Home and Welensky appeared to be less important than the risk of armed conflict with the Africans.

As in Central, so also in East Africa, constitutional advance was considerably accelerated in 1960. As arranged by Macleod's predecessor, talks about the future of Kenya began in January. The participants were the Colonial Secretary, Blundell's New Kenya Party (NKP) and other Europeans, as well as 14 elected African members of the colony's legislative council. Macleod hoped to achieve a significant shift in favour of the Africans by extending the franchise, while reaching agreement in principle upon certain safeguards for the whites.[83] Macmillan was worried about the effects on Southern Rhodesia, but Macleod replied: 'I am afraid there is naught for their comfort wherever Southern Rhodesians look in Africa today.' The pace of events in East Africa and – maybe even more so – in the Congo was bound to have serious effects on the future of the CAF. Furthermore, Macmillan's 'wind of change' speech had been well received by all British newspapers, which commented that things in Africa could never be the same again. The government had to 'try and get this into the heads of the men in Salisbury'.[84] Not to move out of fear of repercussions elsewhere would certainly lead to disaster. The pace of events was overtaking the timetables drawn up under Lennox-Boyd, and accordingly they should be revised. In the end Macmillan caved in and Macleod was authorised to make his proposals.

Early in February 1960 the Kenya talks were on the point of breakdown, since both the settlers and the Africans had rejected

Macleod's proposals. The Colonial Secretary worked out a compromise: the franchise was to be enlarged on the Tanganyikan model and the number of African ministers to be raised to four, while the Governor would continue to appoint the members of the council of ministers. There was to be no adult suffrage, nor the abolition of reserved seats in the legislature, but at least an extended common roll that would allow the Africans to secure 33 of the 65 elective seats. At the same time, the government would begin to provide funds to purchase land in the 'white highlands' for redistribution to African farmers, thus responding to a major Kikuyu grievance while also allowing European farmers to withdraw if they were unwilling to accept the new order. The Africans accepted the proposals. The NKP was ready to accept them provided there were constitutional safeguards for the rights of minorities. These safeguards were given, but it was still not good enough for many of Kenya's whites. They were alarmed by the results of the conference, which coincided with the Belgian announcement that the Congo would become independent within a few months. House and share prices tumbled, and the prospect of the settlers, with their capital and skills, leaving the country threatened the government's plans for a stable multi-racial Kenya. The situation worsened when the first refugees from the Belgian Congo arrived in summer 1960, spreading stories about atrocities and the break-down of law and order. Because of this development Macleod decided that Jomo Kenyatta, the leading nationalist arrested for alleged involvement in the Mau Mau uprising, would not be released from detention. The Colonial Secretary would have preferred to release him in order to have a prominent African to counter white representation, but realised that it was equally important to reassure the white population.

In the meantime events in Tanganyika went much faster than originally planned. During a visit to East Africa in December 1959, the Colonial Secretary managed to establish a good rapport with Nyerere; afterwards, he reported to the Prime Minister that it would probably not be necessary to hold a special conference, since the ideas put forward by the Tanganyikan leader were 'almost exactly those that in any case we intended to offer'.[85] In fact, Macleod and Nyerere were able to finalise Tanganyika's constitution, during talks in the Colonial Secretary's flat in London in the spring of 1960. Macleod reported enthusiastically that Nyerere had shown 'excellent cooperation' as well as 'a complete understanding of the economic needs of his country and the need for keeping British administration and Western capital and knowledge'. There was no reason why Tanganyika should not continue to 'go forward and prosper', even without British supervision – the transfer of power would not end the close links existing between the two countries.[86] Despite his apparent optimism, Macleod soon began to have second thoughts: Nyerere was not ready to go as slowly as he had hoped. Rather he moved 'pretty well in line with the pressures of his "wild men" while at the same time adroitly preserving his reputation as an "enlightened" nationalist'.[87] However, since public opinion seemed not to be inclined to accept the lack of native administrators as a reason for resisting TANU demands, the Colonial Secretary concluded that it was best to give in, i.e. to grant independence not as originally planned in 1968, but in 1962, as requested by Nyerere.

In the elections with an extended franchise held in September 1960, TANU achieved an overwhelming victory. Having tried in vain to delay the transfer of power until at least March 1962 in order to allow time for the necessary administrative arrangements, the Colonial Secretary at last agreed to the new date proposed by Nyerere, i.e. December 1961, which the Cabinet accepted without any major resistance. After all, Tanganyika was 'very much our showpiece … and we must not be suspected of dragging our colonial heels'.[88] Ministers were relieved that the transfer of power took place in cooperation with a moderate, friendly nationalist apparently eager to maintain the British connection. It was hoped that this step would reduce international criticism (thus allowing some delay in the more sensitive territories) while serving as a positive example for other territories in the region.

'Too Clever by Half': Growing Resistance Against Early Decolonisation

Having been in office for 15 months, the Colonial Secretary continued to push his colleagues to accept faster constitutional advance in Kenya and the CAF. 'We have, I think, come through 1960 reasonably well', he reported in January 1961. Despite the many contrary pressures, the government had managed to hold to a pace of change which was 'not as fast as the Congo and not as slow as Algiers'. All emergencies in colonial territories had ended, but the risk remained of a break-down in Kenya and of a violent escalation in the CAF. The government had to strive to succeed 'in doing what the Prime Minister once defined as "turning an Empire into a family"'.[89] After the independence of the French and Belgian colonies, the pressure from the United Nations would increasingly concentrate on Britain. And there would be 'echoing voices … from both the extreme right and the extreme left in this country'; 1961 was therefore sure to be 'a year of drama and decision in the colonial field'.

Accordingly, Macleod set out to find a solution for the two remaining problems: Kenya and Southern Rhodesia. This, however, was no easy task since he had to face increasing resistance not only from the settlers, but also their allies in Britain. Macmillan began to have doubts about the wisdom of advancing at the speed envisaged by his Colonial Secretary: in October, he replaced him with Maudling, hoping the latter would prove less radical. However, as the Prime Minister was soon to find out, this was not the case: the new Colonial Secretary followed in the footsteps of his predecessor and even advocated further acceleration.

In January 1961 the inauspicious Northern Rhodesian constitutional conference finally opened in London. The Governor-General of the Federation, Lord Dalhousie, issued a strong warning: pressing the whites 'beyond the point they will go' (a statement he did not bother to clarify) would result in the 'immediate and certain break-up' of the CAF. Welensky had threatened to sever relations with Britain and 'go his own way independently whatever this means'. He had even perhaps considered holding some areas by force.[90] The conference proceeded despite these warnings, but the Colonial Secretary was unable to reach any compromise. The problem was the number of Africans allowed to vote and, consequently, the number of non-European representatives. According to Macleod's proposal, Africans were to hold 16 elected seats in the legislative assembly, while the Europeans would have 14 plus some six nominated officials who would in effect hold casting votes. This would have secured white supremacy, at least in the transitory phase, but it still went too far for the colony's Europeans. For them, two Africans did not 'make a white – you need at least six!' (which was a gross understatement: after all, only one in 31 of Northern Rhodesia's population was white; for the settlers it took more than 30 Africans to make a white).[91]

Macmillan began to fear a *coup d'état* which would make it necessary for British troops to intervene. On 24 February 1961 the Prime Minister noted that the government was preparing for 'the worst event' – a white rebellion – by drawing up the necessary legislative, administrative and military plans.[92] Macmillan now began to have second thoughts about the wisdom of accelerating the transfer of power against the will of the whites. He was particularly worried about the 'differences, almost tensions which may easily build up inside the Cabinet and the Party' and criticised the Colonial Secretary for having leaned over 'too far towards the African view'.[93] Macmillan's fears of a rebellion at home were nourished by the growing resistance the Colonial Secretary encountered in the Conservative Party, an overwhelming majority of which had supported his policy until early 1961. Now, however, there was increasing anxiety about the fate of the whites. At a meeting on 9 February 1961 of the back-bench Commonwealth affairs committee, Macleod had to face criticism from almost 50 MPs who pressed him to slow down the pace of change in Northern Rhodesia.[94] An early-day motion to the same end attracted nearly 90 signatures. Home and Salisbury mobilised all their resources in the fight against any concessions which were deemed to discriminate against the white minority. Pressure groups like the Monday Club and Salisbury's watching committee lobbied against any 'premature' withdrawal from East and Central Africa, arguing that white administration was the only source of stability. Chaos and tribal wars would inevitably follow upon a rapid withdrawal of colonial rule. In the House of Lords, Salisbury launched a fierce personal tirade against Macleod, denouncing him as 'too clever by half' and accusing him of implementing a completely wrong policy.[95]

Macmillan tried to find a way of accommodating Welensky without offending the Africans. The Prime Minister was ready to make far-reaching concessions, but he was not willing to concede all Welensky's demands. If he did the government would lose the confidence of the Africans, making it impossible to preserve the Federation 'except by force', which was unthinkable, not only because of the resulting international criticism but also because Britain could not afford to squander scarce resources. On the other hand, he was not ready to confront the whites. He feared that Welensky would come to London to put his case to parliament and public opinion, possibly even demanding independence – 'a most serious situation would then arise, which might lead to violence and perhaps civil war'.[96] Accordingly, he tried to lure Welensky into a compromise. For some time nothing moved. By June 1961 the Prime Minister noted in frustration that 'every idea we put up is opposed either by Welensky or by Governor Hone – usually by both'.[97] However, in July a compromise was reached. The Prime Minister conceded many but not all of Welensky's demands – most notably a white majority in the legislature. Macmillan ignored Macleod's protests and thought he had defused the situation. Kaunda, however, expressed disappointment at receiving less than neighbouring Nyasaland or Tanganyika, and vowed to fight for more rights.

At the beginning of August, some districts of Northern Rhodesia were rocked by arson attacks and violent disturbances. Macleod warned that to ignore Kaunda's demands would inevitably force him either to join with 'the UNIP hotheads' in a violent campaign against the government, or to withdraw from the territory. In both cases his moderating influence was likely to be lost. The July proposals should be changed in favour of the Africans. This, however, was too much for Macmillan. He preferred *'no change'*, both because of possible repercussions on Southern Rhodesia and because of the impression it would create, namely that Britain was yielding to force.[98] The Prime Minister feared that any concession would only lead to further attempts to blackmail Britain. Once more the situation was in abeyance. In Nyasaland, on the other hand, the political situation developed in a way few would have foreseen two years earlier. Banda won a large majority of votes in August 1961. This was followed by a demand for secession from the CAF in 1962. For the time being, though, Britain hesitated to take such a step, since it would have major repercussions on Northern Rhodesia. Despite this delay the situation remained free of major tensions, probably because Banda sensed that independence was within arm's reach if only he waited for a little while.

Alongside Northern Rhodesia, ministers also discussed the future of Kenya. Home argued that it was 'politically impossible' to disengage as rapidly as envisaged by the CO. Britain should maintain formal rule for another eight to ten years. This would allow sufficient time to prepare the Africans for independence. The cost of conducting a rescue operation for the Europeans as a result of handing over power to a African majority too soon was likely to be much higher than that of maintaining British rule over a longer period. The loss of confidence in the East African Territories as well as the speed at which they were advancing towards independence already gave rise to the grave threat of administrative breakdown. Expatriate officials would start leaving as soon as their territory achieved internal self-government. Between then and the date of independence, the United Kingdom would be directly responsible only for external affairs and defence. But in fact Britain would retain ultimate responsibility for the whole administration. If there was a breakdown Britain would have a moral responsibility to intervene, and this might lead to a delay of independence well into the 1970s. Any further loss of confidence would also lead to a flight of capital on a large scale. In Tanganyika this would lead to the gradual deterioration of the economy, but in Kenya it would result in disintegration culminating in civil war. Assuming that an administrative breakdown could be averted, the basic problem in East Africa and in Northern Rhodesia over the next few years would be to carry through agricultural and educational development programmes that would eliminate those countries' dependence on European expatriates.[99]

While Home was above all concerned about the fate of the white minority, the Colonial Secretary thought the key to future stability lay in securing the goodwill of the Africans. Of course it would be 'splendid' if the government still had seven or eight years at its disposal, but this did not fit in with 'the facts of life in Africa today'. Kenya should move as slowly as possible. But this did not mean eight years, and if the government tried to impose this it would in less than a year have another Cyprus on its hands. The success in Tanganyika had been largely due to Britain's willingness to consider an early transfer of power. Britain still had a chance to reach a similar success in Kenya. But it was essential not to hesitate. It would not be acceptable to Kenyans to be deprived of constitutional advances that were at least comparable to those in other East African territories just because 1 per cent of the population was European. Most Africans did not want disturbances or bloodshed. However, there was an extremist group which wanted African domination at any cost, if necessary at the cost of economic chaos and the expulsion of all Europeans. A more powerful and moderate group wanted independence but it also wanted to administer Kenya as a modern state complete with its developed economic structure, i.e. including the whites. The problem was to build up these moderate leaders and help them get these ideas across.[100]

According to Macleod, the preservation of African goodwill was not the only argument in favour of a rapid transfer of power. Another point was the fact that the economy was on the point of break-down because of the drastic fall of external investment.[101] Its restoration depended on a return of confidence. This did not depend (as claimed by Home) on a delay of seven to eight years, but rather on the quick establishment of a stable African majority government pursuing policies favourable to private investment. The more successful Britain was in attaining this objective, the better the chances of British trading and investment interests being maintained and of Kenya remaining within the Western camp. Therefore it was important to move rapidly towards independence (which was to be achieved in 1964), while making reassuring gestures to the Europeans, for example by continuing the construction of military bases. Any falling off in the volume of work would immediately be interpreted as a sign that the government was thinking of pulling out. This would strike a severe blow to white confidence. The loss of confidence in 1960 had already led to 'embarrassingly large outflows of capital' with Britain having had to prop up the Kenyan budget to avoid cuts in essential social services.[102] All ministers, Macleod stressed, had agreed that 'our main objective overriding all others' was to hold the East African territories as 'firm and faithful friends of the free world'. And all the governors had advised that there was a greater possibility of securing this objective if the government was prepared to move 'reasonably quickly with the African tide'. If HMG sought to delay or to qualify independence by keeping some form of physical presence, however, the new states were sure to gravitate towards the Soviet Union or China. Lord Home's anxieties were understandable, but Macleod was convinced that the path Britain had embarked on was the right one:

> It isn't enough to say that it is full of danger. Of course it is. But so is every other path in colonial affairs, as you well know. All we can do is to try and follow the road that seems the safest in front of us.[103]

The Lord Chancellor, David Kilmuir, supported Macleod: the government's dilemma was to find a solution which was beneficial to Kenya and East Africa, provided the maximum protection for the settlers and their property, and was recognised by the Conservative Party as being 'intellectually respectable and positive action, and not merely a drift into surrender'.[104] Independence in 1964 would pose an obvious danger to settlers who risked the expropriation of their property. But many officials on the spot advised that any attempt to lengthen the 'period of incubation' for independence would make expropriation even more likely. It could also lead to rebellion and bloodshed in addition to a loss of goodwill. Since it was difficult to believe that the situation would be appreciably better in 1967 or 1968, there was no point in slowing down Kenya's advance to independence. The most important thing was not to forget that Britain's 'inspiration and achievement in the twentieth century' was making 'nations who voluntarily remain our friends'. Of course the African territories were not yet ready for independence, but early independence was the only realistic option. Britain could not hold these territories by force, and the risks in moving quickly were far less than the risks of moving slowly.[105]

In elections held in February 1961, the Kenyan African National Union (KANU), campaigning on the claim that it would not take office unless Kenyatta was freed, won twice as many votes as the more moderate Kenya African Democratic Union (KADU). Nonetheless, the Governor was able to form a minority government of KADU, Blundell's NKP and Kenyan Asians. This was in accordance with Macleod's strategy which aimed to attract the support of moderate Europeans for a phased transition to African majority rule. But the Colonial Secretary was aware of the need to maintain the goodwill of the black population. Vital for this was the release of Kenyatta, a move he began to prepare carefully – against the strong resistance of Governor Peter Renison. At the same time the Colonial Secretary hinted that Kenya might reach internal self-government not as originally planned in 1963, but even earlier. Given the experience in other territories, it was more than likely that events would soon develop an impetus of their own. There would be 'pretty consistent pressure' from KADU for rapid constitutional progress on the grounds that this was necessary if its members were not to be branded as 'stooges' by KANU.[106] After further arguments between Macleod and the Governor, Kenyatta was finally released in August 1961. Lord Swinton warned the Prime Minister that the prospect of Kenyatta's release was 'utterly repugnant to decent-minded people'. There would be a revolt in the Tory party and Swinton himself would be among the rebels.[107] However, Macmillan backed his Colonial Secretary. The revolt failed to materialise, and public reactions were mostly positive. In November 1961 Kenyatta came to London, and made a good impression on politicians and civil servants as well as on Kenyan Europeans, by claiming that property rights would be safeguarded and foreign investment encouraged.

Despite the successful release of Kenyatta, Macmillan was not yet convinced that power should be transferred as quickly as envisaged by the CO. As concerned the Rhodesias, the Prime Minister still worried about domestic reactions to Macleod's policy. He noted that in some ways, Kenya was 'more difficult *at home* even than Central Africa'. The people were not yet accustomed to the idea that, sooner or later, the government would have to concede independence. But even those who accepted that it would come sooner or later thought it would be later rather than sooner. From the party point of view, therefore Kenya was going to create a big problem: 'We might even split on it.'[108] Throughout the year the Prime Minister tried to balance the different pressures, allowing Macleod some advance, while making sure that this did not go further than a majority of the party (and his ministers) would tolerate. In theory, Macmillan knew that by early 1961 there was no alternative to a rapid withdrawal. But while he acknowledged that Macleod's policy was sound, he was reluctant to implement it to the full. Fearing a major upheaval in the party, he replaced Macleod with Maudling in October 1961 and hoped that the latter would be less insistent on rapid change than his predecessor. This was not the case: after a few months Macmillan ruefully noted that the new Colonial Secretary was *'plus noir que les nègres*, more difficult and intransigent than his predecessor'.[109] Macleod's move from the CO proved to be helpful in another respect though: many Conservative critics of the government's African policy tended to put the blame on the personality of the Colonial Secretary, not on events on the spot itself. After October 1961 resistance against early decolonisation slowly began to abate – not least because it was realised that the speed of decolonisation was not the result of one of Macleod's fancies. But a change of mood had been in the offing for some time. Even those colonial administrators who until mid-1961 had opposed Macleod's policy finally came around to his point of view, sometimes adopting even more radical positions. The British Resident in Zanzibar, for example, had in early 1961 still been 'very unhappy' about the prospects of what he called a scuttle. By September he was convinced that an early withdrawal was 'the lesser risk out of a series of risks which are very great indeed'.[110]

'Plus noir que les nègres': Maudling and the End of British Africa

Macleod had initiated the acceleration of constitutional development, but his successor increased its momentum even further, mainly because of developments on the ground. In order to avoid a clash with the growing nationalist sentiment among Africans, the new Colonial Secretary was determined to pressure the whites into accepting the loss of their political predominance. In January 1962 he threatened to resign over the pace of reform in Northern Rhodesia. Nothing less than the immediate grant of majority rule would suffice to secure African cooperation – and if this cooperation was not secured, any new constitution was likely to be frustrated at the outset by a recrudescence of violence.[111] Astonishingly enough, Macleod now accused Maudling of advancing too hastily. The new Colonial Secretary, he argued, took an 'extreme view'.[112] Maudling's proposals would lead to a row with Welensky at a time when relations were already far from easy. It is not clear whether this reaction was the result of Macleod's dislike of Maudling or his sincere conviction (which seems less likely). But despite his critical remarks, he was willing to resign with the Colonial Secretary over the franchise. This was not necessary, since by then Macmillan too was determined to break free of the colonial problems in Central Africa.

In February 1962 the French President Charles de Gaulle finally managed to negotiate a solution with the Front de Libération Nationale (FNL) in Algeria, which made Algerian independence a probability in the near future. Once it had come about, the Prime Minister calculated, attention would focus on the remaining colonial territories in Africa. The pressure on Britain would then increase considerably. He realised that it was not possible to reach a compromise acceptable to both Welensky and the Africans. Macmillan decided that, on broad political grounds, it was better to antagonise the former rather than the latter. He foresaw 'hideous trouble' if the government did not accept the inevitable disintegration of the Federation.[113] The only possible means of maintaining the *status quo* was force. This, however, was ruled out by the example of Algeria and Britain's limited resources. In North Africa the French had a million men under arms, and they had suffered a humiliating defeat – it was 'too simple a reasoning of history to think that you can exercise control simply by the use of power'. The CAF's Prime Minister, Macmillan reckoned, had killed multi-racialism by his brutality and his talk. Unless Nyasaland and Northern Rhodesia were allowed to secede and become self-governing under an African-dominated government, there was no way out from civil war or an African revolution.[114]

Also most other ministers were now convinced that the Federation could not be permitted to drag on much longer. The risk of an African uprising, leading to widespread international criticism and necessitating costly counter-insurgency measures, seemed too great. A new franchise for Northern Rhodesia, making African majority rule a certainty, was announced in the House of Commons in February 1962. One month later Macmillan appointed R.A. Butler to head the newly created Central African Office, which was to take over the Rhodesian problem from the CO and the CRO.[115] Some ministers, among them Duncan Sandys, briefly toyed with the idea of breaking up Northern Rhodesia into three parts, thus allowing the economically vital Copper Belt to become part of Southern Rhodesia.[116] This project was not supported by the Prime Minister, since it was clear that it would not be tolerated by the Africans, the United States or the United Nations (not least because of possible repercussions in the Congo, where United Nations troops were fighting against the secessionist Katanga region). Should Welensky try to retain the Copper Belt by force, Britain could bring enough pressure upon the Federation, for example, by withholding investment capital, to make him reconsider his actions. Southern Rhodesians would not wish to see their economy destroyed for the sake of a federal adventure and would certainly not support him.[117]

Over the next few months, Butler struggled in vain to find some common ground between politicians in Salisbury, Zomba and Lusaka. In October he had to inform British ministers that the secession of Nyasaland and Northern Rhodesia could not be delayed much longer. Kaunda and Banda were not willing to continue in the Federation. The only way in which Nyasaland and Northern Rhodesia could be brought to understand the advantages of federation was for them to stand alone. If secession was refused, serious unrest was likely to break out soon, and federal troops would have to be brought in to deal with the situation. This would hardly improve relations with the Africans and was likely to be highly embarrassing for Britain. The Foreign Secretary Lord Home argued that it was possible to control the situation by force (the Nyasas were 'a docile people' and respected firmness), but his colleagues were weary of the prospect of having to deal with 'another Cyprus'.[118] Therefore Nyasaland and Northern Rhodesia were to be allowed to secede. In the meantime, feelings in Southern Rhodesia had changed, too: the Europeans were no longer interested in federation if it meant having to deal with African-dominated governments. This new attitude was confirmed by the victory of the right-wing Dominion Party in the Southern Rhodesian elections held in December 1962.[119] A few days after the elections, Butler announced that Nyasaland would be permitted to secede from the CAF. The statement was received quietly in Commons; some harsh remarks were made in the Lords, with Salisbury being 'very rude and difficult'.[120] But, generally speaking, the government did not have to face any serious challenge.

Once elections in Northern Rhodesia had produced a black government demanding secession and independence, Butler announced that the territory would be allowed to secede.[121] The Federation was formally dissolved at the end of 1963, and in 1964 Nyasaland and Northern Rhodesia became independent. The Southern Rhodesian government also demanded independence, with its existing constitution ensuring white predominance. Butler was in favour, but Macmillan feared that this would split the Cabinet and the Conservative Party. If the white minority regime was given independence, the government would be blamed by 'all progressive and even moderate opinion'. All African (and probably some Asian) states would leave the Commonwealth.[122] The problem, Macmillan reckoned, was that if Southern Rhodesia was *not* given independence, the Africans would not benefit either. The country would be forced under the influence of South Africa, and probably issue a unilateral declaration of independence. This would mean 'a bloc of White power from the Cape to the Zambesi. Is it a good thing or not?'[123] The issue was left undecided, since neither Macmillan nor his successors could persuade the government in Salisbury to accept at least some token concessions in favour of the Africans; it was not even ready to make a declaration of intent to move towards an extension of the franchise before independence.[124] Finally, in November 1965, the Ian Smith government unilaterally declared Southern Rhodesia's independence, thus depriving Britain of its (always rather shaky) control over

Central African affairs – but also freeing HMG of the embarrassment of having to deal with an African rebellion or of being obliged to force the white minority to make more concessions.

In January 1962 Maudling called for a transition to African majority government in Northern Rhodesia. At the same time he also recommended a further acceleration of the transfer of power in Kenya. He acknowledged that in political maturity, the indigenous people were 'far behind the West Africans'. Rapid independence was risky, since there were few trained administrators, and tribal antagonisms jeopardised the stability of the country. Theoretically, it would be better to wait, but confidence was disappearing and the local economy was rapidly going downhill. European farmers and administrators, upon whom the country depended, had little incentive to stay – 400 of them were already leaving every month.[125] It was important to preempt a stampede out of Kenya: if the European officers left, the administration would crumble. If the farmers left, other investors' confidence would disappear as well, leading to total collapse. But even without such a stampede the financial outlook was extremely sombre. Kenya was heading for complete bankruptcy. HMG would have to subsidise the country to the tune of some £30 million per annum by the date of independence, and the figure was unlikely to drop, at any rate for some years thereafter.[126] The cost of compensating European settlers for their land alone would amount to about £140 million. This was a large sum, but it was essential for the resettlement of landless Africans; the alternative would involve 'a mass exodus of frightened and embittered Europeans combined with a free-for-all seizure of European land by Africans, probably leading to tribal warfare'.[127] The cost of the resulting rescue operations and compensations would be much higher than present sums. It was important to make reassuring noises and to secure constitutional safeguards for the whites. But looking to the future, the great question was whether the constitution would remain in force after independence or whether it would collapse and lead to a breakdown of law and order on a major scale. The longer Britain waited, the more likely the prospect of a political crisis. Although a federal system of government might be held to offer the best hope of protection for minorities, it would be very costly and Kenya could not possibly afford it. It would therefore be necessary to find other safeguards for the interests of minorities.

The best Britain could hope to achieve was an orderly transfer of power to 'a securely-based and African-dominated Government' which was 'genuinely anxious' to avoid civil war and a relapse into tribalism, and to respect the rights of individuals of any race. It was not likely that such a government would be 'actively pro-Western'. The most Britain could expect was a government which was not committed to either side in the East–West struggle and which, because it was reasonably stable, did not offer too many opportunities for penetration by the communist bloc.[128] It was not in Britain's interests to attempt to delay independence beyond the date which 'political and administrative practicabilities' indicated. Any suggestion that the government was deliberately dragging its feet was likely to unite African opinion against Britain. This would prejudice the government's chances of achieving its 'ultimate objective', that is a stable successor state with the white minority staying on after independence. It would neither improve the economic position of the country nor be in the ultimate interests of the European community if the government gave any impression that it was the settlers' presence which had led to Kenya to progress less rapidly towards independence than Tanganyika and Uganda. Besides, such a delay might give the 'Kikuyu extremists' an excuse for adopting terrorism once more.

Another important point which had to be kept in mind was the situation in the United Nations: the 'deliberate and concerted campaign' to use the organisation as a weapon of anti-colonialism contained great dangers; it was vital to deprive Britain's enemies of arguments that could be used against it.[129] Ministers should be ready to make generous concessions. It would clearly be an advantage if the 'moderate' wing of KANU could be separated from 'the extreme group – men of violence and of Communist contacts'. The more moderate elements might then enter into a coalition with KADU. But this could only be achieved if the advance to black majority rule was not obstructed. The longer the government waited, the more opportunity there was for 'the more extremist negative elements to undermine the more reasonable ones'. Independence would have to be granted at the latest in 1964, and

> from the standpoint of making the country more mature, better educated, and with a wide economy, two years is neither here nor there. Proceed swiftly and the Africans may regard our economy as an asset; proceed slowly and they may try to pinch it.[130]

When ministers discussed the issue, Home argued that the threat to Kenya's economic stability put the colony into a special category. The transfer of power should be delayed since Kenya had no reasonable prospect of becoming economically viable. A frank explanation of the colony's economic difficulties would be regarded by world opinion as justifying delay. A majority of ministers, however, saw the danger that this might cause the Soviets to offer the economic aid needed to support an independent Kenya. The government would then be obliged to grant early independence in less than fortunate circumstances.[131] Another attempt by Home and like-minded policy-makers to prolong Britain's hold over the settlers' fate was the proposal to retain the so-called 'coastal strip' of Kenya (which was not an integral part of the colony, but belonged to Zanzibar) under British sovereignty. This, they argued, would allow Britain to protect the European community and to restore law and order if the new state collapsed. The mere presence of British troops would exercise 'a moderating influence' and work against a communist penetration of East Africa. A firm base would also be useful for possible inter-ventions in the Middle East.[132] Maudling, Macmillan and most other ministers rejected the idea: not only would it be costly to maintain British sovereignty over a small part of East Africa, but it would also be difficult to defend the decision in public. International opinion would turn against Britain, and African goodwill (which, after all, was one of the prime motives for the early transfer of power) would be lost. In addition, the plan might bring about the situation it was de-signed to prevent, i.e. hostile actions against the white minority.[133]

The Prime Minister acknowledged that colonial rule could not be prolonged for much longer. But he was still worried about the consequences of an early withdrawal for Kenya's whites as well as for his government. He would have preferred a transition period of five years, but realised that this might provoke a violent African reaction which would further accelerate Kenya's economic collapse. On the other hand he feared that to leave Kenya wholly in the hands of African politicians would sooner or later lead to a break-down as in the Belgian Congo.[134] Since formal rule had to be ended, though, the government should try to find other ways of stabilising the area. One possibility was the creation, with US backing, of a Commonwealth ad-visory committee to assist newly independent countries in 'the twilight period between Independence and true nationhood'. An alternative might be to involve the United Nations in the country's administration. Not much came out of these deliberations. Officials advised that sharing responsibility for any territory with the Commonwealth or the United Nations was in the interest neither of the colony nor of Britain.[135] It was better to transfer power and to use the resulting goodwill to exercise a moderating influence after inde-pendence – a conclusion accepted by an overwhelming majority of the Cabinet.

At the second constitutional conference in London in the spring of 1962, agreement was reached on a constitution and the formation of a

KADU–KANU government, with the heads of the two parties acting as joint premiers. Britain also agreed to provide a large sum of money to buy out the farms of white settlers who refused to accept African rule.[136] Independence was scheduled for early 1965. But in January 1963 the government was persuaded by Malcolm MacDonald, the new Governor, to speed up the transfer of power from two years to 11 months. Riots among minority tribes and unrest among landless Kikuyu, the former Commissioner-General to south-east Asia argued, made it advisable to go ahead faster than planned. To wait any longer would only further undermine the already shaky confidence of settlers and foreign investors.[137] In elections held in April 1963 KANU won an overwhelming majority, enabling Kenyatta to be sworn in as prime minister at independence in December.

Although Kenya's independence came much faster and under circumstances that were radically different from those envisaged in 1959, Macmillan had reason to congratulate himself: he had avoided a break-down as in the Belgian Congo as well as a 'futile military campaign' like the one in Algeria. A majority of the Conservative Party, the British public, and even the settlers had been reconciled with the end of empire in East Africa. In addition, in the international sphere, there was one less target for Britain's anti-colonialist critics. Given the manifold uncertainties facing the government with regard to future developments, Kenya's independence was not an insignificant achievement on the part of Macmillan and his Colonial Secretary – even though their success is clearly attributable to the fact that there were only relatively small numbers of white settlers. In Southern Rhodesia, the Prime Minister was not able to achieve a comparable breakthrough (nor did he or his Colonial Secretary really press for one).

'The Sooner We Get These People Out of Our Hair the Better': Smaller Territories

Macmillan's second premiership successfully resolved not only the problem of East and Central Africa, but also that of the smaller territories, which became independent even though they had once been considered unviable. The price for this was a further increase in the number of Commonwealth members, leading to a transformation of the club into a 'minor UN'. But policy-makers thought it more important to rid Britain of what by the early 1960s was considered a stigma, that is, its status as a colonial power. In order to end international criticism, power was transferred wherever possible, and as soon as was possible, without risking the creation of a power vacuum.

In 1960 the idea of statehood was finally dropped: an official working party concluded that any form of 'half-way house' between colonial status and independence was unacceptable for the territories concerned. Self-government and Commonwealth membership should be granted to all colonies (except the fortress territories) which demanded it, irrespective of their size, since the criterion of viability was clearly 'out of date'.[138] Refusing to do so, officials argued, would seem to be a device to prevent dependent peoples from attaining independence – and 'we all agreed that, in the second half of the 20th century, this would be trying to swim against the tide'.[139] Initially it was still hoped that at least the territories in the Caribbean could be persuaded to accept inclusion in a federation, thus making it possible to keep down the number of new Dominions. However, it soon became obvious that regional jealousies and vested interests were too strong to permit a lasting union.

In September 1961 a majority of Jamaica's population voted against the federation. Macleod advised ministers that given the precedents set by Cyprus and Sierra Leone, Jamaica should be granted independence. The Cabinet endorsed his proposal, and in August 1962, the island became independent. Over the following years, the other Caribbean territories achieved separate independence as well.[140] Thereafter there was no longer any need to maintain that certain territories were too small to attain independence. On the contrary: policy-makers concluded that international factors made the ending of colonial rule, even in small territories, all the more urgent. Not only was the role of a colonial power an uncomfortable one for Britain which was subjected to 'a continuous barrage of criticism and attack', but it also coloured other international issues. Britain should do all it could to remove the colonial label as soon as possible. Although the focus for the time being was on East and Central Africa, the time would come when the United Nations would take a similar interest in the destinies of smaller territories. If they could be removed from the purview of the United Nations in the next few years, much 'needless interference and trouble-making by the anti-colonial faction' might be avoided.[141]

Britain now scrambled to end colonial rule, by almost scrapping the principle of viability. Territories like the Gambia or British Guiana came to be seen as public-relations liabilities that should be shed as soon as possible. Whereas at the end of the 1950s such a withdrawal had been considered 'degrading', it now seemed the best solution. A good example of this change was reflected in the case of British Guiana. Macleod's successor at the CO, Maudling, concluded that the government had no strategic or economic reasons for delaying independence.[142] As long as the territory remained under British sovereignty, the tendency in the United States and elsewhere would be to regard Britain as primarily responsible for aid and assistance, while criticising the territory's colonial status. The aid sought by British Guiana, however, was on a scale beyond Britain's resources. The sooner the colony was put in a position where it could tap other sources of financial assistance, and which would force the United States to recognise that the territory was 'more vital to their interests than ours', the better. The Commonwealth Secretary welcomed the proposal, since British Guiana was 'a running sore'.[143] Given the strength of international anti-colonialism, it was probably best to grant independence: 'the sooner we get these people out of our hair the better'.[144]

It is interesting to note the curious change of roles that took place between the various ministers in this case. Now it was the Chancellor of the Exchequer, not the Colonial or Commonwealth Secretaries, who urged a delay. Independence should not be conceded unless the local leader, Dr Cheddi Jagan, acknowledged his country's liabilities, i.e. to pay compensation and pensions to former British civil servants of the colonial administration. Selwyn Lloyd, who had moved to the Treasury in 1960, recognised the difficulties of 'hanging on where we are not wanted, and where there is very little reason for us to stay'. But he warned that the financial consequences of Guiana becoming independent without a binding agreement could be very serious[145] – a strange echo of Dalton's remarks made in 1947, with the difference that the impetus was now on the necessity to stay, not to leave. If encouraged by Guiana, others might well refuse to adopt compensation schemes or default on schemes already in existence. The sums of money involved were very large. If Jagan's example should spread, the whole bill would fall on the Exchequer. These arguments (as well as an intervention by the US Secretary of State Dean Rusk) alarmed Macmillan and led him to opt for a delay. It was only after the financial questions had been resolved (and American fears about another 'Cuba' in their backyard assuaged) that power was transferred in 1966.

It was to take some years before Aden, as well as most of Britain's other remaining territories in the Caribbean and the Pacific, attained independence; some outposts such as St Helena, the Falkland Islands or Gibraltar remained under British control.[146] Apart from Aden, these delays were not due to Britain's desire to retain the territories out of an economic or strategic interest – with the possible exception of some scarcely populated islands in the Indian Ocean which could be used as military bases without prompting local or international criticism. As has been demonstrated above, in the mid-1960s British strategy came to rely almost exclusively on carriers and land-based facilities where the local political scene had no 'anti-colonialist or anti-Western complexes', or, preferably, where there were no inhabitants at all.[147] The 'delayed' independences of the 1970s and 1980s thus reflect the lack of local demand for self-government and the difficulties of arranging a transfer of power in these territories, rather than any longing to continue formal rule. Even though the smaller territories were increasingly considered a political and financial liability, policy-makers were still anxious not to create a power vacuum or to leave chaos behind.[148]

Britain's sudden willingness in the early 1960s to grant independence to most of the smaller territories may be attributed to several factors. First, it became clear that even smaller states could maintain themselves economically (not least because of the emerging system of international aid and Britain's new approach towards Commonwealth assistance). Second, a stable international environment made the life of independent smaller territories safer. Last, but not least, the Commonwealth was opened up to all former British colonies, thus removing the final obstacle to formal inde-pendence for smaller territories, that is, Britain's desire to preserve the club as an association of nations which mattered on the international scene. These factors *made it possible* to grant independence. In addition, others were pushing Britain towards transferring power: internal and international pressure rendered colonial rule more bur-densome, and, therefore, just as in the larger territories independence was conceded in part to rid Britain of the stigma of being a colonial power – while also reducing the burden on the Exchequer. Furthermore, after the break-up of the West Indian Federation and the independence of Cyprus and Sierra Leone, it was difficult to claim that other territories of comparable size were not viable – a logic quickly acknowledged by British officials.

Conclusion

From late 1959 onwards international developments became increasingly important for colonial policy. The sudden independence of the Belgian Congo as well as of most of France's colonies left Britain isolated on the international scene as one of the last colonial powers. At the same time, international criticism of 'colonialism' and racial inequality grew ever stronger. These developments made it more difficult to stick to old timetables, a fact also acknowledged by the CO.

Colonial Secretary Macleod therefore decided to move ahead. The remaining 'normal' colonies were rushed to independence, even if there was no strong demand for it. Macleod moved also towards African majority rule in East and Central Africa. However, his original intention had not been to end formal rule as quickly as it did. Both Macleod and Macmillan were anxious to find a middle way between another 'Algeria' and another 'Congo', i.e. a revolt of the settlers or their flight out of the country.

In Tanganyika, local dynamics led to a radical shortening of the timetable. Independence had been planned for 1968, but Nyerere's strong position allowed him to manoeuvre Britain into transferring power in December 1961. In Kenya and Northern Rhodesia, things at first continued to move slowly; while the risk in Central Africa was that of a white *coup d'état*, the problem in Kenya was the dependence of the national economy on the settlers. In addition, at home there was growing resistance to Macleod's policy. Macmillan therefore did not allow any substantial changes. In October 1961 Macleod was replaced with Maudling. The Prime Minister hoped that this would reconcile the imperial wing of the party and reduce the pressure for change emanating from the CO.

Contrary to Macmillan's expectations, the demand for ever faster advance did not diminish under the new Colonial Secretary. Local as well as international developments led Maudling to call for a rapid move towards black majority government in Northern Rhodesia. After some hesitation Macmillan realised that it was no longer possible to try to maintain special privileges for the settlers. Otherwise Britain would soon have to deal with another emergency at a very high cost to the metropole and without any prospect of winning international approval. The risk of a white rebellion in Central Africa now looked relatively small in comparison, especially since Southern Rhodesia had increasingly lost interest in the CAF. The Federation was dissolved, and Nyasaland and Northern Rhodesia achieved independence in 1964.

In Kenya, it was the prospect of economic breakdown rather than the risk of rebellion which led to accelerated decolonisation. An early transfer of power coupled with generous financial assistance was to ensure that moderate African nationalists remained in control of a country with a viable economy (which depended on the continued presence of the white settlers). After some wavering Macmillan realised that it was neither realistic nor advisable to stand against international opinion and the African majority. By the time he left Downing Street, Britain's African problem had been largely solved – except for the thorny case of Southern Rhodesia. In the other colonies, the hoped-for safeguards for the white minorities could not be assured, but the transfer of power had taken place as the result of peaceful negotiations and with African goodwill largely intact. Most of the whites accepted their fate, and Britain had once more 'come out with honour'.

During Macmillan's second term in office (1959–63), the problem of the smaller territories was also resolved. Policy-makers concluded that it was preferable to end colonial rule as soon as possible, since international criticism made Britain's position as a colonial power a rather uncomfortable one. The criterion of viability was abandoned partly because of changed international conditions, partly because of Britain's concerns about its international standing. This attitude was most evident in the case of Guiana. The Colonial Secretary wanted to rid Britain of this 'running sore' in order to reduce international criticism as well as the burden on the metropole – and his idea was welcomed by nearly all ministers. Except for a few scattered islands and the special case of Gibraltar, all smaller territories thus became self-governing over the following years.

THE COMMONWEALTH

During Macmillan's second premiership, policy-makers began to consider Britain's membership of the EEC (albeit on special terms) as essential for the maintenance of its Great Power status and its special relationship with the United States. This shift was not causally related to any downward reassessment of the Commonwealth. Policy-makers acknowledged that the club no longer had its former cohesion and unanimity, but they still thought it was a useful institution. I do not share the view, advanced by Wolfram Kaiser, that Macmillan wanted to replace the Commonwealth with Europe because the latter had taken over the former's role as the *fons et origo* of political, military and economic power.[149] The decision to seek entry into the EEC did not reflect a deliberate turning away from the Commonwealth. Archival evidence suggests that the first application under Macmillan was the result of a tactical shift, not a strategic one. The United Kingdom's position as a global power was still thought to rest on three pillars, that is, the special relationship, the Empire-Commonwealth and Europe. Although their relative importance may have changed by the early 1960s, they were still not considered to be exclusive of one another, but in fact, interlinked. As will be shown, disillusionment with the Commonwealth's political role set in only *after* Britain had decided to make an application for EEC membership.

The Commonwealth in the Early 1960s

In July 1959 CO, CRO and Treasury officials presented a joint memorandum on the development of the Commonwealth over the next ten years.[150] The basic question underlying their report was whether in political and economic terms, the club was more of a liability than an asset to Britain. The paper acknowledged that the association had changed considerably since the war. It was no longer a single defence unit. Grand totals of its military strength were therefore rather pointless, except as an indication of 'the overall potential of a group of countries who if not wholly with us, are not against us'. Newly independent countries remained suspicious of Britain and were not necessarily very helpful on the international scene. While the Commonwealth was no longer a direct source of military or economic power, the club was still a considerable asset. It was 'a very important potential source of political influence' and of unique significance in the relationship between advanced and backward countries.[151] Britain's influence depended to a large extent on its position as the centre of the Commonwealth, i.e. on its 'knack of being able most of the time to get on particularly well with, and to maintain the respect and cooperation of, most of the peoples in other continents whom we have ceased to govern'.[152] The Commonwealth was probably the main reason why the United States listened closely to Britain. If it broke up, the United Kingdom would become in the eyes of the United States 'no more than one among a dozen or so smallish countries competing for her attention'. The Commonwealth was also good business. It was by far the largest source of overseas investment income and an important trading partner. This was not merely due to imperial preferences. More important were the hidden preferences which Britain derived from sharing a common language with its customers as well as established trade links. All this was helped by the Commonwealth.

While the joint paper drew a rather rosy picture of the club's importance, it did not necessarily represent the views of all departments concerned. In stark contrast to the views prevailing in the CO and the CRO, officials in the FO were increasingly sceptical about the Commonwealth's real importance. This change of attitude was closely linked to the FO's reorientation towards Europe. Since Britain's links with the Commonwealth was one (if not *the*) main argument put forward against any *rapprochement* with the EEC, officials in the FO set out to demonstrate that the club was not worth the effort necessary to hold it together. All the papers produced in the CRO or the CO failed to analyse why and how the Commonwealth should be vital for Britain's role as a great power.[153] Certainly, it enhanced its influence with the United States, but the assertion that it created this influence required, 'at the very least', some justification.

As concerned the economic aspect, FO officials thought the extent of Commonwealth solidarity prevailing in other ministries 'rather embarrassing' since it narrowed Britain's room of manoeuvre in negotiations on matters such as Europe or GATT.[154] Commonwealth membership was only one among many factors influencing the direction of trade. It did not make members buy products they did not want nor were non-members deterred from buying British products as long as they were competitive.[155] Historically, the greater part of British overseas investments had been made in the Commonwealth, and investors in other regions, for example, Latin America or the Middle East, had burned their fingers. But the value of British investment in the United States was greater than in any Commonwealth country except Australia and Canada. It was doubtful whether investment in the Dominions was necessarily any safer or more profitable than investment elsewhere. The club's past stability might have helped investments survive, but this was no reason why it should be of great importance in the future. There was no reason to believe that a disintegration of the Commonwealth would mean a confiscation of British assets.[156] All this led to the conclusion that the club would never be a source of power comparable with the United States or western Europe. With some luck and the right policies it could enhance the power and prestige of the United Kingdom. Conversely, 'if we are unlucky or make bad mistakes' it might become more of a weakness than an asset. Any attempt on behalf of the CO or the CRO to equate the Commonwealth with the United States in terms of absolute power or of its value to the United Kingdom should be strongly resisted: 'Sentiment is irrelevant to either side of such an equation.'[157]

At the end of the 1950s, this criticism was not yet shared by other ministries. A majority of officials continued to underline the Commonwealth's importance, but with a change of emphasis. According to these officials, it was not so much the Commonwealth's bearing on the special relationship or the economic links which mattered, but the possibility of retaining newly independent states in the Western camp. Admittedly, there were some drawbacks. Since the club was a conglomeration of often disparate and occasionally incompatible elements, it could rarely be used with any force or precision. Sometimes it was even more of an embarrassment than an asset, for example, when British policies had to be diluted to take account of the views of various members which did not regard themselves as part of the Western camp.[158]

At the same time, it demonstrated to coloured peoples the possibility and advantage of an independent but close relationship with the West, and allowed Britain to maintain a special relationship with them. The Commonwealth thus played an important role in the Cold War. Officials concluded that Britain had much to lose, in terms both of direct economic interest and of wider political considerations, if the club fell apart. This belief in the importance of the Commonwealth was shared by the Prime Minister. Fearing a row over South Africa's apartheid politics, he wrote: 'Once the Commonwealth begins to disintegrate I feel it is really finished.'[159]

Macmillan's feeling was shared by many of his colleagues. Britain's position as leader of the Commonwealth was still seen, alongside the special relationship, as 'the main mark of our standing as a world power'.[160] Without the United States, Britain would be defenceless, without western Europe it would be poorer, but without the Commonwealth its position in the world would rapidly decline. The United States would pay much less attention to what Britain had to say; Canada, Australia and New Zealand would become satellites of the United States, while India might be 'cut off altogether from the West'.[161] The admission of African and Asian states had profoundly changed the nature of the Commonwealth, and the imminent entry of smaller territories would further exacerbate the trend of turning the club into a 'minor UN'. But it was hoped that the increase would continue to be gradual, and that the new members would adapt to club life. In addition, policy-makers argued, the Commonwealth assumed special importance in the Cold War struggle for influence and power in the countries outside Europe. The club offered opportunities for the propagation of Western (and, above all, British) ideas and ideals, and for intimate association with developing countries. As such helped to 'keep away from communist clutches' a large part of the world's population.[162]

In 1960 the Commonwealth still held an important position in the mind of many policy-makers. The FO had come to identify Europe as the future base of British power and influence, and did indeed consider the club as dispensable. But this view was not yet accepted in most other ministries. On both the official and the ministerial level, there was considerable resistance against anything which smacked of abandoning the links with the club in favour of the Continent. The importance of the EEC was not undervalued, but membership was to be compatible with Britain's wider obligations and connections. Ministers acknowledged that for economic reasons, Britain should join the Common Market. While it might have to persuade other Commonwealth countries to relinquish some of their special advantages in the United Kingdom market, it should certainly not press that to the point where it threatened the Commonwealth partnership. The latter was still considered as having considerable economic and political importance.[163]

It was only from 1961 onwards that the Commonwealth finally lost its attraction for all those who until then had still believed in its importance for Britain. The new African members, most notably Ghana and Tanganyika, proved far more anti-colonialist and critical of Britain and far less amenable to British influence than had been hoped. This development made it impossible to prevent the departure of South Africa, an event greatly regretted by the Prime Minister and his entourage – 'perhaps my first real defeat', as Macmillan said.[164] Another factor was the immigration of coloured people, mostly from the West Indies and the Indian subcontinent, which was increasingly perceived as a social problem. The year 1958 saw the first race riots. In 1960 the number of immigrants stood at 58,000; by 1962 it had reached 136,000; and later that year an immigration act imposed restrictions on the right of Commonwealth citizens to settle in the United Kingdom. A few years earlier, such restrictions had still been considered dangerous. In the early 1960s, however, the domestic aspects of the issue outweighed anxieties about repercussions on the cohesion of the Commonwealth.[165]

A third factor making the Commonwealth less attractive was the entry of many smaller territories, a development not foreseen at the end of the 1950s. In 1960 Macleod had still spoken of only three new members over the next ten years. In reality the intake proved to be much higher. Most of the new members had very little international importance and therefore hardly increased the club's standing in the world. Instead they contributed to its transformation into an amorphous conglomeration of states whose only common trait was the fact that at one time they had all been governed by Britain. Last but not least, the United States demonstrated that it did not consider the Commonwealth sufficiently important a factor in international affairs to justify Britain's privileged position. Owing to these developments, policy-makers increasingly considered the Commonwealth a chimera and its Afro-Asian members 'ungrateful, grasping, and unsympathetic'.[166] In a letter to the Australian Prime Minister Robert Menzies, Macmillan confided that he shrank from any Commonwealth meeting 'because I know how troublesome it will be'. In the old days, he said, a prime ministers' conference used to be a pleasant occasion: 'One met old friends and discussed business; whilst the latter discussion might not perhaps be very serious, the ties between countries were strengthened by the social contacts.' Unfortunately, this was no longer the case. The Commonwealth had many members, not all of whom were particularly desirable colleagues. The only reason for keeping the association together, Macmillan explained, was the feeling that at some later point it might be used to exert some influence. For the time being, though, it was difficult to find any positive or constructive purpose for it.[167]

By the end of Macmillan's second term as Prime Minister, it was obvious that the Commonwealth could serve none of the purposes policy-makers had expected. Plans for closer strategic and diplomatic cooperation had been buried long ago. Those aimed at reviving the economic links between members hardly fared any better. A proposal to revive economic cooperation by creating a Commonwealth free trade area, launched after the French veto of Britain's application to the EEC, was immediately rejected by the Board of Trade. Officials pointed out that any attempt to create such a free trade area would strike the Dominions as palpably unrealistic, while arousing grave misgivings in EFTA.[168] It would be flying in the face of the determination of all members to develop their own industries and to foster their trade relations with countries other than Britain. Moreover, attempting to maintain imperial preference would entail a substantial change in Britain's basic approach to the new GATT round on trade liberalisation. In addition, it would further limit Britain's freedom on agricultural policy, effectively preventing it from entering the EEC so long as the new agreements were in force. Free-trade arrangements with the Commonwealth would thus largely be incompatible with a policy of reducing trade barriers on a worldwide basis or of seeking closer integration with Europe. But even if new arrangements were feasible, they could not substitute membership of the Treaty of Rome which was of crucial economic importance to Britain.[169] The BoT's verdict was accepted without any major controversy, and the idea of reviving Commonwealth trade finally vanished in the mid-1960s.

The same applied to the political sphere. The physical institutions were growing weaker, and some even expected the Commonwealth relationship eventually to disappear, leaving only its 'hard rock foundation', i.e. Canada, Australia and New Zealand.[170] Nearly all policy-makers knew that a return to the old Commonwealth was not feasible. The Commonwealth, far from being a buttress for post-colonial Britain, turned out to be an arena in which Britain itself could be pilloried. Its failure to underpin Britain's continuing greatness led to deep disappointment among many of its former supporters, sometimes even to profound antipathy. However, as the following section will demonstrate, this development was not causally linked to increased British interest in joining the EEC – the disenchantment with the relics of empire set in *after* the government had decided to apply for membership. Moreover, British policy-makers never believed that the two commitments were mutually exclusive. Rather they expected them to interact to Britain's advantage. Even after the Commonwealth had lost most of its attraction, the British approach to Europe did not change fundamentally: policy-makers never accepted that the United Kingdom might content itself with the role of a purely European power, and continued to underline the importance of their country's links with the United States and the extra-European world.

Europe and the Commonwealth

By the end of the 1950s Europe became increasingly important for policy-makers. This shift was linked to the apparent success of the Six in coordinating their economic and political strategies, and to the realisation that Britain's relative importance in Washington was declining. The United States had demonstrated that it fully supported the EEC and did not regard an agreement with EFTA as necessary or desirable.[171] At the same time, de Gaulle's veto on cooperation between EFTA and the EEC destroyed all hopes for a situation that would have allowed Britain to make the best of both worlds without committing itself to any political association. Apparently, it was time to make a choice. In 1959 the FO began to argue for closer links with Europe. Britain might end up isolated and ignored by the United States if the effort to establish a community succeeded 'without our being associated with the new alignment of power'.[172] Exclusion from an integrated western Europe would also reduce Britain's importance in NATO. The special relationship would be destroyed if the United States believed Britain's influence to be less than that of the six members of the EEC. This was not unlikely, since, at least economically, Germany threatened to overtake Britain. Meanwhile de Gaulle's attempt to establish France as a fourth nuclear power (alongside the United States, the Soviet Union and Britain) was also undermining Britain's claim to a special position next to the two superpowers.[173] Both emotionally and rationally, the United States was attracted to the idea of a strong, united Europe: if faced with the choice between a failing United Kingdom, which remained aloof from this ideal of unity, and a resurgent western Europe which eagerly embraced it, if would no longer regard Britain as its principal ally. The disastrous consequences of such a development were all too obvious:

At the best we should remain a minor power in an alliance dominated by the United States and the countries of the EEC; at the worst we should sit helplessly in the middle while the two power blocs drifted gradually apart.[174]

This was a development Britain had to prevent by all means. A 'fundamental rule' of British policy was to avoid having to make a definite choice between the two sides of the Atlantic.[175] In order to be able to avoid such a choice Britain had to ensure the continuity of a US presence in Europe and the development of a wide economic and political community of interests embracing both continents (the North American and the European) – something which was best achieved through closer links with the Treaty of Rome states.[176] However, even though officials in the FO concluded that the political arguments in favour of joining the Community were strong, their instincts were against it. The Permanent Under-Secretary, Frederick Hoyer Millar, commented: 'Although one's mind thinks one ought to join, one's heart is against it.'[177] Apparently, even the Foreign Office, which often chided the CO and the CRO for being irrational and emotional, was not free of these faults.

At the end of 1959, Macmillan also began to envisage a *rapprochement* with the Six, even though he was still suspicious of 'the Jews, the Planners, and the old cosmopolitan element' among Continental politicians who wanted a supra-national Europe. While he envisaged a shift towards the Continent, he was still determined to ensure that Britain did not enter the Common Market as just another member. It had to preserve its position as 'a Great nation with world-wide responsibilities'.[178] The aim should be a tripartite system, based on the United States, Britain and France. This would make it possible to organise the free world against communism, lure away France from Germany (thus making the latter more vulnerable) and secure Britain's special relationship with the United States.[179] This was to be complemented with membership of the EEC – albeit on special terms which would allow the maintenance of the United Kingdom's links with EFTA and the Commonwealth.[180] While the Prime Minister slowly made up his mind about the advantages of joining the Six, most of his colleagues were not yet inclined to consider such a step.

A memorandum by the Chancellor of the Exchequer D. Heathcoat Amory explained that EEC membership was no option since it would it make it necessary to discriminate against Commonwealth products. It would also undermine Britain's agricultural policy and lead to a loss of sovereignty to an organisation that could develop into a supranational federation.[181] However, officials in other ministries began to follow the lead given by Macmillan and the FO. The BoT, in particular, feared Britain's exclusion from an increasingly dynamic market. The economic steering committee for Europe, made up of FO, Treasury and Board of Trade officials, advised that 'near-identification with the Common Market' was the right objective to pursue.[182] Some of the economic and commercial consequences ruled out simple adhesion, but the long-term objective had to be EEC membership, albeit on special terms. Staying aloof would not only have commercial, but also political repercussions: 'our influence and standing in the world at large – including the Commonwealth and the uncommitted countries – would be bound to diminish'.[183]

In July 1960 ministers rehearsed the arguments for and against joining the EEC. They acknowledged that the arguments in favour of such a step were strong. If Britain remained outside, its political influence in Europe and the rest of the world was likely to decline. If it became part of the Community, it would be greatly enhanced. There were also economic advantages. Britain would not only avoid tariff discrimination against British exports, but would also be able to participate in a large and rapidly expanding market. However, ministers found the arguments against joining to be at least as strong as those in favour. Britain would surrender control of its commercial policies to a European bloc. This could jeopardise Britain's worldwide trading interests. Ministers feared that on entering Europe, Britain's special economic relationship with the Commonwealth, including free entry for Commonwealth goods and the preferential system, would have to be given up. It could even become necessary to discriminate actively against the Commonwealth, leading to widespread resentment in the Dominions. The cost of living would increase, since the government would have to give up Britain's traditional agricultural policy under which the burden of support for the farmers was carried by the Exchequer, not the consumer. Last, but not least, Britain would have to sacrifice its 'loyalties and obligations' to the members of EFTA, some of whom would find it impossible to join the EEC as full members.[184] The Chancellor of the Exchequer summed up the discussion by proposing the exploration of an intermediate course which would allow Britain to maintain close links with Commonwealth and EFTA while moving closer to the Community. A decision to join the EEC would be 'essentially a political act with economic consequences, rather than an economic act with political consequences'. Britain should join the Community only if it could do so without substantially impairing its relations with the Commonwealth. It could not accept membership on the terms of the Treaty of Rome, but had to be granted special terms.

After further deliberation, Macmillan and the Chancellor of the Exchequer concluded that the balance of economic advantage lay in favour of moving closer to Europe. The FO advised that the balance of political advantage pointed in the same direction. Participation in the 'inner circle' of the Six was essential to secure Britain's position as the link between the United States and Europe. The United States wanted not only economic, but also political cooperation in Europe – the US President, Dwight D. Eisenhower, encouraged Macmillan to seek membership of the EEC. This as well as unproductive talks with Germany finally removed the possibility of using EFTA as 'a battering ram to reshape Europe on Britain's preferred terms'.[185] By early 1961 most policy-makers believed that the advantages to be gained from entering the Common Market (albeit on special terms) were more important than the drawbacks. Britain would be the most powerful member and might be able to exercise 'a strong and sometimes a decisive influence' upon the policies of the Community. British manufactured goods would gain free access to a large and rapidly expanding market. If it did not join, however, Britain would inevitably enter into a period of relative decline. Not only would its industry and agriculture suffer, but also its influence in the Commonwealth and the world generally.[186] In July 1961 ministers therefore decided to apply for full membership 'if satisfactory arrangements can be made to meet the special interests of the United Kingdom, of the Commonwealth and of the European Free Trade Association'. The terms of the announcement made it clear that Britain was far from abandoning its links with the wider world, in particular the Commonwealth, for the sake of Europe.[187] Entry into the EEC was desired, but only on British terms. Although the British Ambassador in Bonn warned that the French had 'no intention of letting us into their private Europe', officials still believed that Britain could afford to impose certain conditions.[188]

In January 1963 the negotiations over Britain's entry into the Common Market collapsed in the face of a French veto. This was greatly regretted by the Prime Minister. De Gaulle's 'no' did vital damage to Macmillan's plans of reviving Britain's role as a world power. Britain was excluded from the lucrative European market as well as denied a new source of political prestige and power, while the Commonwealth drifted apart. The special relationship was only a pale shadow of its former self – a fact underlined by Dean Acheson's disrespectful remark that Britain had 'lost an Empire, [but] not yet found a role'.[189] The ex-US Secretary of State denounced Britain's attempt to play a special role, counting on its links with the United States and the Commonwealth, an organisation without structure, unity or political strength. Apparently this was also what Macmillan felt, since he noted: 'We have lost everything. All our policies at home and abroad are in ruins.'[190]

The Adoption of Quasi-Automatic Commonwealth Membership

Macmillan's disappointment over de Gaulle's veto stemmed not just from Britain's exclusion from the EEC, which deprived it of vital leverage on European (and US) policy-making. Equally important was his realisation that the Commonwealth had failed to fulfil the hopes he had projected onto it. The rush of new, mostly smaller members in the early 1960s contributed to the disenchantment of policy-makers with the Commonwealth as a factor bolstering Britain's prestige and influence in the world.

In the summer of 1960, an official working party was appointed to consider the future development of the club. It concluded that any form of 'half-way house' between colonial status and full membership was unacceptable.[191] Therefore Commonwealth membership should be granted to all independent territories, irrespective of size. This was 'most consistent both with the aspirations of the new nations and with the general ethos of the Commonwealth'. However, officials still hoped that the increase 'may not be unmanageable'.[192] The working party was confident that the Commonwealth would not become a kind of smaller United Nations.[193] The Commonwealth had no public deliberations or decisions taken on a one-country, one-vote basis, so there was no danger of the adoption of anti-British resolutions. But its members could nonetheless constitute a formidable bloc in the United Nations. Some territories currently behaved in an irresponsible way. But as they entered the club, they were exposed to 'positive influences'. It was reasonable to hope that in time their leaders would absorb 'Commonwealth habits of reason and good sense'. In any case, they were less likely to be irresponsible within the club than without.

The recommendations of the working group were accepted by ministers. After the admission of Cyprus, Commonwealth membership thus became quasi-automatic for all territories acceding to independence, irrespective of their size. However, it was assumed that at least in the near future, it would be possible to maintain the Commonwealth as a more or less exclusive club that boosted Britain's international standing and diplomatic influence. In 1960 it was still assumed that the only additions in the near future would be Sierra Leone as well as the West Indian and Central African Federations. The number of new members would thus remain relatively low and the increase would continue to be gradual.

In 1962, the break-up of the two federations and the independence of the East African territories were imminent. This raised the prospect of many more smaller territories joining the Commonwealth than had been expected two years earlier. Norman Brook alerted the Prime

Minister to a situation in which Britain would be faced with 'another rush of candidates'. Since the 1960 report the advances to independence had become more rapid (and numerous) than 'anything we had envisaged'. If this influx was permitted, the club was destined to become 'a relatively large association including a number of relatively small countries'.[194] The majority of its members would be made up of countries with little international significance. Moreover, some of them would be neutral in the 'secular struggle of East versus West' or sympathetic to the anti-colonialist cause. At the urging of Brook a new working group was appointed to consider the possibility of reducing (or at least retarding) the intake.

An interim report proposed designating certain territories which could not be considered suitable for independence. Such territories might be dissuaded from applying. Others might become protected states within the Commonwealth (like Brunei) or outside it (like the Gulf States). But officials advised that all this was unlikely to keep down the number of possible candidates. The only options were to persuade other members to set a limit to the number of acceptable applicants or to decide that the advantages of opening up the club outweighed the disadvantages. After some deliberation, it was concluded that only the second option was realistic:

> having regard to our declared Colonial policy of aiming at inde-
> pendence within the Commonwealth as the constitutional goal for
> our dependent territories; the climate of opinion in the Afro-Asian
> Commonwealth; the difficulty of not admitting to the
> Commonwealth States which would inevitably be accepted as
> members of the United Nations; and our moral obligation to
> launch our dependencies into independence with the support that
> can be given by the Commonwealth association, we cannot hope to
> avoid a considerable influx of new Commonwealth members in the
> next decade.[195]

Any attempt to restrict membership would provoke serious criticism from inside and outside the Commonwealth. It would also lead to a serious deterioration of relations with the territories concerned. Policy-makers consoled themselves with the knowledge that enlargement was not necessarily a disadvantage. Far from diluting the Commonwealth, they thought, the intake had increased the number of independent countries open to Western influence: 'The Russians must certainly envy our opportunities.'

Brook feared that, in admitting new members, Britain could 'hope for no more than that they are willing to join us rather than go over to the other side'. But in the eyes of many policy-makers, this in itself was already an important gain. As Macmillan stated in his 'wind of change' speech, 'the great issue' in the second half of the twentieth century was whether the uncommitted peoples of Asia and Africa would swing to the East or to the West.[196] If the Commonwealth helped to tip the balance in favour of Britain and the West, it was a success. Despite his pessimistic outlook, even Brook had to admit that the enlargement of the Commonwealth had two advantages: firstly that new members, on attaining independence, were choosing voluntarily to preserve the British connection and 'though they may not be actively with us in the East–West struggle', were 'at least refraining from joining the other side'. Secondly, the new Commonwealth demonstrated that peoples of different races could cooperate in a multi-racial association in 'an atmosphere of mutual tolerance'. In a world of increasing racial tension this would be a valuable contribution to peace and might even ease the transition to self-government among multi-racial communities in East and Central Africa.

The issue was finally settled at a meeting of Cabinet ministers in May 1962. The Colonial and Commonwealth Secretaries advised that there were no criteria of eligibility such as size, population or wealth. After the admission of Cyprus and Sierra Leone, it would be logical to give full membership to all colonies attaining independence.[197] The Prime Minister agreed, proposing that the enlargement should be compensated for by a modification of the methods of consultation between members. Even though the idea of a formal two-tier Commonwealth was thus finally buried, that of having some members which were more equal than others was not. As concerned political and strategic cooperation, the Commonwealth was effectively reduced to its 'hard-rock foundation', i.e. Canada, Australia and New Zealand. At the same time, the facade of a multi-racial organisation linking Britain with its former colonies was maintained.[198] By the mid-1960s, the Commonwealth had, therefore, almost become a Cold War propaganda weapon, which demonstrated that African and Asian states could remain in the Western camp without prejudicing their newly won independence. There was a short revival of the Commonwealth ideal under Harold Wilson, who believed that the club could provide Britain with a disproportionate global influence, particularly in Asia and Africa, but even then the club did not regain its former importance for the majority of British policy-makers.[199]

Conclusion

From 1959 onwards policy-makers entertained increasing doubts about the value of the Commonwealth. The FO, in particular, deemed it an obstacle in future negotiations on Europe and GATT. Moving towards the EEC would be more advantageous than trying to hold together a group of heterogeneous countries that had little in common but their former association with Britain. For the CRO, however, the club was essential for Britain's international standing, and for fostering trade with former colonies. Moreover, it helped to link the West with non-aligned countries in Asia and Africa. At the end of the 1950s, this point of view was still shared by a majority of policy-makers. Britain was to seek membership of the EEC, but should not press its point if it threatened the Commonwealth partnership.

From 1961 onwards Britain's attachment to the Commonwealth grew increasingly weaker. This development was due to several factors: the critical stance of the new members (leading *inter alia* to the departure of South Africa), rapidly growing immigration from brown and black Dominions, the accession of many smaller territories and the United States openly displayed preference for the EEC. By the end of Macmillan's second term in office, the Commonwealth therefore was considered mainly a façade. Cooperation with the older Dominions increasingly took place in other spheres, while entering the Common Market (albeit still on special terms) was considered vital to preserve Britain's economic and political interests.

NOTES

1. D.J. Morgan, *The Official History of Colonial Development: A Reassessment of British Aid Policy, 1951–1965, Vol. 3* (Basingstoke: Macmillan, 1980), p. 211.
2. Dilwyn Porter, 'Downhill All the Way: Thirteen Tory Years 1951–64', in R. Coopey, S. Fielding and N. Tiratsoo (eds), *The Wilson Governments 1964–1970* (London: Pinter, 1993), p. 18f.
3. Memorandum, 'Defence and Economic Aid: the Resources Balance Sheet' (FP (A) (59) 11), Treasury to steering committee, 23 December 1959. CAB 134/1930 (PRO).
4. Treasury memorandum, 'United Kingdom Balance of Payments Situation' (FP (A) (61) 3), 10 August 1961. CAB 134/1932 (PRO).
5. Note of a meeting of ministers at Admiralty House (GEN 740/1st meeting), 5 July 1961. CAB 130/177 (PRO).
6. Foreign Secretary to Prime Minister, 9 May 1959. PREM 11/2753 (PRO).
7. 'Report of the Working Party on Government Overseas Defence Expenditure' (FP (A) (61) 1), 18 July 1961. CAB 134/1932 (PRO).
8. Memorandum, 'Our Foreign and Defence Policy for the Future' by Macmillan, 29 September 1961. CAB 134/1929 (PRO).
9. FP (A) (61) 1st meeting, 24 July 1961. CAB 134/1932 (PRO).

10. FP (A) (62) 2nd meeting, 7 September 1961. CAB 134/1932 (PRO).
11. FO/MoD report, 'Future Policy in the Persian Gulf' (GEN 745/4), 25 September 1961. CAB 130/178 (PRO).
12. Official report, 'Military Expenditure Overseas' (FP (A) (61) 4), 1 September 1961. CAB 134/1932 (PRO).
13. FP (A) 1st meeting, 4 January 1962. CAB 134/1933 (PRO).
14. Official report, 'Defence of the Persian Gulf' (D (60) 46 annex B), 23 September 1960. CAB 131/24 (PRO).
15. Report, 'Future Developments in South East Asia' (D (60) 50) by official committee on future developments in south-east Asia, 12 October 1960. CAB 131/24 (PRO).
16. FP (A) (62) 1st meeting, 4 January 1962. CAB 134/1933 (PRO).
17. Minutes of a meeting of ministers (GEN 754/1st meeting), 9 November 1961. CAB 130/179 (PRO).
18. Minutes of a meeting of ministers (GEN 754/3rd meeting), 21 March 1962. CAB 130/179 (PRO).
19. D (62) 1st meeting, 12 January 1962. CAB 131/27 (PRO); CPC (62) 4th meeting, 16 February 1962. CAB 134/1561 (PRO).
20. D (63) 3rd meeting, 9 February 1963. CAB 131/28 (PRO).
21. Minute, 'Aden', Burke Trend to Prime Minister, 6 February 1963. PREM 11/4678 (PRO).
22. Note, 'The Implications of Withdrawal from the Middle and Far East' (GEN 796/2) by chairman of the official overseas co-ordinating committee, 7 May 1963. CAB 130/190 (PRO).
23. Minutes of a meeting held in Burke Trend's room (GEN 796/2nd meeting), 21 May 1963. CAB 130/190 (PRO).
24. Note, 'The Middle East' (GEN 796/2 annex A) by official overseas co-ordinating committee, 9 May 1963. CAB 130/190 (PRO).
25. Note, 'The Far East' (GEN 796/2 annex B) by official overseas co-ordinating committee, 9 May 1963. CAB 130/190 (PRO).
26. Minute, 'Aircraft Carrier Programme', Kockaday to Bligh, 22 July 1963. PREM 11/4731 (PRO).
27. Memorandum, 'Future Defence Policy' (D (63) 24), Chancellor of the Exchequer to defence committee, 5 July 1963. CAB 131/28 (PRO).
28. CM 48 (63), 25 July 1963. CAB 128/37 (PRO).
29. D (63) 9th meeting, 10 July 1963. CAB 131/28 (PRO).
30. D (63) 8th meeting, 19 June 1963. CAB 131/28 (PRO).
31. Minute, 'Future Defence Policy', Burke Trend to Prime Minister, 9 July 1963. PREM 11/4731 (PRO).
32. Memorandum, 'Future Defence Policy', Burke Trend to Prime Minister, 18 June 1963. PREM 11/4731 (PRO).
33. Memorandum, 'Future Defence Policy' (D (63) 23), Minister of Defence to defence committee, 2 July 1963. CAB 131/28 (PRO).
34. Memorandum, 'Future Defence Policy' (D (63) 22), Foreign Secretary to defence committee, 17 June 1963. CAB 131/28 (PRO).
35. Memorandum by W. Stevens, 19 July 1963. FO 371/170165 (PRO).
36. Peter Catterall (ed.), 'Witness Seminar: The East of Suez Decision', *Contemporary Record* 7 (1993), p. 612. In 1965 there were 55,000 troops stationed east of Suez, and 15 per cent of the defence budget was spent on maintaining them (David Sanders, *Losing an Empire, Finding a Role: British Foreign Policy since 1945* (Basingstoke: Macmillan, 1990), p. 123).
37. Minute, 'Repercussion on British Policy in South East Asia of the Separation of Singapore from Malaysia' (OPD (65) 131), 21 September 1965. PREM 13/1833 (PRO).

38. Report, 'Military Tasks in the Indo-Pacific Area' (MISC 94/1 (final)) by interdepartmental official working party, 22 November 1965. CAB 130/252 (PRO).

39. Note, 'Defence Review: Aden', Greenwood to Minister of Defence, 2 August 1965. PREM 13/113 (PRO).

40. Minutes of official working group on economies in overseas expenditure (MISC 121 (66) 1st meeting), 15 June 1966. CAB 130/294 (PRO).

41. Malcolm Chalmers, *Paying for Defence: Military Spending and British Decline* (London: Pluto Press, 1985), p. 87.

42. *The Guardian*, 4 July 1998. For a detailed description of the debates on the role of the Royal Navy after 1945 see Andrea Ellner and Anthony Gorst, 'The British Surface Fleet since 1945', unpublished paper, September 1999 (personal communication).

43. Keith Kyle, *The Politics of the Independence of Kenya* (New York, NY: St Martin's Press, 1999).

44. Speech at Conservative Party conference, 11 October 1961, quoted in Shepherd, *Iain Macleod*, p. 254; Lord Douglas-Home in an interview with Brian Lapping, quoted in Lapping, 'Did Suez hasten the End of Empire?', p. 33.

45. Philip E. Hemming, 'Macmillan and the End of the British Empire in Africa', in Aldous and Lee (eds), *Harold Macmillan*, p. 118.

46. Despatch, Dean to Home, 4 January 1962. FO 371/166819 (PRO).

47. CP (O)(60) 1, annex A, 30 March 1960. CAB 134/1552 (PRO).

48. Poynton to colonial governors, 29 September 1960. CO 936/678 (PRO).

49. Paper, 'United Kingdom Policy in the United Nations on Colonialism and Target dates' by J. Martin, 1 June 1961. CO 936/680 (PRO).

50. Macleod to Poynton, 10 August 1961. CO 936/681, quoted in Hemming, 'Macmillan and the End of the British Empire', p. 113.

51. Ryrie to Jerrom and Eastwood, 8 May 1961. CO 936/680 (PRO); minute by Ryrie, 16 May 1961. ibid.

52. CPC (60) 2, 18 March 1960. CAB 134/1559 (PRO).

53. Hargreaves, *Decolonization in Africa*, p. 196.

54. Macmillan to Brook, 1 November 1959. Macmillan Archives, quoted in Horne, *Macmillan*, p. 185.

55. Note of a meeting in the room of the Colonial Secretary, 16 November 1959. CO 822/1451 (PRO).

56. CPC (59) 6th meeting, 20 November 1959. CAB 134/1558 (PRO).

57. Governor of Tanganyika to Gorell Barnes, 12 May 1959. CO 822/1449 (PRO).

58. Memorandum, 'Constitutional Development in Tanganyika' by Colonial Secretary (CPC (59) 20), 12 November 1959. CAB 134/1558 (PRO).

59. Macleod to Prime Minister, 29 December 1959. PREM 11/2586 (PRO).

60. Turnbull (Tanganyika) to Monson, 25 October 1959. CO 822/1450 (PRO); minutes of a meeting at the CO, 20 May 1959. CO 936/572, quoted in Louis and Robinson, 'The Imperialism of Decolonization', p. 486f.

61. Minute by F. Webber, 5 November 1959. CO 822/1448 (PRO).

62. 'Report of the Kenya Constitutional Conference', Cmnd 960, February 1960, PP (1959–60) X, 891 (Porter and Stockwell, *British Imperial Policy*, II, 78).

63. 'A Plan for East and Central Africa' by D. Stirling, 20 May 1959. PREM 11/2583 (PRO).

64. Speech at Conservative Party conference, 11 October 1961, quoted in Shepherd, *Iain Macleod*, p. 253.

65. Minute, 'Nyasaland', Macleod to Macmillan, 3 December 1959. PREM 11/3075 (PRO); 'Note for the Prime Minister on the Emergency in Nyasaland', Macleod to Macmillan, n.d. (January 1960). PREM 11/3075 (PRO).

66. Macleod to Sandys, 15 November 1960. PREM 11/3080 (PRO).
67. CM (60) 6th, 9 February 1960. CAB 128/34 (PRO).
68. Speech by Macmillan to both Houses of the Parliament of the Union of South Africa, Cape Town, 3 February 1960 (Porter and Stockwell, *British Imperial Policy*, II, 77). Already in 1957 Macmillan had warned that nationalism had become a 'tidal wave surging from Asia across the ocean to the shores of Africa. ... Of all political forces, the new rise of nationalism is the most powerful, swift and elemental ... It can be led: but it cannot be driven back'. Quoted in Dan Horowitz, 'Attitudes of British Conservatives towards Decolonization in Africa', *African Affairs*, 69 (1970), p. 16.
69. Quoted in Robert Hyam, 'The Parting of the Ways: Britain and South Africa's Departure from the Commonwealth, 1951–61', *Journal of Imperial and Commonwealth History*, XXVI, 2 (1998), p. 162.
70. Memorandum, 'Policy towards South Africa: The United Nations Items', Commonwealth Secretary to Prime Minister, 17 December 1959. T 236/4873 (PRO).
71. Macmillan diary, entry for 14 December 1960, quoted in Horne, *Macmillan*, p. 209.
72. Quoted in Hemming, 'Macmillan and the End of the British Empire', p. 101.
73. CPA, CRD, 2/53, SC/45, 23 June 1959. PREM 11/2583, quoted in Shepherd, *Iain Macleod*, p. 158.
74. Macmillan diary, entries for 22 and 23 March 1960, quoted in Horne, *Macmillan*, p. 203. On 21 March 1960, 67 African demonstrators were killed at Sharpeville by South African police.
75. Macmillan diary, entry for 22 February 1961, quoted in Horne, *Macmillan*, p. 389.
76. All quotes from Macleod to Macmillan, 31 March 1960. PREM 11/3076 (PRO).
77. Home to Macmillan, 10 June 1960. CO 1015/2254 (PRO).
78. Macleod to Macmillan, 3 April 1960. PREM 11/3076 (PRO).
79. Macmillan to Macleod, 6 August 1960. PREM 11/3077 (PRO).
80. Macleod to Sandys, 15 November 1960. PREM 11/3080 (PRO); Report of the Advisory (Monckton) Commission on the Review of the Constitution of Rhodesia and Nyasaland, Cmnd. 1148, October 1960. PP (1959–60) XI, 21 (Porter and Stockwell, *British Imperial Policy*, II, 79).
81. Minute by P. Ramsbotham, 20 November 1959. FO 371/143700 (PRO).
82. Note by Wyndham, 13 November 1960. PREM 11/3080 (PRO).
83. Macleod to Butler, 15 January 1961. PREM 11/3030 (PRO).
84. Quotes from Macleod to Macmillan, 8 February 1960. PREM 11/3030 (PRO).
85. Macleod to Macmillan, 16 February 1960. PREM 11/3031 (PRO).
86. Macleod to Macmillan, 31 May 1960. PREM 11/3240 (PRO).
87. W. Monson to J. Martin, 21 July 1960. CO 822/2299 (PRO).
88. Macleod to Prime Minister, 22 November 1960. CO 822/2300 (PRO).
89. Memorandum, 'Colonial problems in 1961' by Colonial Secretary (CPC (61) 1), 3 January 1961. CAB 134/1560 (PRO).
90. Dalhousie to Macmillan, 31 January 1961. PREM 11/3485 (PRO).
91. WP 389/3, 'Statements at Press Conference, Salisbury', 29 September 1960, quoted in Murphy, *Party Politics and Decolonization*, p. 83.
92. Macmillan diary, entry for 24 February 1961, quoted in Horne, *Macmillan 1957–1986*, p. 389.
93. Macmillan to Lord Chancellor, 8 January 1961. PREM 11/4083 (PRO); Macmillan diary, entry for 22 February 1961, quoted in Horne, *Macmillan 1957–1986*, p. 389.
94. Shepherd, *Iain Macleod*, p. 220.

95. Shepherd, *Iain Macleod*, p. 225.
96. Macmillan to Macleod, 26 February 1961. PREM 11/3488 (PRO).
97. Macmillan diary, entry for 21 June 1961, quoted in Horne, *Macmillan*, p. 394.
98. Macleod to Hone, 6 August 1961. PREM 11/3493 (PRO); Macmillan to Bligh, 28 August 1961. PREM 11/3493 (PRO).
99. CPC (61) 1, 5 January 1961. CAB 134/1560 (PRO); AF (60) 3, 21 December 1960. CAB 134/1356 (PRO).
100. Minutes of a meeting between the Colonial Secretary and the East African governors (EAC (61) minutes 1), n.d. (January 1961). PREM 11/4083 (PRO).
101. Macleod to Prime Minister, 6 January 1961. PREM 11/4083 (PRO).
102. Macleod to Minister of Defence, 12 January 1961. FO 371/146498 (PRO).
103. Macleod to Prime Minister, 6 January 1961. PREM II/4083 (PRO).
104. Note, 'The East African Problem – Concentrated on Kenya', Lord Chancellor to Prime Minister, 11 January 1961. PREM 11/4083 (PRO).
105. 'Trouble in Africa', leading article by Iain Macleod, The *Spectator*, 31 January 1964 (Porter and Stockwell, *British Imperial Policy*, II, 82).
106. Colonial Secretary to P. Renison (Nairobi), 19 May 1961. CO 822/2241 (PRO).
107. Home to Macmillan, 18 April 1961. PREM 11/3413 (PRO).
108. Macmillan diary, entry for 20 January 1961, quoted in Turner, *Macmillan*, p. 200.
109. Quoted in Murphy, *Party Politics and Decolonization*, p. 195.
110. Monson to J. Martin, 11 September 1961. CO 822/2327 (PRO).
111. Lord Chancellor to Prime Minister, 29 December 1961. PREM 11/3942 (PRO).
112. Butler to Macmillan, 18 January 1962. PREM 11/3942 (PRO).
113. Horne, *Macmillan*, p. 408.
114. R. Welensky, *4000 Days: The Life and Death of the Federation of Rhodesia and Nyasaland* (London: Collins, 1964), p. 323; Macmillan diary, entry for 19 February 1962, quoted in Horne, *Macmillan*, p. 408.
115. Memorandum, 'The Problem in Central Africa' (C (62) 59), Secretary of State for the Home Department to Cabinet, 3 April 1962. CAB 129/109 (PRO).
116. Note by Butler, 13 March 1962. RAB F97, fol. 25 (TCC).
117. Duncan Sandys to Saville Garner, 24 February 1962. PREM 11/3943 (PRO).
118. Minutes of a meeting of ministers at Admiralty House, 22 February 1962. PREM 11/3943 (PRO); minutes of a meeting of ministers (GEN 775/1st meeting), 24 October 1962. CAB 130/189 (PRO).
119. Horowitz, 'Attitudes of British Conservatives', p. 12.
120. Butler to Macmillan, 19 December 1962, quoted in Lamb, *Macmillan Years*, p. 277.
121. Minute, 'Central Africa', Burke Trend to Prime Minister, 16 January 1963. PREM 11/4419 (PRO).
122. Memorandum, 'Meeting of Ambassadors and High Commissioners from Tropical Africa, 21st–24th May, 1963' (C (63) 106 annex), Commonwealth Secretary to Cabinet, 20 June 1963. CAB 129/114 (PRO).
123. Macmillan diary, entries for 23 and 24 April 1963, quoted in Horne, *Macmillan*, p. 411f.
124. Minutes of a meeting of ministers (GEN 792/1st meeting), 23 April 1963. CAB 130/190 (PRO).
125. Memorandum, (C (62) 22), Colonial Secretary to Cabinet, 6 February 1962. CAB 129/108 (PRO).
126. AF (61) 10th meeting, 8 December 1961. CAB 134/1357 (PRO); CPC (62) 3rd meeting, 2 February 1962. CAB 134/1561 (PRO).
127. Memorandum, 'Kenya Constitutional Conference' (C (62) 53), Colonial

Secretary to Cabinet, 19 March 1962. CAB 129/109 (PRO).

128. Memorandum, 'Kenya Constitutional Conference' (CPC (62) 3), Colonial Secretary to Cabinet colonial policy committee, 30 January 1962. CAB 134/1561 (PRO).

129. Colonial Secretary to Home, 5 January 1962. FO 371/166819 (PRO).

130. Quoted in Gary Wasserman, *Politics of Decolonization: Kenya Europeans and the Land Issue 1960–1965* (Cambridge: Cambridge University Press, 1976) p. 95.

131. CM 12 (62) 5, 8 February 1962. CAB 128/36 (1) (PRO).

132. Salisbury to Home, 9 February 1962. PREM 11/4886 (PRO).

133. Memorandum, 'Constitutional Development in Zanzibar' (CPC (62) 2), Colonial Secretary to colonial policy committee, 14 February 1962. CAB 134/1561 (PRO).

134. Macmillan to Foreign Secretary, n.d. (31 January 1962). FO 371/166850 (PRO).

135. AF (62) 5th meeting, 29 March 1962. CAB 134/1359 (PRO).

136. Minutes of meeting of ministers at 10 Downing Street (GEN 810), 17 October 1963. CAB 130/192 (PRO).

137. Sanger, *Malcolm MacDonald*, p. 396.

138. C (60) 122, 11 August 1960. CAB 129/102 (PRO).

139. Brook to Prime Minister, 28 July 1960. PREM 11/3649 (PRO).

140. Barbados and Guiana attained independence in 1966, the Bahamas in 1973, followed a year later by Grenada. British rule in Dominica ended in 1978; Antigua, Barbuda and British Honduras followed suit in 1981. The British Virgin Islands remain under colonial rule, while others chose the status of Associated States, i.e. that of territories whose external relations are dealt with by Britain. These are the Cayman Islands, Montserrat, St Kitts, Nevis, Anguilla and the Turks and Caicos Islands.

141. Memorandum, 'The Problem of the Small Colonial Territories' (PFP (62) 19), CO to Cabinet committee on future policy in the Pacific, 30 November 1962. CAB 134/2402 (PRO).

142. Memorandum, 'British Guiana Independence' (CPC (61) 32), Colonial Secretary to colonial policy committee, 15 December 1961. CAB 134/1560 (PRO).

143. M. Cary to Prime Minister, 4 April 1962. PREM 11/3666 (PRO).

144. Commonwealth Secretary to Prime Minister, 11 January 1962. PREM 1/3666 (PRO).

145. Minute, 'British Guiana Independence', Chancellor of the Exchequer to Prime Minister, 11 January 1962. PREM 11/3666 (PRO).

146. In 2001, the following territories were still dependent on the United Kingdom: Anguilla, Bermuda, British Antarctic Territory, British Indian Ocean Territory, British Virgin Islands, Cayman Islands, Falkland Islands, Gibraltar, Montserrat, Pitcairn Islands Group, St Helena and Dependencies (Ascension and Tristan da Cunha), South Georgia and South Sandwich Islands, Turks and Caicos Islands.

147. Minute, 'British and American Strategic Interests in Area of South East Asia and the Indian Ocean', Butler to Prime Minister, 20 April 1964. PREM 11/4907 (PRO).

148. Paper, 'The Political Future and Economic Need of the British Territories' (PFP (62) 4), CO to Cabinet committee on future policy in the Pacific, 3 January 1962. CAB 134/2402 (PRO).

149. Wolfram Kaiser, 'To Join, or not To Join: The "Appeasement" Policy of Britain's First EEC Application', in Brian Brivati and Harriet Jones (eds), *From Reconstruction to Integration: Britain and Europe since 1945* (Leicester:

Leicester University Press, 1993), p. 149.

150. Memorandum, 'The Commonwealth 1960–1970' by CRO, CO and Treasury, 30 July 1959. CAB 134/1935 (PRO).
151. FP (A) (59) 5, 10 November 1959. CAB 134/1930 (PRO).
152. Memorandum, 'The Commonwealth 1960–1970' by CRO, CO and Treasury, 30 July 1959. CAB 134/1935 (PRO).
153. C. O'Neill (FO) to W. Clark (CRO), 12 and 31 August 1959. CO 1032/74 (PRO).
154. UEE 1011/68, 2 July 1959. FO 371/141138, quoted in Jacqueline Tratt, *The Macmillan Government and Europe: A Study in the Process of Policy Development* (Basingstoke: Macmillan, 1996), p. 146.
155. Selwyn to Williamson, 25 August 1958. CO 1032/74 (PRO).
156. C. O'Neill (FO) to W. Clark (CRO), 12 August 1959. CO 1032/74 (PRO).
157. All quotes from Dean to Foreign Secretary, 15 March 1960. FO 371/152133 (PRO).
158. FP (A) (59) 1 (revise), 26 October 1959. CAB 134/1930 (PRO).
159. Macmillan to Butler, 25 March 1960. Macmillan Archives, quoted in Horne, *Macmillan*, p. 204.
160. Brook to Prime Minister, n.d. (January 1961). PREM 11/3325 (PRO).
161. FP (60) 1st, 23 March 1960. CAB 134/1929 (PRO).
162. FP (A) (60) 5, 15 January 1960. CAB 134/1930 (PRO).
163. CM 41 (60), 13 July 1960. CAB 128/34 (PRO).
164. Quoted in Horne, *Macmillan*, p. 393.
165. Andrew Roberts, *Eminent Churchillians* (London: Phoenix, 1995), p. 228.
166. D.A. Low, 'Little Britain and Large Commonwealth', *Round Table*, 298 (1986), p.111.
167. Macmillan to Menzies, 8 February 1962, PREM 11/3649 (PRO).
168. Memorandum, 'Extension of Bilateral Trade Arrangements with Commonwealth Countries' (MISC 56/1) by Board of Trade, 11 May 1965. CAB 130/229 (PRO).
169. Chancellor of the Exchequer to Home, 7 January 1964. PREM 11/4640 (PRO); memorandum, 'Commonwealth Policy' (CP (64) 6) by Prime Minister, 3 January 1964. CAB 129/116/1 (PRO).
170. Memorandum, 'The Future of the Commonwealth Relations Office' by G. Cunningham, 28 January 1964. Mss.Brit.Emp. s 332, 4/3 (RHL).
171. Anthony Adamthwaite, 'Britain, France and the Integration of Western Europe, 1957–1961', in Dockrill (ed.), *Europe within the Global System*, p. 137.
172. CM 37 (57) 4, 2 May 1957. CAB 128/31 (1) (PRO).
173. Memorandum, 'The Future of Anglo-American Relations' by Planning Section, 5 January 1960. PREM 11/2986 (PRO).
174. Memorandum by FO Planning Section, n.d. (Autumn 1959). PREM 11/2985 (PRO).
175. FP (A) (59), 10 November 1959. CAB 134/1930 (PRO).
176. Dean to Gladwyn Jebb (Paris), 5 April 1960. FO 371/152132 (PRO); H. Caccia (Washington) to F. Hoyer Millar, 29 June 1960. FO 371/152133 (PRO).
177. Quoted in Lee, 'Staying in the Game?', p. 140.
178. Minute of meeting of ministers at Chequers, 29 November 1959. PREM 11/679 (PRO).
179. Memorandum by Prime Minister, 29 December 1960–3 January 1961. PREM 11/3325 (PRO).
180. Memorandum, 'The Future of Anglo-American Relations' by Planning Section, 5 January 1960. PREM 11/2986 (PRO).
181. Memorandum Heathcoat-Amory to Cabinet, 20 February 1959. CAB 129/96/27 (PRO).

182. ES (E) (60), 23 May 1960. CAB 134/1852 (PRO).
183. ES (E) (60) 14, 27 June 1960. CAB 134/1853 (PRO).
184. CM 41 (60), 13 July 1960. CAB 128/34 (PRO).
185. Porter and Stockwell, *British Imperial Policy*, II, p. 37.
186. Minutes of European economic association committee, 17 May 1961. CO 852/1935 (PRO).
187. *Hansard* (House of Commons Debates) 645, column 1481.
188. Quoted in Adamthwaite, 'Britain, France and the Integration of Western Europe', p. 138.
189. *The Times*, 6 December 1962. In his speech given at West Point on 5 December 1962, Dean Acheson did not present an official view; but in Britain his comments provoked a public outcry – the speech was seen as an insult, and Macmillan especially feared that it would do further damage to Britain's standing. (Douglas Brinkley, 'Dean Acheson and the "Special Relationship": The West Point Speech of December 1962', *Historical Journal*, 33, 3 (1990), p. 603).
190. Harold Macmillan, *At the End of the Day, 1961–63* (Basingstoke: Macmillan, 1973), p. 367.
191. C (60) 122, 11 August 1960. CAB 129/102 (PRO); 'Future Expansion of the Commonwealth', CO brief for Secretary of State, n.d. (1960). CO 1032/224 (PRO).
192. Report of group of Commonwealth officials, 23 July 1960. CAB 133/200 (PRO).
193. Note, 'Smaller Colonial Territories' (revised version) by Lintott, n.d. (June 1960). DO 35/7876 (PRO).
194. Brook for Prime Minister, 6 February 1962. PREM 11/3649 (PRO); note, 'Evolution of the Commonwealth' by Brook, 24 April 1962. PREM 11/3649 (PRO).
195. PMM (UK) (62) A1, 27 August 1962, CAB 133/263 (PRO).
196. Quoted in Max Beloff, 'The End of the British Empire and the Assumption of World-Wide Commitments by the United States', in Wm Roger Louis and H. Bull (eds), *The Special Relationship: Anglo-American Relations since 1945* (Oxford: Clarendon Press, 1989), p. 255.
197. Minutes of a meeting at Admiralty House, 18 May 1962. PREM 11/3649 (PRO).
198. Although full membership became quasi-automatic in 1962, some territories opted voluntarily for a special status, very similar to that developed by the CRO and the CO (see note 140). However, these were the exceptions rather than the rule: 27 members of the Commonwealth have a population of 1,000,000 or less.
199. Chris Wrigley, 'Now you see it, now you don't: Harold Wilson and Labour's foreign policy 1964–70', in R. Coopey, S. Fielding and N. Tiratsoo (eds) , *The Wilson Governments 1964–1970* (London: Pinter, 1993), p. 124.

— 6 —

Conclusion

THE ANALYSIS of British attitudes towards the Empire-Commonwealth from 1945 to 1963 has shown how important it is to differentiate between three clearly distinct units making up the 'Empire-Commonwealth', that is, the informal empire, the formal empire and the Commonwealth. Although the ideas and objectives underlying British policy in all three areas were closely related, there was no policy covering the ensemble. Each area had its own function, structure and problems. Decisions with regard to the informal empire in particular have to be clearly separated from those taken with regard to the formal empire. It is futile to lump the two together under the heading of 'imperial' policy and then point to supposed contradictions – their subjective value, as well as the methods that were thought to be appropriate to protect them simply were not the same. Even within each group, a differentiation has to be made in order to avoid misleading generalisations. This applies particularly to the formal empire: no government had a colonial policy that can be said to have been universally applied to all dependent territories. In various colonies, different approaches were implemented at the same time, either because of feelings of loyalty to a certain group, for example, white settlers and specific strategic interests, or of a good understanding with local nationalists – imperial policy was always more a matter of feeling and sentiment rather than of rational calculation.

The extent of informal empire is by definition hard to grasp: it was not based on formal rule, but on 'power' and influence, mostly sustained by the presence of armed forces. Because of its elusive nature, it is difficult to say whether and when it ceased to exist. In the late 1950s Britain's hold on the Middle East had already become rather shaky, and it is unclear to what extent one can really speak of an 'empire' in this case. However, given the definition employed in this book, i.e. of informal empire as Britain's military commitments in the Middle and Far East, it is possible to sketch the history of the concept from 1945 to 1963. In the immediate post-war period, the informal empire was very much centred on the eastern Mediterranean and the

Red Sea. Britain controlled Palestine and Jordan and had a substantial military presence in Egypt. Protection of the Suez Canal was a main function of informal empire. Twenty years later, its centre of gravity had shifted to the Persian Gulf and the protection of British oil interests. Britain's military presence was now much more thinly spread. Moreover, non-military ways of promoting British influence had acquired more importance. Nonetheless, a strong showing was still considered essential, and Britain was ready to make important sacrifices in order to render it possible.

Throughout the period under consideration, the *raison d'être* of the informal empire was repeatedly challenged. The two basic questions around which these discussions revolved were, first, to what degree military, economic and political strength were interlinked, and second, how leadership could be exerted. There were always two major groups which opposed each other over these issues, but they were not necessarily identical in each case. As regards the interdependence of political, economic and military strength, there were those who argued that a military presence overseas was essential to maintain Britain's political and economic position. According to this group (which had the upper hand most of the time), the United Kingdom could only remain a major power as long as others *thought* it was. Confidence in Britain's capacities ensured that sterling continued to play an important role in the international financial system, that the United States granted it privileged treatment and that other countries respected British assets. The other group argued that only a balanced budget and a favourable balance of trade could ultimately guarantee Britain's economic and political strength. Cutbacks were made throughout the period, but no government ever dared to implement to the full the demands put forward by this group. With regard to exertion of leadership, policy-makers generally agreed that Britain had to compensate its economic and military weakness with other assets that would allow it to exert influence: these were reckoned to be Britain's experience in international affairs as well as its prestige and standing. But there was some disagreement with regard to the extent to which Britain should attempt to woo Asian or Arab nationalists. Some thought this would impair Britain's dignity and attacked anything smacking of 'scuttle' – Bevin and India and Churchill and the Suez Base agreement are cases in point. For them, the use of force was still a legitimate means of asserting Britain's claim to be a world power. However, a majority of policy-makers believed Britain would gain rather than lose by attempting to come to an amicable settlement. Not only were Britain's resources limited but the use of force was increasingly difficult to defend on the international scene. Moreover, it would achieve no lasting settlement and only serve the ends of the Soviet Union.

Probably the most dangerous attack launched on the informal empire from within the policy-making structure came from Attlee in the immediate post-war period. Based on a mixture of strategic, economic and ethical arguments, it questioned the purpose of Britain's widespread overseas commitments, at least those in the Middle East. Faced with the fierce resistance from Bevin and the Chiefs of Staff, Attlee eventually backed down. He realised that the United Nations would not be able to guarantee the protection of British interests, that the Soviet Union was not ready to compromise, and that it was necessary to impress the United States so that it would continue to pay particular attention to British views and needs.

The ambitious rearmament programme in the wake of the Korean War and the ensuing financial difficulties led Butler to launch a new onslaught that was immediately countered by Eden and Macmillan. They as well as most other policy-makers still saw a close link between Britain's overseas commitments, its international standing and its economic and financial strength. Nonetheless, Eden strove to reach an agreement with Egyptian nationalists – without, however, being willing to accept anything that could be regarded domestically and internationally as approaching humiliation. After Suez, the Treasury began to call for a withdrawal of all troops east of Suez. But it was not able to overcome the united resistance of the FO, MoD and Prime Minister. Despite the move towards greater mobility, aircraft carriers and non-military means for promoting and protecting British interests, policy-makers remained convinced that Britain had to make a strong showing in the Persian Gulf and Malaysia if it wanted to remain a Great Power.

The value of the informal empire was intangible, but its importance was taken for granted: many policy-makers considered it *the* symbol of Britain's status as a Great Power. To lose it, they feared, would condemn the country to an ignoble future among other European middle powers. This, they thought, was simply not appropriate for Britain – although they were rarely (if ever) able to prove their point in discussions with policy-makers who considered informal empire to do more harm than good. (For the sake of fairness it should be said that the arguments of their adversaries were not based on hard facts either.) Often they were also unable to say exactly *why* Britain would suffer unspeakable damage if it ceased to be a Great Power. It was simply assumed that Britain had to continue being one if it did not want to succumb to irresistible economic, political, and even moral decline. The debate about the informal empire therefore was mostly about assumptions and stereotypes rather than hard facts.

Informal empire had five essential functions: to preserve Britain's prestige and standing in the world; secure its privileged position in relation to the United States; make a contribution to the containment of communism; protect British assets, for example, overseas investments and oil companies; and – last but not least – to ensure the stability of the pound. For policy-makers in Britain the most important functions were to preserve the position of the pound and to secure the special relationship, although it should be pointed out that all five functions were thought to be interdependent. Without US support, for example, it would, they supposed, have been impossible to preserve sterling's position, while Britain's standing in the world depended on its influence in the United States.

Throughout the period under consideration policy-makers assumed that, in order to preserve Britain's status as a Great Power with a leading currency, Britain had to continue to play a major role on the international scene, in particular by maintaining a military presence overseas. In order to ensure the continued use of the pound as an international currency, sterling's reserve role (which depended on international confidence in its stability) had to be maintained at all costs. A strong pound was believed to generate price stability and employment. It was also seen to reflect confidence in the British economy and to support traders and merchants in the City. Without a strong pound, many imports would have to be paid for in dollars (which Britain never had enough of), and its creditors would attempt to exchange their sterling balances into hard currency. Most policy-makers were convinced that the confidence of foreign governments and investors did not so much depend on a sound balance of payments, but rather on a show of strength on the international scene. They feared that investors would not put their money in a weak currency (or that of a country which *appeared* to be weak), and without their confidence, Britain would lose its invisible exports, i.e. the income from loans, investments, and insurance that supplied an important percentage of its foreign exchange and reserves. In addition, the holders of sterling balances might decide to withdraw them – a course that was particularly dangerous after the introduction of full convertibility in 1958. The belief that a strong economy would result from a strong currency, and not the other way round, had firm roots in the official mind.

The second crucial function of the informal empire was to prop up the special relationship. Britain believed that without the United States, it would not be able to maintain itself as a Great Power, be it in financial, diplomatic or strategic terms. Therefore it was determined to maintain its overseas commitments, even at the cost of cutbacks in domestic sectors such as education or social expenditure. Policy-makers were convinced that Britain had to demonstrate that it was a worthwhile partner; therefore it was thought necessary to make a significant contribution to Western defence – not only in Europe (with the commitment of forces in Germany) or through the nuclear deterrent, but also in the wider world.

Although there were some readjustments, the five functions of the informal empire remained the same over the period under consideration, i.e. 1945–63. In 1945 as in the mid-1960s, the capability to intervene worldwide, i.e. to project military power in distant areas, was considered vital. The objective remained the same, even though the means employed changed: aircraft carriers and rapid intervention forces replaced coaling stations, gunboats and large concentrations of troops in the two pillars of informal empire, the Middle East and south-east Asia. Despite the Treasury's consistent pressure for cutbacks, Britain continued to spend a comparatively large proportion of its GNP on defence expenditure, a considerable part of which was needed for overseas commitments. At the same time, more money was spent on non-military Cold War measures in order to maintain Britain's influence and to secure the voluntary cooperation of local regimes. Therefore, while the appearance of the informal empire changed, its basic nature remained the same.

The inertia of the imperial idea in the official mind is not surprising. Far from being merely the remnants of a system which had lost its *raison d'être* with the end of the Raj (as argued, for example, by Philip Darby), overseas commitments were thought to play a vital role for the maintenance of Britain's role as a world power and for the protection of British interests. Not only was a military presence in the Middle and Far East considered necessary to preserve US goodwill but policy-makers were also convinced that a British withdrawal would lead inevitably to a take-over by a hostile power in Malaysia or the Persian Gulf. There were dangerous rivals such as Egypt, Iraq and Indonesia, and local collaborators did not seem strong enough to resist great pressure. In addition, there was always the risk of Soviet (or Chinese) penetration. Since the supply of oil was vital for the West (and its sale through British companies an important contribution to the United Kingdom's balance of payments), policy-makers were reluctant to risk withdrawal. Consequently, overseas commitments were maintained, even at the price of cutbacks at home. While Kennedy and Chalmers might be right in arguing that in the end, this policy proved counter-productive, they are mistaken in assuming that this should have been obvious to policy-makers at the time.

Whereas the informal empire had, or at least was thought to have, direct advantages for Britain, policy-makers found it more difficult to say what the colonies (apart from the fortress territories) were good for. Attachment to them was based more on romantic, paternalistic visions of Britain's role as the colonies' protector and tutor than on any clear-cut interest: colonial rule was considered to be for the good of the natives rather than that of the metropole (an interpretation which did not keep policy-makers from attempting occasionally to tip the balance more in Britain's favour). The jolting course of British colonial history has to be seen as the result of the difficulties linked with arranging an orderly transfer of power rather than any intention on the part of British officials to keep control over the colonies for their own sake. In many territories the problem was the lack of any convincing alternative to colonial rule. Bernard Porter claims that especially in the first years after the war, 'there was a great deal to keep Britain in her colonies'.[1] In fact, there was more often than not a lack of convincing arguments to push Britain *out* of its colonies rather than any concrete interest to keep it in. Most colonies still had to be developed economically and politically before they could stand on their own feet, particularly in Africa, where there was initially no sufficiently strong, educated elite. Given the unsettled international situation after the Second World War (and the expectation of an imminent showdown with the Soviet Union), this state of affairs offered bleak prospects in the event of colonial rule ending precipitately – not only for the territories themselves, but also for Britain as the power responsible for them.

Under the Attlee governments the colonies were already being seen as territories in need of support and protection, i.e. as at best a responsibility, at worst a burden. Plans for the development of colonial resources were rapidly abandoned once policy-makers realised the difficulties related to it. Trade liberalisation came to be seen as more in Britain's interests than any attempt to maintain the disintegrating imperial economy. The colonies' strategic importance (which in any case had never been overwhelming) diminished because of technical advances such as nuclear bombs, wireless stations and long-distance planes. Yet these factors were not sufficient to push them towards independence: what was needed were changes on the international scene as well as on the periphery. Although most colonies were not material assets, policy-makers initially considered it important to maintain formal rule. This was due as much to a feeling of responsibility as to the fear of losing prestige if Britain failed to fulfil its trust. Over the years, however, an increasing number of policy-makers concluded that a rapid transfer of power was the best means of ensuring future cooperation, preventing emergencies and thwarting a communist take-over, even in smaller territories or in colonies with white minorities (the only temporary exception being fortress territories such as Aden). Not only would any alternative course lead to a clash with local nationalists who were expected to mushroom everywhere sooner or later, but the changing international climate would also make it impossible to maintain Britain's privileged position in relation to the United States. In the 1950s, the international scene had become more static and the use of force less acceptable: the Cold War was being increasingly fought in the United Nations rather than in Malaya or Korea. In this context, the question of self-government became a crucial issue. Whereas in the 1940s global war still seemed a distinct possibility, a decade later the emphasis was on fighting the Cold War. For this, the possession of large colonial territories was not necessary; on the contrary, policy-makers concluded that maintaining formal rule against strong local and international criticism was not in Britain's interest. If more or less friendly local forces could take over, British objectives would be equally well served. Under these circumstances it was the transfer of power to local elites rather than as in the past the acquisition, pos-session and defence of empire, which held out the prospect of maxi-mising metropolitan influence and standing in the world. The new world order not only pushed Britain to dismantle its formal empire – it also allowed it to do so without losing face.

Decolonisation did not so much reflect a change in British perception of the colonies as underdeveloped regions in need of assistance and supervision (although policy-makers realised that the locals were not necessarily as incapable of governing themselves as they had initially thought), as the growing belief that formal rule was dangerous for Britain's international standing. In some parts of the empire developments were somewhat delayed – either because of feelings of loyalty *vis-à-vis* white kith and kin, or because of strategic interests which might be endangered by unreliable local collaborators, or simply because some territories were not considered viable. However, by the time Macleod became Colonial Secretary, anti-colonialism had become such a strong factor in international affairs that it decisively influenced the decisions taken with regard to East and Central Africa, as well as (after a little delay) the smaller territories. Concerns about Britain's standing gained the upper hand over feelings of responsibility and racial solidarity. In the early 1960s the CO dropped its insistence on viability and the emergence of racial unity, hoping that aid and cooperation within the Commonwealth could compensate for the end of British rule and supervision. After the first hesitant steps in the Gold Coast and Malaya, decolonisation soon became a scramble proper – this time not *for* Africa, but rather *out* of it. This acceleration was not only due to changing international circumstances. Equally important was the logic of events on the spot. These led policy-makers to transfer power much earlier than foreseen in order to avoid a difficult transition period or a clash with local nationalists (whose goodwill after independence was considered crucial). Decolonisation was a learning experience, and policy-makers were eager not to repeat the mistakes (supposedly) made in India.

In the case of 'normal' colonies, the exact timing of independence as well as the circumstances of the transfer of power depended largely on the strength of nationalist demands and developments in neighbouring territories. The withdrawal from India and Burma took place in order to avoid a civil war or an armed rebellion that would have tied up scarce military and financial resources desperately needed in other places. The transfer of power in both cases was hardly ideal, but policy-makers were satisfied that they had 'come out with honour'. Ceylon, on the other hand, seemed to demonstrate how rapid decolonisation could pre-empt a crisis and even further British interests. Power was transferred with the mutual agreement of both parties, before there was any serious conflict. Thus Britain's international prestige was enhanced while its interests were secured through politicians apparently susceptible to British influence. The island therefore set an example for the transfer of power in other colonies, including the Gold Coast and Malaya. British concluded that it was better to concede too much too early than too little too late.

In East and Central Africa, there was some hesitancy as to the right course. While the whites were not to gain unrestricted control, they were not to be subjected to African majority-rule either. For some time, the colonies' future was in a limbo. This was possible since there was neither strong local nor international pressure. In the late 1950s, the FO came to favour rapid decolonisation in order to improve Britain's position in the international arena; the CO continued to insist on 'good government' and economic stability. After some delay, however, the CO also realised the risks of attempting to hold the situation for much longer; not only was international pressure increasing, but in the territories themselves everything was moving towards a confrontation with the Africans. In Kenya, there was also the risk that the white settlers and administrators would leave, thus leading to an economic break-down. This would have destroyed the prospect of creating a stable successor state able to withstand communist inroads. Having vainly tried to create multi-racial societies, British officials decided that, on balance, African goodwill and democratic credibility were more important than securing the interests of their white kith and kin. Policy-makers were afraid that after de Gaulle's sudden decision to grant independence to most French colonies, their country would lag behind along with Portugal in the shift towards decolonisation. This would focus international criticism on Britain and injure its relationship with the United States and Afro-Asian nations. In addition, it could lead to conflict with the Africans. There was some discontent within the government and the Conservative Party, but in the end most policy-makers realised that it was no longer either feasible or advisable to try and maintain a privileged position for the whites.

The smaller territories were at first thought to be incapable of ever attaining self-government, whether because they were too small, or whether because of their strategic importance to Britain. In the early 1960s, however, Britain began to rush them towards independence. This change of strategy had various causes. The so-called 'fortress territories' lost importance because military planners moved increasingly towards a strategy based on aircraft carriers and bases in Australia and Britain. The emergence of a new world order as well as international aid made it possible for smaller territories to survive even without a 'big brother'. International criticism rendered colonial rule more of a burden. Finally, the Commonwealth was opened to all of Britain's colonies, thus allowing it to transfer power and thereby rid itself of the onerous status of a colonial power.

It was not the economic, strategic or geopolitical value of a colony that determined whether and when it should become independent, but the value policy-makers attached to the imperial relationship in each case. The most important thing, at least in the case of 'normal' colonies, was the presumed reliability of local nationalists: as soon as there were any doubts that they would not be able to protect their country against local rivals or communist subversion, the British hesitated. If the colonies fulfilled the right criteria, however, the transfer of power went ahead. British policy-makers were, above all, interested in stability in order to prevent Soviet penetration and guarantee freedom of trade and investment. Goodwill and voluntary cooperation were considered the best safeguards for these interests. Therefore power was transferred as soon as the natives showed sufficient interest in and were capable of being in charge of their own affairs. In fact, Britain pursued a double-edged strategy: on the one hand it tried to lure local politicians to its side by making concessions, on the other it cracked down on those who appeared to be linked to the Soviet Union or China. Constitutional concessions were made in order to back moderate nationalists and reduce pressure from extremists. As long as nationalist movements were not openly hostile or pro-communist, policy-makers did all they could to find a *modus vivendi*.

Britain believed that in most cases its interests could not be secured by force. This belief went hand in hand with the conviction that after independence, Britain would still have 'a worthy and continuing part' to play in its former colonies.[2] The end of formal rule was not to mean the end of economic, political and cultural links. Metropole and periphery were to remain closely linked. In fact, Britain held a firm belief in its capacity to lead – and in the usefulness of replacing control with influence. For Britain, the latter was 'a very much finer and more durable and more eternal thing than power'. The latter had served Britain since the days of Clive, but the former, 'if we could use it aright in the changed conditions of the 20th century, would serve us better'.[3] Coercion was to be replaced with cooperation, which would allow Britain to maintain a privileged position in its former dependencies while winning praise for its liberal policy.

The belief in Britain's capacity to influence development in its colonies faded in the 1950s once it realised that Asian and African nationalists were far less malleable than it had assumed. Although this did not necessarily lead to a change of policy in the remaining colonies, policy-makers still thought it better to maintain local goodwill rather than try to govern by force. It is important to point out that at no point did the belief in Britain's ability to influence lead policy-makers to expect the empire to continue under a new guise. 'Formal empire' was not merely to be transformed into 'informal empire': it was always acknowledged that the new states could not be obliged to walk in step with Britain – even though it was hoped that they would recognise sooner or later that close links with the United Kingdom were in their own interest. Certainly, 'the failure to construct the expected close post-colonial partnership with the new states'[4] was disappointing, but it was not considered a tragedy. Darwin, Owen and others do not sufficiently evaluate this liberal aspect of British policy which they discard as mere rhetoric.

The claim that the end of empire 'undermined long-held convictions of the superiority of European technology and government and touched the raw nerve-ends of national humiliation and decline'[5] has not been substantiated by the material consulted for this book. In general it was not the end of formal rule itself which really mattered, but the manner in which it ended. The problem was not *whether* power should be transferred, but *how* and to *whom*. One of the prime objectives of British colonial policy was to hand over power in a spirit of amity and goodwill. This was to ensure that after independence, the territory maintained a friendly attitude towards the United Kingdom which would allow continuous cooperation and help Britain to save face. Policy-makers considered it crucial to avoid humiliation and at least to *appear* to be in control of events. Imperial greatness was mostly 'a matter of style and perception rather than concrete interest',[6] and often it was possible to end formal rule without jeopardizing British interests – provided it was done in an honourable fashion. Prestige was a key element in metropolitan thinking, even though it was not 'the crucial reference point against which everything was judged'.[7] For policy-makers it went without saying that the position and influence of their country depended to a large extent on what other countries thought of it. Therefore they were determined to avoid any impression of 'scuttling'. They feared humiliation in a colony because of its consequences for the government's standing – not only at home, but also in the wider world.

Policy-makers paid particular attention to the way power was transferred and its perception by the public. Officials were willing to end colonial rule, but they did not want to be 'shouted out'.[8] If Britain appeared to have been forced to agree to a transfer of power, it would be considered a defeat, even if there were no important interests at stake. Therefore the peoples concerned and the world at large had to be convinced that Britain was not 'yielding step by step to pressure', but was 'sincerely following out an enlightened policy'.[9] If the transfer of power could be presented as an act resulting from British generosity and liberality, much had been won. Prestige and standing were considered important values *per se*, indispensable for a Great Power like Britain. However, it is important to underline that the attention paid to these values was also due to quite concrete, material interests. With regard to the informal empire, the stability of sterling, Britain's standing on the international scene, the loyalty of the Dominions as well as the special relationship were all thought to be influenced by Britain's performance in the colonial field. To give an appearance of weakness, it was feared, would have far-reaching repercussions. It would start a crumbling process, which would destroy the whole imperial fabric and undermine the foundations of Britain's economic and political strength. Therefore formal rule had to be ended in a dignified way, even where it had no importance in terms of real power.

British colonial policy after 1945 did not follow any grand strategy, but was the result of *ad hoc* decision-making process. Policy-makers were mostly reactive, responding to pressures on the periphery and the international scene rather than grasping the initiative. The increasingly fast advance towards independence in the early 1960s, still unthinkable in the 1940s, was due to the double concern of 'coming out with honour' and of securing local and international goodwill, as well as due to the dynamics developing at the periphery. Britain felt responsible for the well-being of the locals and wanted to prepare the countries properly for independence. On the other hand, it was eager to avoid difficult transition periods in which it might lose control. In the end, it was the latter concern which prevailed. Bad self-government, most British officials reasoned, was better than good colonial government – except in cases where vital strategic interests were at stake. Thus for the most part, decolonisation was neither an 'unpredictable erosion of position after position' nor a 'selective shrugging off of commitments',[10] but rather the attempt to secure Britain's position (both on the international scene as well as in the colonies) by making it adapt to changing circumstances.

Given the conclusions drawn above, it is necessary to rethink those theories which see the explanation for Britain's imperial withdrawal in a rational balancing of economic advantages and drawbacks. Admittedly throughout the 1940s and 1950s Britain was concerned to ensure that colonial sterling balances were reduced in an orderly fashion. Sterling balances had some influence on colonial policy, but not in a negative sense: they made policy-makers consider the preservation of goodwill as their highest objective. It was feared that to grant independence too late or with too many strings attached might lead the colonies to leave the sterling area or run down their balances faster than was in Britain's interest. Therefore everything was done to appease local politicians showing a minimum degree of readiness to cooperate – a pattern which was particularly evident in the case of Malaya and the Gold Coast, which were the first colonies to reach independence in the 1950s, and incidentally also the most important ones in the sterling area. Thus it was clearly not the declining importance of a colony for the sterling area that was decisive for the timing of its independence.

The same applies to trade interests. As Robinson and Gallagher have shown, commercial motives for acquiring colonies, particularly in Africa, were weak; they were no stronger when formal rule was relinquished. In the first decade after the war, only about 10.2 per cent of British imports came from the colonies, and roughly 13 per cent of all exports went to them. Moreover, by 1951 the United Kingdom was generally paying open-market prices for its purchases of colonial produce.[11] This as well as Britain's conviction that goodwill was the best guarantee for metropolitan interests demonstrates that the British had no reason to delay independence for economic reasons. Nor was it the diminishing of the colonies' already rather marginal importance for British global economic interests that led to a rapid end to formal rule. Already in the early 1950s policy-makers had realised that imperial development and trade-links did not necessarily represent the best option for Britain – but they did not decolonise because of this insight.

Similarly, no clear link can be detected between the mounting cost of administering, developing and defending the colonies and the acceleration of the transfer of power. In Malaya, for example, financial and military assistance continued long after independence. To state that Britain withdrew because the colonies had lost their former political, strategic or economic value makes sense only if it is assumed that the formal empire had been acquired because it was useful. Admittedly, there were colonies which benefited the metropole – but there were many others that made no direct contribution whatsoever. At the same time, there were areas of high importance where there was neither formal nor informal empire. This contradiction can only be re-solved by regarding the decisive element in Britain's decision to grant independence to lie in the value of the imperial relationship in an international context, rather than in the value of a colony itself. It is equally necessary to be cautious about the argument that it was nationalists who forced Britain to decolonise. In some cases, they proved a nuisance, in others it was the prospect of a strong nationalist movement emerging which prodded Britain towards action. More often than not, however, the demands of nationalist groups only somewhat accelerated constitutional advance without being at the root of any radical changes. In general, it was not the strength of indigenous nationalism that led Britain to react. It was rather the Cold War inter-national environment with its rapidly increasing hostility against any form of colonial rule as well as the insight that rule by force could not (and should not) be maintained for long, that led British policy-makers to search for a *modus vivendi* with indigenous politicians.

It was not only the role of the colonies, but also of the Commonwealth that changed considerably in the period under con-sideration. The idea of developing the Commonwealth into a third force, fostered for a short time after 1945, had to be given up relatively quickly. Policy-makers still hoped that the club could provide a satisfactory framework for strategic, economic and diplomatic coop-eration. But it soon became obvious that the other members were not willing to take over a bigger share of the defence burden, and that in strategic terms they considered the United States, not the United Kingdom, to be their ultimate reference point. The club's economic importance also diminished, although more slowly. A large percentage of British trade was still carried out with the Dominions, but policy-makers realised that these would turn increasingly to other markets. It was also clear that, for Britain, trade liberalisation was more advantageous than imperial preferences. The political aspect, however, remained important until the early 1960s, although in a less clear-cut fashion.

In the 1940s, policy-makers still thought it possible to substitute empire with Commonwealth, an association that was to be stronger than the old empire since it was based on voluntary association. Labour's concept of a multi-racial Commonwealth was conditioned by the expectation that the new members could be persuaded to play a positive role in imperial defence and in buttressing sterling – and thereby accept British guidance in international affairs. Thus the Commonwealth, far from being merely the negation of empire, would give Britain vital strategic advantages enabling it to remain in the top international league.[12] At the time, acceptance of Commonwealth membership was seen as the outward expression of a state's intention to maintain close relations with Britain (hence, Mountbatten's enthusiasm about India accepting Dominion status). The Commonwealth system was vague and informal, but nonetheless it was thought useful in stemming the decline of Britain's weight in the world. By the mid-1950s, and certainly after Suez, hardly anyone believed that it would be possible to restore the cooperation of the inter-war period. It was recognised that, at best, the Commonwealth would help maintain a façade of continuity: the empire did not cease to exist, but was rather transformed into a family of (English-speaking) nations. In terms of real strength, the club had become insignificant. Cooperation with the old Dominions was still important, but no longer necessarily took place within the framework of the Commonwealth.

Until the early 1960s it was still hoped that the Commonwealth would continue to enhance Britain's prestige, particularly *vis-à-vis* the United States, and in the Cold War, even a façade like the Commonwealth was considered useful. Throughout the post-war period, links between members grew weaker, partly because of domestic developments within the old colonies, partly because of the admission of new members. The latter initiated a profound transformation of the Commonwealth from a white man's club to a minor United Nations. The enlargement of membership was accepted because Britain expected the club to contribute to the maintenance of close relations with its former colonies, which went beyond traditional relations with 'foreign' states; it was to allow continuous contacts and consultation, and facilitate aid and assistance. At the same time, policy-makers tried to devise means of compensating for the resulting loss of intimacy. Most important in these deliberations was the idea of second-class membership. After much soul-searching, the idea was finally dropped in 1962. All Britain's colonies could now become full members at independence. Policy-makers realised that a two-tier Commonwealth would not be accepted by the newly independent states, and that the old club could not be preserved since it was disappearing regardless of the admission of non-European members – Canada, Australia and New Zealand were increasingly going their own way, and South Africa's racial policies put it at odds with most other members. If some of the old links with the white Dominions survived, this was not due to the club, but to a feeling of racial and cultural closeness.

Policy-makers regretted that the new members were less willing to follow Britain's guidance than had been expected, but they were eager not to bring the Commonwealth into disrepute by making it appear as an instrument of neo-colonialism. Therefore any attempt at openly influencing former colonies was refrained from in the hope that they would realise sooner or later who their true friends were. Even when this failed to occur it was still regarded as more advantageous to keep the new states in the club than to see them drift into the US or Russian spheres of influence. By 1962 policy-makers concluded that the Commonwealth had played out its role as a source of international standing: the United States had demonstrated that it preferred the Treaty of Rome, and the new members proved to be rather un-comfortable company on the international scene. Nonetheless, the club remained important in the context of the Cold War. It assumed special importance in the 'ideological and economic struggle for influence and power in the countries outside Europe'. Indeed, this was the major function of the Commonwealth 15 years after the war: keeping out of 'Communist clutches' a large part of 'the world's more backward populations'.[13]

Until the early 1960s there was strong resistance against any *rapprochement* with Europe on the grounds that it would damage the Commonwealth. This was not due to any objective calculation about the club's economic or political value. The reason was rather the conviction of many policy-makers that Britain had to remain a power with world-wide interests and commitments. The Commonwealth was only one aspect of this world role, although its 'Britishness' (as opposed to Europe's 'foreign-ness') also mattered. The importance of developments on the Continent was not underestimated: by 1960 many policy-makers realised that the EEC was a new fount of prestige and power. But it was still thought important to maintain overseas links; these were expected to strengthen the special relationship. In addition, there was still a strong *feeling* that Britain's true vocation lay overseas rather than on the Continent: policy-makers abhorred the idea of their country being reduced to the level of just another European power.

Throughout the two decades under consideration, there was an astonishing continuity of policy, largely independent of political affiliations and personalities. Both Labour and Conservative ministers initially talked of implementing a 'left-wing' or 'right-wing' policy respectively, but their exuberance soon died down – rarely were there any profound disagreements between the two major parties. Policy was dictated by developments in the wider world as well as by Britain's weak position in material terms, not by any party programmes. In general, colonial policy was pragmatic, not ideological. Even if officials and politicians are taken together, it is striking to see how the circle of policy-makers involved in imperial decisions was always rather small, marked by a high continuity and homogeneity in their definition of national interests. There were certainly differences of opinion within the government, but in general the Prime Minister managed to remain in control. Policy-makers were wary of acting if they expected their decisions to go against opinion prevailing in public (or in their party), but this stance was more often than not based on vague assumptions rather than on concrete observations. And if a certain course, which they considered to be in the best interests of the country, was expected to be unpopular (as were the hasty withdrawals from India and Kenya), policy-makers implemented it regardless of resistance even while attempting to present their decision in a favourable light.

It has been repeatedly pointed out that the Empire-Commonwealth should be considered as consisting of three clearly distinct units with different functions and different rules. However, there were also traits the three units had in common. The Empire-Commonwealth was more than just a collection of territories in various degrees of dependence on Britain. It was an attempt to create a British world order that guaranteed peace and stability, a *pax Britannica*. In general, the difference between formal empire and Commonwealth was only gradual. Certainly policy-makers felt much closer to the 'white' Dominions and considered them more mature than any of the colonies. But in principle (at least from 1953 onwards), all colonies were expected one day, to become, self-governing members of the club. The colonies were thought to have acquired a certain 'Britishness' through their links with the United Kingdom. Therefore they were considered less 'foreign' than most European countries. The end of formal rule, policy-makers assumed, would not substantially change the relations between metropole and periphery.

The informal empire in the Middle East was different. Britain did not think it possible (or advisable) to transform it into a Commonwealth. This was due to several factors. In the Middle East and, to a lesser degree, in south-east Asia, Britain had stronger economic and geopolitical interests than in most of its other colonies. Defending these interests was deemed to be vital to Britain's economic survival but also to the special relationship. Local regimes were considered neither totally reliable nor strong enough to resist outside encroachments without British assistance. Moreover, the Middle East was believed not to have the same degree of 'Britishness' as, for example, India. However, there is one trait the informal empire had in common with its formal counterpart. Wherever strong nationalist movements emerged (as in Egypt or Persia), Britain tried to find a *modus vivendi*. As long as Britain could avoid losing face, it was willing to make concessions.

In the two decades after the war, it was crucial for British policy-makers to maintain international confidence in sterling and to preserve Britain's standing as a Great Power. Without these two factors, the United States would supposedly have ceased to regard Britain as a privileged partner, and the Dominions would have turned to the United States. Many other countries would drift into the Soviet orbit or confiscate British assets, and sterling would cease to be an international currency. In other words, the foundations of Britain's economic and political strength would be destroyed, and it would be reduced to a second-rate power. In order to avoid such a development, policy-makers had to proceed very cautiously (or, as Macmillan said, 'bicycle along a tightrope') while trying to balance opposing interests. Economies clearly had to be made – but not at the price of leading other countries to think the United Kingdom was no longer a power they needed to reckon with. Because of the international constellation after 1945, which led to increasing criticism of 'colonialist' and 'imperialist' powers and of the two blocs' (the United States and the Soviet Union) currying favour with non-aligned countries, international opinion and its interpretation of Britain's imperial policy mattered strongly. The new world order led Britain to consider cooperation with, not domination of, Asian and African nationalists with, as the key to success – provided this was not interpreted as a 'scuttle'.

The period under consideration in this book was subject to a new world order, with its predominance of two superpowers and a marginalized Europe. Colonial emancipation was *inter alia* a consequence of this new constellation. It led to a sea change in international discourse that had begun long before the war.

Domination of other peoples (at least by the Europeans) as well as the use of force against them were no longer considered legitimate. If Britain did not want to risk its standing *vis-à-vis* the United States, it had to conform to this rule. In the late nineteenth century the best way of excluding (potentially) hostile powers from Britain's spheres of influence and interest had seemed to lie in formal rule. The 1950s and 1960s rather called for a dismantling of the imperial relationship in order to keep out the enemy – whom, after all, it was now much easier to identify. Whereas a hundred years earlier nearly every other power was a potential rival, Britain now considered itself part of a 'Western' alliance opposed to the Soviet Union. This limited the possibility of independent action, but also offered new opportunities of promoting and protecting national interests. Adaptation to this new order was slow and uneven, and it is still an ongoing process – but decolonisation was clearly a part of it.

The end of formal empire was noted with a slight regret. But as long as the transfer of power was peaceful and no hostile power could take over, the worst had been avoided. The shrinking of the informal empire was the result of the need to make economies but also of a new bipolar world order, which made the use of force as well as interventionist policies less acceptable. On the one hand, this reduced Britain's freedom of action, on the other, it guaranteed stability without a military presence being necessary. The transformation of the Commonwealth led to some more bitterness, but in the end it was acknowledged to be the inevitable result of Britain's policy of keeping the door wide open in order to maintain a façade of continuity. Britain's adaptation to the post-colonial world can thus be said to have been relatively successful.

In the case of informal empire, in particular, myths and stereotypes influenced policy-making; but in general imperial policy was flexible and capable of change. This was due to the fact that the Empire-Commonwealth was always a way to promote British interests, not an end in itself. After 1945 its use became increasingly difficult because of the Cold War and a climate of political correctness, which condemned the use of force and intervention (at least by anyone other than the two superpowers). This development made it at once advisable *and* possible to look for alternative ways of protecting and promoting British interests. Empire was no longer an asset. But the new world order also meant that Britain could do without it. After all, one of the functions of empire had always been the physical protection of British investments and trade interests – this task was now performed by the *pax Americana*. Although the United States did not always act in Britain's interests, British policy-makers were nonetheless convinced

that their country's special relationship with the United States offered
the best chance of securing Britain's survival as a major power.

Once the post-war order had begun to crystallise, the problem was
not so much the loss of formal rule: it was rather to find a way by
which Britain could honourably divest itself of old obligations. This
task was exceedingly difficult. Since there were no precedents for the
transfer of power to non-European nationalists, decolonisation was,
by necessity, a learning experience. Consequently some mistakes were
made, especially in the beginning. But, all told, Britain managed its
task rather well. It might have chosen an over-hasty retreat, leaving
the colonies to their own devices (as Belgium did in the Congo), or
tried to maintain old privileges and racial inequality by force (as
France did in Algeria). Instead it steered a middle course, naturally
giving pride of place to national interests, but also attempting to
secure the well-being of its colonial subjects. In the 1940s and 1950s,
policy-makers did not have the impression of giving away an empire.
Rather they believed that they were transforming it into something
new: a family of nations united in the Commonwealth. By the 1960s,
this had been achieved and, like so many parents, Britain had to
realise that its offspring were increasingly going their own way and
failing to show it the respect it had expected. The handling of informal
empire was also a learning experience. Given the insecurity about
future developments as well as the assets at stake, it is understandable
that there were many hesitations, sometimes even mistakes. But, in
general, the task was handled without any major crisis. The
predominant feeling among British officials (despite Suez) therefore
was not one of defeat or retreat, but rather the belief that Britain had
bowed gracefully to the inevitable.

In a book with a wide chronological and thematic scope, there
should be a brief concluding remark about the role of decolonisation
in the wider framework of world history. Many forms of cultural or
economic dependence might have survived the end of formal rule, but
it nonetheless profoundly changed the settings in which Britain (and
other world powers) had to operate: the 'colonial world' was replaced
with a 'world of nations'. The emerging 'Third World' was a new,
more or less independent actor on the international scene; East and
West had to try to curry favour with it. Decolonisation signalled Britain's readiness to accept new rules in international relations, particularly in its relations with underdeveloped countries. Policy-makers
acknowledged that metropolitan interests overseas could not be
secured by force, and that the best way of protecting them was to win
local goodwill. Notwithstanding all the necessary reservations, British
policy can be said to have been relatively liberal, particularly if

compared with that of other colonial powers. The idea of transforming 'an Empire into a family' might have been unrealistic, but it
testifies to an astonishing maturity with regard to the kinds of force
and exercise of power still considered permissible.

Finally there should be a brief remark about the direction of future
research. There are three main points, detailed study of which would
help to gain a better understanding of Britain's changing relationship
with the 'imperial' circle. First, there is the question of how relations
between Britain and its former colonies developed after
independence: what did the transfer of power change in the attitudes
of metropolitan policy-makers? There is very little authoritative literature on these post-colonial '*états d'âmes*'. They are hard to reconstruct,
but they definitely merit more attention than has hitherto been paid to
them. A second topic is aid for less developed countries that Britain –
like most other Western (and Eastern) powers – began increasingly to
hand out from the 1950s onwards. It is questionable whether this new-
found generosity really represented a new approach to the non-
European world. It might be argued that it only helped conceal
continuities in Britain's strategic objectives that had survived the dismantling of formal (and informal) empire. Future research should
therefore examine to what extent this aid was expected to help project
a certain image of Britain in the world and preserve British influence.
What was its role in the Cold War and the containment of Soviet influence? How far did its functions differ from the role of the old empire?
In this context it would also be rewarding to analyse the role the
Commonwealth was expected to play in the post-colonial age of the
1960s and 1970s.

A third point to be studied in more detail is the fate of Britain's
'informal' empire in the late 1960s and early 1970s. With many
relevant sources accessible, it is now possible to attempt a detailed
reconstruction of the withdrawal 'east of Suez'. To what extent did
Britain remain involved in the Middle and Far East after 1970? What
had really changed? The various policy-reviews executed under
Macmillan always stated that Britain should move towards informal
(and non-military) means of protecting its interests. How were these
ideas implemented? Future research should focus on the means that
were by then considered appropriate to foster Britain's influence and
to protect its interests – and how these interests were defined. Thus it
would be possible to elaborate continuities and discontinuities in
economic, military and diplomatic strategies, helping us to
understand further how Britain managed (or failed) to adapt to the
new order of a post-colonial world.

NOTES

1. Porter, *The Lion's Share*, p. 328.
2. Lyttelton to Templer, 1 February 1952. PREM 11/639 (Stockwell, *Malaya*, II 268).
3. Both quotes cited in Kathryn Tidrick, *Empire and the English Character* (London: I.B. Tauris, 1992), p. 242; quoted in Nicholas Mansergh (ed.), *Documents and Speeches on British Commonwealth Affairs, 1931–52*, Vol. 2 (London: Oxford University Press, 1953), p. 700.
4. Darwin, *Britain and Decolonisation*, p. 330.
5. Nicholas Owen, '"More Than a Transfer of Power": Independence Day Ceremonies in India, 15 August 1947', *Contemporary Record*, 6 (1992), p. 418.
6. Robert Holland, '"Greatness" and the British in the Twentieth Century', in Jansen and Lehmkuhl (eds), *Großbritannien, das Empire und die Welt*, p. 38.
7. Brasted, Bridge and Kent, 'Cold War', p. 23.
8. Hankey to A.V. Alexander, 2 April 1959. AVAR 5/18 (CC).
9. 'British Foreign Policy in the Far East', report by Cabinet Far Eastern civil planning unit, April 1946. FO 371/54052, quoted in Rolf Tanner, *'A Strong Showing': Britain's Struggle for Power and Influence in South-East Asia, 1942–1950* (Stuttgart: Steiner, 1994), p. 110.
10. J. Darwin, 'British Decolonization since 1945: A Pattern or a Puzzle?', in R.F. Holland and G. Rizvi (eds), *Perspectives on Imperialism and Decolonization: Essays in Honour of R.F. Madden* (London: Frank Cass, 1984), pp. 187–209.
11. Herward Sieberg, *Colonial Development: Die Grundlegung moderner Entwicklungspolitik durch Großbritannien 1919–1949* (Stuttgart: Steiner, 1985), p. 555; Feinstein, 'The End of Empire', p. 224.
12. Fieldhouse, 'The Labour Governments', p. 84.
13. FP (A) (60) 5, 15 January 1960. CAB 134/1930 (PRO); C (60) 107, 6 July 1960. CAB 129/102 (1), quoted in Lawrence J. Butler, 'Winds of Change: Britain, Europe and the Commonwealth, 1959–61', in Brivati and Jones (eds), *From Reconstruction to Integration*, p. 163.

Bibliography

SOURCES

Unpublished Documents

Public Record Office (PRO) (London)

Cabinet: CAB 21: registered files, Prime Minister's briefs
    CAB 127: private and official papers of Edwards Bridges
    CAB 128: Cabinet minutes
    CAB 129: Cabinet papers
    CAB 130–4: Cabinet committees

Colonial Office: CO 54: Ceylon
    CO 537: Colonies (general)
    CO 554: West African Department
    CO 822: East African Department
    CO 852: Economic General Department
    CO 859: Social Service Department
    CO 926: Mediterranean Department
    CO 936: International Relations Department
    CO 967: Southeast Asian Department
    CO 999: Colonial Development
    CO 1015: Central African and Aden Department
    CO 1025: Finance Department
    CO 1027: Information Department
    CO 1032: General Department

Ministry of Defence: DEFE 5: Chiefs of Staff Committee: Memoranda
    DEFE 7: registered files: general series
    DEFE 10: minutes and papers of major committees and working parties
    DEFE 13: Private Office: registered files

Commonwealth Relations Office: DO 35: General Correspondence
DO 121: Commonwealth membership
DO 142: India and the Commonwealth

Foreign Office: FO 371: General Political Correspondence
FO 800: private papers (various)
FO 1110: Information Research Department

Prime Minister's Office: PREM 8: Correspondence and Papers (1945–51)
PREM 11: correspondence and papers (1951–64)
PREM 13: correspondence and papers (1964 ff.)

Treasury: T 220: Imperial and Foreign Division: Registered Files
T 236: Central Economic Planning Staff

British Library Oriental and India Office Collections (London)

Mss.Eur.D.: 621 (manuscripts)
670 (manuscripts)
714 (manuscripts)
724 (manuscripts)
1030 (manuscripts)
Mss.Eur.F: 200 (manuscripts)
230 (manuscripts)
Photo.Eur.: 212 (manuscripts/photographic reproductions)

Bodleian Library (Oxford)

Papers of the Conservative Party's Research Department (CRD)

Private Papers

Addison papers (Bodleian Library, Oxford)
Alexander of Hillborough papers (Churchill College, Cambridge)
Attlee papers (Bodleian Library, Oxford)
Attlee's draft memoirs (Churchill College, Cambridge)
Bevin papers (Churchill College, Cambridge; PRO)
Butler papers (Trinity College Library, Cambridge)
Creech Jones papers (Rhodes House Library, Oxford)
Churchill papers (Churchill College, Cambridge)
Dalton papers (London School of Economics)
Gordon-Walker papers (Churchill College, Cambridge)
Gorell Barnes papers (Churchill College, Cambridge)
Halifax papers (Churchill College, Cambridge)
Hetherington papers (London School of Economics)

Ismay papers (Liddell Hart Centre for Military Archives, King's College, London)
Lennox-Boyd papers (Bodleian Library, Oxford)
Noel-Baker papers (Churchill College, Cambridge)
Selwyn Lloyd papers (Churchill College, Cambridge)
Swinton papers (Churchill College, Cambridge)
Turnbull diary (Churchill College, Cambridge)

Published Documents

Bullen, Roger and Pelly, M.E. (eds), *Documents on British Policy Overseas*, series II, Vol. II (London: HMSO, 1987) (*DBPO*).

De Silva, K.M. (ed.), *Sri Lanka*, 2 vols (London: HMSO, 1997) (De Silva, *Sri Lanka*, I–II).

Goldsworthy, David (ed.), *The Conservative Government and the End of Empire, 1951–1957*, 3 vols (London: HMSO, 1994) (Goldsworthy, *Conservative Government*, I–III).

Hyam, Robert (ed.), *The Labour Governments and the End of Empire 1945–1951*, 4 vols (London: HMSO, 1992) (Hyam, *Labour Government*, I–IV).

Kent, John (ed.), *Egypt and the Defence of the Middle East*, 3 vols (London: HMSO, 1998) (Kent, *Egypt*, I–III).

Mansergh, N. (ed.), *Documents and Speeches on Commonwealth Affairs, 1931–52*, 2 vols (London: Oxford University Press, 1953).

——(ed.), *Documents and Speeches on Commonwealth Affairs, 1952–1962* (London: Oxford University Press, 1963).

Mansergh, N. and Lumpy, E.W.R. and Moon, E.P. (eds), *Constitutional Relations between Britain and India: The Transfer of Power, 1942–47* (London: HMSO, 1970–83) (Mansergh *et al.*, *Transfer of Power*, I–XII).

Porter, A.N. and Stockwell, A.J. (eds), *British Imperial Policy and Decolonization 1938–64*, 2 vols (Basingstoke: Macmillan, 1987), (Porter and Stockwell, *British Imperial Policy*, I–II).

Rathbone, Richard (ed.), *Ghana*, 2 vols (London: HMSO, 1992), (Rathbone, *Ghana*, I–II).

Stockwell, A.J. (ed.), *Malaya*, 3 vols (London: HMSO, 1995) (Stockwell, *Malaya*, I–III).

Tinker, H.R. (ed.), *Burma: The Struggle for Independence, 1944–1948*, 2 vols (London: HSMO, 1983–84) (Tinker, *Burma*, I–II).

Other Published Sources

Attlee, Clement R., *As it Happened* (New York, NY: Viking, 1954).
Barnes, John and Nicholson, David (eds), *The Empire at Bay: The Leo*

Amery Diaries 1929–55 (London: Hutchinson, 1988).

Dalton, Hugh, *Memoirs, 1945–60: High Tide and After* (London: Muller, 1962).

Dupree, Marguerite (ed.), *Lancashire and Whitehall: The Diary of Sir Raymond Streat, Vol. 2: 1939–57* (Manchester: Manchester University Press, 1987).

Eden, Anthony, *Full Circle* (London: Cassell, 1960).

Harris, K., *Attlee* (London: Weidenfeld & Nicolson, 1982).

Hinden, Rita, *Empire and After: A Study of British Imperial Attitudes* (London: Essential Books, 1949).

Macmillan, Harold, *Riding the Storm 1956–1959* (Basingstoke: Macmillan, 1971).

——*Pointing the Way 1959–1961* (Basingstoke: Macmillan, 1972).

——*At the End of the Day: 1961–63* (Basingstoke: Macmillan, 1973).

Moon, E.P. (ed.), *Wavell: The Viceroy's Journal* (London: Oxford University Press, 1973).

Williams, F., *A Prime Minister Remembers: The War and Post-War Memoirs of the Rt. Hon. Earl Attlee* (London: Heinemann, 1961).

Secondary Sources

Adamthwaite, Anthony, 'Britain and the World, 1945–49: The View From the Foreign Office', in J. Becker and F. Knipping (eds), *Power in Europe? Great Britain, France, Italy and Germany in a Post-War World, 1945–1950* (Berlin: de Gruyter, 1986), pp. 9–25.

——'Overstretched and Overstrung: Eden, the Foreign Office and the Making of Policy, 1951–5', *International Affairs*, 64 (1988), pp. 241–59.

——'Suez Revisited', *International Affairs*, 64 (1988), pp. 449–64.

——'Britain, France and the Integration of Western Europe, 1957–1961', in M. Dockrill (ed.), *Europe within the Global System 1938–1960. Great Britain, France, Italy and Germany: From Great Powers to Regional Powers* (Bochum: Brockmeyer, 1995), pp. 133–43.

Aldrich, Richard J., (ed.), *British Intelligence, Strategy and the Cold War, 1945–51* (London: Routledge, 1992).

——'British Strategy and the End of Empire: South Asia, 1945–51', in Richard J. Aldrich (ed.), *British Intelligence, Strategy and the Cold War, 1945–51* (London: Routledge, 1992), pp. 275–307.

Aldrich, Richard and Coleman, Michael, 'Britain and the Strategic Air Offensive Against the Soviet Union: The Question of South Asian Air Bases, 1945–1949', *History*, 242 (1989), pp. 400–26.

Andrew, Christopher, 'L'Empire Britannique et le Commonwealth, facteurs de puissance mondiale de 1938 aux années 1960', in Jean-Claude Allain (ed.), *La Moyenne Puissance au XXe siècle: Recherche d'une définition* (Paris: Institut d'Histoire des conflits contemporains, 1988), pp. 251–64.

Ashton, Stephen, 'British Official Documentary Perspectives on Decolonisation: A Case Study of the Gold Coast', in *Décolonisations européennes: Actes du colloque international 'Décolonisations comparées', Aix-en-Provence, 30 septembre–3 octobre 1993* (Aix-en-Provence: Université de Provence, 1995), pp. 111–29.

Ball, Simon J., 'Macmillan and British Defence Policy', in Richard Aldous and Sabine Lee (eds), *Harold Macmillan and Britain's World Role* (Basingstoke: Macmillan, 1996), pp. 67–96.

Bangura, Y. *Britain and Commonwealth Africa: The Politics of Economic Relations 1951–75* (Manchester: Manchester University Press, 1983).

Becker, J. and Knipping, F. (eds), *Power in Europe? Great Britain, France, Italy and Germany in a Post-war World, 1945–1950* (Berlin: de Gruyter, 1986).

Beloff, Max, 'The End of the British Empire and the Assumption of World-Wide Commitments by the United States', in Wm Roger Louis and H. Bull (eds), *The 'Special Relationship': Anglo-American Relations since 1945* (Oxford: Clarendon Press, 1989), pp. 249–60.

Betts, Raymond F., *France and Decolonization 1900–1960* (Basingstoke: Macmillan, 1991).

Bowring, Walter, 'Great Britain, the United States, and the Disposition of Italian East Africa', *Journal of Imperial and Commonwealth History*, XX (1992), pp. 88–107.

Boxer, Andrew, *The Conservative Governments, 1951–1964* (London: Longman, 1996).

Brasted, H.V., and Bridge, C., 'Labour and Transfer of Power in India: A Case for Reappraisal?', *Indo-British Review*, 12 (1987), pp. 70–90.

Brasted, H.V., Bridge, C. and Kent, J.: 'Cold War, Informal Empire and the Transfer of Power: Some "Paradoxes" of British Decolonisation Resolved?', in M. Dockrill (ed.), *Europe within the Global System 1938–1960. Great Britain, France, Italy and Germany: From Great Powers to Regional Powers* (Bochum: Brockmeyer, 1995), pp. 11–30.

Brinkley, Douglas, 'Dean Acheson and the "Special Relationship": The West Point Speech of December 1962', in *Historical Journal*, 33, 3 (1990), pp. 599–608.

Burgess, Simon and Edwards, Geoffrey, 'The Six plus One: British Policy-Making and the Question of European Economic Integration, 1955', *International Affairs*, 64 (1988), pp. 393–413.

Burke, Kathleen, 'Britain and the Marshall Plan', in Chris Wrigley (ed.), *Warfare, Diplomacy and Politics: Essays in Honour of A.J.P. Taylor* (London: Hamilton, 1986), pp. 210–30.

Burridge, Trevor David, *Clement Attlee: A Political Biography* (London: Cape, 1985).

Butler, Larry J., 'The Ambiguities of British Colonial Development Policy, 1938–48', in Anthony Gorst, Lewis Johnman and W. Scott Lucas (eds), *Contemporary British History 1931–61: Politics and the Limits of Policy* (London: Pinter, 1991), pp. 119–40.

Butler, Lawrence J., 'Winds of Change: Britain, Europe and the Commonwealth, 1959–61', in Brian Brivati and Harriet Jones (eds), *From Reconstruction to Integration: Britain and Europe since 1945* (Leicester: Leicester University Press, 1993), pp. 157–65.

Cable, James, 'Inquest on Empire', *International Relations* 11 (1992), pp. 57–67.

Cain, P.J. and Hopkins, A.G., *British Imperialism: Crisis and Deconstruction 1914–1990* (London: Longman, 1993).

Carruthers, Susan, *Winning Hearts and Minds: British Governments, the Media and Colonial Counter-Insurgency, 1944–1960* (Leicester: Leicester University Press, 1995).

Catterall, Peter (ed.), 'Witness Seminar: The East of Suez Decision', *Contemporary Record*, 7, 3 (1993), pp. 612–53.

Cell, J.W., 'On the Eve of Decolonization: the Colonial Office's Plans for the Transfer of Power in Africa, 1947', *Journal of Imperial and Commonwealth History*, VIII (1979/80), pp. 235–57.

Chalmers, Malcolm, *Paying for Defence: Military Spending and British Decline* (London: Pluto Press, 1985).

Croft, Stuart, *The End of Superpower: British Foreign Office Conceptions of a Changing World, 1945–51* (Aldershot: Dartmouth, 1994).

Darby, Philip, *British Defence Policy East of Suez, 1947–1968* (London: Oxford University Press, 1973).

Darwin, John, 'British Decolonization since 1945: A Pattern or a Puzzle?', in R.F. Holland and G. Rizvi (eds), *Perspectives on Imperialism and Decolonization: Essays in Honour of R.F. Madden* (London: Frank Cass, 1984), pp. 187–209.

——'The Fear of Falling: British Politicians and Imperial Decline since 1900', *Transactions of the Royal Historical Society*, 5th series, 36 (1986), pp. 27–43.

——*Britain and Decolonisation: The Retreat from the Empire in the Post-War World* (Basingstoke: Macmillan, 1988).

——*The End of the British Empire: The Historical Debate* (Oxford: Black-well, 1991).

——'The Central African Emergency, 1959', *Journal of Imperial and*

Commonwealth History, XXI (1993), pp. 217–34.

Dean, D.W., 'Final Exit? Britain, Eire, the Commonwealth and the Repeal of the External Relations Act, 1945–1949', *Journal of Imperial and Commonwealth History*, XX (1992), pp. 391–418.

Deighton, Anne (ed.), *Britain and the First Cold War* (Basingstoke: Macmillan, 1990).

Dodds, Klaus, 'The End of a Polar Empire? The Falkland Islands Dependencies and Commonwealth Reactions to British Polar Policy, 1945–61', *Journal of Imperial and Commonwealth History*, XXIV (1996), pp. 391–421.

Dooley, Howard J., 'Great Britain's "Last Battle" in the Middle East: Notes on Cabinet Planning During the Suez Crisis of 1956', *International History Review*, 11 (1989), pp. 486–517.

Ebersold, Bernd, *Machtverfall und Machtbewußtsein: Britische Friedens- und Konfliktlösungsstrategien, 1918–1956* (Munich: Oldenbourg, 1992).

——'"Delusions of Grandeur": Großbritannien, der Kalte Krieg und der Nahe Osten, 1945–1956', in Hans-Heinrich Jansen and Ursula Lehmkuhl (eds), *Großbritannien, das Empire und die Welt: Britische Außenpolitik zwischen "Größe" und "Selbstbehauptung", 1850–1990* (Bochum: Brockmeyer, 1995), pp. 139–68.

Ellner, Andrea and Gorst, Anthony, 'The British Surface Fleet since 1945' (unpublished paper, September 1999, pers. comm.).

Fforde, John, *The Bank of England and Public Policy, 1941–1958* (Cambridge: Cambridge University Press, 1992).

Feinstein, Charles H., 'The End of Empire and the Golden Age', in Peter Clarke and Clive Trebilcock (eds), *Understanding Decline. Perceptions and Realities of British Economic Performance* (Cambridge: Cambridge University Press, 1997), pp. 212–33.

Fieldhouse, David K., 'The Labour Governments and the Empire-Commonwealth, 1945–51', in Ritchie Ovendale (ed.), *The Foreign Policy of the British Labour Governments, 1945–1951* (Leicester: Leicester University Press, 1984), pp. 83–120.

——*Black Africa 1945–80: Economic Decolonization and Arrested Development* (London: Allen & Unwin, 1986).

Flint, John, 'The Failure of Planned Decolonization in British Africa', *African Affairs*, 82 (1983), pp. 389–411.

Fraser, Cary, 'Understanding American Policy towards the Decolonization of European Empires, 1945–64', *Diplomacy & Statecraft* 3, 1 (1992), pp. 105–25.

Furedi, Frank, 'Britain's Colonial Wars: Playing the Ethnic Card', *Journal of Commonwealth and Comparative Politics*, XXVIII (1990), pp. 70–89.

——'Creating a Breathing Space: The Political Management of

Colonial Emergencies', *Journal of Imperial and Commonwealth History*, XXI, 3 (1993), pp. 89–106.

Gallagher, John and Robinson, Ronald, 'The Imperialism of Free Trade', *Economic History Review*, 2nd series, 6, 1 (1953), pp. 1–15.

Gifford, Prosser and Louis, Wm Roger (eds), *The Transfer of Power in Africa: Decolonization 1940–1960* (New Haven, CT: Yale University Press, 1982).

——*Decolonization and African Independence. The Transfers of Power, 1960–1980* (New Haven, CT: Yale University Press, 1988).

Goldsworthy, D., *Colonial Issues in British Politics 1945–1961. From 'Colonial Development' to 'Wind of Change'* (Oxford: Clarendon Press, 1971).

——'Keeping Change within Bounds: Aspects of Colonial Policy during the Churchill and Eden Governments, 1951–1957', *Journal of Imperial and Commonwealth History*, XVIII (1990), pp. 81–108.

——'Britain and the International Critics of British Colonialism, 1951–56', *Journal of Commonwealth and Comparative Politics*, XXIX (1991), pp. 1–24.

Gorst, Anthony, "We must cut our coat according to our cloth": The making of British defence policy, 1945–48', in Richard J. Aldrich (ed.), *British Intelligence, Strategy and the Cold War, 1945–51* (London: Routledge, 1992), pp. 143–65.

Gupta, Partha Sarathi, *Imperialism and the British Labour Movement, 1914–1964* (Basingstoke: Macmillan, 1975).

——'Imperialism and the British Labour Government of 1945–51', in J.M. Winter (ed.), *The Working Class in Modern British History* (Cambridge: Cambridge University Press, 1983), pp. 99–124.

——'British Strategic and Economic Priorities during the Negotiations for the Transfer of Power in South Asia, 1945–47', *Bangladesh Historical Studies*, VII (1983), pp. 39–51.

Hack, Karl, 'Screwing Down the People: The Malayan Emergency, Decolonisation and Ethnicity', in Hans Antlöv and Stein Tønnesson (eds), *Imperial Policy and Southeast Asian Nationalism 1930–1957* (Richmond: Curzon Press, 1995), pp. 83–109.

Hanes, W. Travis, *Imperial Diplomacy in the Era of Decolonization. The Sudan and Anglo-Egyptian Relations, 1945–1956* (Westport, CT: Greenwood Press, 1995).

Hargreaves, John D., 'Les techniciens de la décolonisation: l'évolution de la politique de la Grande-Bretagne en Afrique, 1936–1948', in *Les chemins de la décolonisation de l'empire colonial français: Colloque organisé par l'I.H.T.P. les 4 et 5 octobre 1984* (Paris: Centre Nationale de Recherche Scientifique, 1986), pp. 83–93.

——*Decolonization in Africa* (London: Longman, 1988).

Hartley, Anthony, 'The Lost Vocation', *Journal of Contemporary History*, 15 (1980), pp. 67–79.

Hemming, Philip E., 'Macmillan and the End of the British Empire in Africa', in Richard Aldous and Sabine Lee (eds), *Harold Macmillan and Britain's World Role* (Basingstoke: Macmillan, 1996), pp. 97–121.

Hennessy, Peter and Laity, Mark, 'Suez – What the Papers Say', *Contemporary Record*, 1 (1987), pp. 2–8.

Hinds, Allister E., 'Sterling and Imperial Policy, 1945–1951', *Journal of Imperial and Commonwealth History*, XV (1986/87), pp. 148–69.

——'Imperial Policy and Colonial Sterling Balances, 1943–56', *Journal of Imperial and Commonwealth History*, XIX (1991), pp. 24–44.

Holland, Robert, 'The Imperial Factor in British Strategies from Attlee to Macmillan', *Journal of Imperial and Commonwealth History*, XII (1984), pp. 165–86.

——*European Decolonization 1918–1981: An Introductory Survey* (Basingstoke: Macmillan, 1985).

——'Did Suez Hasten the End of Empire?', *Contemporary Record*, 1 (1987–88), p. 39.

——*The Pursuit of Greatness. Britain and the World Role, 1900–1970* (London: Fontana, 1991).

——'Never, Never Land: British Colonial Policy and the Roots of Violence in Cyprus, 1950–54', *Journal of Imperial and Commonwealth History*, XXI, 3 (1993), pp. 148–76.

——'"Greatness" and the British in the Twentieth Century', in Hans-Heinrich Jansen and Ursula Lehmkuhl (eds), *Großbritannien, das Empire und die Welt: Britische Außenpolitik zwischen 'Größe' und 'Selbstbehauptung', 1850–1990* (Bochum: Brockmeyer, 1995), pp. 31–40.

——'The British Experience of Decolonization', *Itinerario*, 20 (1996), pp. 51–63.

Hopkins, Anthony Gerald, *An Economic History of West Africa* (Harlow: Longman, 1973).

Hopkins, Tony, 'Macmillan's Audit of Empire, 1957', in Peter Clarke and Clive Trebilcock (ed.), *Understanding Decline. Perceptions and Realities of British Economic Performance* (Cambridge: Cambridge University Press, 1997), pp. 234–60.

Horne, Alistair, *Macmillan, 1957–1986. Volume II of the Official Biography* (London: Macmillan, 1989).

Horowitz, Dan, 'Attitudes of British Conservatives towards Decolonization in Africa', *African Affairs*, 69 (1970), pp. 9–26.

——*Anticolonialism in British Politics: The Left and the End of Empire 1918–1964* (Oxford: Oxford University Press, 1993).

Hyam, Ronald, 'Africa and the Labour Government, 1945–1951', *Journal of Imperial and Commonwealth History*, XVI (1988), pp. 148–72.

——'The Geopolitical Origins of the Central African Federation: Britain, Rhodesia and South Africa, 1948–1953', *Historical Journal*, 30 (1987), pp. 145–72.

——'The Parting of the Ways: Britain and South Africa's Departure from the Commonwealth, 1951–61', *Journal of Imperial and Commonwealth History*, XXVI, 2 (1998), pp. 157–75.

Kaiser, Wolfram, 'To Join, or not To Join: The "Appeasement" Policy of Britain's First EEC Application', in Brian Brivati and Harriet Jones (eds), *From Reconstruction to Integration: Britain and Europe since 1945* (Leicester: Leicester University Press, 1993) pp. 144–56.

——*Großbritannien und die Europäische Wirtschaftsgemeinschaft 1955–1961: Von Messina nach Canossa* (Berlin: Akademie Verlag, 1996).

Kelly, Saul, 'Transatlantic Diplomat: Sir Roger Makins, Ambassador to Washington and Joint Permanent Secretary to the Treasury', *Contemporary British History*, 13, 2 (1999), pp. 157–77.

Kennedy, Dane, 'The Expansion of Europe', *Journal of Modern History*, 59 (1987), pp. 331–43.

Kennedy, Paul, *The Rise and Fall of the Great Powers* (New York, NY: Random House, 1987).

Kent, John, 'Bevin's Imperialism and the Idea of Euro-Africa, 1945–49', in Michael Dockrill and John W. Young (eds) *British Foreign Policy 1945–56* (Basingstoke: Macmillan, 1989), pp. 47–76.

——'The British Empire and the Origins of the Cold War, 1944–49', in A. Deighton (ed.), *Britain and the First Cold War* (Basingstoke: Macmillan, 1990), pp. 165–83.

——*British Imperial Strategy and the Origins of the Cold War 1944–49* (Leicester: Leicester University Press, 1993).

Killingray, David, 'The Idea of a British Imperial African Army', *Journal of African History*, 20 (1979), pp. 421–36.

Krozewski, Gerold, 'Sterling, the "Minor" Territories, and the End of Formal Empire, 1939–1958', *Economic History Review*, XLVI (1993), pp. 239–65.

——'Finance and Empire: The Dilemma Facing Great Britain in the 1950s', *International History Review*, 18 (1996), pp. 48–69.

Kunz, Diane B., 'The Importance of Having Money: The Economic Diplomacy of the Suez Crisis', in Wm Roger Louis and Roger Owen (eds), *Suez 1956: The Crisis and its Consequences* (Oxford: Clarendon Press, 1989), pp. 215–32.

——*British Post-War Sterling Crises* (Austin, TX: University of Texas

Press, 1992).

Kyle, Keith, *The Politics of the Independence of Kenya* (New York, NY: St Martin's Press, 1999).

Lamb, Richard, *The Macmillan Years, 1957–1963: The Emerging Truth* (London: Murray, 1995).

Lapping, Brian, 'Did Suez Hasten the End of Empire?', *Contemporary Record*, 1, 2 (1987), pp. 31–3.

Lavalie, Alpha Mohamed, 'The Transfer of Power in Sierra Leone: British Colonial Policy, Nationalism and Independence, 1945–61', unpublished PhD thesis, University of London, 1989.

Lee, J.M., *Colonial Development and Good Government: A Study of the Ideas Expressed by the British Official Classes in Planning Decolonization, 1939–1964* (Oxford: Clarendon Press, 1967).

Lee, Sabine, 'Staying in the Game? Coming into the Game?', in Richard Aldous and Sabine Lee (eds), *Harold Macmillan and Britain's World Role* (Basingstoke: Macmillan, 1996), pp. 123–47.

Lieven, Dominic, 'Dilemmas of Empire 1850–1918: Power, Territory, Identity', *Journal of Contemporary History*, 34, 2 (1999), pp. 163–200.

Louis, William Roger, *The British Empire in the Middle East, 1945–51: Arab Nationalism, the United States and Post-War Imperialism* (Oxford: Clarendon Press, 1984).

——'American Anti-Colonialism and the Dissolution of the British Empire', in Wm Roger Louis and Bull Hedley (eds), *The 'Special Relationship': Anglo-American Relations since 1945* (Oxford: Clarendon Press, 1986), pp. 261–83.

——'The Anglo-Egyptian Settlement of 1954', in Wm Roger Louis and Roger Owen (eds), *Suez 1956: The Crisis and its Consequences* (Oxford: Clarendon Press, 1989), pp. 43–71.

——*'In the Name of God, Go!' Leo Amery and the British Empire in the Age of Churchill* (New York, NY: Norton, 1992).

Louis, Wm R. and Robinson, Ronald, 'The Imperialism of Decolonization', *Journal of Imperial and Commonwealth History*, XXII (1994), pp. 462–511.

Low, D.A., 'Little Britain and Large Commonwealth', *Round Table*, 298 (1986), pp. 109–121.

——*Eclipse of Empire* (Cambridge: Cambridge University Press, 1991).

MacKenzie, John M., 'European Imperialism: Comparative Approaches', *European History Quarterly*, 22 (1992), pp. 415–29.

Marx, Roland, 'Le Commonwealth et les choix européens de la Grande-Bretagne de 1948 à 1975', *Relations internationales*, 55 (1988), pp. 361–76.

McIntyre, W. David, 'The Admission of Small States to the Commonwealth', *Journal of Imperial and Commonwealth History*,

XXIV (1996), pp. 244–77.

——*The Significance of the Commonwealth, 1965–90* (Basingstoke: Macmillan, 1991).

Moore, Robin J., 'The Demission of Empire in South Asia: Some Perspectives', *Journal of Imperial and Commonwealth History*, II, 1 (1972/73), pp. 79–94.

——*Making of the New Commonwealth* (Oxford: Clarendon Press, 1987).

——'The Transfer of Power: An Historiographical Survey', *Indo-British Review*, 14 (1988), pp. 108–17.

Morgan, D.J., *The Official History of Colonial Development: A Reassessment of British Aid Policy, 1951–1965,* Vol. 3 (Basingstoke: Macmillan, 1980).

Morgan, Kenneth O., *Labour in Power, 1945–1951* (Oxford: Clarendon Press, 1984).

Morris-Jones, W.H. 'The Transfer of Power, 1947: A View from the Sidelines', *Modern Asian Studies*, 16 (1982), pp. 1–32.

Morris-Jones, W.H. and G. Fischer (eds), *Decolonization and After: The British and French Experience* (London: Frank Cass, 1980).

Morvay, Werner, 'Decolonization: British Territories', in *Encylopaedia of Public International Law* (Amsterdam: North Holland, 1987).

Munro, J. Forbes, *Britain in Tropical Africa, 1880–1960. Economic Relationships and Impact* (Basingstoke: Macmillan, 1984).

Murphy, Philip, *Party Politics and Decolonization: The Conservative Party and British Colonial Policy in Tropical Africa, 1951–1964* (Oxford: Clarendon Press, 1995).

Neuberger, Benyamin, 'The Withdrawal "South of Suez" – Great Britain and Postcolonial Africa', *Asian and African Studies*, 26 (1992), pp. 95–100.

Newton, S., 'The Sterling Crisis of 1947 and the British Response to the Marshall Plan', *Economic History Review*, 2nd series, XXXVII (1984), pp. 391–408.

——'Britain, the Sterling Area and European Integration, 1945–50', *Journal of Imperial and Commonwealth History*, XIII (1984–85), pp. 163–82.

Nye, Joseph S., 'The Changing Nature of World Power', *Political Science Quarterly*, 105 (1990), pp. 177–92.

Ovendale, Ritchie, 'Britain and the Cold War in Asia', in Joseph S. Nye (ed.), *The Foreign Policy of the British Labour Governments, 1945–1951* (Leicester: Leicester University Press, 1984), pp. 121–48.

——'Macmillan and the Wind of Change in Africa, 1957–1960', *Historical Journal*, 38 (1995), pp. 455–77.

Owen, Nicholas, 'The End of Empire 1945–51', *Contemporary Record*, 3

(1990), pp. 12–16.

——'"More than a Transfer of Power": Independence Day Ceremonies in India, 15 August 1947', *Contemporary Record*, 6 (1992), pp. 415–51.

Pandey, Bishwa, Nath: *The Break-Up of British India* (Basingstoke: Macmillan, 1969).

Paul, Kathleen, '"British Subjects" and "British Stock": Labour's Post-War Imperialism', *Journal of British Studies*, 34 (1995), pp. 233–76.

Peden, George C., 'Economic Aspects of British Perceptions of Power on the Eve of the Cold War', in J. Becker and F. Knipping (eds), *Power in Europe? Great Britain, France, Italy and Germany in a Post-War World, 1945–1950*, (Berlin: de Gruyter, 1986), pp. 237–60.

Pelling, Henry, *The Labour Governments, 1945–51* (Basingstoke: Macmillan, 1984).

Pickering, Jeffrey, *Britain's Withdrawal from East of Suez: The Politics of Retrenchment* (Basingstoke: Macmillan, 1998).

Porter, Bernard, *The Lion's Share: A Short History of British Imperialism, 1850–1995* (London: Longman, 1996).

——*Britannia's Burden: The Political Evolution of Modern Britain 1851–1990* (London: Arnold, 1994).

Porter, Dilwyn, 'Downhill All the Way: Thirteen Tory Years 1951–64', in R. Coopey, S. Fielding and N. Tiratsoo (eds), *The Wilson Governments 1964–1970* (London: Pinter, 1993), pp. 10–28.

Rasler, Karen A. and Thompson, William R., *The Great Powers and Global Struggle, 1490–1990* (Lexington, KY: University Press of Kentucky, 1994).

Reynolds, David, *Britannia Overruled: British Policy and World Power in the Twentieth Century* (London: Longman, 1991).

Roberts, Andrew, *Eminent Churchillians* (London: Phoenix, 1995).

Robinson, Ronald, 'The Moral Disarmament of African Empire, 1919–1947', *Journal of Imperial and Commonwealth History*, VIII, 1 (1979), pp. 86–104.

——'Imperial Theory and the Question of Imperialism after Empire', *Journal of Imperial and Commonwealth History*, XII, 2 (1983/84), pp. 42–54.

——'The Excentric Idea of Imperialism, with or without Empire', in W.J. Mommsen and J. Osterhammel (eds), *Imperialism and After: Continuities and Discontinuities* (London: Allen & Unwin, 1986), pp. 267–89.

Sanders, David, *Losing an Empire, Finding a Role: British Foreign Policy since 1945* (Basingstoke: Macmillan, 1990).

Sanger, Clyde, *Malcolm MacDonald: Bringing an End to Empire* (Liverpool: Liverpool University Press, 1995).

Saville, John, *The Politics of Continuity: British Foreign Policy and the Labour Government, 1945–46* (London: Verso, 1993).

Schenk, Catherine R., 'The Sterling Area and British Policy Alternatives in the 1950s', *Contemporary Record*, 6, 2 (1992), pp. 266–86.

——*Britain and the Sterling Area. From Devaluation to Convertibility in the 1950s* (London: Routledge, 1994).

——'Decolonization and European Economic Integration: The Free Trade Area Negotiations, 1956–58', *Journal of Imperial and Commonwealth History*, XXIV (1996), pp. 444–63.

——'Finance and Empire: Confusion and Complexities: A Note', *International History Review*, 18 (1996), pp. 869–72.

Schmidt, Gustav, 'Die politischen und die sicherheitspolitischen Dimensionen der britischen Europapolitik 1955/56–1963/64', in Gustav Schmidt (ed.), *Großbritannien und Europa – Großbritannien in Europa: Sicherheitsbelange und Wirtschaftfragen in der britischen Europapolitik nach dem Zweiten Weltkrieg* (Bochum: Brockmeyer, 1989), pp. 179–252.

Shuckburgh, E., *Descent to Suez: Diaries 1951–1956* (London: Weidenfeld & Nicolson, 1986).

Sieberg, Herward, *Colonial Development: Die Grundlegung moderner Entwicklungspolitik durch Großbritannien 1919–1949* (Stuttgart: Steiner, 1985).

Shepherd, Robert, *Iain Macleod: A Biography* (London: Pimlico, 1994).

Shipway, Martin, 'British Perceptions of French Policy in Indochina from the March 1946 Accords to the Inception of the Bao Dai Regime 1946–1949: A Meeting of "Official Minds"?', in Charles-Robert Ageron and Marc Michel (eds), *L'ère des décolonisations: Sélection de textes du colloque 'Décolonisations comparées', Aix-en-Provence, 30 septembre–3 octobre 1993* (Paris: Karthala, 1995), pp. 83–96.

Singh, Anita Inder, 'Economic Consequences of India's position in the Commonwealth: The Official British Thinking in 1949', *Indo-British Review*, 11 (1984), pp. 106–11.

——'Keeping India in the Commonwealth: British Political and Military Aims, 1947–49', *Journal of Contemporary History*, 20 (1985), pp. 469–81.

——'Post-Imperial Attitudes to India: The Military Aspect, 1947–51', *Round Table*, 296 (1985), pp. 360–75.

Smith, Alison, 'The Immigrant Communities (I): The Europeans', in D.A. Low and Alison Smith (eds) *History of East Africa*, vol. 3 (Oxford: Clarendon Press, 1976), pp. 423–66.

Smith, R. and Zametica, J., 'The Cold Warrior: Clement Attlee Reconsidered, 1945–7', *International Affairs*, 61 (1985), pp. 237–52.

Stockwell, A.J., 'British Imperial Strategy and Decolonization in South-East Asia, 1947–1957', in D.K. Bassett and V.T. King (eds), *Britain and South-East Asia* (Hull: Hull University, Centre for South-East Asian Studies, 1986), pp. 79–88.

——'Insurgency and Decolonisation during the Malayan Emergency', *Journal of Commonwealth and Comparative Politics*, XXV (1987), pp. 71–81.

——'Malaysia: The Making of a Neo-Colony?', *Journal of Imperial and Commonwealth History*, XXVI, 2 (1998), pp. 138–56.

Stockwell, Sarah, 'Decolonisation beyond the Public Record Office: Non-Official Sources for Studying the End of Empire', *Contemporary Record*, 6 (1992), pp. 557–66.

——'Political Strategies of British Business during Decolonization: the Case of the Gold Coast/Ghana, 1945–57', *Journal of Imperial and Commonwealth History*, XXIII (1995), pp. 277–300.

Strange, Susan, *Sterling and British Policy: A Political Study of an International Currency in Decline* (London: Oxford University Press, 1971).

Tanner, Rolf, *'A Strong Showing': Britain's Struggle for Power and Influence in South-East Asia, 1942–1950* (Stuttgart: Steiner, 1994).

Tarling, Nicholas, '"An Empire Gem": British Wartime Planning and Post-War Burma, 1943–44', *Journal of South-East Asian Studies*, 13 (1982), pp. 310–48.

——'Lord Mountbatten and the Return of Civil Government to Burma', *Journal of Imperial and Commonwealth History*, XI, 2 (1982/83), pp. 197–226.

——*The Fall of Imperial Britain in South-East Asia* (Singapore: Oxford University Press, 1993).

Taylor, Philip M., 'Power, Propaganda and Public Opinion: The British Information Services and the Cold War, 1945–57', in Ennio Di Nolfo (ed.), *Power in Europe? II: Great Britain, France, Germany and Italy and the Origins of the EEC, 1952–1957* (Berlin: de Gruyter, 1992), pp. 445–61.

Throup, David, 'The Historiography of Decolonization' (unpublished paper given at the Institute of Commonwealth Studies, 31 January 1991).

Tidrick, Kathryn: *Empire and the English Character* (London: I.B. Tauris, 1992).

Tignor, Robert L., 'Decolonization and Business: The Case of Egypt', *Journal of Modern History*, 59 (1987), pp. 479–505.

Tinker, Hugh, 'The Contraction of Empire in Asia, 1945–48: The Military Dimension', *Journal of Imperial and Commonwealth History*, XVI (1987–88), pp. 218–33.

Tomlinson, Brian Roger, 'India and the British Empire, 1935–1947', *Indian Economic and Social History Review,* XIII (1976), pp. 331–52.

——*The Political Economy of the Raj 1914–1947: The Economics of Decolonization in India* (Basingstoke: Macmillan, 1979).

——'The Contraction of England: National Decline and Loss of Empire', *Journal of Imperial and Commonwealth History,* XI (1982), pp. 58–72.

Tomlinson, Jim, 'The Attlee Government and the Balance of Payments, 1945–51', *Twentieth Century British History,* 2 (1991), pp. 47–66.

——'Inventing 'Decline': The Falling Behind of the British Economy in the Post-war Years', *Economic History Review,* XLIX (1996), pp. 731–57.

Tratt, Jacqueline, *The Macmillan Government and Europe: A Study in the Process of Policy Development* (Basingstoke: Macmillan, 1996).

Turner, John, *Macmillan* (London: Longman, 1994).

Twaddle, Michael, 'Decolonization in Africa: A New British Historiographical Debate?', in Bogumil Jewsiewicki and David Newbury (eds), *African Historiographies: What History for Which Africa?* (Beverly Hills, CA: Sage, 1986), pp. 123–38.

Warner, Geoffrey, 'Britain and Europe in 1948: The View from the Cabinet', in J. Becker and F. Knipping (eds), *Power in Europe? Great Britain, France, Italy and Germany in a Post-War World, 1945–50* (Berlin: de Gruyter, 1986), pp. 447–59.

——'Aspects of the Suez Crisis' in Ennio Di Nolfo (ed.), *Power in Europe? II: Great Britain, France, Germany and Italy and the Origins of the EEC, 1952–1957* (Berlin: de Gruyter, 1992), pp. 43–65.

Wasserman, Gary, *Politics of Decolonization. Kenya Europeans and the Land Issue 1960–1965* (Cambridge: Cambridge University Press, 1976).

Weiler, Peter, 'British Labour and the Cold War: The Foreign Policy of the Labour Governments, 1945–1951', *Journal of British Studies,* 26 (1987), pp. 54–82.

Welensky, Roy, *4000 Days: The Life and Death of the Federation of Rhodesia and Nyasaland* (London: Collins, 1964).

White, Nicolas J., 'Government and Business Divided: Malaya, 1945–57', *Journal of Imperial and Commonwealth History,* XXII, 2 (1994), pp. 251–74.

Wrigley, Chris, 'Now You See It, Now You Don't: Harold Wilson and Labour's Foreign Policy 1964–70', in R. Coopey and S. Fielding and N. Tiratsoo (eds), *The Wilson Governments 1964–1970* (London: Pinter, 1993), pp. 123–35.

Young, John W., 'Churchill's "No" to Europe: The "Rejection" of European Union by Churchill's Post-War Government,

1951–1952', *Historical Journal,* 28 (1985), pp. 923–37.

——*Cold War Europe 1945–1991: A Political History* (London: Arnold, 1991).

Zametica, John, *British Officials and British Foreign Policy 1945–50* (Leicester: Leicester University Press, 1990).

Index